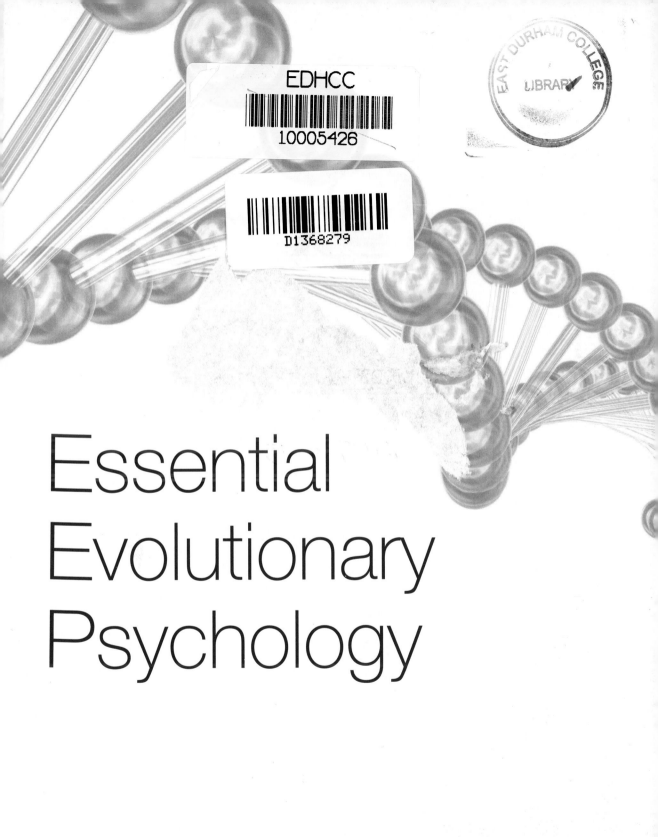

Essential
Evolutionary
Psychology

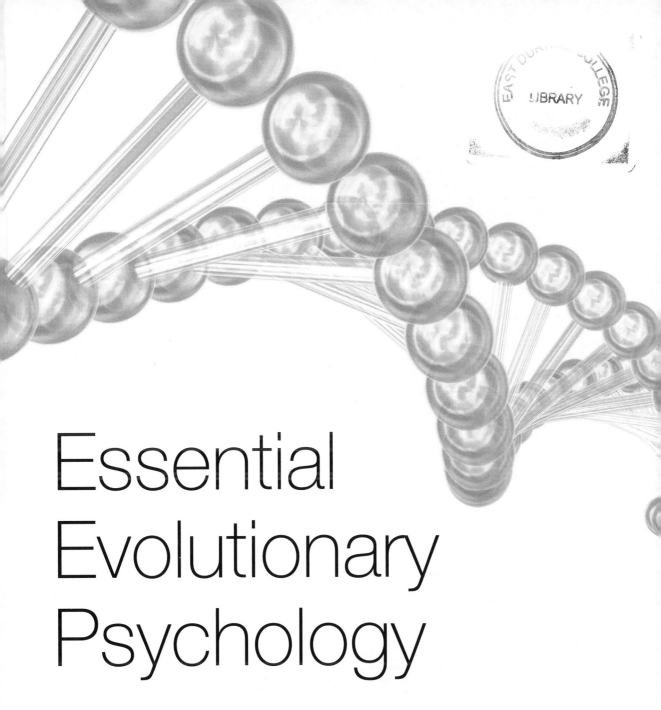

Essential
Evolutionary
Psychology

Simon Hampton

Los Angeles | London | New Delhi
Singapore | Washington DC

SAGE Publications Ltd
1 Oliver's Yard
55 City Road
London EC1Y 1SP

SAGE Publications Inc.
2455 Teller Road
Thousand Oaks, California 91320

SAGE Publications India Pvt Ltd
B 1/I 1 Mohan Cooperative Industrial Area
Mathura Road, Post Bag 7
New Delhi 110 044

SAGE Publications Asia-Pacific Pte Ltd
33 Pekin Street #02-01
Far East Square
Singapore 048763

Library of Congress Control Number: 2009941373

British Library Cataloguing in Publication data

A catalogue record for this book is available from the British Library

ISBN 978-1-4129-3584-5
ISBN 978-1-4129-3585-2 (pbk)

Typeset by C&M Digital (P) Ltd, Chennai, India
Printed and bound in Great Britain by TJ International Ltd, Padstow, Cornwall
Printed on paper from sustainable resources

Mixed Sources
Product group from well-managed forests and other controlled sources
www.fsc.org Cert no. SGS-COC-2482
© 1996 Forest Stewardship Council

DEDICATION

This book is dedicated to Abigail, Susanna, and Edward.

CONTENTS

LIST OF FIGURES

LIST OF TABLES

LIST OF BOXES

PREFACE

This book works on and from the following assumptions. One, that academic psychology and the social sciences are very largely secularised. This means that they do not invoke metaphysical concepts such as 'god', 'gods', 'spirit' or some other conception of a supreme being or grand designer in order to explain how people think and behave. And the second assumption is that psychology and the social sciences embrace a secular view of life and humanity which encompasses a more-or-less explicit acceptance that life forms on earth, including human beings, and that there is at least tacit acceptance that evolution has come about by the process of **natural selection**.

Subscribing to these assumptions, this book goes one step further and adopts the view that an evolutionary approach to the human mind and human behaviour is fruitful and can compliment other approaches. There are, of course, streams and schools of thought in psychology and social science which have and continue to explicitly exclude evolutionary and biological considerations and explanations. And some proponents of an evolutionary approach have made much of the antagonisms and disputes. Herein the antagonisms and disputes are acknowledged but not given centre stage. Rather, the focus will be the literature which shows us that in psychology, and the social sciences more widely, a Darwinian approach has long been entertained as serious and useful by a visible cohort of thinkers and researchers.

There are advantages to this approach. First of all it encompasses the fact that evolutionary explanations to mind and behaviour are not really new. **Evolutionary psychology** and allied theoretical viewpoints really ought to be considered as contemporary manifestations of a mature and persistent way of thinking which has an interesting history within psychology and the social sciences. Also, the history can be used as a guide to which have been the more and less useful lines of inquiry. Second, it enables us to see an evolutionary approach as a **meta-theory** or grand-**paradigm** rather than as an alternative to many of the specific theories that comprise psychology and the social sciences and which populate general textbooks. A prime objective of this book is to equip readers with a 'way of seeing', with a way of thinking about common behaviours. An explicit acceptance of the idea that humans have evolved can allow us to use the theory to evaluate more specific theories. And a third advantage to seeing evolutionary psychology as part of a long and fruitful tradition is that it enables us to place evolutionary psychology within the wider context of psychology and the social sciences and our attempts to explain ourselves to ourselves. It enables us to contextualise controversy that surrounds evolutionary psychology against the controversy that surrounds any concrete claims that are made about the human condition.

Appreciating the fact that evolutionary psychology is not new, that it can be used as a meta-theory, and that it is bound to be contentious just by virtue of its subject matter may facilitate another objective of this book which is to 'normalise' evolution in psychology. What is meant by 'normalise' is to make evolutionary theory a part of the fabric of psychology and social science, to make it one of the common-or-garden ways of thinking about thought and behaviour, to make it a part of your intellectual tool box. This objective will have been achieved if this book manages to get its readers to move from an acceptance that it is at the very least highly likely that our brains and minds have evolved to an exploration of what this may mean and to which aspects and facets of human psychology evolutionary theory is most usefully applied. In treating evolutionary approaches as an established school of thought we are hitching it to the claim that the major schools of thought in psychology that have persisted have done so because they are useful in that they describe and explain something about mind and/or behaviour.

EVOLUTION AND PSYCHOLOGY

As the phrase 'evolutionary approaches to mind and behaviour' that I used above suggests, the contemporary scene is comprised of slightly different ways of formulating and addressing hypotheses in what can be called 'the Darwinian tradition' or paradigm. We will be looking at the different approaches in Chapter 2 'Evolutionary approaches to thought and behaviour?' and again during the course of the book as and when the differences between the approaches help us to nuance our thinking and appreciation of evidence.

As we will see, the term 'evolutionary psychology' is just one of the ways of formulating and addressing hypotheses and it has a specific meaning. However, the term 'evolutionary psychology' has been used in the title of the book because it also has a general connotation: the Darwinian tradition of approaches in psychology and the social sciences has come to be most widely labelled as 'evolutionary psychology'. The title of the book, then, has come about by popular consent. The point to be made is that while adopting the term 'evolutionary psychology' the content of the book and the literature it reviews and examines is not constrained by the specific meaning of the term.

AIMS

This book has been prepared for readers with no prior knowledge of evolutionary approaches to psychology and social science. However, it is assumed that most readers (if not all) will have a more-or-less reliable working understanding of who Darwin was and the basic tenets of evolutionary theory. In light of these considerations the aim of the book is to take the reader to a level whereupon she or he should:

- Be conversant with and confident enough to give an exposition of the fundamentals of evolutionary theory and neo-Darwinism.
- Be able to evaluate arguments which claim an evolutionary basis for common human behaviours and conditions.
- Be able to evaluate the conceptual foundations of research conducted in the name of evolutionary theory.
- Be able to apply the theory to the day-to-day behaviour of individuals, groups and modern society as a whole with a view to generating testable hypotheses.
- Have an appreciation of debates within and objections to a Darwinian approach to mind and behaviour.

OUTLINE OF THE CONTENTS

The book comprises of 12 chapters. Chapter 1 is an explication of contemporary evolutionary theory, and Chapter 2 is an explication of how the theory has been and is used in psychology and the social sciences. There then follows two chapters which detail what is known about the evolution of humans and an outline of the development and functional structure of the mature human brain. Chapter 3 includes a cautionary tale about the use and abuse of the fossil record and **palaeontology**, and Chapter 4 explains why some think that the terms 'brain' and 'mind' refer to very different things. In Chapters 5, 6, 7 and 8 we move onto an introduction to evolutionary accounts, theories and research which purports to explain four central pillars of human behaviour: cooperation, families, mate selection, and aggression. Chapters 9, 10 and 11 address less obvious uses of evolutionary thought, namely, evolutionary accounts of abnormal behaviour, language and culture. And the closing chapter will look at wider objections to the very notion of evolutionary psychology and how evolutionary psychology may develop in the future.

INDEPENDENCE AND INTERDEPENDENCE OF THE CHAPTERS

Chapter 1 'Darwin's argument and three problems' is a 'must read' if you are not familiar with the theory of evolution by natural selection as it was presented by

Charles Darwin and as it has developed since. I say 'must read' for one simple reason: to paraphrase Theodosius Dobzhansky, nothing much in evolutionary psychology makes sense if you are not familiar with the tenets of the theory. Accordingly, nothing much in the rest of the book will make sense if you are not familiar with the ideas expounded in Chapter 1.

Apart from a dependence on Chapter 1 (or existing knowledge that you have which is equivalent to it), the remainder of the chapters should be self-contained and can be read alone and in any order. That said, most chapters contain cross-references wherein ideas and evidence in other chapters are referred to. For example, Chapter 11 'Evolution and culture' begins with a list of examples derived from previous chapters of how evolutionary psychologists invoke social conditions and circumstances to explain how evolved mental mechanisms **function** in modern environments.

LITTLE EXTRAS TO AID YOUR LEARNING

Each chapter is prefaced by a list of questions that are addressed in the chapter. The idea behind presenting you with questions before material that provides some answers is to get you actively thinking about what the content of the chapter might be and what sort of purpose it might serve. You may also find that your existing knowledge allows you to have stab at some of the questions. For example, theories that you have encountered and first- and second-hand experience might have left you with the confidence to answer a question such as 'What do women find attractive in men?' Some of the questions may bring to mind knowledge that you already have but may have forgotten that you know; e.g. why might an evolutionary theorist broadly agree with the sentiments behind the claim that blood is thicker than water? Also, in such cases you can use the text that follows the questions to check if what you think you know is sound. In those instances where the questions that preface the chapters make no sense or seem very complicated you may need to take a little extra care over the text so to develop your knowledge.

Each chapter is also prefaced by a list of learning objectives. Think of these as targets which the text is supposed to hit, of things I hope you come to understand or be able to do come the end of the chapter. And each chapter is also prefaced by a list of key terms and concepts. You may already have noticed that some terms in the text are in bold. You can also find definitions and examples of these key terms and concepts in the glossary at the end of the book. You may find it useful to look at these definitions before you begin each chapter and as you go along because it may either remind of what they mean, or give you a modest headstart. You will also find that definitions of key terms given in the chapters are worded differently from those given in the glossary. This is not designed to confused but rather to give you two ways of getting to grips with the meaning of key terms.

For a similar reason you will find text boxes dotted throughout the book. Some of these are headed 'Try it this way'. Experience both as a student and as a lecturer has taught me that it should be possible to present or explain the same idea in more than one way. This is a good thing because any one given way of explaining something doesn't make sense to everyone. Paraphrasing Abraham Lincoln this time, a given way of explaining or defining an idea will make sense to some people first time, all people sometimes, but it won't make sense to all people every time. Typically through metaphors and analogies the 'Try it this way' boxes offer a different way of thinking about concepts. The hope is that if you already get the idea your understanding will be enhanced, and if you don't get the idea the 'Try it this way' boxes give you a second shot at it.

You will also find boxes headed 'Before we continue, ask yourself . . .' dotted throughout the book. These boxes are filled with questions that appeal to your own experience and, in most cases, you ought to be able to offer a reply. The purpose of the questions is to link the associated content to your own experience, to show that the text has something to say about the world around you, and to help you tap into yourself as a resource in your own learning. The use of yourself as a resource is possible courtesy of the fact we live, work, and play amongst the phenomenon that psychology and social science studies.

THE END OF THE BEGINNING

It is probable that you have read this far because you have, or are planning to, enrol on a course about evolution and psychology and the relevance of one for the other. The very existence of such courses tells us that the idea that the two are mutually relevant is at large. This fact alone makes this book worth reading. Having read it you may come to the conclusion that evolution can tell you nothing about yourself or others. But I am confident that should you reach such a conclusion you will have been challenged by some of the most thought provoking and powerful ideas in psychology and the behavioural sciences along the way.

ACKNOWLEDGEMENTS

I am indebted to all who have taught me. Special thanks go to those who have encourged me to think a little harder than is my natural inclination – Alfred Newman, Erroll Cooke, Margaret O'Sullivan, Richard Mansfield, Alan Marks, Margaret Mynott, Andrew Wells, Bradley Franks, Robert Farr, Christopher Badcock, Jim Good and Anne Campbell. And I am indebted to those who have created the space in which this book could be written. Special thanks on this count must go to David Howe, Gillian Schofield and Neil Cooper.

PUBLISHER'S ACKNOWLEDGEMENTS

The author and publishers wish to thank the following for the permission to use copyright material:

We thank Custom Digital Maps for granting us permission to use Figure 2.3 *Map of Africa*. Maps courtesy of customdigitalmaps.com. Copyright © Custom Digital Maps 2009.

We thank David Orban for granting us permission to use Figure 4.6 *Daniel Dennett*.

We thank Elsevier for granting us permission to use material from the following articles:

Figure 1 from Daly, M. and Wilson, M.I. (1994) Some differential attributes of lethal assaults on small children by stepfathers versus genetic fathers. *Ethology and Sociobiology*, 15: 207–217. Copyright © 1994 Elsevier Science Inc. All rights reserved.

Table 1 from Pawlowski, B. and Koziel, S. (2002) The impact of traits offered in personal advertisements on response rates. *Evolution and Human Behaviour*, 23(2): 139–149. Copyright © 2002 Elsevier Science Inc. All rights reserved.

We thank Kathryn Tosney for granting us permission to use Figure 4.1 *Induction of the Neural Tube*. Garrett, B. (2009) *Brain and Behaviour: An Introduction to Biological Psychology* (2nd edn). SAGE Publications Inc. Courtesy Kathryn Tosney, University of Miami.

We thank Pearson for granting us permission to use Figure 4.2 *Neural Proliferation and Migration*. Toates, F. (2001) *Biological Psychology: An Integrated Approach*. Harlow: Prentice Hall.

We thank SAGE Publications for granting us permission to use Figure 4.4 *Saggital Section of the Human Brain*. Garrett, B. (2009) *Brain and Behaviour: An Introduction to Biological Psychology* (2nd edn). SAGE Publications Inc.

1 DARWIN'S ARGUMENT AND THREE PROBLEMS: HERITABILITY, SEXUAL SELECTION AND ALTRUISM

Some of the questions addressed in this chapter:

- What is natural selection?
- What problems did the theory of natural selection face after Darwin's death?
- How were the problems addressed?
- What are the laws of inheritance?
- What is sexual selection?
- How can we account for altruistic behaviour according to natural selection?

SOME KEY TERMS AND CONCEPTS

Adaptation; Altruism; Chromosomes; Darwinism; Fitness; Function; Genes; Heritability; Lamarck(ism); Mendel(ian); Natural selection; Reproductive success; Sexual selection; Variation.

LEARNING OBJECTIVES

Having studied this chapter you should be better able to:

- Outline the theory of natural selection.
- Indicate which parts of the process Darwin did not fully understand.
- Outline the mechanisms which underlie evolution.

INTRODUCTION

In this chapter we will look at Darwin's argument for the theory of natural selection and its logic. We will see that it is a good theory in that it offers a parsimonious account of the fact that animal and plant species are typically well designed to survive and reproduce in the environments in which they occur. Soon after its presentation, Darwin's theory gained currency in the scientific community and was widely accepted as a plausible account of how species come about and evolve over time. However, it still faced a number of problems. It wasn't entirely clear how characteristics of parents were passed to offspring, why some characteristics seemingly detrimental to long-term survival persisted in various species, and why all organisms were not relentlessly selfish. These problems were tackled in time and we will briefly review the solutions.

DARWIN'S ARGUMENT

BOX 1.1 ARE YOU A DARWINIAN?

Before we begin, ask yourself:

Do you believe that humans have evolved?
Do you accept that that you are the product of evolution?
Do you believe that humans are adapted?
Do you accept that you are fitted to, or designed to survive in, certain specific environments?
Do you believe that what we are adapted to and for can be addressed by our natural history?
Do you believe that the physical form that you take is explicable in terms of past selection pressures?

I suggest that if you either do or are inclined to say 'yes' to these questions then you are indeed a Darwinian.

Charles Darwin's argument for the natural selection of evolved life forms is not complicated and is based on observations. As was suggested soon after the publication of his *On the Origin of Species by Means of Natural Selection, or the Preservation of Favoured Races in the Struggle for Life* (Darwin, 1859), Darwin's interpretation of his evidence appears, on hindsight, to be obvious. The theory of natural selection can be presented as comprising three basic premises: the variation premise, the **heritability** premise and the adaptation premise. Together these premises led Darwin to the conclusion that life forms on earth evolved by a blind process he called natural selection. Let us look at the premises a little more closely.

VARIATION

The **variation** premise is based upon the observation that organisms within a species differ in their physical and behavioural characteristics. Following the conventions of common language, Darwin called identifiable differences between individuals of the same species 'variations'. Variation is demonstrated by the fact that no two instances of a species are physically (save the possibility of monozygotic siblings, more commonly called 'identical twins') or behaviourally identical.

INHERITANCE

The **inheritance** premise is based on the observation that variations between members of a species are frequently transmitted from parent to progeny. This is simply to say that identifiable characteristics of individual organisms are passed on to their offspring such that the offspring are distinct from others by virtue of the characteristics. This observation allows us to say that, *ceteris paribus* (all things being equal), offspring will resemble their progenitors more than they will any other randomly selected member of the species population.

ADAPTATION

The **adaptation** premise is based on the observation that organisms are 'fitted' to their environments. To say an organism is fitted to its environment is to say that in the wild (as opposed to in a zoo or a laboratory) it exhibits physical and behavioural characteristics which enable it to cope with and exploit features of the environment in which it lives. These features Darwin called 'adaptations'.

DARWIN'S CONCLUSION

Having established that organisms vary, that the variations can be inherited, and that species were adapted to the environments in which they are naturally found, Darwin inferred that not all variations are 'equal'. What he meant by saying they are not equal is that not all individual differences fitted the carrier equally well to the environment and the problem of reproduction. Darwin argued that as a result of variations some members of a species not only survived longer than others but, crucially, some produced more offspring than others. Invoking the observable fact that variations are heritable, Darwin concluded that variations which facilitate survival and reproduction will be more numerous in the next and future generations than others. The continual and inevitable reiteration of the process wherein some members of a species reproduce and pass on the characteristics which enabled them to survive and reproduce is what we call natural selection. The iteration of this process shapes and reshapes a species over time. Such shaping and reshaping is what we call evolution.

DARWIN'S PROBLEMS

As straightforward as it appeared to those of his contemporaries such as Thomas Huxley who proselytised on Darwin's behalf, Darwin himself and critics within the scientific community identified problems with his theory of evolution by natural selection. One of the problems concerned the observable fact that many typical features of different species appeared to hinder rather than help them to survive. The male peacock's tail is, perhaps, the most salient and oft-given example. Its size and visibility makes it expensive to produce in metabolic terms and renders the bird vulnerable to predators. We will call this the 'problem of non-**fitness**'. Darwin solved the problem himself in his volume *The Descent of Man and Selection in Relation to Sex* (Darwin, 1871) with his theory of **sexual selection** but his solution was not widely accepted until the 1930s. A second problem was the mechanism of inheritance. Darwin accepted that he did not know how it was that adaptive variations were transmitted from parent to offspring. He also did not know that the mechanism and rules of inheritance had, to a considerable extent, been discovered by Gregor Mendel. And a third problem, and one that Darwin said made him feel 'sick', was that of **altruism**. According to the theory, organisms should behave purely in their own self-interest but innumerable observations suggested that this 'rule' was routinely broken by any number of different species. The solution to the problem of altruism was presented in the 1960s by William Hamilton. The problem of altruism was solved by seeing the correct level at which natural selection operates – the genetic level. Let us now look at the solutions to the problems of non-fitness, heritability and altruism in turn. What we learn here will be essential to our understanding of later analyses of the evolutionary basis of human thought and behaviour.

THE PROBLEM OF NON-FITNESS AND SEXUAL SELECTION THEORY

As we have noted, many organisms, including humans, exhibit physical and behavioural characteristics that are typical of the species but appear to be detrimental to the bearer's prospects of survival and longevity. An example that we will examine in more detail in Chapter 8 'Competition, aggression and violence' is what has been called the '**young male syndrome**' – the apparently unnecessarily risky, and often life-threatening, behaviour exhibited by post-pubescent human males (Wilson and Daly, 1997). Being typical of a species any such characteristics are, according to theory, evolved and therefore, naturally selected. But, if the characteristics mitigate against survival and longevity how could they be repeatedly selected for and why would they persist?

In *The Descent of Man and Selection in Relation to Sex* Darwin reinforced his argument that evolution does not favour longevity *per se*, but it favours **reproductive success**. Now, while any given organism has to survive for some period of time – a minimum enough time to reach reproductive maturity – its reproductive success determines how many of its characteristics will be represented in the next generation rather than its life span. Of course, there is a relationship between the two given that longevity is likely to aid reproductive success. However, the maxim 'Don't count the candles on the cake, count the kiddies' holds. What we now call **Darwinian fitness** – the long-term survival over evolutionary time of any given heritable characteristics – is determined by the reproductive success of an organism and not the length of its life. In the currency of natural selection it is of no use if an organism lives very much longer than other members of her or his species if he or she does not reproduce.

With this insight in mind let us now outline sexual selection theory. Sexual selection theory argues that physical and behavioural traits that mitigate against longevity – that is, carry a cost to the bearer with regard to overall life expectancy – but facilitate reproduction – that is, aid the bearer in attracting mates and parenting viable offspring – can persist in a population over time. Let us return to the peacock's tail for an example. While the large and elaborate plumage of the male bird is costly to grow and makes the animal vulnerable to potential predators it also makes it visible and attractive to pea hens. In the case of peacocks the trade-off between the cost to longevity and the gain for reproductive success have favoured the elaborate tail which characterises the birds we see today. In short, sexual selection theory argues that the existence of variable heritable traits which seem to be useless or disadvantageous to survival can be explained if it can be shown that they confer an advantage with respect to reproductive success.

Sexual selection and natural selection are not necessarily mutually exclusive. A trait that enables an organism to enjoy reproductive success may also enable it to live longer. For example, better than average eye sight may enable an organism to spot predators, prey *and* this ability might make that organism more appealing to members of the opposite sex. However, to be confident that a given trait has evolved by sexual selection an analysis of its function should show that the trait is neutral or detrimental with regard to longevity and that it clearly facilitates reproductive success.

This is the reasoning behind the solution to the apparent problem of non-fitness. When we see that success over evolutionary time is determined by reproduction rather than survival we can also see that physical and behavioural characteristics which appear non-fit in survival terms may be fitness enhancing in reproductive terms.

As has been suggested, Darwin's proposal was not readily accepted when first introduced and it was further undermined by its rejection by the co-founder of evolutionary theory, Alfred Wallace (1823–1913). We might suppose that the emphasis on sex in the natural history of humans, and Darwin's emphasis on how the choices and preferences of females shape the evolution of most mammalian species including humans, was not well received in the late nineteenth century due to the sensitivities of the time. Sir Ronald Fisher (1890–1962) is, perhaps, most responsible for putting sexual selection at the centre of the theory of evolution and giving it nuance. His *The Genetical Theory of Natural Selection* (Fisher, 1930) proposed what has come to be known as '**runaway selection**' (also occasionally referred to as 'Fisherian selection'). Based on sexual selection theory, runaway selection theory further explicates how a non-fit characteristic can come about, evolve and become species typical. It explains how sexual selection can accelerate the evolution of characteristics beyond that which would be possible via natural selection by supposing that once a preference for a trait (often a female preference for a trait in males) becomes established only those males showing extreme forms of the trait get to reproduce. The only limiting factor on the evolution of the trait is it metabolic cost and/or negative impact on longevity.

We will be revisiting, expanding upon, and elaborating the theory of, and examining research inspired by, sexual selection theory in a number of subsequent chapters, especially Chapter 7 'Mate selection', Chapter 8 'Competition, aggression and violence' and Chapter 11 'Evolution and culture'.

THE PROBLEM OF HERITABILITY

BOX 1.2   THE DIFFERENCE BETWEEN PROCESSES AND MECHANISMS

TRY IT THIS WAY …

Darwin and Mendel:

As has been pointed out (Plotkin, 2002) Darwin explained the *process* by which change came about over time but he was unable to explain the *mechanisms* which embodied the process. To understand the distinction between process and mechanism consider the difference between the set of rules which govern how your essays or research reports are assessed and the actual work that is done – reading, appraising, commenting – in order to assess them. The rules provide an abstract description of the process that has to be gone through. The appraisal is the observable mechanism that instantiates the rules. Contemporary evolutionary theory is a synthesis – a marrying together – of the process that Darwin described and the mechanisms that Mendel and his successors have described.

Darwin was not the first to suggest that variations exhibited by individuals of a species are heritable and he was not the first to propose a theory of evolution. Probably the most influential of his predecessors was the French thinker and scientist Jean-Baptiste Lamarck (1744–1829). Lamark's theory of evolution was presented in a book whose English translation is *Zoological Philosophy: Exposition with Regard to the Natural History of Animals* published in 1809 (Richards, 1987) Lamarck proposed that evolution comes about via a process of **inheritance of acquired characteristics** – an idea also known as **Lamarckism**. The idea is that parents (of whatever species) pass on changes that have occurred in their physical make-up during the course of their existence to their offspring. Here we can appeal to another well-worn but illustrative example – that of the blacksmith who acquires larger than ordinary arm muscles and then passes on these acquired characteristics to his sons. Despite Lamark's failure to offer evidence in its favour it persisted through the nineteenth century and retains a certain appeal to this day. Why was this so?

There are at least three reasons. First, it was the first forcefully articulated theory of evolution by a respected naturalist in an age wherein the developing scientific community was amenable to the general idea that life had come about and evolved courtesy of forces other than the divine intervention of a god-like being. Second, when applied to humans the idea of acquired characteristics suggested that evolution, when thought of as 'improvement', was possible in response to human striving. And, third, when seen as the accumulation of useful knowledge and functional traditions, social and cultural evolution appears to fit the term 'acquisition of characteristics'. In the rapidly changing Europe of the late eighteenth and early nineteenth centuries it seemed to make sense to say that the hard-won characteristics that defined certain persons and social classes were bequeathed to their children, i.e. that the diligence, thrift, educational and moral outlook acquired by the expanding middle classes in newly industrialised European cities would be handed down to and exhibited by

Figure 1.1   Jean-Baptiste Lamarck

their children. In the absence of a plausible mechanism that would accommodate the transmission of heritable characteristics over multiple generations, through successive editions of the *Origin* Darwin drifted towards a Lamarckian position towards the end of his life (Badcock, 1994). Today Lamarck's theory is seen to be an inadequate account of change through time because the selection courtesy of use or disuse is not sophisticated enough to accommodate the innumerable very finely grained adaptations that comprised even simple organisms.

Unbeknown to Darwin, the problem of inheritance had, in essence, already been solved. In 1865 Gregor Mendel (1822–1884) presented his research to the Natural History Society of Brünn – Brünn being a town in Bavaria, Germany. Mendel published his findings a year later in the Society's journal. Mendel's idea was that organisms are composed of more-or-less discrete and fixed characteristics in much the same way that any machine is. What have come to be known as 'Mendel's Laws' can be derived from the evidence he accumulated. We will briefly consider the 'Laws' before moving on to see how Mendelian genetics solves Darwin's problem of heritability.

LAW OF SEGREGATION

An organism which reproduces via sexual reproduction transmits unchanged to its sex cells (or **gametes**) one of two sets of instructions it carries for any given discrete characteristic. Sex cells in humans are male sperm and female ova. Also called 'factors' or 'traits' these instructions are what we call genes. Reproduction involves the passing on of some of these fixed characteristics to their offspring via sex cells. While he did not use the term 'gene' (it was introduced by Wilhelm Johannsen in 1909), Mendel claimed that the sex cells from the two parents carried very specific instructions concerning the characteristics that the new offspring would exhibit. From a Darwinian point of view the key point is that the inherited factors or traits are passed on unchanged. What this means is that the offspring may look like a 'blend' of the parents – like a cocktail of blue and yellow paints producing green – but in actuality it is a recombination of fixed characteristics. The new mixture looks green but on closer examination we see that it is still made up of blue components and yellow components. Part of the uniqueness of the new individual comes not from blending characteristics but from but from a recombination of particular characteristics.

LAW OF INDEPENDENT ASSORTMENT

Applying to both prospective parents, the factors or traits are randomly assigned to any given sex cell – sperm or ovum. Look at Table 1.1 'Law of independent assortment'. We can think of what happens with independent assortment by imagining that the pairs of letters underneath 'Pop's Genome' represent all of his genes. The capitalised letters represent one variant of the gene, and the lower-case letters represent another. Let us say that the 'as' represent one part or feature of Pop, the 'bs' another, and so on. The same goes for 'Ma's Genome'. Independent assortment refers to the process whereupon when Pop produces a sex cell (a sperm in humans) a random selection of one of each type of gene goes into the sex cell. In the example shown it is a **B** c **D** e, but it could be ABCDE or abcde, or any other combination. Again, the same applies to Ma's sex cell. These two cells then combine to produce the new genotype.

Table 1.1   Law of independent assortment

Pop's Genome	Ma's Genome	Baby's Genome
Aa	aA	aA
Bb	bB	**Bb**
Cc	cC	cC
Dd	dD	**Dd**
Ee	eE	eE

Sperm – a **B** c **D** e   Egg – A **b** C **d** E

The importance of the **law of independent assortment** for **Darwinism** comes in its ability to explain how offspring vary from the parents and all other members of the species (save a monozygotic twin) when looked at as a whole while retaining discrete and unchanged traits from parents.

Before moving on to look at the **law of dominance** we will pause here to introduce a little more formal terminology. The variety of forms a factor or trait can take is called an **allele**. For the 'alpha' factor or trait in the imaginary example above possible alleles are **A**, A, **a** and a. There could be many others in the population such as *A A a* and *a.* Each one codes for a specific characteristic of the organism such as hair or eye colour, size of a particular anatomical structure or the physiology of a structure. The set of alleles which a new individual organism ends up is called its **genotype**. It is the genotype – the collection of alleles – which codes for and builds the mature organism which is also known as the **phenotype**.

LAW OF DOMINANCE

As we can see from the illustration in Box 1.3, alleles are paired and offspring receive one version of each from each parent. However, only one gene gets expressed. This means that only one is 'turned on' and codes for the particular characteristic. That which is expressed is called the **dominant gene**. That which is not expressed is called the **recessive gene**. We should note that the terms 'dominant' and 'recessive' do not mean and should not be taken to imply 'better' or 'worse'. They mean only expressed or not expressed, activated or not-activated.

The important point about dominant and recessive genes from a Darwinian perspective is that they demonstrate that a preponderance of observable expressed characteristics in a population of organisms can hide the fact that an equal number of genes coding for a different variation of the trait exist in a population and that the expression of recessive genes (often after many generations) shows that traits cannot be 'blended' out of existence.

To recap, Mendel's Laws, based on the notion that fixed and particular characteristics are inherited from parents via sex cells, show how variations could persist unchanged in organisms which, taken as a whole, appeared to be unique. However, Mendel's finding also raised a further problem for Darwinism. Given the seemingly fixed and permanent properties of genes, how do we account for evolutionary change in species as opposed to endless variations of the same basic template or design? The answer comes in the form of genetic mutations and the fact that the genes passed from parent to offspring are not always absolutely identical.

MUTATION

Mutation refers to the imperfect replication of a gene. A mutated gene is an inexact copy of that held by a parent which ends up in a gamete and, subsequently, in a new genome. See Table 1.2 for an illustration.

Here we have the same schematic as in Table 1.1. The difference in detail can be seen in the genes in Pop's sperm and Ma's egg. While Pop is carrying a B c D and e he donates *a* B c D *e* because a and e have mutated to *a* and *e*. Similarly, while Ma is carrying A b C d E she donates A b *C* d E because C has mutated to *C*. The outcome is an offspring which is not a collection of genes identical to those which reside in its parents. On the assumption that these mutations are novel (and let us do so for the sake of the illustration), what we have here is not simply an organism which is a variation on an established template or design but a new form of the species.

Table 1.2   Mutations

Pop's Genome	Ma's Genome	Baby Genome
Aa	a**A**	*a*A
Bb	b**B**	**B**b
Cc	c**C**	c*C*
Dd	d**D**	**D**d
Ee	e**E**	*e*E

Sperm – *a* **B** c **D** *e*   Egg – A **b** *C* **d** E
Where the italicised letters refer to mutated genes, and upper-case
letters refer to dominant genes.
Notice that only dominant genes get expressed and thus only one of the
three mutations in the new genome in this case would be expressed.

For our purposes there are three things to note about genetic mutations. One, the evidence suggests that they are rare and genes copy from donor to gamete with fidelity almost all of the time. Two, mutations are normally deleterious to the carrier – expressed mutations very rarely 'improve' the final phenotype in terms of its Darwinian fitness. And three, mutations – errors in the copying mechanism of genes – are the driving force in evolution. The rare mutations that do improve the fitness of the final phenotype which they code for can out-replicate alternatives alleles with the result that over very many generations a species can evolve into something different.

Mendel's discoveries allowed Darwinism to replace Lamarckism as the favoured theory of evolution because the idea that the inheritance of naturally selected particulate characteristics replaced the inheritance of acquired characteristics. Mendel also provided a scientifically well-attested means by which inheritance took place, it allowed evolution to be 'natural' or blind rather than purposive or teleological, and it provided a mechanism for variation and change that was slow, random and sex linked just as Darwin had proposed.

THE PROBLEM OF ALTRUISM

A third problem for Darwin concerned the apparent lack of selfishness exhibited by many of the species he observed. To understand the problem it is useful to look at one of the key notions which had influenced Darwin.

Before formulating the theory of natural selection in the 1840s Darwin had read Thomas Robert Malthus' (1766–1834) *An Essay on the Principle of Population* which was first published in 1798. Malthus' *Essay* is, essentially, a political treatise concerned with population growth. Population growth was a topic of great interest in eighteenth-century Britain where it had quadrupled in less than 100 years (Woods, 1995). Of particular interest to Darwin was Malthus' assertion that food supply can only grow at an arithmetic rate while population grows at a geometric rate: i.e. that agricultural advances can only increase food supply incrementally by fractions but population can grow by multiples.

Figure 1.2 Thomas Robert Malthus

The general message that Darwin gleaned from Malthus was that population growth for any species is constrained by resources and the constraint is omnipresent. The arithmetic warranted the conclusion that the capacity for reproduction will always outstrip the resources required to sustain the resultant population. To be successful in such circumstances it seemed to follow that organisms cannot not compete with one another for the resources which sustain life. Accordingly, ever-persistent resource shortages allied to the necessity of competition for the limited resources implies that organisms should be profoundly selfish. According to natural selection, if an organism sacrificed itself or any resource needed for survival and reproduction (and this could be time and space as well as nutrients) to the benefit of another then that proclivity would, axiomatically, not be passed on to others. The conclusion seemed obvious: over evolutionary time selfishness will out-compete and eradicate selflessness.

However, Darwin saw it himself and the evidence from observations of various species in their natural settings contradicted the selfish selection formulation of natural selection. Altruism and apparent cooperation amongst species as diverse as ants, birds and primates offered what seemed to be sound reasons for believing that many individual organisms behaved in such as way as to promote the survival of the species to which they belonged. These observations and this thinking gave rise to **group selection** – the idea that members of a species acted for the good of the species.

It is not too difficult to see why group selection has an appeal over and above the evidence which gives it licence. It takes some of the 'tooth and claw' out of an evolutionary view of the natural world. With humans in mind, group selection seemed to offer grounds for optimism. Perhaps the highpoint of the group selection theory came with Wynn-Edwards' volume *Animal Dispersion in Relation to Social Behaviour* (1962).

There are a number of conceptual and empirical problems with group selection theory and we will be examining some of them as well as looking at further reasons why the idea was, and remains, popular in Chapter 5 'Cooperation and Interdependence'. Now we will look at William Hamilton's solution to the apparent conundrum of altruistic behaviour and one of the most important ideas in contemporary evolutionary theory – **kin selection theory** (also known as **inclusive fitness** theory).

KIN SELECTION THEORY

Recall from our discussion of Mendelian inheritance that parents pass on to their offspring, and that which persists over time, are genes – instructions for particular and discrete characteristics. It is always tempting to think of natural selection as something that operates at the level of the individual – that it is you, me, Tom, Dick or Harriet that gets selected for or against. However, we need to remember that natural selection operates at the level of the gene. Why? Because natural selection works imperceptibly slowly, its winnowing process sifting characteristics favouring reproductive success through innumerable generations, it couldn't work at the individual level simply because individuals do not persist long enough, and, because we do not clone ourselves, we do not reproduce ourselves. But our genes do persist, replicate and clone. However, if we accept that the unit of selection is the gene, the following reformulation of the problem of altruism presents itself: how can one explain the existence of a gene that aids the reproduction of other genes?

As with much in evolutionary theory the answer may seem obvious when presented. And the answer, presented by William Hamilton (1936–2000) in two papers in the mid-1960s (Hamilton, 1964a, 1964b), rests on the observation that any given gene is selfish but not necessarily unique. Identical alleles are expected to be extant in a number of individuals. Furthermore, where there are multiple copies of genes, given the Mendelian rules of inheritance, the proximity of exact copies are likely to be found most frequently in families or kin groups. With this in mind, we can see that a gene that motivates the phenotype it helps to build to help other phenotypes which carry a copy of itself assists in its own replication, and vice versa. The conclusion is that natural selection could favour acts of altruistic helping on the condition that the helper is genetically related to the person helped. Should you and the person next to you share half your genes in common then any reproductive success that they enjoy amounts to reproductive success for you when looked at from the genetic level of analysis.

BOX 1.3   FORMULA FOR KIN SELECTION

Kin selection is formalisation as follows:
$Br>C$
Where **B** = benefit to the reproductive success of the actor.
Where **C** = cost to the actor in terms of its own reproductive success.
Where **r** = the degree of relatedness between the benefactor and the benfitee.

In ordinary language it means that altruistic acts of helping can pay off for the helper provided the cost incurred is not greater than the benefit received by the related individual. To illustrate, it will pay Tom to help his sister Harriet if the help to her is worth more in terms of her final reproductive success than twice the cost to him in terms of his final reproductive success given that, all thing being equal, they share half their genes in common courtesy of common descent. To reiterate courtesy of a parent–child scenario, it will pay Thomasina to help her child Dick if the help facilitates his reproductive success to more than twice the extent that it inhibits hers given that they share half their genes in common courtesy of common descent. The general point is that provided there is some degree of relatedness, there is always some potential that it will benefit the actor to jeopardise her own reproductive success provided the success of the other is enhanced.

Given that species with much smaller central nervous systems and far less elaborate cognitive abilities than humans appear to operate according to its edict it is supposed that, psychologically, all that is required for kin altruism to work is that an individual is able to identify others that carry the clone. This could be a simple counterfactual rule such as '*If raised with X then help*', or we need only invoke some sort of proximity calculation/rule such as '*Help those who look/smell like others around you*'. It is not necessary to suppose that either we or other species formally calculate who is and who is not related to us and to what degree we share which genes in common (Dawkins, 1979). The rough-and-ready way in which we calculate degrees of genetic relatedness has important implications. It may allow for what we might call 'virtual kin altruism' wherein we treat as kin others who we come to know well. We will look at the notion of virtual kin altruism in more detail in Chapter 5 'Cooperation and interdependence'.

Hamilton's solution to the problem of altruism has four-fold appeal to Darwinism. First, the problem of how altruism could exist dissolves. Second, it is solved by invoking the same unit and level of selection as the unit of inheritance and the source of variation – the gene. Third, seeing the individual as potentially altruistic but the gene as selfish accommodates the selfish logic insisted on by Darwin. A fourth way in which Hamilton's solution adds weight to Darwinism comes in the way it facilitated analysis of seemingly altruistic acts between non-kin. Kin altruism enables us to see how pro-social, cooperative, interdependent behaviour can come about and become common in a whole population of organisms (Maynard-Smith, 1982). We will conclude this chapter with an overview of Robert Trivers' theory of reciprocal altruism.

RECIPROCAL ALTRUISM

Further consideration of Hamilton's ideas suggests to us that altruism among kin is something of an illusion. The care provided by a parent to its child may look like it is unconditional, but from the gene-eye view, the parent is merely helping itself, aiding its own Darwinian fitness. We can see apparently unconditional assistance extended to brothers and sisters, cousins and grandchildren in a similar way. Trivers' account of how Darwin's theory can accommodate assistance given to unrelated others – **reciprocal altruism** theory – also invites some confusion because of the terminology used (Trivers, 1971). *Prima facie*, 'altruism' implies a one-way, unconditional act of giving whereas 'reciprocal' implies a two-way conditional exchange. It is the second notion which is at the heart of Trivers' idea. Strictly, perhaps, we ought not use the term 'altruism' because reciprocal altruism theory claims that exchanges of favour can become common amongst members of a species (and, indeed, between species) provided favours are reliably and consistently repaid. According to Trivers and others, reciprocal altruism – or what we might also call mutual assistance – can and has evolved to be a typical characteristic of many species, including humans, because it pays those who engage in it in terms of their reproductive success. It is especially apt to work well in species wherein the assistance of others can enable an organism to achieve a goal that would be either difficult or impossible to achieve alone. For example, it is easier to get another to scratch your back than it is to do it yourself, and vice versa. Sexual reproduction itself is an example wherein the goal cannot be achieved with some sort of cooperation from another party, and there are many others. In Dennett's words, reciprocal altruism is a 'good trick', a mutually beneficial, cost-effective way of gaining desirable pay-offs (Dennett, 1995). In fact, so good a trick is mutual assistance that it can be a positive disadvantage not to engage in it, or to dodge debts if the consequence is a withdrawal of aid.

As we shall see when we explore the mechanics, arithmetic and psychology of kin selection and reciprocal altruism in further detail in Chapter 5 'Cooperation and interdependence', the claim that apparently altruistic acts are underpinned by genetic gain does not mean that an act of giving between kin does not feel like an expression and outcome of unconditional love, or that favours exchanged between acquaintances are not also expressions of care and affection. Evolutionary psychologists argue that evolution has shaped us to feel and think in ways which mask the biological functions being served. While the functions served are real, so too are the psychological states that serve them (Trivers, 1983).

SUMMARY OF CHAPTER 1

Darwin's theory of evolution by natural selection rests on three observations. The first is that members of a species vary. The second is that offspring inherit characteristics from their parents. And the third is that species are adapted to their natural environments. From these observations Darwin concluded the accumulation of inherited variations that better fitted some organisms to solve the problem of survival and reproduction resulted in change in the species over time.

The emphasis on the need to reproduce allowed Darwin to explain why some characteristics of species seemed to be an impediment to their chances of surviving. What we have called the 'problem of non-fitness' is solved when we see that the overarching problem is not survival but reproduction and some characteristics persist because they assist reproduction at the cost of longevity.

However, Darwin did not know how inheritance worked, or why selfless behaviour was so commonplace. The solutions to the problem of inheritance and the problem of altruism lay in the concept of the gene. Mendel's work led to the identification of genes as the mechanism by which inheritance works. And the work of Hamilton showed that because genes clone themselves they can code for organisms that assist others to their own benefit. The result was kin selection theory and it provides the rationale behind the notion of the selfish gene. Trivers applied similar cost–benefit thinking to the issue of mutual self-assistance. His theory of reciprocal altruism explains how non-related members of a species can come to cooperate with one another.

FURTHER READING

Apart from the references in this chapter you may find it interesting and useful to consult one or more of the following:

Cronin, H. (1991) *The Ant and the Peacock*. Cambridge: Cambridge University Press – see Chapter 2 'A world without Darwin'.

Fisher, R.A. (1997/orig. 1930) The nature of adaptation. In Ridley, M. (ed.) *Evolution*. Oxford: Oxford University Press – see pp. 112–115.

Hume, D. (1997/orig. 1751) The argument from design. In Ridley, M. (ed.) *Evolution*. Oxford: Oxford University Press – see pp. 387–389.

Huxley, T.H. (1894) *Man's Place in Nature and Other Essays*. London: Macmillan and Co. – see Chapter XIV 'The Darwinian hypothesis'.

Williams, G.C. (1997/orig. 1966) Adaptation and natural selection. In Ridley, M. (ed.) *Evolution*. Oxford: Oxford University Press – see pp. 115–118.

2 EVOLUTIONARY APPROACHES TO THOUGHT AND BEHAVIOUR

Some of the questions addressed in this chapter:

- What is the history of Darwinism in psychology and social science?
- What is 'instinct'?
- How can the past tell us about the present?
- How can the present tell us about the past?
- To what extent is evolutionary psychology a 'new science'?
- How do psychologists and social scientists use evolutionary ideas to explain thought and behaviour?

SOME KEY TERMS AND CONCEPTS

Adapted mind; Adaptive mind; Conceptual integration; Environment of evolutionary adaptation (EEA); Ethology; Human behavioural ecology; Instinct theory; Modularity; Sociobiology; Standard social science model.

LEARNING OBJECTIVES

Having studied this chapter you should be better able to:

- Detail what is meant by the term 'evolutionary psychology'.
- Outline the precursors to evolutionary psychology.
- Be able to distinguish between different ways of using evolutionary theory to explain human thought and behaviour.

INTRODUCTION

In the preface to this book it was said that the term 'evolutionary psychology' has a specific meaning and that it differs from other approaches which utilise Darwinian ideas to understand

and explain human thought and behaviour. And it was said that the title of this book glosses over these different approaches, choosing to use the term 'evolutionary psychology' because it has become the name of popular choice when referring to applications of evolutionary theory to mind and behaviour. In this chapter we will stop to pause and look more carefully at what evolutionary psychology proper purports to be. And we will look at how it is similar to and different from the line of thinking and research from which is has emerged and other contemporary approaches.

We will begin with an overview of what has been called the '**instinct debate**' (Hampton, 2004b). The instinct debate refers to a protracted series of debates and discussions which took place amongst psychologists, social scientists and philosophers between *c.* 1890 and *c.* 1930. At its broadest, the discussion was about how to use and apply Darwin's theory in psychology, sociology and anthropology. More narrowly it was a debate about how to properly define the term 'instinct'. Instinct theory gave way to more experimentally orientated approaches in the 1930s. Most notable amongst them was behaviourism which was especially influential in America where the greatest concentration of academic psychologists was to be found.

We will then look at **ethology**. Ethology was initiated in Europe in the 1930s and it sought to examine and analyse the behaviour of organisms and species in situ, in their natural setting, in the wild. While not specifically about humans, and situated outside of schools and departments of social science and psychology, as a discipline ethology was always relevant to human psychology. For example, Lorenz's *On Aggression* (Lorenz, 1966) became and remains a staple reference for students of social psychology. And Bowlby's series of books about human attachment remains influential in developmental psychology (Bowlby, 1969).

As we saw in Chapter 1, the work of William Hamilton is taken to have solved one of Darwin's problems – altruism. His kin selection theory gave Darwinism a new impetus and two new strands of Darwinian psychology subsequently emerged. The first of them that we will consider is **sociobiology**, and the second is **human behavioural ecology**.

Our brief review of past and present varieties of Darwinian psychology will lead us to an explication of evolutionary psychology – arguably the most influential attempt to provide a Darwinian paradigm for psychology. The formulation of evolutionary psychology that we will focus upon is that presented by John Tooby and Leda Cosmides. Their essay 'The psychological foundations of culture' (1992) and the papers that presaged and preceded it, 'Evolutionary psychology and the generation of culture, part I: theoretical considerations' (1989), and 'The past explains the present: emotional adaptations and the structure of ancestral environments' (1990), and subsequent iterations (see Tooby and Cosmides, 2005) 'have informed virtually all work being conducted in the field of evolutionary psychology' (Buss, 2005:1), and Tooby and Cosmides are considered the 'architects' of evolutionary psychology (Pinker, 1997) and described as 'true pioneers' (Buss, 2005).

It is worth noting that the discussion in this chapter is largely uncritical of evolutionary approaches to thought and behaviour. The view has been taken that it is more useful, and less confusing, if concepts, theories and findings are laid out and understood before being subject to a critique. Or, to put the point another way, one can only sensibly and seriously criticise ideas after they have been fully explicated. We will be looking at empirical and conceptual difficulties in Chapter 12 'Some problems with evolutionary approaches'. You are, of course, free to look at that chapter at any point of your choosing.

BOX 2.1   DARWIN AND DARWINISM

Apparently Karl Marx once said that he was not sure what Marxism was but he was sure that he wasn't a Marxist. What could he have meant? Presumably he saw some of the interpretations and variations of his theory of political and social change as being insufficiently true to his own position. Marx seemed to take some of the ways in which his name was applied to ideas to be illegitimate uses of what might think of as his 'brand'. The same situation is probably true for other famous theorists and thinkers – Freud for example. Is it true of Darwin? Is what we call 'Darwinism' and the 'Darwinists' who trade on the Darwin 'brand' today true to Darwin?

THE INSTINCT DEBATE

The idea that humans come into being equipped with certain sorts of knowledge, with certain proclivities and abilities which subsequently mature and can be seen in the child and adult, has been an issue in psychological and behavioural thought since Aristotle, and the notion of 'instinct' is of equal vintage (Beach, 1955; Drever, 1917; Hobhouse, 1901; Richards, 1987; Robinson, 1981; Wilm, 1925). If we were to accept the orthodox view and accept that psychology proper emerged as a distinct academic specialty in the late nineteenth century (see Farr, 1985), it would be reasonable to say that at that time the concept of instinct was as salient and considered as important as any other idea in the discipline. Many researchers and theorists who today's historians of psychology take as representative of academic psychology in its infancy contributed to what we can call 'the instinct debate' (e.g. Allport, 1924; Angell, 1906, 1907; Dewey, 1896, 1930; Dunlap, 1919, 1922, 1932; James, 1890; Lloyd-Morgan, 1894; McDougall, 1908; Mead, 1934; Thorndike, 1911; Titchener, 1914; Tolman, 1922, 1923, 1932; Watson, 1913, 1919, 1931; Yerkes, 1911 – see Hampton, 2004b). This debate was inspired by Darwin's theory, given impetus by William James in his influential *Principles of Psychology* (James, 1890), and, more widely popularised by William McDougall courtesy of his textbook *An Introduction to Social Psychology* (McDougall, 1908). Darwin discussed instinct in *The Origin of Species*, and again in *The Descent of Man* and *The Expression of Emotion in Man and Animals*. Although he stated 'I will not attempt a definition of instinct', he did, in effect, produce a guarded definition by writing:

> An action, which we ourselves require experience to enable us to perform, when performed by an animal, especially by a very young one, without experience, and when performed by many individuals in the same way, without their knowing for what purpose it is performed, is usually said to be instinctive. (Darwin, 1859: 191)

Furthermore, Darwin clearly took instincts to be a phenomenon suitable for psychological inquiry by adding, 'It would be easy to show that several distinct mental actions are commonly embraced by this term' (ibid.,: 191).

Figure 2.1   William McDougall

Perhaps Darwin did not say enough. He certainly left open much room for further discussion and elaboration. The attempt to define instinct – to say exactly what counted as an instinct, to specify what it was that constituted an instinctive act or thought – fractured into a series of oppositions, schools and, in the end, antagonisms (Hampton, 2006). Anglo-Saxon psychologists eventually lost patience with what seemed to be a slide back into the methods and prospects that the discipline faced when it was still a branch of philosophy of mind (Richards, 1987).

For our purposes we need to note that the attempt to establish the concept of psychological instincts was explicitly Darwinian. That is, the scholars mentioned above and many others took themselves to be Darwinians and to be working on and working out Darwin's suggestion that his theory would become the foundation stone for psychology (Hampton, 2004b). Furthermore, instinct theory was psychological in that instincts were supposed to be a property of our minds – conscious or unconscious, in concert with or in opposition to intelligence – that governed our thought, motivations and social behaviour. Among the instinct theorists who classed themselves as psychologists few were of greater importance than William McDougall (Hampton, 2005a). This is how McDougall defined instinct: 'The human mind has certain innate or inherited tendencies which are the essential springs or motive powers of all thought and action … These primary innate tendencies … are probably common to the men of every race and every age' (McDougall, 1908: 19). And:

> We may, then, define an instinct as an inherited or innate psycho-physical disposition which determines its possessor to perceive, and to pay attention to, objects of a certain class, to experience an emotional excitement of a particular quality upon perceiving such an object, and to act in regard to it in a particular manner, or, at least, to experience an impulse to such action. (ibid.,: 29)

In due course we will see that the contemporary approach which calls itself evolutionary psychology is really quite similar to McDougall's formulation.

BOX 2.2 OBJECTIONS TO EVOLUTIONARY PSYCHOLOGY: EUGENICS

When the term 'eugenics' was coined in the latter part of the nineteenth century it meant 'well born', and it was used to refer to persons of 'good stock', and it connoted 'health'. When the term was politicised it came to represent the view that evolutionary theory could be used to determine and control who could and should reproduce (Galton, 1979; Jones, 1998). There are two very good reasons why me might object to eugenics, and, in the process object to the theory which gives it its licence.

Nazism took eugenics to be the study and practice of improving the human race by controlled selective breeding. And we know the outcome – the Holocaust and the many other terrible abuses committed by the Third Reich. Carlos Blacker, the General Secretary of the Eugenics Society between 1931 and 1952, argued that the crimes of the Nazis would come to be seen as the most important event in the history of eugenics. Blacker thought that objections to the historical events would lead to objections to the ideas that brought them about (Blacker, 1952).

Eugenics also invites a further and even more profound objection to evolutionary theory. The very idea that there is such a thing as 'well bred' person of 'good stock' is abhorrent to some. Mere utterance of such terms implies a deep-rooted, unalterable inequality between those who exhibit properties deemed good and those who do not. Accordingly, we might argue that the truth or falsity of the notion of biological fitness is irrelevant, and that we must ignore evolutionary theory and organise ourselves on the assumption that we are all born the same. On this view eugenics provides us with grounds to reject evolutionary approaches to thought and behaviour because they violate the belief in offering the same opportunities and striving for equality of outcome for all.

ETHOLOGY

Whereas the notion of instinct fell out of favour in America and The United Kingdom in the 1930s, it found a home amongst naturalists and zoologists in Europe in the same decade. Whereas psychology at that time used animals to cast light on human psychology, ethology was much more specifically the study of animal behaviour in general with an interest in humans only in so far as it took us to be just another type of animal. Just as Darwin had hinted that instincts were unlearned while habits were acquired, ethology was interested in unlearned and inherited behaviour rather than learned and habitual behaviour.

Konrad Lorenz, Karl von Frisch and Nikolaas Tinbergen are generally recognised as the founders of ethology, a recognition cemented by their receipt of the Nobel Prize in 1973. Desmond Morris, Irenäus Eibl-Eibesfeldt, Robert Hind and Patrick Bateson have also been influential in the field and are better known for their application of the principles of ethology to human behaviour. Desmond Morris' volume *The Naked Ape* (Morris, 1967) may be taken to mark the point at which an ethological approach to human thought and behaviour became of interest to the wider reading public and it is still in print today.

BOX 2.3 SEX AND THE SAVANNAH: *THE NAKED APE* GOES BANANAS

The BBC claimed that the world was 'stunned' when Desmond Morris published *The Naked Ape* which went about describing humans in the same manner as did zoologists when discussing any other animal. The content of the book did not disappoint those who found the title provocative.

While not wholly concerned with sex, many reviewers chose to emphasis some of Morris' claims about human reproduction. For example, amongst all the claims the book makes, some which became more well known and talked about include:

- We have the largest penis and the largest breasts as well as the largest brains in the primate world
- Penises and breasts have been shaped by sexual selection to act as a signal to prospective mates.
- We are the most sex obsessed amongst the primates.
- Our unique ear-lobes are erogenous zones that can be the source of orgasms in both sexes.

The book was a marked success. It was serialised by a British tabloid newspaper and became a bestseller in Europe and America. So successful was *The Naked Ape* that Morris became a tax exile. The book is still in print today. In less than a decade another bestselling book about the biological basis of human behaviour would 'stun' the world – Richard Dawkins' *The Selfish Gene* (1976).

Figure 2.2 *The Naked Ape* **first published in 1967**

Ethology has a legacy in psychology. Common in the introductory textbooks with which most psychology students are familiar with is a treatment of Lorenz's notions of 'fixed action patterns', 'innate releasing mechanisms' and 'imprinting' (Lorenz, 1981). **Fixed action pattern** refers to a functional sequence of behaviours which is typical of a species and is triggered by a specific stimulus – the **releasing mechanism. Imprinting** refers to phase-sensitive learning wherein a certain sort of event needs to take place during what is known as a 'critical period'. These concepts are still used in ethology today and they have been applied in human developmental psychology. For example, when we talk of the first hours after birth as being a critical period during which mother and child 'bond' we are supposing that mother and child act as a stimuli to one another which triggers a pattern of thought and behaviour which can be conceived of as attachment behaviour (Bowlby, 1969). As with the term 'instinct', evolutionary psychologists do not readily appeal to the terms 'fixed action patterns', 'innate releasing mechanisms' and 'imprinting', but it does appeal to the underlying concepts. Contemporary evolutionary psychology subscribes to the idea that we have innate behavioural repertoires, that they are triggered by internal and external stimuli, and that the appearance of these behaviours is contingent on environmental conditions (Tooby and Cosmides, 1992).

Perhaps the most useful theoretical tool in ethology came from Tinbergen and his contention that we should ask four sorts of question when analysing the behaviour of organisms from an evolutionary point of view (Tinbergen, 1963). In no particular order, Tinbergen suggests that we should ask:

1 What is the function of a given typical or common behaviour? How does it relate to and solve the (more or less) immediate problems of survival and reproduction?
2 What is the cause of the behaviour? Which stimuli trigger the behaviour or what are the precedents of it?
3 What is the ontogeny of the behaviour? How does it come to develop in the individual during its life course?
4 What is the phylogeny of the behaviour? How has it come to be selected for and evolve in the species?

The utility of the distinctions are various. First, they can help us to locate and refine questions. Second, they can help us to decide what sort of evidence would address which sort of question. Third, distinctions between types of 'why?' question can help us to make sense of existing evidence. And fourth, they help us to expand and elaborate our questions. For example, suppose that we were interested in the phenomenon wherein children typically come to be orientated towards their peer group as the most explicitly and consciously salient and influential persons in their environment at about the age of 10 (Harris, 1998; Maccoby, 1998). Tinbergen's 'four whys' suggest that a rounded evolutionary account needs to show if and how the shift in orientation impacts upon the long-term fitness of the child, what happens so the that we might reasonably say what is a cause or necessary condition for the change, how the change comes about over the life course of the child and how an orientation towards peers evolved so to become species typical of human children.

Evolutionary psychology has adopted Tinbergen's scheme, but it has recast it into a distinction between ultimate and proximate mechanisms. The former entails a focus on the functional history of the psychological adaptations that organise our behaviours in the here and now. The latter entails a description of how the adaptations work in real time.

SOCIOBIOLOGY

While first use of the term 'sociobiology' appears to have been in a volume published in 1949 called *Principles of Animal Ecology* (Alled et al., 1949), its fame (and, for some, notoriety) came with the publication of E.O. Wilson's *Sociobiology: The New Synthesis* in 1975 and Richard Dawkins' *The Selfish Gene* which followed in 1976. Widely cited within academia and beyond, these two books mark the beginning of sociobiology as a school of thought and a research programme with a definite identity.

As the term implies, sociobiology analyses the social behaviour of species from a biological, and, more precisely, from a gene's-eye, point of view. Like ethology, sociobiology isn't exclusively or especially interested in humans. Wilson demonstrated this by devoting just one chapter of 27 to humans. In essence sociobiology is a working out of Hamilton's insights and solution to the problem of altruism, and Robert Trivers' theories of reciprocal altruism and **parental investment** (Trivers, 1985).

Evolutionary psychology and sociobiology are seen by some as being of a piece, and it has been suggested that the former is merely a re-branding of the latter (Rose, 2000; Rose and Rose, 2000). However, leading proponents of evolutionary psychology claim that there is a critical difference between the two approaches. The claim is that sociobiology adheres to the assumption that organisms work toward the maximisation of their inclusive fitness – they are 'fitness maximisers' motivated by the grand objective of maximum reproductive success and ought to be analysed as such. In contrast evolutionary psychology adheres to the assumption that our thought and behaviour is determined by short-term goals which, if achieved, add up to reproductive success (Buss, 1995; Tooby and Cosmides, 1992). We will explore this supposed difference and work out some of the implications in due course, and most especially in Chapter 10 'Evolution and Abnormal Psychology'.

Few theories of human behaviour have evoked as much controversy as sociobiology. While it has attracted thoughtful and valuable critiques such as Philip Kitcher's *Vaulting Ambition* (1987), it has also attracted a hostility that does not really address the quality of the theory and its explanation of evidence (Wilson, 1994). It has been argued that while evolutionary theory had developed enough to be extended to an analysis of the social behaviour of humans, psychology and the social sciences had not (Pinker, 2002).

HUMAN BEHAVIOURAL ECOLOGY

Human behavioural ecology (sometimes abbreviated as HBE) applies evolutionary theory to the study of human behaviour in its natural or spontaneous contexts and is a branch of anthropology. Like ethology, HBE is interested in behaviour in situ. It typically works on the assumption that humans are adaptive in that our behaviour is organised around a wider unconscious strategy to optimise our inclusive fitness (Laland and Brown, 2002). The different strategies adopted and developed in differing ecological and social environments to the end of maximal inclusive fitness give rise to individual, group-level and cultural diversity. HBE looks to establish the adaptive advantages of individual, group and cultural traits, rituals and means of solving problems. It also adopts a life-history approach to see how behaviours change in light of the differing adaptive problems that come and go during the course of an individual life. In other words, 'The principal goal of human behavioural ecology is to account for the variation in human behaviour by asking whether models of optimality and fitness-maximisation provide good explanations for the differences found between individuals' (Laland and Brown, 2002: 112).

Importantly, for HBE 'An overriding assumption is that human beings exhibit an extraordinary flexibility of behaviour, allowing them to behave in an adaptive manner in all kinds of environments' (Laland and Brown, 2002: 112). This assumption and the emphasis on flexible means towards the end of Darwinian fitness has led to HBE being called the '**adaptive mind**' approach (Hampton, 2004a). As we will see, this is to be contrasted with evolutionary psychology which emphasises the adapted nature of the human mind.

Behavioural ecologists accommodate differences in the expressed behaviour of persons in a group and between different groups courtesy of **life history theory**. Life history theory is based on the assumption that the life of any organism, including a human, involves a trade-off between what is called somatic effort and reproductive effort and that effort devoted to the former cannot be devoted to the latter, and vice versa. Somatic effort refers to all time and energy expended in the development and maintenance of the body – i.e. to survival. Reproductive effort refers to all time and energy devoted to mating, parenting and inclusive fitness. It is supposed that life is a trade-off between the two classes of expenditure and effort and the trade-off is shaped by age, sex, local mortality rates, mate value, **sex ratio**, resource base and ecological constraints. The flexing and alterations of behaviour according to local conditions in order to come to the best trade-off between somatic and reproductive effort, and to adopt the best somatic and reproductive strategy amounts to the particular life history of the organism. Human behavioural ecologists work on the premise that one might predict the life history of a given organism or group if one assumes that the organism will work towards optimal inclusive fitness in the circumstances it finds itself (Kaplan and Gangestad, 2005).

EVOLUTIONARY PSYCHOLOGY

Evolutionary psychology is sometimes referred to as the '**adapted mind**' approach (Hampton, 2004a). The reason for this is straightforward. The volume which cemented together thinking and research into what we might call a school or new movement is called *The Adapted Mind: Evolutionary Psychology and the Generation of Culture* (Barkow et al., 1992), and it may be regarded as 'one of the first and most important collections of essays on modern evolutionary psychology' (Badcock, 2000: 17). It is regarded as 'first' because it claims to introduce a novel approach. And its importance flows from its ascription as being 'the seminal publication in th[e] field' (Corballis and Lea, 1999b: v).

Evolutionary psychology is grounded in the evidence-based conviction that human beings are an evolved species just like any other. It shares this conviction with the instinct theorists of the early twentieth century, with the ethologists in the mid-part of the century, sociobiologists in the 1970s and 1980s, and human behavioural ecologists today. Like instinct theory, evolutionary psychology is centred on the supposition that evolved psychological dispositions generate human behaviour and culture. Like ethology it is amenable to comparative evidence from other species. Like sociobiology it seeks to establish evolutionary theory as the pre-eminent guiding orientation in psychology and the social sciences. And like human behavioural ecology it takes the view that traditional, non-industrialised societies may be of special importance to our understanding of our evolved traits. According to Barkow et al., evolutionary psychology:

> ... unites modern evolutionary biology with the cognitive revolution in a way that has the potential to draw together all of the disparate branches of psychology into a single organised system of knowledge ... [our goal] is to clarify how this new field, by focusing on the evolved information-processing mechanisms that comprise the human mind, supplies the necessary connection between evolutionary biology and the complex, irreducible social and cultural phenomena studied by anthropologists, sociologists, economists, and historians. (Barkow et al., 1992: 3)

Of the 19 papers that comprise *The Adapted Mind*, four are wholly theoretical. Of the theoretical papers, Tooby and Cosmides' 'The psychological foundations of culture' is the cornerstone and it has been the most influential. For example, in Pinker's view 'John Tooby and Leda Cosmides ... forged the synthesis between evolution and psychology' (1997: x). Tooby and Cosmides make four main claims in their essay which, together, constitute their argument for an evolutionary approach to psychology and society.

In order of original presentation, the four claims are that psychology and the social sciences should be conceptually integrated with biology and the natural sciences, that psychology and the social sciences have been dominated by what they call the 'standard social science model', that to understand the present condition of humans and their psychology we must appeal to our natural history, and that humans minds are comprised of psychological adaptations which can be thought of as discrete information-processing machines. Let us unpack and examine each of these claims in a little more detail and look at the role each plays in evolutionary psychology.

BOX 2.4   BACKWARDS AND FORWARDS: THE ADAPTED MIND AND THE ADAPTIVE MIND

TRY IT THIS WAY ...

A distinction between two contemporary approaches which use evolutionary theory to understand and explain psychology and behaviour can be thought about by looking at human behavioural ecology as a 'backward' approach and evolutionary psychology as a 'forward' approach (Reeve and Sherman, 2007; Sherman and Reeve, 1997).

(Cont'd)

Evolutionary psychology – the forward approach:

1 Describe the features of the past (the proper domain).
2 Using our knowledge of the past, stipulate the likely fitness utility of a proposed pattern of thought or behaviour 'X' in the past.
3 Establish the frequency of 'X' in the present (the actual domain).
4 If 'X' would have had fitness utility in the past and is typical in the present then we can conclude that 'X' has been selected for.

In other words, the forward approach says that we should evaluate the present in terms of the past – the past explains the present.

Human behavioural ecology – the backward approach:

1 Describe the features of the present (the actual domain).
2 Evaluate the fitness utility of a given pattern of thought or behaviour 'X' in the present.
3 Postulate the likely fitness utility of 'X' against a model of the past (the proper domain).
4 If 'X' has a fitness utility in the present and it would have had a fitness utility in the past then we can conclude that 'X' has been selected for.

In other words, the backward approach says that we should evaluate the past in terms of the present – the present explains the past.

CONCEPTUAL INTEGRATION

Conceptual integration as a claim belongs to the philosophy of science. It is a particular view on the way in which we should acquire an understanding of our thought, behaviour and societies. According to Cosmides et al., conceptual integration:

> … refers to the principle that the various disciplines within the behavioural and social sciences should make themselves mutually consistent, and consistent with what is known in the natural sciences as well … A conceptually integrated theory is one framed so that it is compatible with data and theory from other relevant fields. (1992: 4)

And, according to Cosmides et al., 'As a result' of the failure of social scientists to adhere to the principal of conceptual integration, 'one finds evolutionary biologists positing cognitive processes that could not possibly solve the adaptive problem under consideration, psychologists proposing psychological mechanisms that could never have evolved, and anthropologists making implicit assumptions about the human mind that are known to be false' (ibid.,: 4).

Barkow et al. (1992) liken conceptual integration to 'vertical integration'. Vertical integration amounts to a philosophy of knowledge that is reductionist in the most commonly understood sense wherein physics is privileged as a source of knowledge (Chalmers, 1999).

In this scheme integration is necessitated by causation, and causes flow vertically upwards from more precise levels of analysis. Every scientific claim is explicable and consistent with what is known in the science immediately below it in a hierarchy. The hierarchy is determined by the precision of physical detail and prediction. Thus, 'the laws of physics apply to chemical phenomena, and the principles of physics and chemistry apply to biological phenomena, but not the reverse' (Cosmides et al., 1992: 4).

Conceptual integration amounts to a slight softening of the position inherent in vertical integration. Sciences as a whole are a family of bodies of knowledge that form a cluster rather than an 'epistemological or status hierarchy' (ibid.,: fn. 13). The criterion of mutual consistency remains but the difference between the hierarchy of vertical integration and the 'heterarchical relationships' (ibid.,: fn. 14) encouraged by conceptual integration comes with the reciprocal influence between sciences that the conceptual integration permits. So, while the causal chain that evolutionary psychology proposes is: natural selection > evolution > adaptations > psychological mechanisms > culture, and, it follows, there is no suggestion that culture is responsible for psychological mechanisms in the manner that psychological mechanisms are responsible for culture, the demand that culture be consistent with psychological mechanisms is matched by the demand that psychological mechanisms must be consistent with culture. In principle, a cultural 'fact' can cast doubt on a psychological theory.

BOX 2.5   A COMPARISON OF HUMAN BEHAVIOURAL ECOLOGY AND EVOLUTIONARY PSYCHOLOGY

	Human behavioural ecology	Evolutionary psychology
Primary focus	Behavioural strategies	Psychological adaptations
Affiliated with	Social anthropology	Cognitive and social psychology
Location of key cause	Ecological variables	Cognitive mechanisms
Hypothesis generation	Optimality models	Inference from past selection pressures
Primary methods	Quantitative observation	Survey and experiment
Outcomes measured	Overall fitness	Expressed preferences, cognitive responses
Favoured topics	Subsistence, reproduction	Mate choice, sex differences

Human behavioural ecology seeks to formulate hypotheses regarding variations in the behavioural strategies of individuals trying to maximise their inclusive fitness whereas evolutionary psychology seeks to formulate hypotheses that specify the operation of the adapted psychological mechanisms that shape and drive behavioural response and choice. Let us a look at an example. HBE has since its inception in the mid-1970's been concerned with foraging behaviour in traditional cultures (Winterhalder and Smith, 2000). Courtesy of optimal foraging theory and working on the assumption that a given forager has as his or her objective the maximum return as measured by calorific and nutritional value, human behavioural ecologists look to predict what foods will be searched for over which range and for how long. Looking at the same phenomenon the evolutionary psychologist would seek to specify the cognitive mechanisms that underlie the observed behaviour, demonstrate their operation in a controlled setting, and ask if it is plausible to say that they can be characterised as psychological adaptations.

THE STANDARD SOCIAL SCIENCE MODEL

The **standard social science model** is a thesis in the history of ideas. As presented by Tooby and Cosmides, the standard social science model (hereafter the SSSM) is all that evolutionary psychology is not. If for no others reason, then, it is worth our while seeing what the SSSM is because it should help us to see what evolutionary psychology is.

The standard social science model is, according to Tooby and Cosmides, 'The consensus view of the nature of social and cultural phenomena that has served for a century as the intellectual framework for the organisation of psychology and the social sciences and the intellectual justification for their claims of autonomy from the rest of science' (1992: 23). Tooby and Cosmides argue that the autonomy of the psychological and social sciences from the natural sciences is grounded in the belief that 'a "constant" (the human biological endowment observable in infants) cannot explain a "variable" (inter-group differences in complex adult mental or social organisation)' (ibid.,: 26). Accordingly,

> ... the SSSM concludes that 'human nature' (the evolved structure of the human mind) cannot be the cause of the mental organisation of adult humans, their social systems, their culture, historical change, and so on... . Whatever 'innate' equipment infants are born with has traditionally been interpreted as being highly rudimentary ... Because adult mental organisation (patterned behaviour, knowledge, socially constructed realities, and so on) is clearly absent from the infant, infants must 'acquire' it from some source outside themselves in the course of development. That source is obvious: this mental organisation is manifestly present in the social world ... the social (or cultural or learned or acquired or environmental) ... contains everything complexly organised ... The cultural and social elements that mould the individual precede the individual and are external to the individual. The mind did not create them, they created the mind ... [the] action of the social world on the individual is compulsory and automatic – 'coercive' to use Durkheim's phrase ... (ibid.)

Tooby and Cosmides argue that the 'cognitive turn' in the 1950s and 1960s offered the SSSM a new, technical cloak and jargon in the form of the metaphor of mind as being a general-purpose information-processing machine that obtains its programs from culture. The essential features of the standard model view were retained in that 'human nature is an empty vessel, waiting to be filled by social processes' (ibid.,: 29).

Though specific in their portrait of an intellectual tradition, Tooby and Cosmides are general with regard to disciplinary focus. With specific reference to psychology, they claim:

> In the SSSM, the role of psychology is clear. Psychology is the discipline that studies the process of socialisation ... Thus the central concept in psychology is learning. The prerequisite that a psychological theory must meet to participate in the SSSM is that any evolved component, process, or mechanism must be equipotential, content free, content independent, general purpose, domain-general, and so on. Moreover, their structures must themselves impose no particular substantive content on culture. (ibid.,: 29)

Tooby and Cosmides' SSSM thesis can be summarised as a set of commitments that are said to have dominated psychology and the social sciences more generally. These are: (a) that mind, aside its capacity to learn, is a *tabula rasa*; (b) that culture is the cause of mental content; (c) that culture is independent of mind; and (d) that psychology should be concerned with the study of enculturation. These four notions are, then, the fundamental propositions – be they explicitly stated or implicitly assumed – that constitute social science. According to Tooby and Cosmides they are commitments in that they are subscribed to by social scientists.

The occurrence of the instinct debate, ethology and sociobiology suggests that standard model depiction of the history of psychology is not reliable. However, for present purposes, criticisms of the SSSM thesis are of limited value and importance. This is because the SSSM in the overall scheme of evolutionary psychology is not essential, and the validity of evolutionary psychology does not ride on the historical accuracy of the SSSM. Still, the SSSM idea does play a part in the story of the rise of evolutionary psychology. The contrast between the standard model and the evolutionary model which evolutionary psychologists propose legitimises the claim that, as a whole, evolutionary psychology is a new approach. As Rose and Rose (2000) have indicated, as a component of evolutionary psychology, the SSSM is one of the elements which distinguishes it from sociobiology and human behavioural ecology. And, as a thesis in the history of ideas, the SSSM, since being introduced by Tooby and Cosmides, has been adopted by a number of authors (Hampton, 2004b) and discussed by evolutionary psychologists 'as though it were a technical abbreviation rather than a rhetorical device' (Kohn, 1999: 19).

THE ENVIRONMENT OF EVOLUTIONARY ADAPTEDNESS

The **environment of evolutionary adaptedness** (EEA) is a methodological tool based on a depiction of our natural history. The term 'environment of evolutionary adaptation' was coined by the developmental psychologist John Bowlby. He used the idea to explain how patterns of attachment between infants and caregivers can be thought of as adaptive responses in infants to differing parenting practises (Bowlby, 1969). As a tool the EEA concept was developed and its utility in evolutionary psychology made explicit by John Tooby and Leda Cosmides (1990, 1992). There are various synonyms of the term and they include ancestral environment, environment of selection and the general references to the **Pleistocene** era in **palaeoanthropology**. The time period typically evoked by reference to the EEA is most often taken to be the *c.* 1.8 million-year period since the emergence of the genus *Homo* through to either appearance of *Homo sapien c.* 150 000 years ago or to the beginning of the Holocene period *c.* 10 000 years ago – a period marked by the emergence of agriculture and a pastoral mode of existence. Occasionally the time period said to mark the beginning of the EEA is relaxed to cover the *c.* 6 million year period since the emergence of the *Australopithecines* and a family of species known as **hominids**.

The key point is that evolutionary psychology takes the EEA to amount to the set of past selection pressures responsible for any given extant adaptation. In Tooby and Cosmides' words, 'one can define the environment of evolutionary adaptedness for an adaptation as that set of selection pressures (i.e. of the ancestral world) that endured long enough to push each allele underlying the adaptation from its initial appearance to near fixation (1996: 122).

The place, or location, of the EEA is Africa. More precisely, it is predominantly eastern and, to a lesser extent, southern African (Wilson and Cann, 1992). This placing of the EEA follows the majority view of palaeoanthropologists that modern humanity is 'Out of Africa' (Tattersall, 1997). What this means is that we evolved in eastern Africa and subsequently migrated from that region to others on that continent and around the world. However, we cannot be as sure of the location of the EEA as we can its duration for there is some debate on the matter of where hominid development prior to modern man took place (Stringer, 1992). A view known as the **multi-regional hypothesis** does have adherents and it argues that modern humans evolved in various parts of the globe. In practice most evolutionary psychologists do not embroil themselves in detailed palaeoanthropological debates and their research does not rest upon assumptions that could reasonably be called precise when specifying the time and place of a supposed selection pressure and subsequent adaptation.

Accordingly, we may take the following as a workable rule: the EEA (or a functional equivalent) is invoked when any given account of our past or hypothesis concerning extant psychological adaptations makes an assumption(s) about a species of *Homo*, and/or the environment to which it was adapted, and/or the environment to which it needed to adapt. For example, were we to claim that, say, modern humans have an evolved tendency to behave generously towards their family members we would be making the assumption that, as a matter of fact, such behaviour was exhibited by hominids prior to modern humans and that such behaviour was adaptive and fitness enhancing in past environments.

The utility of the EEA concept for evolutionary psychology is that an explicit appeal to our evolutionary past holds out the promise of an account of psychology that is specifically human. Here we need to keep in mind that evolution is a general theory, ultimately mathematical in nature, which claims to account for the functional features of all species. It is not specifically about humans. In fact, applied to all the distinct species that have ever existed, the human story would be difficult to find such would be the size of the library. Motivated as such, the EEA is a tacit admission that evolutionary theory in and of itself is not entirely adequate as a generator of hypotheses about human psychological characteristics or adaptations. Reference to our evolutionary history overcomes this problem. We can use knowledge about our past to generate hypotheses about our psychological adaptations, mechanisms and/or dispositions. Moreover, it helps us to think in a more or less disciplined way about what sorts of psychological adaptations humans might have. Reference to our natural history puts a human face on evolutionary theory and in doing so facilitates the prospect of a normative general theory of human nature. And, reference to our past is

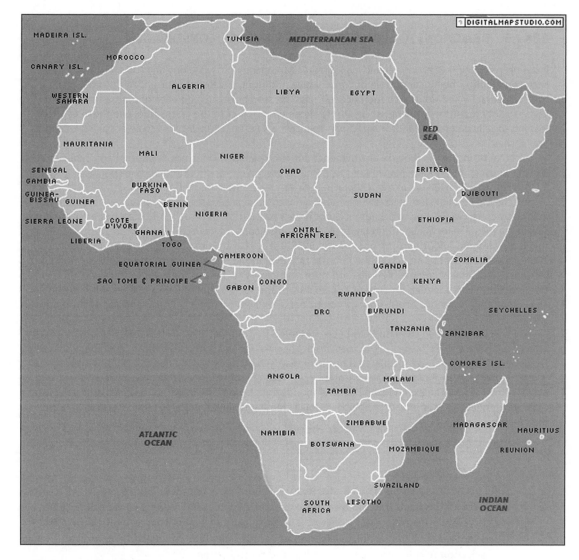

Figure 2.3 Map of Africa
The Out of Africa hypothesis claims that modern humans first evolved in then migrated out of Eastern Africa about 150,000 years ago.
Copyright © Custom Digital Maps 2009. http://www.customdigitalmaps.com/

of a piece with conceptual integration – the proposal that the psychological and social sciences should be mutually consistent – by providing a common ground for hypothesis generation and confirmation.

BOX 2.6   OBJECTIONS TO EVOLUTIONARY PSYCHOLOGY: CONSERVATISM

It has been argued that biological and evolutionary approaches in psychology and the social sciences are seen by default as being supportive of conservative and right-of-centre political views (Pinker, 2002). In turn, conservative and right-of-centre political views are seen as being a defence of the status quo in any given society (Campbell, 1999a). Accordingly, those who object to the status quo, and those of a left-leaning, socially progressive and/or egalitarian political persuasion will be inclined to object to evolutionary approaches.

In actuality, insofar as there is any evidence for such claims it does not support them. Tybur et al. (2008) surveyed 168 US students working for a PhD in psychology and found that those purporting to be adaptationists – 37 in all – were more liberal in their views than non-adaptationists.

Still, the idea that evolutionists are inherently conservative fails to see that evolutionary theory is not inherently conservative simply because it is not driven by political values. Evolutionists *en masse* are not seeking to preserve inequalities and hierarchies. Of course, some of its proponents will be right wing. But this is a statement about persons not the theory. But it is also true that some are left wing (Richards, 2005). Indeed, Singer has argued that contemporary evolutionary theory, founded on kin selection and reciprocal altruism, is compatible with socialism and ought to be inculpated into left-wing thinking because it provides a secular account of human nature and social organisation, and does not reply upon an ungrounded optimism about how we might behave given the right physical and social conditions (Singer, 1999).

An interesting twist on this issue has been presented by Thornhill and Fincher (2007) who argue that attachment style and life history act to mediate political values and that conservatism and liberalism can be viewed as 'functional and socially strategic in human evolutionary history' (ibid.,: 215). Their hypothesis is that highly secure individuals who experienced low childhood stress become conservatives, and avoidant individuals who experienced high childhood stress become liberals. They report that tests which scale attachment style, conservatism-liberalism, social dominance and right-wing authoritarianism support their theory.

The next chapter 'The natural history of humans' examines some of the evidence which licenses the claim that modern humans have evolved, and in doing so we will flesh out the details of this important concept. The next section in this chapter will characterise the claim that our minds are a collection of specific adaptations shaped by natural and sexual selection to solve problem of survival and reproduction.

MINDS ARE COMPOSED OF ADAPTATIONS

The claim that minds are composed of adaptations is a particular philosophy of mind derived from evolutionary theory. The idea is that our minds are made up of evolved psychological adaptations that each of them serve particular and discrete functions. With this claim we come to the aspect of evolutionary psychology which, on the one hand, ties it most closely to the general thrust of the instinct debate and attempts to discern and classify the components which constitute human psychology, and, on the other, differentiates it from ethology, sociobiology and behavioural ecology. To grasp what it is that evolutionary psychologists mean by saying that our minds are a suite of discrete adaptations it will help to review the argument that the mind is modular.

In the most general terms, for any kind of system, or machine, to be modular it must consist of functionally and/or physically separable units. These units, or modules, are (more or less) specialised. On the one hand, the system – the whole – is nothing more than the sum of its parts (nothing more than its modules). On the other hand, the system achieves a concert beyond that which isolated modules might suggest. There are a number of ideas in psychology that converge toward the modularity view. Let us look as some of them.

Anatomically, the human brain, quite literally, looks modular. Neuroanatomy presents it as a collection of cortices, lobes and hemispheres (Crossman and Neary, 2005). For example, the occipital lobe is at the back of our brains and it facilitates vision. The occipital lobe is to a considerable degree isolated from the parietal lobes at the sides of our brain. The parietal lobes facilitate the control of movement. Similarly, the cerebellum at the base of the brain facilitates vegetative and homeostatic functions and can be isolated from the frontal lobes at the front of the brain facilitate higher-order 'intelligent' thought. Neurology shows us that different parts of the brain are critical for certain processes and these parts are (more or less) unique in their exhibition.

BOX 2.7 MODULARITY AND THE MOTOR CAR

TRY IT THIS WAY …

Cars are modular machines. They are made up of many components, each of which does a particular job. For example, the headlights perform a function distinct from head restraints. The headlights can fail leaving the head restraints intact to perform their function, and vice versa. Some components are more important than others with regard to the overall job of the car. The engine, for example, is critical if a car is to get from one place to another. Something as apparently simple as a brake cable is critical if it is to do so safely. The point is that the car as a whole is made up from a myriad of distinct parts and their functional relations.

While such neuroanatomical considerations facilitate the claim that minds are modular, evolutionary psychology is not concerned with the anatomy and physiology of the central nervous system *per se*. Rather, it is concerned with cognitive processes (the demand for mutual compatibility withstanding). Its focus is on mental or cognitive modularity as opposed to physical modularity.

Advocates of cognitive modularity stress its ecological plausibility and its consistency with evidence from studies of patients with brain damage. Such evidence also suggests that modular systems can suffer local failures without a subsequent global failure. That is, we can suffer physical damage to certain anatomically discrete parts of our brain which, in turn, eliminates or impairs our ability to perform certain cognitively discrete functions, but other functions remain unimpaired. This point is one of the reasons why modularity suits evolutionary psychology – it amounts to good engineering (Pinker, 1997; Tooby and Cosmides, 1992).

There are other ways in which modularity meshes with evolutionary psychology. The most important of these is with the claim that mind is a suite of adaptations. In principle, modular processes should dovetail with solutions to adaptive problems. Tooby and Cosmides argue that if the mind was other than a suite of modular specialised systems – were it to be a general purpose computer which was programmed by experience – it would be too clumsy to be effective in natural environments in real time (Tooby and Cosmides, 1992). Evolutionary psychologists believe the human mind is a complex system of computational mechanisms selected for and shaped by natural and sexual selection. These mechanisms may be readily compared to other organs in our bodies in that they are products of selection pressures designed to perform specific functions. In principle, mind taken to be an adaptation is no different from, in the widest sense, say, gills, and in the narrower sense, say, opposable thumbs. Thus, 'The human mind consists of a set of evolved information-processing mechanisms … these mechanisms … are adaptations, produced by natural selection over evolutionary time in ancestral environments' (Tooby and Cosmides, 1992: 24).

These considerations are distilled in a proposed method for studying thought and behaviour from an adaptationist standpoint. Tooby and Cosmides have laid out a scheme that ought to be followed in order to find and detail the operation of psychological adaptations (Tooby and Cosmides, 1992). We can illustrate the scheme by providing examples drawn from Cosmides' social contract theory which proposes that one of our psychological adaptations is a 'cheater detector' which has been selected for and evolved to enable us to spot others who do not reciprocate favours (Cosmides, 1989).

1   First, we need to establish 'an adaptive target': this amounts to a description of what counts as a biologically successful outcome in a given situation. For example, if we are to engage in reciprocal exchanges we need to avoid those who do not reciprocate.
2   We need to establish the 'background conditions': this amounts to a description of the features of the EEA that are relevant to the adaptive problem. For example, we need to have some confidence that cheating was common enough to have been a recurring problem through our evolution.
3   We need to establish a 'design': this amounts to a description of a cognitive processes which would solve the problem. For example, we need to specify how our ancestors would go about detecting cheaters.
4   We need to conduct a 'performance examination': this amounts to an experimental analysis of what happens when the proposed solution interacts with the proposed problem.

For example, if we say that spotting cheaters involves an up-to-date recollection of who has reciprocated equitably in the past and who has not courtesy of an analysis of the value of assistance exchanged we need to see how well such a mechanism works in experimental conditions.

5 We need to conduct a 'performance evaluation': this amounts to an analysis of how well (or how poorly) the proposed design managed to produce the adaptive target (the biologically successful outcome) under circumstances paralleling ancestral conditions. The better the mechanisms performs, the more likely it is that one has identified an adaptation. For example, if we do not need to suppose that anything other than spotting cheaters involves an up-to-date recollection of who has reciprocated equitably in the past and who has not courtesy of an analysis of the value of assistance exchanged in order to account for how people manage not to get cheated most of the time in ordinary day-to-day circumstances, which, we may reasonably suppose, are much like those that our ancestors encountered, then we can conclude that we have found and described a psychological adaptation.

The five steps detailed above amount to an answer to the question 'What is evolutionary psychology?' It is the search for the evolved species typical modes of thought that underpin our behaviour. As we can see, and as the as the central place of the EEA in evolutionary psychology suggests, the place to start the search is with the adaptive target – the biologically beneficial outcome thought to have been regularly achieved in the past. The construction of ancestral conditions, including the condition of the species in question at the time, then allows us to move on and hypothesise a design. It is to the past – to the natural history of humans – that we will now turn.

SUMMARY OF CHAPTER 2

'Evolutionary psychology' is used as a general term which connotes the use of evolutionary theory in psychology and the social sciences. But it also has a specific denotation wherein it refers to a particular way of thinking about and studying thought and behaviour. It is often touted as being a 'new science' but it has a number of predecessors. These include instinct theory, ethology and sociobiology. It is also not alone in the contemporary landscape of Darwinian approaches that include human behavioural ecology.

While differences do exist between the different approaches and we have also seen that there are clear links between them. Evolutionary psychology shares with instinct theory an emphasis on psychological dispositions, aversions, tastes and proclivities. It shares with ethology a distinction between explanations which emphasis how organisms operate in the here and now and why they have come to exhibit the behaviours that they do. Like sociobiology, evolutionary psychology takes a gene's-eye view of adaptations, and like human behavioural ecology it is interested in using depictions of our natural history to define, refine and test hypotheses.

FURTHER READING

Apart from the references in this chapter you may find it interesting and useful to consult one or more the following:

Cosmides, L. and Tooby, J. (1992) Cognitive adaptations for social exchange. In Barkow, J.H., Cosmides, L. and Tooby, J. (eds) *The Adapted Mind: Evolutionary Psychology and the Generation of Culture.* Oxford: Oxford University Press. pp. 163–228.

Dewsbury, D.A. (1999) The proximate and the ultimate: past, present and future. *Behavioural Processes,* 46(3): 189–199.

Krebs, J.R. and Davies, N.B. (1997) *Introduction to Behavioural Ecology* (4th edn). Oxford: Wiley/Blackwell.

Plotkin, H.C. (2004) *Evolutionary Thought in Psychology: A Brief History.* Oxford: Wiley/Blackwell.

Smith, E.A., Borgerhoff-Mulder, M. and Hill, K. (2001) Controversies in the evolutionary social sciences: a guide for the perplexed. *Trends in Ecology and Evolution,* 16(3): 128–135.

Smith, E.A. and Winterhalder, B. (eds) (1992) *Evolutionary Ecology and Human Behavior.* New York, NY: Aldine de Gruyter.

3 THE NATURAL HISTORY OF HUMANS

Some of the questions addressed in this chapter:

- How are humans placed in the wider scheme of animal species?
- What evidence do we have that modern humans have evolved?
- How many species of human have there been?
- Why have new species evolved?
- How did our ancestors behave?
- What constraints does the evidence place on what we can reasonably say about our natural history?

SOME KEY TERMS AND CONCEPTS

Australopithecus; Competitive replacement; Holocene; Hominid; *Homo*; Hunter-gatherers; Pleistocene; **Pliocene**.

LEARNING OBJECTIVES

Having studied this chapter you should be better able to:

- Locate the place of modern humans in the animal kingdom and describe our phylogenetic tree.
- Outline the natural history of *Homo*.
- Generate hypotheses about the evolved dispositions, proclivities and behaviours of modern humans.

INTRODUCTION

In this chapter we will concentrate on the natural history of modern humans. An emphasis on the past is central to most forms of evolutionary explanation. However, courtesy of concepts such as the environment of evolutionary adaptedness, evolutionary psychologists rely on depictions of past selection pressures to a greater extent than did instinct theorists, and than do ethologists, sociobiologists and human behavioural ecologists.

To come to a more developed understanding of our natural history we will begin with our roots as some sort of great ape, and trace the development of our lineage through to about 20,000 years ago and the beginning of the **Holocene** and the advent of agriculture. The purpose of doing this is two-fold. First, it is necessary to look at the actual evidence that we have evolved, for it is logically respectable to hold that all species other than humans are a product of natural and sexual selection. Second, the evidence that we have evolved is our guide to the particulars of the environment of evolutionary adaptedness (EEA) and the selection pressures that have shaped our bodies and minds.

Our review of the evidence will bring us to consider the appearance, development and extinction of a number of species that may have been the ancestors of modern humans. In order to help us frame and place these species in the wider context of life on earth our tour will begin with a discussion of **taxonomy** – the science of classifying living things. We will end this chapter by considering what it is we can say with confidence about the EEA. We will see that it is all too easy to go beyond what is known with confidence and step into a realm of speculation about the past that the evidence does not warrant.

TAXONOMICS

The Swedish naturalist Carolus Linnaeus (1707–1778) is widely accepted to be the founder of what we now call taxonomy. Taxonomy is the science of stipulating the relations between and naming species of plant and animal. Darwin was influenced by Linnaeus and, in part, Darwin's work may be seen as an attempt to provide a theoretical basis for taxonomy. The lasting contribution of Linnaeus was to establish the conventions for the naming of living things and a hierarchical structure which allows us to place species within it.

At the top of the hierarchy are 'kingdoms'. Kingdoms include plants and animals. Within each kingdom there are 'phylum', or types of animal or plant. Within phylum there are 'classes' of the type. Within each class there are 'orders', or types within each class. And so it goes onto 'families' of order, genus within orders, particular species within a genus and, finally, varieties within a species. Let us now place humans within the system Linnaeus devised. We will do this by beginning at the top of the hierarchy.

From the top we can place ourselves in the animal kingdom (or *animalia*) by virtue of the fact that, among other things, we are multicellular organisms capable of locomotion, and we are heterotrophic – that is we eat other living things for growth and maintenance. Amongst the phylum which comprise the animal kingdom we are classed as a chordate because we are vertebrates with a notochord, or backbone. Of the classes of animal that are chordates perhaps the most familiar to those who are not zoologists are reptiles and mammals. We are a mammal by virtue of the fact that we nourish infants via mammary glands, we are warm blooded and give birth to live offspring. Within the class mammalia there are a number of orders and we belong to the order primate. Broadly speaking, primates are what

Figure 3.1   Carolus Linnaeus

most people think of and would recognise as monkeys. Some of the defining characteristics of the primate order are forward facing eyes, hands (as opposed to claws for example), a pattern of dentition including incisor and molar teeth, and large brains in relation to body mass. Primates come in many shapes and sizes from spider monkeys weighing six kilos to mountain gorillas at 200 kilos and more. There are a number of super-families within the primate order. We are placed within a super-family called Hominoidea. This super-family includes the great apes. Hominoidea are divided into further family groups and that to which we belong is the hominid family. Hominids are characterised by being bipedal and, therefore, they stand upright, their brains are typically bigger than the average for primates, and they have stereoscopic vision. Also, as well as having specialised limbs in the form of arms and legs they also have specialised hands and feet. On this description there is only one extant hominid family – us. It follows that there cannot be more than one genus of extant hominid, and one species of the genus. Our genus is *Homo* – but there have been others. And of the species of *Homo* we are called *Homo sapien* meaning 'clever', or 'intelligent', man.

Here we have glossed over many nuances in ways of classifying and sub-dividing the various taxonomic categories that have emerged since Linnaeus. The nuances and distinction have themselves come about courtesy of the discovery of untold new species. The Linnaean system is a categorical system. That is to say, it demands that any given species can be put into a 'box' which is discrete from all other boxes. This approach made sense when it was devised. While still in use, it makes less sense in light of Darwin's theory and the widespread acceptance of the idea that should we to be in possession of fossils of all the species that had ever lived we would see that they are continuous with one another and not categorically discrete. We will be looking at some of the debates about how to classify hominids and species of *Homo* later in the chapter. Before we look at the phases of human evolution it is only reasonable to let you know that the literature is littered with varying forms of terminology and nomenclature for the different fossils that comprise the record. This reflects the intensity of discussion and debate as to how to properly sort and classify the fossils. That the abundance of evidence leads to debate should not be taken to mean that debate leads to doubt as to whether we evolved. The doubt is over how evolution unfolded not that it happened at all.

LINNEAN TAXONOMICS

Kingdom – Animalia
Class – Mammalia
Order – Primates
Super family – Hominoidea
Family – Hominids
Genus – *Homo*
Species – *Homo sapiens*

A BRIEF GUIDE TO OUR NATURAL HISTORY

A largely unspoken assumption in evolutionary psychology is that the extant species that are closest to us in terms of DNA are also most like our now exstinct ancestors or so like us they may be cosidered living ancestors. Those species are the common chimpanzee (*Pan troglodyte*), bonobo (or pygmy) chimpanzee (*Pan paniscus*), the lowland gorilla (*Gorilla gorilla*) and mountain gorilla (*Gorilla beringei*). This is not to say with certainty that we evolved from any of these extant species for it is not known that any of them existed in their current form when the first hominids appeared. But it is assumed that we evolved from something very similar to those species, and that they provide a living picture of our ancestors. According to palaeoanthropological evidence this assumption is reasonable (Foley, 1987; Richmond and Strait, 2000; Ruvolo, 1997; Tattersall, 1995; Wood, 1992; Wood and Brooks, 1999) and it plays out in a number of ways. For example, when we consider the ways in which human beings pair bond and reproduce in Chapter 7 'Mate selection' we will look at the mating systems of the great apes and ask which of them provides a 'best fit' for humans. In doing so we are assuming that one or another of these African ape species provides us with a model of our mating behaviour in the past. In this chapter the assumption that we have evolved from something akin to the extant African great apes provides us with a starting point from which we can build up a picture of human evolution.

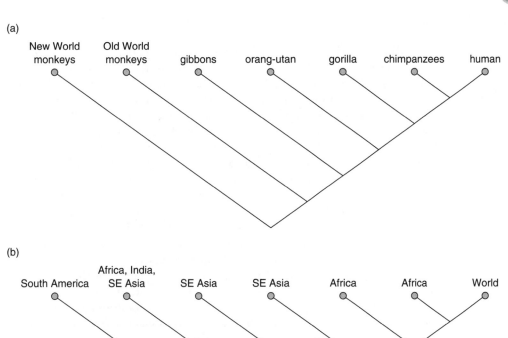

Figure 3.2   Cladogram of the primates

As a guide to our discussion here is an orthodox simplification of human evolution: a new family of ape-like primates which we now call hominids appeared in Africa *c.* 6 million years ago. Their anatomy below the neck was unlike apes and they were bipedal. Above the neck it was ape like and they had ape-sized brains. About two million years ago a genus of hominid called *Homo*, meaning 'man', appeared. *Homo* had a larger brain and used stone tools. Scavenging of meat added protein to an otherwise largely vegetarian diet. About 1.5 million years ago a species of *Homo* migrated out of African and into Europe and Asia. Half a million years ago the brain size of at least one species of *Homo* was close to that of ours, tool technology had advanced and the hunting of large mammals was common. We are the descendants of that species. The following sections will add detail to this preliminary sketch of human evolution.

AUSTRALOPITHECINES

Taking something akin to extant chimpanzees as a starting point, the fossil record suggests that the next stage in human evolution came in the form of a species called *Australopithecus*. The first fossil evidence for this species was discovered in 1925 (Dart and Craig, 1959). Its finder called it *Australopithecus africanus* which means 'southern ape of Africa'. Orthodox taxonomy classes *Australopithecus* as a hominid, and it first appeared in eastern Africa about six million years ago. The skeletal anatomy of the *Australopithecines* tells us that they walked up-right on specialised legs. Known as 'bi-pedalism', this is the defining single characteristic of hominids. However, they also had long arms and long, curved fingers and toe bones. This suggests they were also arboreal, meaning that they were adept climbers and were comfortable moving around in trees. The anatomical hints that they were somewhere between chimpanzees and later *Homo* species does not appear to have extended to their cognitive characteristics. The *Australopithecines* had brains approximately the same size as modern great apes and we have no evidence of a sophistication of tool use that extends beyond what we see in chimpanzees.

The *Australopithecines* persisted for something in the region of three to five million years – at least 20 times as long as we have persisted to date. As we will see, several later species of hominid did not persist for so long. The longevity of *Australopithecus* tells us that they were successfully adapted to their physical environment. The evidence suggests that there may were at least three variants of *Australopithecus* – *afarensis*, *africanus*, and *boisei* – and that they appeared in that order.

One of the more celebrated finds in palaeoanthropology came in 1974 when Donald Johanson and others found an almost complete skeleton of what we now take to be an example of *Australopithecus afarensis*. The skeleton became known as 'Lucy' (Johanson and Edgar, 1996). Other finds support the view that *afarensis* were extant between *c.* 6 and *c.* 2.75 million years ago.

While evidence of *Australopithecus africanus* was found before *afarensis* it is assumed that *africanus* evolved from *afarensis* and was extant between *c.* three–two million years ago. *Africanus* appears to have been taller that *afarensis* and had a slightly larger brain. Its maxiofacial structure was different, with the face being flatter. Dentition too was different and this is taken to mean that the diets of the two species differed (Johanson and Edgar, 1996).

Australopithecus was flexible enough to survive migration into more southerly areas of Africa. Around three million years ago a new form of *Australopithecus* evolved and may have given rise to a further sub-species. While typically classed as *Australopithecus* and given the moniker 'robustus' due to the shape and weight of its skeleton and crania in comparison to afarensis and africanus, some researchers argue that these variants are so different from previous forms they should be thought of a different genus called *Paranthropus* . The robust form, normally labelled *Australopithecus boisei*, was first found and identified in 1959 by Mary Leakey at Olduvi in eastern Africa (Leakey, 1994). The comparison of *boisei* to *afarensis* and *africanus* the has led to the latter being described as 'gracile' forms of *Australopithecus*. *Boisei* was bigger and heavier than its cousins, and its jaw and teeth suggests that it spent an awful lot of time masticating. The skeletal changes are thought to reflect an adaptation to a more fibrous diet and more time spent in open grassland and less in trees. One or more robust variants of *Australopithecus* may have persisted until as recently as one million years ago (Leakey, 1994).

The evidence that we have to date suggests that either the gracile or the robust form of *Australopithecus* subsequently evolved into a different sort of hominid called *Homo*. Current thinking is that it was the original gracile form, more specifically *Australopithecus africanus* (Relethford, 2003). Working on this assumption, we can pause to take stock and consider what we know about our lineage *c.* 2 million years ago. It seems that *africanus* males were markedly larger than the females being, perhaps, 50 cm taller at *c.* 1.5 metres, and twice as heavy at 45 kg (Wood, 1992). 'Sexual dimorphism' refers to such marked and discernible differences in body size between males and females as those seen in *africanus*. The sexual dimorphism of *Australopithecus afarensis* and *africanus* reflects that seen in extant great apes, and is greater than that seen in modern humans. It implies that there was significant amount of intra-sex competition between the males for sexual access to the females. In turn, this implies that the females provided the bulk of parental care to off-spring. Being only marginally greater than that of the apes from which they evolved, the brain size of *africanus* warrants the conclusion that the absence of evidence of tool use invites: they did not use any organised form of technology to exploit their environment. The advent of bi-pedalism is thought to be a response to changes in forestation and not a response to sexual selection pressures.

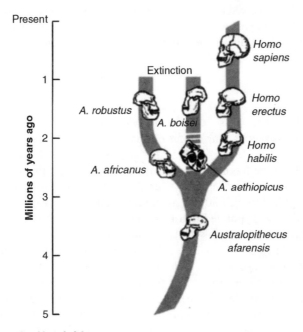

Figure 3.3 Meet the Hominids
The diagram above offers us a conservative estimate of the number of species of *Australopithecus and Homo* may have been extant and when.

HOMO HABILIS

The genus *Homo* includes the species *Homo habilis*, *Homo rudolfensis*, *Homo ergaster*, *Homo erectus*, *Homo neanderthalensis* and us, *Homo sapiens*. We should note that this list is not necessarily exhaustive and that some researchers think that it would be incomplete. However, if not necessarily complete it is, for current purposes, sufficient to illustrate the evolution of modern humans and to flesh out our picture of the EEA.

Habilis is thought to be the first of the genus *Homo* and its immediate ancestor was a gracile form of *Australopithecus*. 'Habilis' means 'able', 'handy' or 'dexterous', and its usage reflects the view that this species was probably the first to systematically use objects as tools. Extant from *c.* 2 million to *c.* 1.5 million years ago in eastern and southern Africa, *habilis* males were larger than the females, with the former being about 130 cm in height and 35 kilos in weight, and the latter being about a metre in height and 30 kilos in weight. There brains were about half the size of ours at *c.* 750 cubic centimetres. We are indebted again to the Leakey family who found and identified the first fossils in the early 1960s in Tanzania (Leakey, 1994).

Habilis' use of stone objects as tools is taken to be evidence of a truly omnivorous diet. They were probably scavengers of meat as well as fruit and nut eaters. The stone tools would have been used to access meat and marrow from decaying carcasses. The move towards increased meat consumption may have been precipitated by environmental changes which was changing even more forest into savannah. The increase in protein consumption would have allowed for the increase in brain size that *habilis* exhibits because the fatty acids in meat and marrow are essential for brain development. The increase in brain growth may have, in turn, allowed for cognitive skills that enabled further procurement of protein.

HOMO RUDOLFENSIS

Unhelpfully the term 'rudolfensis' carries no obvious meaning that assists us in attributing characteristics to this species. Any confusion that may result is reflected in the controversies as to the status of the fossils found by Richard Leakey in 1972 (Leakey, 1994). Leakey declined to attribute the fragments to a genus beyond classing them as *Homo* based on their age and indications of brain size. Valerii Alexee was not so reticent and the term 'rudolfensis' he applied to his find has stuck (Tattersall, 1995). Leakey was undecided but Alexee thought the fossils pointed to a new genus. Others think that *rudolfensis* is just a large male *habilis*, and others think it a large *Australopithecus* (Miller, 2000).

What does appear to be reasonably settled is the claim that this species lived between *c.* 2.4 – 1.7 million years ago across a wide area of east Africa from Ethiopia to Malawi. Like *habilis*, *rudolfensis* was omnivorous but it was larger with the males at *c.*160 cm in height and 60 kg in weight and the females being *c.*150 cm and 50 kg. Its brain too was larger than *habilis*, but this may simply be a reflection of its greater overall size (see the discussion of allometric ratios in Chapter 5 'Cooperation and interdependence').

HOMO ERGASTER AND *HOMO ERECTUS*

Homo ergaster is of special importance. Whereas we cannot be sure which of the *Australopithecus* species or which of the early *Homo* we evolved from, there is some confidence that we are descendants of *ergaster*. Our look at *Homo erectus* will encompass a discussion of another proposed species called *Homo erectus*.

Ergaster persisted from perhaps as long as two million years and until *c.* 30,000 years ago, and certainly for over a million years. Given this time frame it is not surprising that a sub-species may have evolved. *Homo erectus* is thought to be the sub-species. It is also possible that *ergaster* and *erectus* are variants of the same species, and here we will follow the conservative view and say that the name *ergaster* is given to that form of *Homo* which we have found in Africa and *erectus* is given to the same or similar form which has been found outside of Africa. The geographical spread of the long-lived *ergaster* tells us it was a successful adventurer. From the traditional hominid home of eastern Africa *ergaster* migrated south, west and north, and further still into Asia and Europe.

Ergaster means 'workman' and *erectus* means 'upright'. The first appellation reflects an advance in the nature of the tools used and made by this species, and the second reflects distinct changes in the skeleton and especially the pelvis of the fossils given the name. Both *ergaster* and *erectus* were characterised by narrower hips and longer legs than *habilis*. The structure of *Homo ergaster*'s facial bones suggests they had a human-like nose with downward pointing nostrils. This allowed them to add moisture to exhaled air. Allied to this was the ability to sweat. This allowed them to regulate their body temperature without needing to adjust respiration to do so. Together these adaptations meant that they would cover longer distances with increased efficiency. Their improved locomotion over land is thought to be central to their means of subsistence (Tattersall and Schwartz, 2000).

The ability of *erectus* to accommodate new types of terrain, climate and food stuffs as it migrated into Asia and Europe demonstrates a hitherto unprecedented degree of behavioural and cognitive flexibility. Tool use and dentition suggests an omnivorous diet but with increased quantities of meat in comparison with predecessors. Such assumptions are supported by an increase in brain size: *erectus* and *ergaster* had brains about three-quarters the size of modern humans (Falk, 1992).

Ergaster/erectus was also the largest *Homo* up to this point in evolution. Males and females were about as large as modern human men and women outside of the industrialised west. It is thought that *ergaster/erectus* obtained meat by scavenging or by chasing smaller animals until they became exhausted. Animal bones from *ergaster* sites in Africa have been found etched with the characteristic marks of stone tools used for butchery. *Homo erectus* fossils have been found in Asia from Zhoukoudien in China to Sangiran on the island of Java, Indonesia. It is supposed that *Homo erectus* lived in bamboo forests and may have had the ability to use bamboo to make tools such as staffs and spears (Pilbeam, 1986).

HOMO HEIDELBERGENSIS

'Heidelberg Man' – so named because of the location of the find in Germany that led to acceptance that we had come across another species of *Homo* – lived first in Africa *c.* 600,000 years ago, migrated to Europe over the course of the next 200,000 years and appears to have become extinct *c.* 200,000 years ago (Wolpoff, 1999). The males may have been as tall as 180 cm and as heavy as 80 kg on average, with the females at about 155 cm and 50 kg. As we have seen, pronounced sexual dimorphism implies intra-male competition. But the trend toward comparable body size may be taken to suggest that *heidelbergensis* formed enduring pair-bonds.

Also going with trend, *heidelbergensis* was an omnivore but meat was a necessity for healthy growth rather than a luxury. The meat protein content of their diet allowed for both their large brains which were close to the size of ours, and permitted possible evolution of brain size over the course of their presence on earth. It is, perhaps, with *heidelbergensis* that we see the emergence of the **hunter-gatherer** mode of subsistence as opposed to a **scavenger-gatherer** mode. A find at what is today Boxgrove in the south of England suggests that *c.* 400,000 years ago *heidelbergensis* was hunting mammals several times the size of themselves with made-for-purpose tools. The tools include wooden spears made to kill large mammals and stone axes made to butcher the carcasses (Roberts, 1999).

This development is of particular interest to psychology. Their ability to successfully hunt, butcher and use the product of large animals implies an advanced ability to plan their diet, to work in cooperative groups, to develop specialised forms of labour and skill and share precious commodities. Furthermore, all of these abilities may be assumed to expose individual differences, aptitudes and the capacity to learn and modify behaviour. We may assume that if hunting large animals in groups was critical to survival those who did one or more of the component tasks best enjoyed more-or-less direct fitness advantages.

Some have speculated that the hunting and tool making abilities of *heidelbergensis* were so efficient that they allowed for hitherto unseen cultural development (Roberts, 1999). A find at Schöningen in Germany from about the same period as the Boxgrove find suggests that wooden spears appear to have been shaped and weighted so to be thrown like a javelin. Not only does this find provide strong evidence of hunting proper, the condition of the spears suggests that they were unused for what seems to be the intended purpose. Accordingly, room is created for the suggestion that the spears were used for social display or as a part of a ritual or celebration.

Another recent find in Atapuerca, Spain adds grist to the mill. In what has come to be known as 'the pit of bones', the remains of 32 *heidelbergensis* were found in 1997. The condition of the bones suggests that the individuals were in poor health. Regardless of the cause of the deaths, it is assumed that the bodies were placed in the pit. If this was the case then the 'pit of bones' may be evidence of a burial rite and of ritual. Burial rituals are important because they appear to be unique to humans and are certainly characteristics of us. They imply some sort of conception of mortality (Tattersall and Schwartz, 2000).

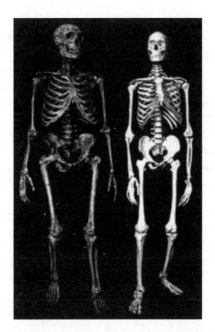

Figure 3.4   Skeletons of a typical adult male *Homo neanderthalis* and *Homo sapien*

The success of *heidelbergensis* as a hunter, tool maker and coloniser tempts us to suppose that modern humans are its descendants. As we will see when we consider the appearance of modern humans, if we are then the orthodox view is that it was from the *heidelbergensis* that remained in Africa that we evolved.

HOMO NEANDERTHALIS

In August 1856 a fossil that has come to be known as Neanderthal 1 was found at Feldhofer in the Neander Valley near Düsseldorf in Germany. The find comprised the top of a skull, two leg bones, three right arm bones, two left arm bones, part of a left hip bone, and fragments of a shoulder blade and ribs. The fossils found their way to a local naturalist called Johann Karl Fuhlrott and an anatomist called Hermann Schaaffhausen. Fuhlrott and Schaaffhausen announced the find and their analysis in 1857.

In fact the Feldhofer fossils were not the first *neanderthal* remains discovered. The remains of what turned out to be a pre-pubescent *neanderthal* had been found in Belgium in 1829 and an adult had been found in Gibraltar 1848. But the Feldhofer fossils did precipitate some sort of acceptance that another species of *Homo* had existed in Europe. In the literature the species was named *neanderthalensis* by William King (King, 1864).

Support for the idea that the *neanderthalis* was a distinct group from prior, contemporaneous and subsequent forms of *Homo* comes from a variety of sources. Certainly, their skeletal and maxiofacial anatomy was distinct. And, importantly, they had very large brains – possibly as much as 15 per cent larger than ours. However, the mass of cortex was orientated more toward the occipital lobe than the frontal lobe in comparison to us. This suggests that they had superior vision but their abstract thinking abilities were not as sophisticated as ours (Stringer and Gamble, 1993). It is thought that *neanderthalis* was capable of speech, but it may have been no more advanced than a **protolanguage** (Bickerton, 1990).

Existing in Europe all the way from the Iberian Peninsula in the west to the Russian Steppes in the east from *c.* 250,000 to *c.* 30,000 years ago (Stringer and Grün, 1991), *neanderthalis* fossils have also been found in Central Asia and the Middle East. Males were larger than females by perhaps as much as 20 per cent. There were shorter but stockier than *ergaster, erectus* and *heidelbergensis* and weighed as much. The fossils suggest that they were heavily muscled and that they were both prone to, but robust against, injury. The injuries may have incurred during hunting and through intra-sexual competition.

To a greater extent than other *Homo* forms, *neanderthalis* was adapted to survive through a cold period, or an 'ice age'. The climate in which they lived meant that there was a relative scarcity of available vegetation and fruit. Their dentition suggests that a major component of their diet was animal protein. In turn, this permits educated guesses about their cognitive abilities and social structure. In particular, we may assume that they were archetypal hunter-gathers. Tool manufacture and use was pragmatically orientated toward animal capture and butchery, and the division of labour between males and females was at least as rigid as any other variant of *Homo*. However – and this may also have been true of *heidelbergensis* – the difference in size between males and females need not be interpreted as meaning that females could not hunt. As has been pointed out, the difference in male–female body size may not have mattered when we consider the size of the prey. Rather, males assumed responsibility for hunting because gestation, weaning and child care made this difficult for females (Relethford, 2003).

The debate that existed in the 1860s concerning the proper status and taxonomic place of *neanderthalis* has never totally abated. Today, the orthodox view would appear to be that something akin to *ergaster* or, perhaps the later *heidelbergensis*, migrated out of Africa into Europe and evolved into *neanderthalis* in situ. Subsequent migrations of pre-sapien *Homo* may have interbred with them but *neanderthalis* did not interbreed with later migrations of Africa *Homo sapiens* who eventually displaced them (Trinkaus and Shipman, 1992). Most scholars would subscribe to the claim that we do not descend from them and that we and they represent distinct though coterminous species (Linz et al., 2007; Smith, 1991). Others argue that it seems unlikely that *neanderthalis* contributed nothing whatsoever to the *sapien* genome (Stringer and Andrews, 2005). This position requires that *neanderthalis* and *sapien* interbred successfully. It may be the case that the two species could have done so in bio-chemical terms but did not see one another as a mating opportunity.

HOMO SAPIEN

Homo sapiens – anatomically modern humans beings – appeared between 200,000 and 100,000 years ago. If we wish to be more precise regarding the date of the appearance of

Homo sapien then a safe bet is to assume that we appeared *c.* 150,000 years ago in Ethiopia (Pilbeam, 1986). By *c.* 110,000 years ago, *sapiens* had expanded their range to South Africa. By *c.* 100,000 years ago we had crossed the Levant land bridge into Southwest Asia, and we show up in Europe and the Middle East *c.* 60,000 years ago. This account assumes that the species of *Homo* that emerged from Africa *c.* 150,000 years ago colonised various parts of the globe is the same species as exists today. It is known as the '**out of Africa**' hypothesis of modern human origins.

Also know as the '**African Eve**' hypothesis, there are a number of lines of evidence which support this view. Amongst the most persuasive is the fact that genetic differences in modern humans support a recent African origin for humanity. More specifically, it is known that mitochondrial DNA (mtDNA) is a type of DNA that is inherited through the maternal line and that the extant genetic types that have accumulated most mutations and changes in mtDNA are African. The inference is that African mtDNA genome types are older than any others. The **bottle-neck theory** takes the relatively small amount of genetic diversity amongst modern humans to suggest that extant human populations were very small before we started to migrate out of Africa (Cann et al., 1987). The out of Africa view has many nuances, but may be simplified as saying that modern humans evolved in Africa and replaced extant populations of *erectus, ergaster, heidelbergensis* and *neanderthalis.*

There is an alternative hypothesis. In Chapter 2, 'Evolutionary approaches to thought and behaviour', it was mentioned that there is something called the multi-regional hypothesis. The multi-regional hypothesis claims that something akin to what we have identified as *Homo erectus* migrated out of Africa much earlier than *c.* 150,000 years ago and evolved in situ. The multi-regional view also has many nuances, but, again at the risk of simplification, it may be said to claim that modern humans are direct descendants and evolved forms of *ergaster* (assuming we keep with the claim that *ergaster* was a variant of *Homo* that evolved and remained in Africa and *erectus* was *ergaster* out of Africa) and we have passed through the intermediate forms that we see in the shape of *heidelbergensis* and, perhaps, others. For example, on the multi-regional view the claim would be that the *erectus* fossils found in China and Indonesian are the direct ancestors of ancient East Asian humans, the *ergaster* fossils found in Africa are the direct ancestors of ancient Africans, and that the *erectus* fossils found in European populations are the direct ancestors of modern Europeans.

BOX 3.1 OBJECTIONS TO EVOLUTIONARY PSYCHOLOGY: RACISM

It cannot reasonably be denied that **racism** is a feature of recorded human history. Furthermore, it cannot be denied that racists have appealed to biological differences between ethnic and social groups in support of their arguments. This is especially true since Darwin proposed the theory of evolution.

(Cont'd)

Perhaps the most infamous and tragic appeal to evolutionary ideas was that made by the Nazis. Perhaps the most pernicious was the eugenics movement which took its licence from the work of Darwin's cousin, Francis Galton (Hampton, 2005b). An outcome of these and other appeals to evolved biological differences is the claim that evolutionary approaches to mind and behaviour are inherently racist.

To address this objection we need to be clear as to what evolutionary theory is being accused of. If the objection is taken to mean, 'Is evolutionary psychology politically motivated towards the end of biologising distinctions between races and or cultures?', the reply is 'No'.

We must keep in mind the objective of the enterprise. The objective is to formulate a *general* theory of human nature and psychological functions. It is not to formulate race specific theories. The licence to formulate a general theory is granted by the assumption that all humans possess essentially identical cognitive adaptations. As a matter of fact, the approaches which comprise evolutionary psychology do not make biologically based distinctions between races or cultures. However, they play down theories such as the multi-regional hypothesis and insist on 'the psychic unity of humankind'. The quarry of the enterprise is the functional organisation of the brain. The assumption is that this organisation must be pan-human because humans are a single species and all members of the species share the same functional organisation of both body and brain.

Still, we may have to accept that race will remain an issue for evolutionary psychology for two reasons. There is that to which we have already alluded – there will be persons who are racist and they will seek to legitimise their views by spurious appeals to science. And, second, the fact that certain genetic differences mark out some populations from others will allow those so motivated to highlight and speculate on the meaning of these differences in contentious and negative ways.

The bulwark against such strategies is a consistent appeal to the evidence which suggest that all modern humans are of the same homogenous species. Individuals differ, families differ, groups may differ, but they do so within the boundaries of a characteristic genome. Contemporary evolutionary approaches to psychology subscribe to the 'out of Africa' hypothesis of human evolution which claims that modern humans have evolved from a single species of human that emerged in eastern Africa approximately 150,000 years ago. Arguing that minds are alike does not deny variation (brought about by recombination, mutation, age, sex, access to social and material resources, injury, disease, etc.). One of things that may make us similar is the desire to be dissimilar – both at an individual and a group level. Stiil, variations within our species are dwarfed by commonalities. An emphasis on the variations may be legitimate for clinical considerations but not for political, economic or moral reasons.

Our ancient history (as opposed to our natural history) suggests that only in recent times – almost certainly at the beginning of the Holocene for the earliest cases and very much later in most cases – have geographically diverse and isolated groups of humans come into regular and sustained contact with one another. The multi-regional view suggests that the various races of human that existed at the beginning of the Holocene *c.* 10,000 years ago had evolved from what had once been *erectus* groups spread across different continents. One implication of the multi-regional view is that what today we see as different races of human were, quite recently, varieties of what had been *erectus* and that racial differences evident in skin and hair colour and gross morphology may have been the early stages of speciation. This implication may be important for the claim that all modern humans are psychologically identical. On the other hand, the out of Africa claim – that a new species of *Homo* evolved, migrated and replaced other species around the globe – carries with it the implication that the phylogeny of modern humans is of limited use to psychology because we are novel and quite different from our ancestors.

We can see that both positions also carry political implications. The multi-regional view invites the accusation that it is fundamentally racist by opening up the possibility that extant races of human are, somehow, unequal or unequally evolved. In contrast, the out of Africa view invites comparison with religious stories which talk of 'genesis' or the idea of Adam and Eve emerging from some sort of paradise. We will consider the narrative structure of evolutionary psychology in Chapter 11 'Evolution and culture'. But now we will return to our natural history.

Some researchers make a distinction between 'archaic' and 'modern' *sapiens*. A find which supports the distinction is of a skull which exhibits the rounded skull case of modern people but retained the large brow ridges of *Homo heidelbergensis* (Stringer, 1992) and that these differences imply behavioural differences not stasis (Mellars, 1990). The distinction between archaic and modern forms of *Homo sapien* suggests that either we have evolved since we appeared or a sub-species of archaic *Homo sapiens* has evolved into what is sometimes referred to as *Homo sapien sapien*. It has also been suggested that the earliest 'archaic' male forms, while modern in biomechanical terms, had heavier bones and greater muscle mass and that the sexes were more dimorphic (Wood, 1992). These differences imply a different diet to that required by modern forms of *Homo sapien sapien* (Aiello, 1992). Although it is accepted that the hominid line as a whole is distinguished by its bipedalism, the pelvic anatomy of all but the immediate precursors to recent modern fossils suggests that they did not enjoy mobility or speed to match our own (Richmond and Strait, 2000). Further support for a distinction between archaic and modern forms of *Homo sapien* comes by way of evidence from archeology which some have interpreted as marking a development in the behavioural repertoire of *Homo sapien*, and, accordingly, a development in our cognitive abilities. This development is referred to as the **Upper Paleolithic transition** and it is said that the appearance of art, signs of ritual and hitherto unprecedented sophistication of tool manufacture and use points to an evolutionary change. The supposed transition coincides with the appearance of modern humans in Europe and the Middle East *c.* 60,000 years ago (Mellars, 1996).

A better-attested transition in our ancient history is the advent of agriculture which some groups of humans developed about 15,000 years ago (Feder and Park, 1997). The control, maintenance and exploitation of land, crops and livestock amounted to a revolution in the ways in which those who practised agriculture organised themselves and lived. Such is the difference in tool manufacture and use, planning, botanical and biological

Figure 3.5   Upper Paleolithic art
http://12.photobucket.com/albums/v25/Hhyaena/neanderthal.jpg

knowledge that underpins agriculture we may be tempted to think that its appearance reflected a further development in our evolution. However, the fossil evidence does not warrant such an inference.

We have come to the end of this brief review of some of the evidence that we are an evolved species. It is now time to draw some conclusion about what we can say about our past and the selection pressures which brought us about.

WHAT CAN WE SAY ABOUT THE PAST?

The aim in this section is to make some general statements about what we are like now based on what we have been like in the past. It begins by examining the claim that modern humans are, in essence, a species of hunter-gatherer and that that mode of existence and subsistence gives us a 'live' window into the past of our species. Following that are some conservative conclusions about the nature of human nature that will serve as assumptions when we move on to to look at particular behaviours in subsequent chapters.

HUNTER-GATHERERS AS A MODEL OF THE PAST

Treating the past as synonymous with the Pleistogene epoch is a way of bracketing a set of selection pressures and adaptive problems. We begin with a picture of our ancestors, the model for which are the African great apes. We then suppose that selection pressures shaped us into what we are now. A way of converting the Pleistocene epoch into a tangible set of pressures and problems that amounted to our past is to suppose that they are well described by the hunter-gatherer mode of existence and subsistence. More precisely, it is common for evolutionary psychologists to précis the archaeological and palaeontological records into an EEA that is more-or-less identical to the suite of problems faced and solved by extant hunter-gatherers. Thus, if our goal is to understand evolved human propensities:

> ... It seems reasonable to seek out those humans today who experienced a social environment most similar to that of our Pleistocene ancestors: Such humans would be most likely to manifest behaviour that provides a window on our human evolutionary heritage. (Miller and Fishkin, 1997: 218)

Turning the EEA into a set of problems more-or-less equivalent to those faced by extant and well documented hunter-gatherer peoples circumvents the difficulty of reconstructing the past for it can be argued that our knowledge of the EEA is scant at best, and not nearly as rich as would be needed to build detailed pictures of selection pressures and subsequent psychological adaptations. A rejoinder to such an observation comes by saying that the past is exhibited in the present (and an extensively recorded recent past) in the form of hunter-gatherers. On this account, the means of subsistence deployed by earlier forms of *Homo*, through to the appearance of *Homo sapien c.* 150,000 years ago and up to the advent of agriculture 10–15,000 years ago was a blend of hunting and gathering. Thus, Cosmides et al. state:

> ... our ancestors spent the last two million years as Pleistocene hunter-gatherers, and, of course, several hundred million years before that as one kind of forager or another. ... The few thousand years since the scattered appearance of agriculture is only a small stretch in evolutionary terms, less that 1% of the two million years our ancestors spent as Pleistocene hunter-gatherers. (1992: 5)

Accordingly, the hunter-gatherer form of living can be seen as a set of selection pressures and those selection pressures have shaped a mind that is adapted to respond to them. The claim is that the modern mind is, essentially, a hunter-gatherer machine by virtue of the fact that it evolved to guide its possessor through that particular form of subsistence. In addition, the forms of social life that are either conducive to, or are a product of (or some combination of the two), hunting and gathering also create social problems that the mind is adapted to negotiate.

This view is taken from and licensed by anthropology. The 'man the hunter' hypothesis became popular in the in 1960s and orthodox following publication of Lee and DeVore's edited volume of the same name in 1968. Subsequent research promulgated this view (Isaac, 1977, 1978), and the hunter-gather hypothesis became the 'consensus view'

(Binford, 1985), an 'axiom' of hominid evolution (Foley, 1988). Since the 1980s the consensus that modern humans are and have evolved from what are called central place hunter-gathers (wherein men hunt, women forage for vegetables and fruit, and both live in a more-or-less fixed settlement) has broken down somewhat. In short, it is thought that the subsistence behaviour exhibited by various extant hunter-gatherer societies is so varied in its details that the unitary term 'hunter-gatherer' becomes strained. In addition, there is not enough evidence to say with certainty that our predecessors exhibited the same complexity and flexibility of behaviour. For example, Foley concludes that it is '… untrue to say that early hominids were full hunter-gatherers in the same way as modern hunter-gatherers' (1988: 211). He goes on:

> Overall, there is a declining willingness among palaeoanthropologists to accept the existence of modern forms of subsistence behaviour among anatomically pre-modern humans. It seems quite probable that the earlier hominids did eat meat, but that this was not integrated into a central place foraging and food-sharing system as found among modern hunter-gatherers…
>
> …Despite being omnivorous there is no reason to assume that their foraging behaviour was of the same level of organisation as modern hunter-gatherers in terms of planning depth, scheduling, subsistence activity and foraging flexibility. In the absence of clear-cut evidence for central place foraging similar to that of modern hunter-gatherers, inferences about the social and sharing behaviour of early hominids must be tentative only. In other words, if the term hunter-gatherer is to mean more than just wild resource omnivory (in which case it would include baboons, chimpanzees and many other animals!), then early hominids were neither human nor hunter-gatherers. (ibid.,: 212, 215)

These considerations weaken the assumption that modern hunter-gatherers provide us with a picture of the EEA. However, they are not fatal and the case that anatomically modern humans have been hunter-gatherers for the bulk of their existence can be maintained. As with fine-grained analysis of human phylogeny, in practice, research conducted in the name of evolutionary psychology absorbs the debates within archaeology and palaeoanthropology about hominid subsistence behaviour by adopting a relaxed or loose conception of hunter-gatherers. For example, in the discussion of mating preferences in Chapter 7 'Mate selection', we will see that, in practice, 'hunter-gatherer' means that *Homos* in the EEA lived in groups of undefined size but not in the thousands; that men did the hunting; that food sharing took place. But it is not said how often they hunted, or precisely who shared what with whom. It means that women did most of the gathering and possibly assisted one another with child care. A relaxed treatment of the term hunter-gatherer is constructed and constrained by importing only those putative forms of meat eating and acquisition provided for us by anthropological studies.

Still, when pushed to say what form of subsistence is characteristic of our species the record tells us that it is hunter-gathering. With this conclusion in mind we can be confident in making a number of statements towards the end of painting a normative picture of humans.

In the most general terms, evolutionary theory tells us that the natural history of any species demanded that the organisms that comprised it sought to reproduce, and extant members of the species come from ancestors that did so successfully. This suggests that extant humans can be thought of and analysed as being powerfully motivated by sex. Inclusive fitness theory tells us that in large, slow-breeding mammalian species such as ours the organism will have exhibited **nepotism**. This suggests that we will behave differently towards kin than we will towards non-kin. And natural selection tells us that we will seek and, if at all necessary, compete for resources that support and promote survival and reproduction.

Our ancestors were hunter-gatherers and/or scavenger-gatherers. This implies a division of labour between the sexes, cooperation between and within the sexes, and both a need for and capacity to exist on a varied diet. Our ancestors probably opted for settled living conditions when possible, but could cope with a nomadic or semi-nomadic existence. They were adapted to low population density in groups which were kin-based. While some resources were privileged over others and wealth could be accumulated in a limited sense through food acquisition and tool manufacture, money is a novel phenomenon and there was no wealth as we understand the term today. Without medicine to speak of, infant mortality was high and life expectancy low. We were vulnerable to the natural environment, predators and disease. Life was orientated around existence and reproduction with little scope for choice and recreation. Males being larger than females probably meant that there was intra-sexual aggression between the males for access to females, and the task of gestating, breast feeding and providing care for offspring probably meant that there was also a marked division of labour between the sexes with regards to parenting.

SUMMARY OF CHAPTER 3

The natural history of modern humans – the environment of evolutionary adaptedness – is central to evolutionary psychology. In this chapter we traced the emergence of a number of species which preceded modern humans and it is thought that some of them are our ancestors. After the assumed split from the lineages of African ape the first hominids to appear were the genius *Australopithecus*. Similar to extant chimpanzees above the neck, *Australopithecus afarensis*, *africanus* and *boisei* were stood more-or-less upright and were bi-pedal. Species of *Australopithecus* persisted from about *c.* 6 million years ago to *c.* 2 million years ago. The genus *Homo* – 'man' – appeared *c.* 2 million years ago. Species including *habilis*, *rudolfensis*, *ergaster* and *erectus*, *heidelbergensis* seemed to have preceded *Homo sapien*. *Home sapien* appeared *c.* 150,000 years ago and lived at the same time as did *Homo neanderthalis*.

There are many debates as to what our predecessors were capable of, how they behaved, why they evolved and why they became extinct. Palaeoanthropologists are not so certain today as they once were that our ancestors were hunter-gatherers in much the same way as are some human populations today. However, evolutionary psychologists assume that they were and that the hunter-gatherer way of life is comprises of similar selection pressures and problems faced and surmounted by our ancestors. This assumption gives rise to the claim that modern hunter-gatherers give us a window into our past.

FURTHER READING

Apart from the references in this chapter you may find it interesting and useful to consult one or more of the following:

Corballis, M.C. (1999) Phylogeny from apes to humans. In Corballis, M.C. and Lea, S.E.G. (eds) *The Descent of Mind: Psychological Perspectives on Hominid Evolution*. New York, NY: Oxford University Press – see Chapter 2.

Crawford, C.B. (1998) Environments and adaptations: then and now. In Crawford, C.B. and Krebs, D.L. (eds) *Handbook of Evolutionary Psychology: Ideas, Issues and Applications*. Mahwah, NJ: Lawrence Erlbaum Associates.

Foley, R.A. (1996) The adaptive legacy of human evolution: a search for the environment of evolutionary adaptedness. *Evolutionary Anthropology*, 4(2): 194–203.

Irons, W. (1998) Adaptively relevant environments vs. the environment of evolutionary adaptedness. *Evolutionary Anthropology*, 6(6): 194–204.

Leakey, R. (1994) *The Origin of Humankind*. London: Weidenfeld and Nicolson – see Chapter 5 'The origin of modern humans'.

Tattersall, I. (2000) We were not alone. *Scientific American*, January: 56–62.

4 BRAINS, MINDS AND CONSCIOUSNESS

Some of the questions addressed in this chapter:

- How does the central nervous system develop after conception?
- What is the functional anatomy of the adult brain?
- What is the mind–body problem?
- How has the mind–body problem been addressed?
- Can the brain be taken as an information-processing device?
- Why would we be self-conscious?

SOME KEY TERMS AND CONCEPTS

Classical cascade; Computational metaphor; Consciousness; Dualism; Idealism; Intentional stance; Materialism; Self-consciousness.

LEARNING OBJECTIVES

Having studied this chapter you should be better able to:

- Describe the development and final form of the human brain.
- Appreciate some of the issues that arise from the distinction between brain and mind.
- Detail some of the ways evolutionary psychology utilises the computational metaphor.

INTRODUCTION

The purpose of this chapter is to outline ways in which evolutionary accounts think about thought. To put it another way, in this chapter we will be considering mind and consciousness and how these difficult concepts relate to brains and are accommodated in a naturalist framework that subscribes to **materialism** – the view that the universe comprises nothing other than matter and the forces that determine its movement.

To achieve this purpose we will begin by looking at the human brain – the organ that is taken to be the source or seat of thought by the majority of psychologists. In particular, we will look at how the central nervous system develops in the days and weeks after conception, and at the functional anatomy of the brain in adult humans. The point of this very brief overview of the brain is to show that its development, anatomy and function are largely invariant between individuals (i.e. we all have very similar brains that develop and mature in very similar ways). Furthermore, on the assumption that the brain and only the brain gives rise to or is responsible for thought, it follows that thought is also largely invariant between individuals (i.e. we perceive, feel, rationalise, believe and remember in very similar ways).

Having looked at the brain as a physical organ, our next task will be to consider what is known in the philosophy of mind and psychology as the 'mind–body problem'. In short, this problem – arguably the fundamental problem in modern psychology – concerns the distinction between mind and brain and how the two interact. We will see that this very long-standing problem (it is at least as old as Plato and in its modern form dates back to the French thinker René Descartes) can be circumvented (if not solved) in a number of ways that are not at odds with an evolutionary point of view. Those that we will discuss rely upon what is known as the 'computational metaphor' – the claim that our brains are information-processing devices.

This chapter ends by looking at consciousness from an evolutionary point of view, examining what consciousness is for and asking what its function might be.

FIRST STAGES OF THE DEVELOPMENT OF THE CENTRAL NERVOUS SYSTEM

BOX 4.1   WHERE ARE YOU?

TRY IT THIS WAY …

Ask yourself this question: If your best friend had a brain transplant where would they then be? In the body that stood before you? Or would your friend now reside in the body which now housed their brain?

Alternatively, ask yourself this: If you had a body transplant where would you now be? In the same bed that you were in when rendered unconscious with anaesthetic before the operation, or wherever your body was taken to?

Most psychology students come to the following conclusion: In response to both questions they say that their best friend and they themselves reside in the body – whatever that body might be like – that houses their brain.

This is not to say that bodies do not matter with respect to the people and personalities we come to be. But it is to say that we are, or reside in, our brains rather than in our bodies. If you want to read more along these lines, begin by consulting Daniel Dennett's essay 'Where am I?' (Dennett, 1978).

Soon after conception the human central nervous system begins to develop. The initial event is called the 'induction of the neural tube' and this term refers to the early stages of physical growth and maturation of what will become the spinal cord and brain. Approximately 18 days after conception the outer dorsal (which means the back and top) layer of the embryo begins to curl in upon itself. This part of the embryo's anatomy is known as the ectoderm and at about 21 days after conception its outer edges fuse together. Once they have done so what is known as the neural tube is formed. This structure will become the spinal cord and brain at about 28 days after conception. When the fusion of the outer edges of the ectoderm is complete the nose, or rostral, end of the neural tube matures into three identifiable chambers. These chambers will become the lateral, third and fourth ventricles of the brain, and the tissue which at this point surrounds them will mature into the forebrain, midbrain and hindbrain. At about 70 days after conception the neural tube is approximately 1.25 cm in length and mostly comprises the fluid-filled ventricles. By 140 days after conception the tube is approximately 5 cm in length and now comprises mostly tissue though the fluid-filled ventricles remain.

Let us now consider what happens from about 50 days through to about 150 days after conception when the broad outline of the adult human brain is discernible.

BOX 4.2 TIMELINE FOR THE INDUCTION OF THE NEURAL TUBE

- 18 days: ectoderm (outer dorsal layer of embryo) forms the neural plate.
- 21 days: the plate curls in upon itself and fuses to form the neural tube.
- 28 days: the tube is closed and its rostral (nose) end develops three chambers – later to become the ventricles – and the tissues around these chambers will become the fore-, mid- and hind brain.
- 50 days: symmetrical division gives way to asymmetrical division – founder neurons produce one other founder cell which stays in place and a neuron which will migrate.
- 70 days: the tube is *c.* 1.25 cm (1 inch) and mostly ventricle.
- 140 days: the tube is *c.* 5 cm (2 inches) and mostly tissue.
- 150 days: the contours of the adult brain are discernible.

FIRST STAGES OF THE DEVELOPMENT OF THE BRAIN

Up to this point we have looked at the development and maturation of the overall anatomy – the super-structure – of the central nervous system. In this section we will consider what happens at the cellular level and look at the proliferation (an event also known as neurogenesis) migration, aggregation, differentiation of neurons, the formation of synapses, the death of neural cells, and the early stages of neural selection and the stabilisation of synaptic connections.

(a)   (b)

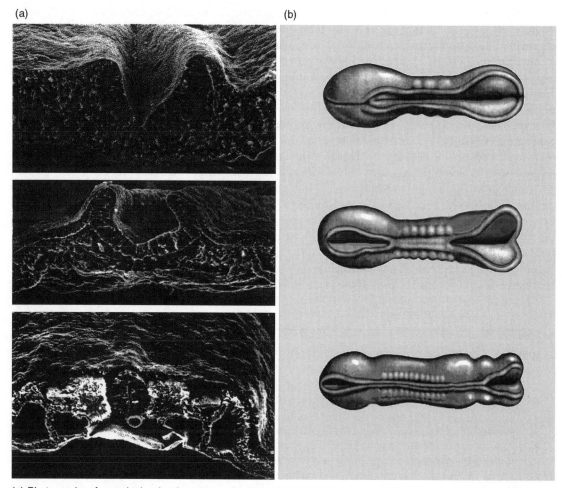

(a) Photographs of neural tube development as the embryo's surface forms a groove, which closes to form a tube.
(b) Diagrammatic representation of the events, viewed from a different angle.

Figure 4.1   Induction of the neural tube
Source: Figure 3.21 (page 72) from B. Garrett (2009). *Brain and Behaviour: An Introduction to Biological Psychology* (2nd edn). Thousand Oaks, CA: Sage.

NEURAL PROLIFERATION

The original and singular cell formed after conception is known as the zygote and it begins to divide within approximately 12 hours. At this point and up to the formation of the neural plate (which will become the neural tube as we have seen) at about 18 days the cells that comprise the neural plate are pluripotent. This means that they could, in principle, go on to become any sort of cells in the human body. At about 18 days these cells become multi-potent. What this means is that they will not, and, it is thought, cannot, become any type of human cell but they could become any type of neuron, or brain cell. At this point in time it is thought that multipotent neurons are produced at the rate of about 250,000 per minute.

NEURAL MIGRATION

Neural migration refers to the events whereby the cells that formed the neural plate and tube and proliferated travel to a position in the maturing physical structure that will become the brain. This process begins approximately 35 days after conception and it follows the proliferation of multi-potent cells. The direction of travel of what will be neurons is from the inside of the neural tube and what will become the lateral, third and fourth ventricles outwards to the extremities of the tube. Accordingly, migration is said to be 'inside-out'. Most neuronal migration is amoeboid and facilitated by radial glia cells (there are a number of different types of glia cells in the human brain and although we do not discuss them here you may wish to consult Box 4.3 'Glia cells' for additional information). What this means is that the neural cells use other cells rather like ropes and they travel along them to their destinations. It is also thought that neuronal cells are guided to their destination by chemicals called neurotropics. At around about 60 days the embryonic stage of maturation ends and the foetal stage begins. The foetal stage is marked the presence of a structurally developed human whereupon all the major organs are present – though not fully developed or mature – in their final anatomical location. At this point almost all neurons have been formed and the physical development of the brain mostly comprises the growth dendrites, axons, glia cells and myelin sheaths.

BOX 4.3   GLIA CELLS

Glia cells are said to be the 'glue' of the brain in that one of their functions is to support neurons. They may be about 10 times as common as neurons, and they are thought to be about one fifth of the size. There a number of different types of glia cells with different functions:

Radial glia facilitate neural migration.
Oligodendrocytes provide insulation for axons.
Astrocytes deliver glucose, water and oxygen to neurons.
Microglia remove waste products from the brain.
Astrocytes and gliosis cells form scar tissue.
Astrocytes contribute to the blood–brain barrier.
Microglia act as the brains immune system.

NEURAL AGGREGATION AND DIFFERENTIATION

When neurons reach their destination after migration they aggregate. Aggregation involves the clustering of neurons at different locations of what will become the mature brain. It is at this point that the eventual role of neural cells is decided. In other words, the neuronal cells become functionally differentiated into aggregates of neurons proper. Differentiation is thought to be driven by two processes – genetic expression and chemical induction. Genetic expression is the result of the cells producing particular types of protein, and chemical induction refers to the influence of neighbouring neurons on the development of axons and dendrites. Once neuronal cells have aggregated and differentiated it is thought that they never again divide.

SYNAPSE FORMATION

Aggregation, differentiation and the functional specialisation that results from those events is consolidated by the formation of synapses between neurons. Synapses can be thought of as the contact point between neurons wherein chemical messages are sent from one cell to another. For a neuron to form a synapse with others it must develop at least one axon and at least one dendrite. Axons are structures that send messengers and dendrites are structures that receive them. We have seen that most neuronal migration occurs courtesy of glia cells and it happens by virtue of structures called a growth cones. After aggregation and differentiation the growth cone develops into an axon. At the end of axons are structures called filopodia, and at the end of these lamellipodia. Theses structures 'reach' for other neurons and in doing so promote the development of dendrites in neighbouring neurons. There are probably (at least) three means by which neurons develop synaptic connections:

- Direct genetic expression: the idea is that the direction filopodia take is genetically determined by instructions coded in the DNA of a given neuronal cell such as take path y for x distance.
- Topographic gradients: the idea is that prior to migration neurons are mapped in relation to one another and execute this spatial relation once aggregated.
- Chemoaffinity: the idea is that neurons attract or repel one another via neurotrophins and/or neurotransmitters.

CELL SELECTION, STABILISATION AND DEATH

It has been estimated that 20–80 per cent of neurons 'die' before becoming part of a functioning nuclei (i.e. a cluster of neurons that serve a particular function) and that most original synaptic connections also die before birth (Edelman, 1987). And it has also been estimated that as many as 50 per cent of neurons die in the first 12–14 years of life after birth, and that a similar proportion of synapses present at 2 years of age die before we reach adulthood. On the assumption that these numbers reflect actual events we might ask ourselves, 'What determines which survive?' Possible answers to this question include the claim that some neurons succumb to PCD – programmed cell death. PCD is also referred to as **apoptosis**. PCD is thought to come about courtesy of 'suicide genes' and the benefit is that the chemical constituents of the dead cells are recycled (Kerr et al., 1972). Another suggestion is that unless neurons make contact with others they do not receive a substance called nerve growth factor which is critical to further growth (Purves, 1994).

Once they have been selected, synaptic connections between neurons are pruned. What this amounts to is that for any given neuron its connectivity is rearranged such that it synapses with fewer other neurons but the complexity of connections that remain is increased.

OHP 27

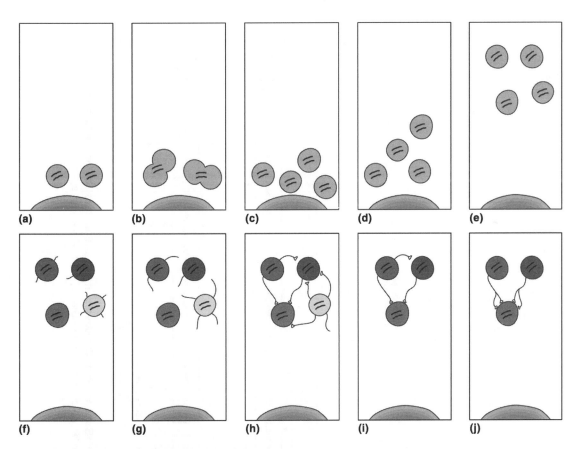

Figure 4.2   Neural proliferation and migration: the basic sequence of events
Development: (a) cells initially located by the ventricle, (b) cells starting to divide, (c) cells divided, (d) start of cell migration, (e) migration complete, (f) start of differentiation, (g) continuation of differentiation, (h) synapses formed, (i) death of some cells and (j) synaptic restructuring.
Source: Figure 6.7 from F. Toates (2001) *Biological Psychology: An Integrated Approach*. Harlow: Prentice Hall.

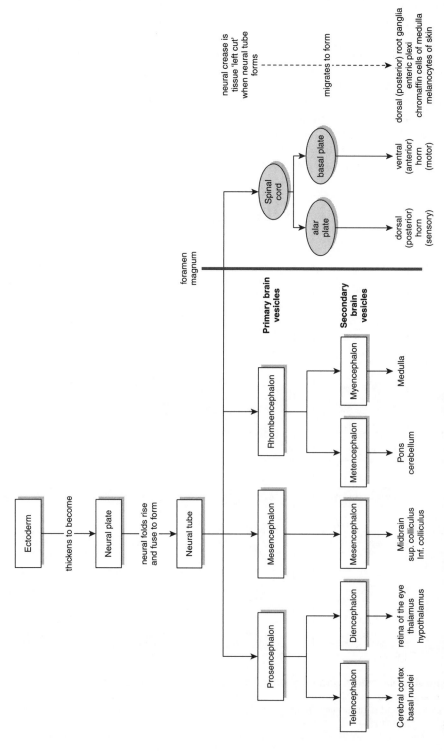

Figure 4.3   Schematic of the development and maturation of the human brain
Source: http://en.wikipedia.org/wiki/File:Development_of_nervous_system.png

FUNCTIONAL ANATOMY OF THE MATURED BRAIN

It is now time to look at the functional anatomy of the matured brain. 'Matured' may sound like an odd term, and it is used here in a purposely vague way: 'matured' in this context means only a more-or-less fully physically developed human brain. Following the anatomical terminology we used when considering the development of the central nervous system, we will parse the brain as a whole into three sub-sections – the forebrain, the midbrain and the hindbrain. And we will see that each of three major sub-components themselves comprise further sub-components. There is almost limitless detail that we could go into when considering which parts of the brain perform which functions. We will be stopping at a level of detail which is more-or-less visible to the naked eye (i.e. will parse the whole into sub-components that can be seen with the aid of microscopes).

FOREBRAIN

The forebrain itself comprises two parts, the telencephalon and the diencephalon. And the telencephalon and the diencephalon are, in turn made up of component parts. The telencephalon is made up of the cerebral cortex, the basal ganglia and the limbic system. The diencephalon is made up of the thalamus and hypothalamus. Let us look at what cognitive and behavioural functions some of these important structures serve.

Cerebral cortex
The cerebral cortex is the outer layer of the brain and it can be readily divided into four lobes.

Frontal lobes
This part of the brain is common to mammals and primates but its size is particular to humans. It is the seat of a range of higher-order abilities including the ability to make and execute extended patterns of goal directed behaviour, and the ability to consider others and form theories of others minds.

Parietal lobes
This part of our brain plans and controls bodily movements and detects bodily sensations such as touch and pain.

Occipital lobes
This part of the brain – as the name suggests – is responsible for vision and object recognition.

Temporal lobes
This part of the brain is implicated in many aspects of memory including the ability recognise familiar faces, sounds and voices, and short-term processing of sensory information.

Beneath the cerebral cortex are two more structures that make up the telencephalon.

Basal ganglia

Courtesy of sub-components known as the caudate nucleus, putamen and globus pallidus, the basal ganglia helps us to organise and control fine-grained voluntary movements such as picking up a cup and putting it to our lips and writing. It also plays a role in our voluntary facial movements such as those involved in a forced smile and speaking. Those who suffer from Huntington's disease have damage to the basal ganglia and the aliment is characterised by involuntary and spasmodic hand, arm, leg and facial movements.

Limbic system

Like the other main anatomical components of the telencephalon the limbic system too comprises sub-components. We will not list them all here, and will not attempt to specify the full range of functions that it is responsible for. However, it is worth making a note of the view that the predominant role of the limbic system is the production and mediation of emotion, which is through a structure called the amygdala, and the formation and storage and of memory principally mediated by a structure called the hippocampus.

Continuing to travel from (roughly) top to bottom, or from the rostral to the caudal ends of the brain (see Box 4.5 'Mapping and labelling the brain'), we next come to the diencephalon and its two major sub-components.

Thalamus

This part of the diencephalon can be thought of as a relay station for sensory information. On the one hand, it can ready us for immediate action by effecting the sympathetic division of the autonomic nervous system via the peripheral nervous system. On the other hand, it sends sensory information to various other parts of the brain including the frontal lobes for further analysis and processing.

Hypothalamus

This part of the diencephalon is critical for the maintenance of homeostasis – overall bodily stabilisation. It controls our body temperature and alerts us to a need for food and water. The hypothalamus also regulates our overall arousal and stress levels courtesy of the triggering of hormones via the pituitary gland.

MIDBRAIN

The midbrain is also known as the 'mecencephalon' and it comprises two main anatomical structures – the tectum and the tegmentum.

Tectum

This term translates as 'roof' and physically it comprises the superior colliculi and the inferior colliculi. The most important function of the superior colliculi is to mediate automatic eye movements in accordance with visual information. In doing this it can generate appropriate responses more quickly than can the visual pathway that ends in the occipital lobe. The inferior colliculi acts as a relay station from cranial nerves which deliver auditory information to the temporal lobes.

Tegmentum

This term translates as 'covering' and physically it comprises the reticular formation, peri-aqueductal grey matter, the red nucleus and the substantia nigra. These anatomical structures serve a number of homeostatic functions, most especially those involved with vigilance, attention, awareness and sleep.

BOX 4.4   OBJECTIONS TO EVOLUTIONARY PSYCHOLOGY: BIOLOGICAL DETERMINISM

Determinism seems to be a dirty word for some students of human thought and behaviour. It refers to a suite of theories that coalesce around the doctrine that all events, including human behaviours and the thoughts, feelings and the decisions that underlie them, are the necessary effects of preceding causes. An objection to evolutionary approaches to mind and behaviour claims that they too take thought and behaviour to be rigidly and unalterably fixed by genes and our biological make-up. Such an objection is facilitated and encouraged by metaphors and analogies which suggest that the human genome is a book or a blueprint wherein our biology and brains are scripted in advance. The inference is that the thoughts and behaviours that make up our lives are written or laid out in advance of them being read or played out. If the human genome is the 'book of life', and if your genome is the book of your life, then, like a book, its story and contents may not yet have been read but the narrative, with its twists and turns, are already decided. But it is not the case that evolutionary approaches to the nature of human nature espouse such a form of **biological determinism**.

While evolutionary psychology assumes that the psychological adaptations at the centre of its interest are coded for by genes – just as is, say, the anatomy and physiology of the human heart – genes do not dictate the day-to-day specifics of their operation. Evolutionary psychology predicts that, all things being equal, thought and behaviour is functional – that it is directed toward end states – but it does not insist on a singular specification of means. Rather, the manner in which adaptations develop in an individual – their **ontogeny** – and the manner of their operation in actual environments depends very much on the environment.

We can also unpack the notion of biological determinism in a slightly different way if we take the objection to mean, 'Does evolutionary psychology assume that thought and behaviour is amenable to causal explanation?' The answer to this question is yes. Evolutionary psychology assumes that thoughts and behaviours are not randomly produced, and that the central nervous system that underpins and allows for them is not randomly produced. Evolutionary approaches assume that what we call a train of thought is more akin to the related images that make up a scene in a film than it is to a set of stills from different scenes spliced together ad hoc. Our thought and behaviour is logical in adaptationist terms. The logic that governs our thought is a product of our natural history which is itself a series of physical events.

HINDBRAIN

The hindbrain comprises the metencephalon and the myencephalon. The metencephalon, in turn, comprises two main anatomical parts, the cerebellum and the pons.

Cerebellum

The cerebellum is a large structure and it can be anatomically and functionally decomposed into a variety of substructures such as the inferior restiform body, the brachium pontis and the brachium conjunctivum; there is also the flocculonodular lobe and the anterior lobe, uvula, pyramis of the paleocerebellum, and the posterior lobe and pontine nuclei of the neo-cerebellum. However, for our purposes we will consider the overall function of the cerebellum which is to execute well-rehearsed coordinated movements that we do not, or do not need to, consciously attend to such as walking, running, bending, standing, stretching and gesturing. Alcohol and other psychoactive drugs affect the cerebellum with characteristic consequences which impair our ability to perform what are usually cognitively effortless actions.

Pons

The cerebellum is connected via the cerebellar penduncles to the other main structure of the metencephalon, the pons. The pons, like other parts of the brain, acts as a connection point between brain regions. In this case it connects the cerebellum to the cerebral cortex, most notably the parietal lobe and the motor areas therein. The pons is also where four cranial nerves junction with the brain. Cranial nerve V, the trigeminal, mediates sensations in the eyes, nose, and mouth and controls mastication. Cranial nerve VI, the abducent, innervates the lateral rectus muscle, which abducts the eye by rotating it outward. Cranial nerve VII, the facial, controls many facial movements and salivation. And cranial nerve VIII, the acoustic/vesibulo-cochlear nerve mediates balance and hearing.

The myencephalon part of the hindbrain comprises a structure called the medulla (also referred to as the medulla oblongata because of its shape) and the medullary reticular formation. This structure extends from the reticular formation of the tegmentum. The medulla controls a number of autonomic and homeostatic functions including the control of respiration, blood pressure, swallowing and vomiting.

This ends our brief tour of the development of the central nervous system and the functional anatomy of the brain. The aim was to give us some idea as to how mechanical is its maturation and how confident we are of which parts perform which roles. Let us now move on and look at some of the reasons why it is said that a description of the brain and its functions does not give us a description of the mind and its workings.

BOX 4.5   MAPPING AND LABELLING THE BRAIN

Our understanding of the functional anatomy of the brain is developing rapidly. As a consequence, parts of the brain large enough to be discriminated from others by the naked eye – the hippocampus which is implicated in memory – are themselves being sub-divided into further functional units. Many of these newly discovered units cannot be discriminated by the naked eye alone. To help name these smaller and smaller functional units a number of terms are used which indicate where they are in relation to the larger part they form part of. Here is a list of such terms and what they refer to:

Ventral or anterior = to the front
Dorsal or posterior = to the back
Lateral = to the side
Medial = to the middle
Distal = to the extremity
Proximal = to the centre
Inferior = from the bottom

Examples of how these terms are used to label functional units in the brain are the ventromedial hypothalamus and the lateral hypothalamus. Both of these sub-structures are a part of the larger hypothalamus and they are implicated in hunger, satiety and eating behaviour. If you look at the list of terms above you can see that 'ventro' means to the front and 'medial' means to the middle. Accordingly, the ventromedial hypothalamus is situated towards the front and middle of the hypothalamus. Similarly, 'lateral' means to the side and the lateral hypothalamus is situated towards the side of the hypothalamus.

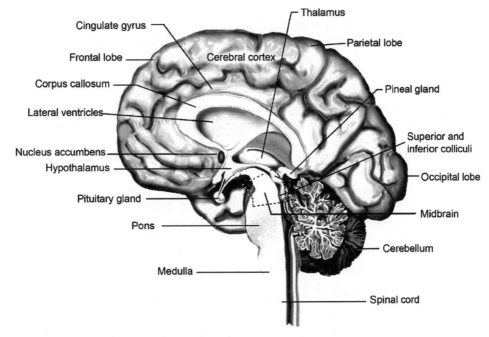

Figure 4.4   Saggital section of the human brain
View of the interior features of the human brain.
Everything above the midbrain is forebrain; everything below is hindbrain.
Source: Figure 3.12 (page 62) from B. Garrett (2009) *Brain and Behaviour. An Introduction to Biological Psychology* (2nd edn). Thousand Oaks, CA: Sage.

THE MIND–BODY PROBLEM

Earlier in this chapter in Box 4.1 'Where are you?' the question was asked: if your best friend had a brain transplant where would they then be? And the answer that most psychologists agree upon is that your friend would not be in the body that once housed their brain but rather they would now reside in the body which now housed their brain. This response to the question illustrates the conviction that we are our brains, that our brains house our personalities and/or that our brains somehow give rise to or cause our mental life and minds. This conviction is licensed by innumerable findings which very powerfully demonstrate that damage to humans brains which is not fatal almost always results in cognitive deficits modest or profound, and that the deficits map relatively neatly on to different regions of the brain. These 'deficits' can also include changes of personality. Similarly, if we introduce psychoactive substances such as alcohol into the brain, the personality – the behaviour, thoughts and feelings – alter in characteristic ways. Furthermore, the evidence that we have suggests that where one finds brains – brains like ours that is – you find minds. And if there are no brains like ours there are no minds. These observations warrant the claim that brains give rise to minds.

So what then is the '**mind–body problem**'? Let us look at that last sentence again: 'brains give rise to minds'. What, exactly, does the term 'give rise to' mean? What does it imply?

To help yourself to think about what answers to these questions might be, consider another question: why does it make sense for someone to say that they have changed their mind, but it does not make sense for them to say that they have changed their brain? For example, suppose that I say that I have changed my mind about what the conclusion to this chapter will be. Now suppose that I say that I have changed my brain about what the conclusion to this chapter will be. Would you agree that the two sentences are not equivalent, that they do not mean the same thing? If you do then an implication is that the terms 'mind' and 'brain' do not mean the same thing. And if they do not mean the same thing then they must refer to two distinct things. So far as our initial question is concerned, 'What does "brains give rise to minds" mean?', the implication is that minds are, somehow, a product of brains but that they are also distinct from them.

This kind of conclusion – the claim that brains and minds are linked but nonetheless distinct – is the basis of the mind–body problem. The mind–body problem arises when we try to spell out how it is that a material thing like a brain gives rise to a non-material or immaterial thing like a mind, and it is compounded when we try to specify how a non-material thing such a mind comes to move or influence a material thing such a brain and vice versa.

Descartes is said to be the father of the mind–body problem as it has been construed in since the advent of academic psychology in the late nineteenth century. Descartes thought that the mind and brain met and influenced one another via the pineal gland. We know now that this view is not plausible. However, some of Descartes' arguments which he took to show that mind and brain are distinct are not easily dismissed (see Kenny, 1968). For example, he argued that the brain is a physical thing that can be seen, measured and weighed, but we cannot see thoughts, talk of them in terms of dimensions, or give them weight.

Figure 4.5   René Descartes and dualism

MIND–BODY SOLUTIONS

A number of ways of dealing with the mind–body problem have been developed in philosophy and psychology. One that you may well have heard of is **behaviourism**. Behaviourism supposes that if psychology is to be a science it must either ignore or wholly deny the notion of unseeable and unverifiable mental states and concern itself only with the seeable and verifiable – with human behaviour (Watson, 1930). It is only behaviour that can be observed, analysed and predicted.

Behaviourism is a form of materialism, and materialism presents other ways of dealing with the mind–body problem. As a general term 'materialism' refers to the point of view which claims that there is nothing other than physical matter in the world and universe. When applied to the mind–body problem, materialism yields the claim that there is no such thing as mind when mind is conceived of as being an immaterial 'substance' which acts upon the physical world or is acted upon by the physical world. Accordingly, there is no mind–body problem. What there is instead is just a brain problem and this problem is to do with how we identify brain states with mental states and replace mental talk with brain talk.

At risk of oversimplification a materialist position known as mind–brain **identity theory** (see Lewis, 1966) claims that when we have an experience of, say, pain we are in a certain physical state: i.e. certain neurons in our brains are in a certain condition and this condition is pain. Ditto any other mental state. And again at risk of oversimplification another materialist position known as **eliminative materialism** (see Churchland, 1981) claims that when I report on my mood state, say, and report that I am feeling, say, 'happy', what I ought to be doing is reporting on the physical properties of my brain such as serotonin and dopamine levels in certain parts of my central nervous system. The essence of each position is that brain states and mental states are one and the same thing.

Another solution to the mind–body problem is to explain away the mind by supposing that it is nothing more than a way of talking about mental events but that it does not exist over and above mental events (Ryle, 1949). For example, at any given moment each of us can report on our mental states such as our mood (good? bad?), physical comfort (warm? cold?) and sensory experience (what colour is the wall in front of you?). However, there is nothing over and above, nothing before or after these mental events. Rather, we use terms such as 'mind' as a form of shorthand to collect mental events together and locate them in persons. Following on from Ryle's analysis, materialists might argue that our 'mentalese', our mind-type terminology, is an artefact of our language and even of our ignorance.

BOX 4.6   CATEGORY MISTAKES AND ABSENCE OF MIND

The term 'category mistaken' was introduced into the mind–body debate by Gilbert Ryle in his book *The Concept of Mind* (1949). The idea is quite simple and quite powerful. Ryle suggests that we give labels to collections of things and come to think that the label stands for something over and above the set of things it was originally introduced to describe. One of his illustrations runs like this. Suppose you offer to show an out-of-town friend your home town: let's call your home town 'HomeTown'. You show your friend the university, the market, the museum, the sports stadium, and so on. Afterwards she asks, 'Where is HomeTown?' In doing so she makes a category mistake because she has assumed that there is some one seeable, touchable thing called 'HomeTown' rather than seeing that there is no such thing as HomeTown over and above the component or constituent parts that, in the abstract, we call 'HomeTown'. We make much the same (harmless) mistake when we say things such as 'The White House announced . . . ' or 'No. 10 Downing Street argues that . . . ' because we are giving life and voice and ontological status to things that do not, as a matter of fact, announce or argue anything not least of all because they don't have the requisite properties. Ryle argues that we make the same mistake when we assume that there is something called 'mind' over and above individual thoughts, feelings, pains and sensations. The fact that mind does not exist as a 'thing' goes some way towards explaining why we have such difficulty defining it and discussing it.

The final solution to the mind–body problem that we will consider in this section is what has come to be known as **'double aspect theory'** (or double aspect monism). The origin of this idea in modern philosophy (i.e. post-Renaissance philosophy) is Benedict Spinoza (Rocca, 1996), and versions of it have been developed by David Hume, William James, Bertrand Russell and Peter Strawson amongst others. The core of this idea is the claim that we are made up of both physical and mental properties. This 'fact' is only a problem to philosophers and theologians who get into a muddle because it is difficult (if not impossible) to conceive of the mental and the physical at the same time: rather like a coin, it is not possible to see both sides at once. But it is also abundantly obvious that each side is of a whole. This can be seen in ordinary (i.e. non-philosophical) discourse. For example, ordinarily we have no difficulty when somebody tells us that they are standing in a kitchen and that they like the kitchen. Notice that in the first part of the statement the person makes reference to their physical self, while in the second part they make reference to their mental self. Strawson (1959) suggests that double aspect theory not only solves the mind–body problem, but also helps to explain why it arises.

It is time now to move away from philosophy and back towards psychology and a conceptual scheme that has been devised to think about what thought is.

THE COMPUTATIONAL METAPHOR

You may be familiar with the major sub-discipline in psychology called cognitive psychology. Cognitive psychologists are interested in the processes that underlie and make up mental functions and thought. For example, it has been cognitive psychologists who have most extensively studies and produced what appear to be our best theories of human memory, its components and the rules that govern its operation (see Baddeley, 2007 for an overview). A more-or-less explicitly stated guiding principle for most cognitive psychologists is the assumption that our minds are like computers. This assumption is known as the **computational metaphor** and it can be seen as being of apiece with previous man – machine metaphors but updated. Viewing the mind as a computer was inspired by the advent of modern digital computers, and they in turn have provided a model of sorts and something akin to an approximation that help us to think about how minds might work.

However, some psychologists and philosophers of mind have taken this assumption further and it has been suggested that the mind is a computer and not just like a computer (Dennett, 1991). In part this claim is justified by thinking through what we mean by the term 'computer' and not being overly bound by the desktop and laptop devices with which we are familiar. The argument is that the digital computers made of silicon and metal and plastic that we use are only examples of a more general class of computational devices. The general class of such devices we can call information processors because that is what they do: process information wherein a defined set of rules manipulate information and produce a result or outcome. According to this view a computer, or information processor, is any device or machine which recognises certain forms of stimuli (key strokes; patterns of sound or light), treats such stimuli as meaningful symbols and then manipulates the symbols according to specific and specifiable rules (i.e. a program). The result of the manipulation is output. Output can be a further stimulus, a symbol, or symbols, an action, or a further state of the machine.

BOX 4.7   INFORMATION PROCESSORS

TRY IT THIS WAY …

To see how simple the concept of an information processor can be let us consider a very ordinary, every-day example of such a thing – a thermostat. A simple thermostat recognises one type of stimuli or information – heat. In response to this stimuli it is in one of two conditions – on or off. By recognising stimuli and by remaining in the same state or changing state in response wherein the change of state is itself a stimuli (to some other part of the heating/cooling system) it acts as an information processor.

THE CLASSICAL CASCADE

According to the view that the mind is a computer and not just like a computer, computation is what is important in cognitive psychology and not computers because computations are the programs, the software, the processors of thought, and computers are just the machinery upon which programs run. This line of reasoning led Marr (1980) to propose an approach wherein the problem of the mind–body relation can be circumvented by seeing the study of thought processors as consisting of three levels of analysis, three types of problem. From the 'top-down' we begin with problem that the system (the person) has to solve. Next we need to say what sort of program (or algorithm) would solve the problem. And next we need to specify what sort of machine (a brain) could run the program in such a way and at such a speed as to solve the problem in the required time. This explanatory scheme has been called the '**classical cascade**' (Franks, 1995; Patterson, 1998), such had been its influence and adoption in cognitive psychology. Let us illustrate the classical cascade with an example:

- Problem: humans need to 'solve' the problem of edge detection.
- Program: what sort of program would allow a human-type animate object to detect edges?
- Physiology: what sort of information-processing device would be required to run the program?

What this scheme says is this. A property that a human brain should have is a program to reliably detect edges in order to avoid them. Once we have specified such a program we have a description of the solution to the given problem. At this point we also have an account which describes the relevant mental processes. It was Marr's contention that the physiological level of explanation need not bother us at this point. In order to make progress in cognitive psychology we can assume that we will be able to describe the information-processing device in neurological terms at some point in the future. The key point about the classical cascade is that the distinction between computations and computers, between hardware and software, can be said to hold between what we typically call mind and brain and we need not know the specification of the machine on which programs run in order to know the programs themselves.

Marr's scheme lacks one key component that an evolutionary viewpoint can supply: how do we know what problems we – the machines – are supposed to solve? It is at this point that we appeal to the past, to the environment of evolutionary adaptedness, which was discussed in Chapter 3. The novel aspect of evolutionary psychology over common-or-garden cognitive psychology is that it claims to know what to look for by way of cognitive functions courtesy of our understanding of the selection pressures that brought us about.

BOX 4.8   THE FRAME PROBLEM

According to Tooby and Cosmides (1992) the early adopters of the computational metaphor in cognitive psychology assumed that the brain was a general problem solver in much the same way that digital computers are general problem solvers in that they can compute anything that can codified in a program. There are a number of problems with this assumption. One of them is that such a machine would be lethally cumbersome in evolutionary terms. Why so?

Well, imagine that all positive goal-directed activity had to be preceded by trial and error experimentation: that we had to truly learn everything and discover anything that had adaptive value. From an evolutionary point of view there are three problems with this:

- Other organisms do not proceed in this manner: they behave as if they come in to the world knowing something or knowing enough to learn adaptive response very quickly.
- The majority of behaviours that we could engage in are deleterious. For example, most of the substances that we could eat would be of no nutritional benefit and most of them would be harmful. Accordingly, our scope for trial and error learning is very limited.
- The reasons above suggest that the 'learner' would not compete well against 'the knower' over time and the knower strategy would out-reproduce the learner strategy.

These considerations have led evolutionary psychologists to suppose that we come into the world with a cognitive frame: a set of presuppositions and/or evaluative criteria within which perception and/or thinking occurs, and which constrains the course and outcome of thought processes. The frame problem is concerned with specifying what the set of presuppositions and/or evaluative criteria are. Evolutionary psychologists claim to have solved the frame problem by supposing that the presuppositions and/or evaluative criteria are the adaptive problems faced by our ancestors.

THE INTENTIONAL STANCE

Another way of thinking about human thought and accommodating the concept of mind in an evolutionary framework has been developed by Daniel Dennett (1987b, 1991). Dennett's scheme breaks up the problem into three related 'stances' or ways of talking about the mind. The three stances are the **intentional stance**, the **design stance** and the **physical stance**. Let us look at each of these conceptual tools in turn.

- The intentional stance involves the assumption that we behave for reasons; that behaviour is driven by purposes.
- The design stance involves the assumption that we are physically structured and organised in the way that is explicable in terms of our purposes; that we are shaped to do something.
- The physical stance involves the assumption that we are physical things and nothing more. Accordingly, our brains are governed and our behaviour is constrained by the causal laws of physics.

Amongst other things, Dennett wants to furnish us with theoretical apparatus and psychological constructs which will facilitate predictions about our behaviour. Accordingly, as important as the design and physical stances are he emphasises the crucial role of the intentional stance and the concomitant assumptions that thinking serves an adaptive purpose, and thoughts have the peculiar property of being about things external to themselves. This property is said to be peculiar because it unique to thoughts. It is known in the philosophy of mind as '**intentionality**' and it is illustrated by Dennett thus: 'Some things are about other things; a belief can be about icebergs, but an iceberg is not about anything; an idea can be about the number 7, but the number 7 is not about anything' (1987a: 383). The key notion is the feature of some things being about other things and that his feature is a hallmark of thought. With this in mind let us now look at how Dennett develops the intentional stance as a way of seeing, explaining and dealing with things that think:

> First you decide to treat the object whose behavior is to be predicted as a rational agent; then you figure out what beliefs that agent ought to have, given its place in the world and its purpose. Then you figure out what desires it ought to have, on the same considerations, and finally you predict that this rational agent will act to further its goals in the light of its beliefs. A little practical reasoning from the chosen set of beliefs and desires will in most instances yield a decision about what the agent ought to do; that is what you predict the agent will do. (1987b: 17)

As you can see, at each point Dennett advises us to assume something about the 'object': assume that anything that behaves is an agent, and that the agent is rational; assume that the behaviour is not random but belief driven, and that these beliefs are rational given the agents experience and objectives. Assume that objective can be taken as desires and that the meeting of desire is what drives the behaviour and confers it with the tag 'rational'.

There are a further three things to take note of here:

1 For Dennett, rationality cannot be pulled apart from beliefs and beliefs cannot be pulled apart from desires. Beliefs and desires confer rationality. We are only rational because we have beliefs and desires. And we only have beliefs and desires because we have purpose. Purpose itself is explicable only in evolutionary and Darwinian.
2 An understanding of beliefs and desires facilitate prediction. In principle, if the exact beliefs and desires of an entity where known we could predict its behaviour with precision. In practice, we are unlikely to know what a person's exact beliefs and desires are and can only offer approximate predictions.
3 The entity of interest may or may not be conscious of its reasons, beliefs and desires. However, we might assume the entity is conscious of its reasons, beliefs and desires for no other reason than that is our own experience.

Figure 4.6   Daniel Dennett

Having now raised the issue let us move on from the classical cascade and the intentional stance and consider consciousness from an evolutionary point of view.

CONSCIOUSNESS

Whether or not mind is something distinct from brain, or whether or not it exists at all, evolutionary psychology is still left with the need to offer an evolutionary plausible account of consciousness. To do this we must, of course, first define this notoriously slippery term.

We are going to keep it (relatively) simple. If we go 'big' and define consciousness as something vast and global power and scope, something into which we are all hooked, something metaphysical, then we lose explanatory traction and push it beyond explanation. So we will go small and say that consciousness is, at bottom, something like awareness, i.e. being aware. To be conscious is to be aware of something.

An evolutionary view encourages such a modest definition of consciousness, and it invites us not to think of it as being something animals either have or do not have. Evolutionary psychology takes the view that adaptations emerge slowly, come into being gradually. On the assumption that consciousness is an adaptation – and its apparent ubiquity in humans and other animals suggests that it does serve an adaptive purpose – then we would expect it to have emerged slowly, to have come into being gradually. This position is supported by the apparent fact that other animals exhibit consciousness because many behave in such as manner as to suggest that they are aware of at least some aspects of the world around them. For example, all healthy mammals respond in predictable and consistent ways to stimuli such as heat, light and noise. For us to support the suggestion that awareness evolved gradually we need only show that there are differences in how much awareness different species exhibit and that at least some animals lower down the phylogenetic scale than us exhibit less of it than we do.

It is also apparent that we enjoy various states of consciousness whereupon we are more-or-less consciously aware of ourselves and the environment: it is not the case that we are either conscious or not in an on-or-off manner. To support this claim we can refer to what we know about patterns of electrical activity in the brain and degrees of awareness – see Box 4.9 'Brain waves and states of awareness'.

BOX 4.9   BRAIN WAVES AND STATES OF AWARENESS

When we are fully awake and mentally active our brains exhibit a pattern of Beta (β) waves. Beta waves signal an active cerebral cortex and a state of focussed attention. Beta waves are marked by irregular, unsynchronised, very low amplitude, high-frequency pattern of electrical waves that occur between about 12 and 50 times per second.

When we are awake and relaxed, perhaps with our eyes closed, our brains exhibit a pattern of Alpha (α) waves. Again the amplitude of these waves is low, but there is greater synchronicity and the waves are less frequent, occurring at about 8 to 12 per second.

Theta (θ) waves are exhibited when we are deeply relaxed, perhaps in the transition period immediately before sleep proper, or in the early stages of a light sleep such as a day-time snooze. Waves are spike-like semi-synchronised, of low to medium amplitude and occur 3 to 7 times per second.

When we are deeply asleep we exhibit Delta (δ) waves. Now masses of cerebral neurons are firing at the same time in large slow waves, the register is regular and synchronised, the waves are of high amplitude, and low frequency – perhaps 5–3 per second.

If we are to accept that to be conscious is to be aware of something, and that this awareness is a more-or-less affair, we are still faced with a problem: why are we aware? What is the point and purpose of awareness? An answer is that awareness facilitates reflection, and reflection facilitates learning and the subsequent modification of behaviour. This answer rests in large part on evidence which suggests that we become consciously aware of stimuli in our environment some time after our central nervous system has logged the presence of the stimuli and initiated a response (Libert, 2003). For example, when we touch something hot action is taken to remove our hand from the stimuli before we feel a sensation of pain. One implication of this finding it that the conscious awareness, coming as it does *after* the central nervous system registers the stimuli and initiates a response, can only serve to influence future behaviour. Granted, the 'future' may be almost immediate, but it is not in real time.

On this account conscious awareness serves to equip us with experience, and experience can be seen as something like a record of stimuli and events in our past that we need to remember because they have fitness consequences. Oscar Wilde suggested that experience is the term we use to name our mistakes and in keeping with his sentiment we are suggesting that consciousness is how we come to be aware of stimuli and events that could, or have, precipitated a fitness-mistake.

BOX 4.10   THE CONTENT OF CONSCIOUSNESS

If to be conscious is to be aware we might ask if consciousness consists of anything over and above aware-ness. The parsimonious answer to this question appears to be 'no' and can be supported by the following consideration of David Hume's:

> For my part, when I enter most intimately into what I call myself, I always stumble on some particu-lar perception or other, of heat or cold, light or shade, love or hatred, pain or pleasure. I never can catch myself at any time without a perception, and never can observe anything but the perception. (1739/1978: I, IV, sec. 6)

What Hume is saying here is that he – and by inference we and other animals that we think to be conscious – are conscious of various sorts of perception and sensation, but that there is nothing over and above these perceptions and sensations to be conscious of. Furthermore, the implication is that nothing over and above the contents of consciousness exists.

SUMMARY OF CHAPTER 4

The concept of mind has long presented a problem for psychology, and evolutionary psychology too. The orthodox view in psychology, and, increasingly, in the philosophy of mind, is that mind and consciousness are a product of the brain – that brains must give rise to consciousness and what we call the human mind. To develop this point we first considered the development and adult form of the human brain. What biology shows us is that the source or seat of thought follows a largely invariant developmental path and takes largely invariant adult form. Working on the assumption that our brains and nothing else gives rise to mind and consciousness we might also argue that the nature of human thought is also largely invariant between individuals – just the point that evolutionary psychology seeks to make.

Evolutionary psychologists also see the mind as an information processor and in doing so go beyond the computational metaphor by taking it in more literal terms. Two ways of using the idea that thought is a series of problem solving computations are the 'classical cascade' and the 'intentional stance'. The classical cascade encourages us to concentrate of the specification of the problems the brain is designed to solve and the algorithmic processes it needs to run in order to so. And the intentional stance encourages us to utilise the folk-notions of beliefs and desires in order to make predictions about our behaviour which, ultimately, is organised around the problems of survival and production.

We need not either ignore or deny that we are conscious animals if we can stipulate a workable definition of consciousness. Here we said it was awareness – to be conscious is to be aware of something. On this account we need only say what function awareness-of-something might serve and a modest and plausible suggestion is that it facilities the accumulation of experience and the modification of future behaviour.

FURTHER READING

Apart from the references in this chapter you may find it interesting and useful to consult one or more of the following:

Blackmore, S. (2003) *Consciousness: An Introduction*. Abbingdon: Hodder and Stoughton.
Carlson, N.R. (2008) *Foundations of Physiological Psychology* (7th edn). Boston, MA: Allyn and Bacon.
Corr, P.J. (2006) *Understanding Biological Psychology*. Oxford: Blackwell.
Dennett, D.C. (2003) *Freedom Evolves*. Harmondsworth: Penguin.
O'Connor, T. and Robb, D. (eds) (2003) *Philosophy of Mind: Contemporary Readings*. London: Routledge.
Priest, S. (1991) *Theories of the Mind*. Harmondsworth: Penguin.

5 COOPERATION AND INTERDEPENDENCE

Some of the questions addressed in this chapter:

- How does evolution account for cooperation?
- Do we do things for the good of the species?
- Are we nepotistic?
- What is 'virtual' altruism?
- Does it pay to be a cheat?
- Are some emotions adaptations for altruism?

SOME KEY TERMS AND CONCEPTS

Game theory; Group selection; In-group; Kin altruism; Reciprocal altruism; Social identity theory; Tragic vision; Zero-sum game.

LEARNING OBJECTIVES

Having studied this chapter you should be better able to:

- Describe the concept of a 'selfish gene'.
- Explain how selfish genes could give rise to organisms that are not selfish.
- Present an argument to show how emotional states might be adaptive.

INTRODUCTION

In Chapter 1 we briefly paused to consider the claim that nature is 'red in tooth and claw'. The phrase is of a piece with a view of evolution as a struggle wherein those that survive are the strongest and most aggressive and that evolution is one enormous and incessant fight to the death. And both the phrase and what it is often taken to connote are of a piece with what has been called the '**tragic vision**' of human nature as something inherently self-serving, myopic and, ultimately, vicious (Pinker, 2002; and see Box 3.1). A certain view of the natural history of humans may augment such a vision. However, as we saw in Chapter 3 'The natural history of humans', many species of hominid have come about, but all bar one is extinct. And, as we have seen, perhaps one of those species was rendered extinct as a consequence of our behaviour. In Chapter 6 we will be adding to this view when we look at competition, aggression and violence, and in other chapters we will also see that an evolutionary view of things we cherish such as our romantic partnerships and families can also yield rather bleak predictions.

This chapter is an antidote to the tragic vision. Look around you. Humans are nested in hierarchies of groups of families, friends, schools, colleges, businesses, towns and cities, regions and nations. These are all groups that depend upon varying degrees and forms of cooperation amongst members. Oddly, even wars can only be fought if the persons who form the competing sides cooperate amongst themselves (Tooby and Cosmides, 1988). Of course, many of us do not cooperate with all others all the time, but this chapter is based upon the premise that most human beings are first and foremost cooperative and interdependent, that social existence is not a **zero-sum game** wherein one either wins or loses, and that self-interest is not inconsistent with mutually beneficial interactions.

BOX 5.1   OBJECTIONS TO EVOLUTIONARY PSYCHOLOGY: PESSIMISM

Is evolutionary theory pessimistic? Since its inception Darwinism has drawn political comment (Degler, 1991; Dennett, 1995; Kitcher, 1987). Here it has been argued that it is not inherently political (or moral or theological). But we might also agree that it has been politicised (see Beckwith, 1981). Perhaps this was and is inevitable given that the purview of the theory of evolution includes humans and can be applied to them. The term 'purview' carries an important and useful implication. Because Darwinism isn't about any species in particular, but organic life in general, it carries the *possibility* of being detached, one might say 'cold', with respect to its subject matter.

For some such an ambition will appear to be misguided. Psychology and the social sciences have long been torn between what are perceived to be two obligations. While on the one hand there is the obligation to be value-free and scientific, there is another obligation and that is to be a '**humaneering**' enterprise which is in the business of making things better (Stainton Rogers et al., 1995). Of course, the two need not be seen as inconsistent: we can only make things better if we know the current state of affairs, i.e. the 'truth'. Here will examine the claim that evolutionary psychology is pessimistic (as opposed to realistic) about both the actualities of the human condition and its possibilities.

To begin, we might ask if evolutionary approaches suggest that humanity, like the rest of nature, is 'red in tooth and claw'. We have encountered and gone some way towards addressing this point in this chapter and we saw that an analysis of cooperation is central to contemporary Darwinism as applied to the human condition. However, if the charge is that evolutionists tolerate a pessimistic view of the human condition and if we do so then we must accept that to be true. The work of and subsequent abundance of research influenced by Daly and Wilson shows that evolutionary psychologists accept that there is a dark side to human behaviour and that it is important to study it. However, this work does not fall prey to the so-called 'naturalistic fallacy' whereupon it mistakes questions about 'what is?' with 'what ought to be?' For example, were we to subscribe to the notion that the temporal and geographical pervasiveness of male sexual aggression can be explained in evolutionary terms we are not condoning it. Evolutionary psychology seeks to find out about the source of negative behaviours but there is no bar on also searching for ways to ameliorate negative behaviour. For example, given that some males are sexually aggressive, an evolutionary analysis may be as useful as any other in discerning the conditions that elicit such behaviours and, in doing so, lead to an ability to predict and control them. The idea that evolutionary approaches are pessimistic is often tied to Darwin's claim that humans are a part of nature. What we need to see is that a tolerance of a pessimistic view of the human condition does not constitute a pessimistic philosophy.

Nor is it the case that evolutionists deny that social change for the better is impossible and it would be absurd to do so. Yes, human societies have shown themselves to be in a state of tension between individual self-interest and the profound need for social alliances and cooperation. This tension is dynamic and creative. Social change is inevitable rather than impossible by virtue of the fact that the individuals who make up society are forever renewed.

Picking up where we left off in Chapter 1, we will look at Hamilton's inclusive fitness theory and kin selection again and in more detail. We will look again at Trivers' theory of **reciprocal altruism**, and we will discuss **game theory** and the notion of **evolutionary stable strategies** – the idea that certain patterns of interaction between members of a species become typical and are reiterated because they work well in terms of the inclusive fitness of the actors (Maynard-Smith, 1982). We will take the conclusion that humans are fundamentally cooperative and explicate a productive and robust theory from social psychology called **social identity theory**. Social identity theory seeks to describe and explain the formation and change within and between groups and the role of groups in the formation of a sense of self and self-concept. This chapter closes with a brief review of the evolution of moral sentiment and begins with further discussion of group selection theory.

GROUP SELECTION

You may recall the term 'group selection' from Chapter 1. It refers to the theory that the feeding, breeding and social behaviour of species can be explained by assuming that the individual members of a species act for the good of the species as a whole. More precisely, it refers to how the members of a specific breeding group act in the interests of the group. Group selection theory claims that individuals act in the interests of the group because alleles can spread and become a fixed characteristic of a breeding population of animals because of the fitness benefits they bestow upon the population irrespective of the fitness consequences for individuals. In his book *Animal Dispersion in Relation to Social Behaviour*, Wynne-Edwards argues that animals regulate their reproduction so as not to over-exploit essential resources. Individuals in a breeding group may eschew reproductive opportunities if and when such decisions lead to a non-optimal population size in relation to the necessary resource base needed to maintain the breeding group. Furthermore, natural selection would favour those populations wherein such behaviour was typical (Wynne-Edwards, 1962).

If for no other reason group selection theory is optimistic and, therefore, attractive to some. It allows us to retain the strict secularism of Darwinian theory while retaining a depiction of ourselves as other-minded and communitarian. It suggests that the individuals of species, ourselves included, either are or can come to be in harmony with one another and with the natural world upon which we depend. Furthermore, this other-mindedness, this group-orientation, is not something we need to be cajoled or forced into. It is a fundamental part of us. It has been chosen by natural selection. It is in our genes and will be in the genes of our children. Unfortunately, it does not appear to fit the facts of our natural history and ancient history. And its theoretical foundations are readily undermined.

In Chapter 3 we saw that our ancestors repeatedly migrated away from what we think was their evolutionary birth place. This implies that population densities repeatedly over-exposed the local resource base. This appears to be true for the gracile *Australopithecus* species, *Homo ergaster* and *Homo sapien*. Originating in eastern Africa, each of these species subsequently migrated. It is reasonable to suppose that they did so because they reproduced at a rate that the immediate environment could not sustain. The orthodox view of *Homo neanderthalis* is that the species became extinct because of **competitive replacement** by *Homo sapien*. This broad macroscopic picture derived from the natural history of hominids is reflected in the microscopic migrations that have been a feature of recorded human history. To this day peoples are displaced from environments because the size of populations place intolerable pressure on the natural resource base. Neither account offers support for group selection theory. Let us now turn to the theoretical considerations of why evolutionists have come to the conclusion a species (or a population therein) cannot come to be for the good of itself.

BOX 5.2   GROUP SELECTION AND THE TRAGEDY OF THE COMMONS

TRY IT THIS WAY ...

An ecologist called Gavin Hardin published a paper called the 'The tragedy of the commons' in the journal *Science* in 1968. In it, and in other publications, Hardin argued that with regard to the consumption of common resources what is logical for each of us is catastrophic for all of us. Here is one of his illustrations of the idea.

The tragedy of the commons develops in this way. Picture a pasture open to all. It is to be expected that each herdsman will try to keep as many cattle as possible on the commons. Such an arrangement may work reasonably satisfactorily for centuries because tribal wars, poaching, and disease keep the numbers of both man and beast well below the carrying capacity of the land. Finally, however, comes the day of reckoning, that is, the day when the long-desired goal of social stability becomes a reality. At this point, the inherent logic of the commons remorselessly generates tragedy.

As a rational being, each herdsman seeks to maximise his gain. Explicitly or implicitly, more or less consciously, he asks, 'What is the utility *to me* of adding one more animal to my herd?' This utility has one negative and one positive component.

1) The positive component is a function of the increment of one animal. Since the herdsman receives all the proceeds from the sale of the additional animal, the positive utility is nearly +1.

2) The negative component is a function of the additional overgrazing created by one more animal. Since, however, the effects of overgrazing are shared by all the herdsmen, the negative utility for any particular decision-making herdsman is only a fraction of −1.

Adding together the component partial utilities, the rational herdsman concludes that the only sensible course for him to pursue is to add another animal to his herd. And another; and another … But this is the conclusion reached by each and every rational herdsman sharing a commons. Therein is the tragedy. Each man is locked into a system that compels him to increase his herd without limit – in a world that is limited. Ruin is the destination toward which all men rush, each pursuing his own best interest in a society that believes in the freedom of the commons. Freedom in a commons brings ruin to all. (Hardin, 1968: 1244).

Group selectionists such as Wynne-Edwards did not invoke explicit rationality to support their claims. Had they have done so they would have encountered Hardin's seemingly inescapable conclusion. As we will see, it turns out that it can be rational to do other than Hardin suggests and escape the 'remorseless working of things' towards collective tragedy.

In short, the reason why group selection does not work is because it is always vulnerable to selfishness from both within the group and from other selfish groups. Within a non-selfish group we still expect genetic transmission rules to operate, for mutations to occur, and we expect that individuals in a group will vary. Short of invoking a special rules for the transmission of the 'for the good of all' trait that maintains the behaviour that sacrifices individual self-interest for the good of the group, we should also expect the trait, or traits, that governs 'for the good of all' to vary. Let us suppose that one such variation led an individual to fail to restrain its direct reproductive effort. This individual would enjoy greater Darwinian fitness than it would have done and, accordingly, the trait would be more numerous in the next generation. This outcome would repeat itself until the trait became common and then typical. In the process the 'for the good of all' rule governing reproductive effort would be broken and eventually collapse.

Similarly, a 'for the good of all' population would be vulnerable from without. A selfless population would be out-reproduced by a competitor population which was identical in all respects bar the selfless trait. To illustrate, imagine a species comprising organisms that exercised a 'for the good of all' rule over food distribution. Let us suppose that, in practice, this rule involved the careful and equitable distribution of food from each individual collector to every other group member. Let us say that this activity doubles the amount of time involved in dealing with food on a daily basis. Now, compare this first group with a second neighbouring group whose members consume what they eat, thus spending half the amount of time dealing with food on a daily basis. Add the assumption that once sufficiently nourished both groups seek to maximise their reproductive success and it is apparent that the second group have more to time to devote to more direct reproduction-related activities than does the first.

The selfish group, even if it remained a separate group and did not interbreed with the self-less group, would expand and exploit the selfless groups' resource base. These considerations lead to the conclusion that while group-orientated traits could work in principle, and that natural selection could work at the level of the group with whole gene pools being selected for, in practice it is not stable against selfishness.

Group selectionist thinking still has some proponents (Jablonka and Lamb, 2006; Soltis et al., 1995; Wilson and Sober, 1994). The optimism that may lead some to it aside, we have already noted why this is so. Human beings are a cooperative, group-dwelling, group-forming species. But for the most part evolutionary psychologists do not subscribe to the idea. There is an important reason for their failing to do so. It is claimed that the selfish-gene view and the theories of kin and reciprocal altruism that it inspires can accommodate pro-social behaviour without needing to suppose one or more additional or alternative levels at which natural selection works.

KIN SELECTION THEORY II

Chapter 1 'Darwin's argument and three problems: heritability, sexual selection and altruism' discussed kin selection theory. It was said that if we accept that the unit of selection is the gene, the problem of altruism represents itself in the form of the question, 'How can one explain the existence of a gene that aids the reproduction of other genes?' And the answer is that while any given gene is selfish it is not necessarily unique. In the course of reproduction genes clone themselves and clones are expected to be extant in related individuals. If related individuals assist one another in ways that enhance one another's fitness then they are increasing the likelihood that some of the genes that they carry will replicate. Let us a look at an illustration of how kin selection could work and how it could favour genes that aid reproduction of their clones.

Let us suppose that the *K* locus on a **chromosome** of a species of sexual reproducers carries alleles that code for exchange relations toward kin. Let us suppose that this allele comes is four forms, **K**, k, **k** and K. And let us suppose that each form codes for a different pattern, or type, of behaviour towards kin. Thus:

- k   We will we call the 'Cheat' pattern because its bearer accepts but doesn't return help.
- **k**   We will call 'Grudger' because its bearer only gives help having been given to.
- K   We will call 'Initiator' because its bearer will give before being given to.
- **K**   We will call 'Altruist' because its bearer will give unconditionally to others with **K**, but otherwise adopts one of the other patterns.

Imagine now that we have the following scenario:

Generation 1

Pop   Ma
Kk   **k**K

Wherein Pop is carrying **K** 'Altruist', and k 'Cheat', and Ma is carrying **k** 'Grudger' and K 'Initiator'. Let us look at a pattern that could then occur in a set of children that Pop and

Ma have. In this hypothetical case – which is one of the many that could occur – the distribution pattern of the *K* allele is thus:

Generation 2

Baby1	Baby 2	Baby 3	Baby 4
Kk	kK	**KK**	k**k**

As we would expect given the laws in inheritance, each Baby has one variant of *K* from each parent, and going with the probabilities inherent in random assortment, each variant of *K* finds itself in the next generation twice. We should also note that any given allele will be expressed in a given Baby if it is dominant against its paired gene.

In our scenario we are supposing that Pop, Baby 1 and Baby 3 will offer unconditional help to one another courtesy of each possessing **K**. All that is required for **K** to out-reproduce other variants of *K* is for **K** to have the effect of enabling other bodies with **K** to have greater reproductive success than will k, k or K in other bodies with k, k or K. For example, let us suppose that Pop's **K** gene helps those children with **K** to have greater reproductive success compared with the other children.

So, if Babies 1 and 3 have, say, six children against an average of, say, four children for Babies 2 and 4, then **K** is likely to have a greater representation in generation 3 than k, k, K and other variants of *K* that come from those that the Babies reproduce with. Again assuming random segregation and assortment, where it to be the case that those with **K** again have 50 per cent more reproductive success than those without courtesy of mutual assistance then we might expect to see in Generation 3 six copies of **K** as opposed to 4 copies of any other variant of *K*. In Generation 4 we might expect to see twice as many **K** as any other variant of *K*. In Generation 5 **K** could be almost four times as numerous as other alleles.

There are conditions that need to be satisfied if our hypothetical illustration is to become a model of what has happened in evolution. We need to have confidence that related individuals remained in contact with one over sufficient periods of time to allow the altruistic pattern to cash out in the form of greater reproductive success for those who exhibited it. We can be confident of this for a number of reasons. First, in the case of parent-to-child kin altruism the period between birth and puberty has probably been at least a decade. Second, in the case of sibling-to-sibling kin altruism because the age gap may have been about 3 to 5 years we can assume that they too had many years wherein they were in contact. And third, mobility between unrelated groups could have been limited. We also need to be confident that related individuals knew that they were related. This condition is harder to satisfy so a discussion of it will be delayed until the end of the next section.

RECIPROCAL ALTRUISM II

The discussion of kin selection illustrated a technique for analysing interactions and their likely success called game theory (Axelrod, 1984; Maynard-Smith, 1982). Game theory refers to a way of studying interactive situations wherein different strategies are pitted against one another with a view to finding out which of them is best. The example used pitted the 'Altruist', which adopted the strategy 'help unconditionally those with who do likewise but only reciprocate with others', against 'Cheat', 'Grudger' and 'Initiator'. 'Best' was measured by counting the number of such strategies in subsequent generations. The essential feature of game theory is the way in which abstract and formal strategies are used to model social situations. Game theory has been influential in evolutionary biology because it offers a way of modelling and mimicking the trillions of interactions that have taken place during evolution. It is of interest to us in this chapter because it helps us to explain why humans are cooperators, so it will now be used again to see how reciprocal altruism could have evolved to become a typical feature of our social interactions.

Recall from Chapter 1 that reciprocal altruism refers to favour-for-favour behaviour – you scratch my back and I will scratch yours. To see how it could come about, imagine a world containing four personality types:

1 The Sucker: this type helps others indiscriminately – it is not choosy about to whom it gives up resources. Sucker also continues to act this way impervious to past experience.
2 The Cheater: this type is all take – it is not choosy about whom it exploits and never returns favours.
3 The Grudger: this type helps only those who have helped it – it will not begin an exchange but will reciprocate on the basis of past favours. It never gets cheated because is always returning a favour, never giving one.
4 The Initiator: this type is prepared to initiate exchanges and extend a favour. However, it remembers past events and whom it has given to, and Initiator refuses to extend a favour a second time if the first was not returned.

Now, let us imagine four different scenarios. In the first we will suppose that the bulk of the population is composed of 'Suckers'. In the second we will suppose that it is mainly composed of 'Cheaters'. In the third it is composed of 'Grudgers'. And in the fourth it is mainly composed of 'Initiators'. Imagine now that each strategy is playing for points and points make for reproductive success. Without being rigidly arithmetical we can conduct an informal thought experiment and see what happens in each scenario when we introduce a small number of each of the minority strategies. We are looking to see which strategy would do well and gain points which would convert into a proliferation of the strategy in the population over time.

Scenario 1: Population of Suckers

- In a population composed mainly of Suckers, Cheats would do well. Their gains will exceed their costs because they have no costs and would meet Suckers most of the time. The Cheat strategy would proliferate mainly at the cost of Suckers.
- Grudgers also do well in a population composed mainly of Suckers. Their gains will also exceed their costs. Meeting Suckers who give but do not insist on reciprocation, the Grudger strategy would also proliferate.
- Initiators will do as well as Cheats by happenstance. They would be ready to give but take without reciprocation from the Suckers they meet most of the time.
- Suckers do relatively badly. They lose more than they gain because although they accumulate gains from other Suckers they give to all.

Scenario 2: Population of Cheats

○—○ Suckers do very badly. They are exploited by the majority Cheats.

○—○ Grudgers would not do well. In a population of Cheats they don't lose because they do not initiate by giving but because Cheats never give Grudgers have limited chances to gain from reciprocal exchanges.

○—○ Initiators would do badly. Although they would only be exploited by any given Cheat strategy once by virtue of their tit-for-tat strategy, they would move from interaction to interaction in a population composed mainly of Cheats and lose from each one.

○—○ Cheats do not do particularly well either. In a population composed mainly of Cheats the Cheat has few opportunities to cheat!

Scenario 3: Population of Grudgers

○—○ In a population comprised mainly of Grudgers Suckers would do fairly well because the majority of favours would be returned by the numerous Grudgers.

○—○ Cheats would not accumulate many points because Grudgers do not give before having taken.

○—○ Initiators would do well because favours would be returned.

○—○ Grudgers would not do so well. Being a Grudger in a population mainly of Grudgers means that few positive reciprocal exchanges would begin.

Scenario 4: Population of Initiators

○—○ Suckers would do well because favours would be returned by the Initiators.

○—○ Cheats would do very well by exploiting the tendency of Initiators to begin exchanges with a favour and responding with nothing.

○—○ Grudgers do well because positive exchanges would be initiated and their response would be reciprocation.

○—○ Initiators would do almost as well as Grudgers – almost because the tendency to initiate means they would be carrying IOUs from Grudgers and would lose against Cheaters.

Where does this thought experiment take us? Well, there are some lessons to be learned. Across the four scenarios we can see that Suckers do not do particularly well. Unconditional giving leaves it vulnerable to Cheats. Suckers hold their own best amongst themselves. Cheats thrive in two of the four scenarios – populations of Suckers and Initiators. But they hit a wall against themselves and Grudgers. Grudgers are immune to Cheats, they thrive amongst Suckers, they accumulate points in exchanges with Initiators, but they too hit a wall against themselves. Initiators appear to fair best. If we assume that reciprocal exchanges are advantageous for both parties in terms of overall fitness then those who engage in more of them win over time. Yes, Initiators are exposed by Cheats. But they gain from Suckers to an equal extent as do Cheats and Grudgers. Initiators trigger beneficial reciprocal exchanges in a population of Grudgers, and they exchange amongst themselves. It is for this reason that it is thought that something like the Initiator strategy can come to be what is called an '+ −' or an Evolutionary Stable Strategy (EES) (Maynard-Smith, 1982). Coming from game theory studies, an EES is a strategy, a pattern of interactions, that is robust against invasion from other strategies. We have seen that group selection is not stable against selfishness. But it is thought that Initiator – a 'tit-for-tat' strategy which begins generously but adopts a 'do unto others as they do unto you hereafter' approach – is (Axelrod, 1984).

At this point we are going to go further back in time than has been and will be usual and ask how the Initiator tendency may have got started. If we make the reasonable assumption that life started out as a population of Cheats and add our consideration as to what happens to Initiators in such a population we may ask how Initiator spread. An answer could lie in kin altruism. Here is how.

Something like a Sucker strategy is not a sucker strategy when it comes to exchanges with kin. Why? Because the exchange is not about giving and taking wherein what is received is then converted into reproductive success. The benefit gained by the giver comes in the form of the reproductive success of the receiver. If I scratch your back, and that allows you to scratch a mate's back in return for a mating opportunity then I gain through the relatedness I have with the resultant progeny. Your reproductive success is mine. Your gain is my pay-off.

At the end of our earlier discussion in this chapter of kin selection theory we left hanging one of the conditions said to be necessary for it to work: how do we identify kin? An answer was hinted at in Chapter 1. We operate by one or more simple counterfactual rules such as *'If raised with X then help'*, or, we work on a proximity rule such as *'Help those who look/smell like others around you'*. This may strike us as unacceptably imprecise. But it is a combination of the imprecision and the pay-offs of unconditional help that creates the conditions in which Initiator could work. The very success of kin altruism as a means of scoring fitness points means that a version of it that is more rather than less giving, more rather than less inclusive could be selected for. We can think of this in terms of a useful idea called '**error management theory**' or EMT (Green and Swets, 1966).

EMT argues that it is sometimes better to overestimate the probability of one outcome and underestimate the probability of another given the costs of being wrong. For example, think of a job interview. Suppose that you really want the job. You reckon that it will take you about half and hour to get from home to the place of the interview. Would it be better to overestimate or underestimate the traffic problems that you might encounter given that the cost of being late is likely to be fatal of your chances of getting the job? It would be better to overestimate it. The cost of doing so may be 15 minutes of wasted time. The cost of wrongly underestimating the traffic problems is the cost of your time getting to and from the place of the interview plus the lost job opportunity.

Let us apply this logic to kin altruism. A.N. Other could be genetically related to you. You could help them out and enjoy a fitness pay-off that would obey the dictum of Hamilton's rule wherein the benefit as a function of the extent to which you are related to A.N. Other is greater than the cost to your own direct fitness. Or you could refuse to help them. All things being equal, it pays to help in the long run if the chances of A.N. Other being related to you is better than 50/50. It pays to operate on the basis of a false positive provided the cost of getting it wrong is small. On this reasoning we might expect to see the evolution of a more rather than a less open or generous form of kin altruism. Because those around you during development are probably kin, because those that resemble you more than do most others are probably kin, you probably land on the right side of the equation when you overestimate the likelihood that those others are kin. It is in a population of such generous kin altruists that Initiator would stand a chance. Furthermore we could apply EMT to the Initiator strategy. There is theory in social psychology that gives us more reason to suppose that the picture that game theory and EMT paints is a plausible picture and provides us with additional tools with which to analyse cooperation and interdependence.

BOX 5.3 RECIPROCAL ALTRUISM, REPUTATION AND GOSSIP

We will be exploring ideas and evidence concerning the link between cooperation and language in more depth in chapter 9 'Evolution and language', but this is a good point to flag up the relationship between reciprocal altruism, reputation and gossip courtesy of some interesting recent studies.

Hess and Hagen (2006) claim that reputation as it is mediated and communicated through day-to-day gossip plays an important role in how, when and with whom we cooperate. They argue that 'If resources were allocated among individuals according to their reputations, competition for resources via competition for "good" reputations would have created incentives for exaggerated or deceptive gossip about one-self and one's competitors in ancestral societies' (Hess and Hagen, 2006: 337). On this view they suppose that we ought to be able to reliably assess the validity of personal information garnered through gossip. Having presented participants with a number of fictional scenarios which offered unverified but plausible information about others they found that:

- Iteration of the same claims made what participants took to be uninteresting information more plausible but this was not the case for interesting or important information.
- Multiple sources made information more plausible.
- The independence of the source (i.e. did he, she, or it have an issue with the subject of the gossip?) increased whereas competition between source and subject decreased the plausibility of the information.
- Benign information was taken to be more plausible.

Hess and Hagen interpret these outcomes as indicating a set of heuristics which we use to assess gossip, and they suggest that an emphasis on multiple independent sources of the same information rather than repeated claims made by interested parties would tend to provide more-or-less valid results in most circumstances.

Piazza and Bering (2008) also worked on the supposition that gossip matters for reputation and reputation matters for cooperation, but they looked at the idea from a very different angle. In their study they asked participants to divide up a fictional sum between themselves and an unknown other. Half of the participants were informed that the person they split the sum with would be discussing their actions with others, and half again of these participants were told that the third party knew of and about them. In other words, amongst all of the participants there was a group whose generosity – or lack of – would be attributed to them and talked about. Piazza and Bering had hypothesised that this 'threat' of exposure and damage to reputation would promote generosity in their decision-making and this is what was found.

SOCIAL IDENTITY THEORY AND VIRTUAL KIN ALTRUISM

Founded in the work of Musafa Sheriff and developed by Henri Tajfel, Michael Billig, Graham Turner and others (Augoustinos and Walker, 1995), Social Identity Theory (SIT) makes three basic assumptions. One, our self-concept consists of personal and social aspects. For example, your name is probably formed of first and sur-components. The first name is yours, the second belongs to your family. Accordingly, insofar as your name makes up part of your self-concept it has personal and social components. Two, SIT assumes that, ordinarily, we are motivated to achieve and sustain a positive self-concept, and, by virtue of that part of it which is derived from our social setting, we are motivated to achieve a positive social identity. For example, we seek to enhance our self-esteem (to see that this is so, imagine how peculiar a person who actively seeks to lower it would seem) and we do so by affiliating with other people. And the third assumption of SIT is that our social identity is built upon the positive identity of the group to which we belong and positive distinctions from and comparisons with other groups. For example, our self-esteem is enhanced if the group(s) with which we affiliate is seen as desirable, popular, prestigious and/or exclusive by and in comparison with other groups.

The important point to note for present purposes is the role of the group in how we think about ourselves. The proposal is that our group memberships are internalised. They are within. Also, studies that gave rise to SIT show that given an opportunity to do so, we categorise ourselves as group member on the flimsiest of pretexts (Tajfel, 1970). We appear to be powerfully inclined to affiliate with others and this inclination is promiscuous in that the need to affiliate overrides the detailed analysis of other group members, and it leads to a further inclination to discriminate in favour of group members (Brown, 2000; Tajfel, 1981). It has been suggested that the need to affiliate, to identify and derive our identities from groups is so great, that when we define ourselves as members of a group we perceive ourselves to be interchangeable with members of that group. Interchangeability carries the implication that we are, in some sense, the same, or identical to the other people and that this applies to members of other groups (Brown, 2000). We can call the outcome of the need to affiliate and discriminate in favour of members of our group '**virtual kin altruism**'. We seem to be prepared to invent 'fictive kin' (Stack, 1974) wherein we bring people and even pets 'into the family' and adopt a way of speaking about non-related persons as if they were family members. For example, it appears to be common for close friends to use kinship language such as 'he/she is like a brother/sister to me'. We also see the use of such language in trade unions and religious groups. It is noticeable how common labels and dress codes typify those groups where the members accept an obligation to make sacrifices for one another and to surrender self-interest in the interests of the collective. Sports teams and armies give us examples.

Given that evolutionary psychology is grounded in Hamilton's theory of kin altruism we should not be altogether surprised by the findings of social identity theory. Both predict favouritism toward an **in-group** over identifiable out-groups. A difference, of course, is that the evolutionary psychology tends to think of a 'group' as a collection of kin, while social

Figure 5.1 Virtual kin altruism

identity theory enforces no such stipulation. Combining the fitness pay-offs of a positive bias toward kin and the probability that those around us over the course of natural history were kin (or, at least, long standing allies) yields the result that a (relatively) indiscriminate 'rule' that includes those that share some or another resemblance could evolve. 'Good tricks' and 'no brainers' are phrases that have been used to refer to solutions that are so effective that evolution was bound to come across them sooner or later and for their utility to be so great that they would spread to fixation in a species (Dennett, 1995).

THE EVOLUTION OF MORAL SENTIMENT

We have seen how the theory of kin altruism does not depend on the acts which confer benefits to others being consciously intended. The claim can be extended to reciprocal altruism. However, Trivers (1971, 1985) has argued that the psychological basis of reciprocal altruism in humans is an evolved sense of fairness, and there are studies which suggest that other primates also have this evolved sense (Brosnan, 2006). Trivers contends that a sense of fairness is an adaptation and it forms the basis of human morality. Most broadly conceived, a sense of fairness has evolved and works as an adaptation because of the benefits that equitable cooperation between conspecifics offers, and, in a population of cooperators, the costs that are incurred by non-cooperators.

More particularly, there are a number of ways in which a sense of fairness could have been selected for and a number of ways in which it is governed. If we see a sense of fairness as simple like-for-like cooperation it can be selected for because those of our ancestors that assisted one another may have enhanced one another's fitness over non-cooperators. If certain positive outcomes can only be achieved with the help of another, cooperation could be critical and, hence, have more pronounced effects on fitness. Seen as a pressure to reciprocate, a sense of fairness would be selected for because the pressure will facilitate reiterated cooperation and help to build enduring relationships. We can also look at a sense of fairness as underlying our ability to detect cheaters. Here it works to help us see not only that we are being fair to others but that they are being fair to us. As part of our ability to detect cheaters the sense of fairness would be selected for because it enables us to avoid cost-negative interactions.

Picking up on Darwin's comments in *The Expression of the Emotions in Man and Animals*, Trivers considers the sense of fairness to be underpinned by a variety of emotions that facilitate the need to engage and operate in complex systems of iterated reciprocation. On the one hand, positive emotions engender expansive altruism and facilitate cooperation that can have benefits over longer periods and with greater rewards. On the other hand, negative emotions can act as a deterrent to the ever present problem of cheating. There are a number of proposed emotional concomitants of reciprocal altruism of both positive and negative types (McCullough et al., 2008). Positive emotions could include warmth which would act as a signal for an initial altruistic move in a possible exchange, sympathy which signals an awareness of another's need for an help, gratitude which signals thanks and acceptance of debt, and forgiveness which marks a hope that another will desist from further cheating. Negative emotions could include guilt which signals an acknowledgement of a violation and/or of indebtedness to another, suspicion which is a result of a calculation that a debt may not be repaid, anger which signals a realisation that a debt will not be honoured and a wish for revenge, and indignation which may be a response to another's accusation of cheating. The general idea is that certain emotions act as some kind of 'reciprocity police' which create pleasant and unpleasant subjective states that condition exchange relations (Gintis et al., 2007).

THE ROAD MOST OFTEN TRAVELLED

The philosopher Thomas Hobbes suggested that human life was 'solitary, poor, nasty, brutish and short', a 'war of all against all' (Hobbes, 1996/1651), and we may be tempted to think that an evolutionary approach to human thought and behaviour augments his view. But this would be an error. Yes, it seems to be the case that we are most fascinated by the tragic, the 'evil', by persons and groups who betray others, and by violence and criminality if the content of much of the news we receive from main stream media sources are anything to go by. But we ought not be beguiled into averting our eyes from the much greater weight of experience and evidence which tells us that we are overwhelmingly civil and sociable towards one another. The vast majority of interactions between humans across time and place, history and cultures, are peaceable and cooperative. The road most of us travel most of the time is a good life wherein we are good to most others most of the time. That is what we are like. Evolutionary theory, and in particular inclusive fitness theory, explains why that is so. It gives us much reason to be optimistic.

SUMMARY OF CHAPTER 5

For many the theory of evolution by natural selection comes with a bleak message. Closer inspection of the theory which underpins modern neo-Darwinism – inclusive fitness theory – brings a different message. Altruism, cooperation and interdependence clearly exist in any number of species, us included. Group selection theory is one way of explaining these observations but it is flawed. It assumes that selection and evolution works at the level of the group, but it is now assumed that selection and evolution works at the level of the gene. We can understand altruism when we see that while genes are selfish replicators they build organisms that can be selfless towards kin and cooperative towards others. The notion of kin implies non-kin. In social psychology we can map this difference onto the in- and out-group preferences illustrated and explained by social identity theory and we can see that two otherwise distinct lines of reasoning and research may be mutually consistent.

FURTHER READING

Apart from the references in this chapter you may find it interesting and useful to consult one or more of the following:

Brown, A. (1999) *The Darwin Wars: The Scientific Battle for the Soul of Man*. London: Simon and Schuster – see Chapter 1 'The deathbed of an altruist'.

Cronin, H. (1991) *The Ant and the Peacock*. Cambridge: Cambridge University Press – see Chapter 12 'Altruism then'.

Dawkins, R. (1989) *The Selfish Gene* (2nd edn). Oxford: Oxford University Press – see Chapter 10 'You scratch my back, I'll ride on yours' and Chapter 12 'Nice guys finish first'.

Nowak, M.A., May, R.M. and Sigmund, K. (1995) The arithmetic of mutual help. *Scientific American*, 6: 50–55.

6 FAMILIES AND PARENTING

Some of the questions addressed in this chapter:

- What are 'mating systems'?
- Are humans serial monogamists?
- What is parent–offspring conflict?
- Should we anticipate sex differences in parenting style?
- Why might female and male children elicit different responses from parents?
- How might family forms influence the personality of adults?

SOME KEY TERMS AND CONCEPTS

Cinderella syndrome; Development; Life history theory; Maternal certainty; Monogamy; Parental investment; Paternal uncertainty; Parent–offspring conflict; Polyandry; Polygamy; Polygyny; *r* and K selection.

LEARNING OBJECTIVES

Having studied this chapter you should be better able to:

- Develop an argument as to which mating system might best describe human behaviour.
- Describe points of tension that might arise when considering the fitness interests of individual in family groups.
- Consider some of the wider implications of parental investment theory.

INTRODUCTION

Grounded as it is in inclusive fitness theory, contemporary Darwinism may be seen as a theory of nepotism insofar as it predicts that biologically related individuals will behave favourably towards one another in comparison to other members of a population. Accordingly, it ought to provide us with insights into family life, how family members think about and behave towards one another, and the motivations behind parenting. The aim of this chapter is to explore some of those insights.

We will begin by looking at *r* **and K selection** and parental investment theory. Together these ideas may explain why we as a species provide more parental care than do most others, and why females provide more parental care than do males. We will also see that we provide parental care because human infants are born profoundly immature and females invest more in offspring because they enjoy **maternal certainty**.

With the conceptual apparatus that *r* and K selection and parental investment theory provide in place we will frame the notion of family within the notion of **mating systems**. Sexual reproducers can be analysed in terms of the broad pattern of mating that they exhibit – the pattern is the mating system. We will look at the systems exhibited by the great apes and ask which one of them may provide the best fit for humans. The potential yield is a model of family form which may underlie the myriad types that we see across cultures and time. In turn, family form gives us clues to parental behaviour. As it turns out, perhaps none of the mating systems exhibited by great apes quite fits us and we have developed a new form which we will call **serial monogamy**.

Our discussion of serial monogamy as a form of mating system which some humans clearly exhibit (especially in western societies where it is permitted most readily) will include a consideration of its fitness benefits for males and females. In turn these considerations open the way for us to think about the implications of us not being true monogamists. While this chapter is founded on the assumption that humans are nepotistic, favouritism amongst kin is neither flawless nor inevitable. Mutation and sexual recombination see to it that each actual individual morph is unique and, it follows, so is any given grouping of them. Amongst other factors, individual differences create the possibility for antagonisms and we will consider the **Cinderella syndrome** and **parent–offspring conflict**. It may be that the very need for protracted and intense kin altruism in family groups can result in conflict and neglect. To illustrate some of these ideas we will close this chapter with a consideration of how Darwinian theory can be synthesised with Freudian theory and in doing so offer another example of how evolutionary psychology can be used to complement rather than replace established lines of thought in psychology and the social sciences.

PARENTAL INVESTMENT THEORY

The term 'parental investment' refers to time, energy and resources that an organism gives in the service of gestating and rearing its offspring. More precisely, it refers to metabolic and material efforts given to offspring that could have been directed towards other problems of survival and reproduction (Trivers, 1973). What an organism invests in its offspring is not reciprocated in terms of a return of time, energy or resources. The return comes in the form of the offspring itself and its reproductive potential. In evolutionary theory, offspring are the object and end-goal of organisms' efforts. From a gene's-eye perspective, the life of an organism is a means towards genetic reproduction.

One way to think about parental investment is to place species on what is known as the *r*–K continuum. *r* selected species provide little or no investment in offspring. K selected species provide lots. *r* selection is about quantity. K selection is about quality. *r* selected organisms produce multiple offspring, few of which survive. K selected species produce few offspring, many more of whom survive in comparison. In species that are K selected offspring are relatively immature and vulnerable at birth, and, undergo a long period before puberty. Consequently, the more K selected a species is the more there is a need for parental investment.

Humans are amongst the most K selected of species. Our infants are born profoundly immature. It is thought that the size of the human neonate's head in relation to the size of the female pelvis necessitates a gestation period very much shorter than might be deemed ideal. Newborns remain so vulnerable and helpless that we may conceive of the first months after birth as an extension of gestation. The intensity of investment in new born babies give rise to one of the most affecting, affectionate, peaceful and recurrent images of human interaction – that of the newborn and his or her caregiver. Typically, that image is of a mother and the child rather than the father. Evolutionary theory offers an explanation as to why this might be so.

To begin with, the minimum 'investment' required of females is to procure a mate, donate an egg, gestate for nine months and give birth; the minimum 'investment' required of males is to procure a mate and donate sperm. Even at the point of gamete donation we can see that the females invest more. **Anisogamy** (or gamete dimorphism) refers to the fact that the gametes (sex cells) of each sex are of markedly different size. The human ovum is the largest and rarest cell to be found in humans (of either sex), and sperm are the smallest and most common cell to be found in humans (of either sex). A human female produces approximately 500 ova whereas a male can produce as many sex cells in a month as he has neurons. The relative 'cost' of sperm compared to an ovum is about 1: 1,00,0000. Pregnancy provides another example. The average new-born is one hundred billion times heavier than the **zygote** (or fertilised ovum) from which it originates. And notice that all of the resources required for this development are directly provided by the mother.

Next, because of the limit eggs and time place on female reproductive potential it is important that the female gets it 'right' – that is, it is important that she sees the offspring through to puberty if at all possible. In contrast, and in theory, because males have (virtually) no limit to their reproductive potential it is not as important that they get it right each time. This

Table 6.1   *r* and K selection

r-selected species tend to be . . .	K-selected species tend to be . . .
Short-lived	Long-lived
Physically small	Physically large
Less intelligent and behaviourally inflexible	More intelligent and behaviourally flexible
Producers of large litters	Producers of small litters
Sexually active soon after birth	Sexually active after an extend period of immaturity
Low investors in offspring	High investors in offspring
High percentage of time devoted to copulation	Relatively low percentage of time devoted to copulation

is not to say that all females invest more than all males. Given the profound vulnerability of human infants and the relatively slow rate at which humans reproduce, we should expect to see what we find: most fathers invest in their offspring. But we should also expect to find that, on average, fathers invest less than do mothers in their offspring.

A further reason why we might predict that females will be more inclined than males to invest in offspring arises from maternal certainty and paternal uncertainty. These complementary terms refer to the fact that, ordinarily, while human females know with certainty that any given child is or is not theirs males do not. The consequences of this so-called 'Mama's baby, Papa's maybe' situation are far reaching. For now we simply need to keep in mind the claim that the limit on female reproductive potential allied to maternal certainty strongly favours maternal solicitude whereas potentially unlimited male reproductive potential allied to paternal uncertainty mitigates against paternal solicitude.

Having set out some ideas which gives us a theoretical framework for parenting and potential differences between the sexes let us now turn to the issue of mating systems and the question as to which, if any, appears to fit humans.

BOX 6.1   WHAT IS CHILDHOOD FOR?

What is the function of childhood (broadly conceived as life before reproductive maturity)? Is it just a spandrel, an incidental by-product of biological constraints which prevents us from becoming sexually mature more quickly? The length of time between birth and reproductive maturity in humans is atypical in comparison to other primates and the great apes. We may be tempted to think of this period as redundant in evolutionary terms – especially so when we think of its percentage of total life expectancy. However, our protracted childhood leave us open to what has been called 'generational deadtime' (Lorenz, 1966). This phrase refers to the exposure of genes between replications. The idea is that any given gene is locked into a given genotype and at the mercy of the subsequent phenotype until (indeed if) it recombines courtesy of the reproductive success. Generational deadtime at one extreme of the r–K continuum can be minutes, at the other it is years. In highly K-selected modern humans generational deadtime exceeds a decade. If we are to take the view that our relatively extended childhood has long-term-fitness benefits and serves a purpose then we might suppose that it is a period of preparation for adulthood (Ellis and Bjorklund, 2005). Looked at this way, it is no different, in principle, to any other problem, period or preamble that must be overcome before the main events of copulation, gestation and parental investment. Just as evolutionary psychologists take the general problem of reproduction to consist of many sub-problems, we may take childhood to be a sub-problem itself comprising further problems. One view suggests that the pay-off for protracted childhood is the opportunity it offers for calibration to the physical and social world.

MATING SYSTEMS

The manner in which a species goes about the generation to generation business of reproducing is its 'mating system'. This term is used to describe a characteristic pattern of contact, courtship, copulation and parenting behaviours. In social group-living species the mating system is influential in shaping the social life of the species in question. The assumption is that natural selection and sexual selection has shaped how organisms orientate themselves towards the opposite sex. Typically there is a difference between the strategies of male and females. Evolutionary psychology takes these points to hold for humans too.

Anthropologists have observed a variety of mating systems in modern humans including **monogamy, polygyny, polyandry** and **promiscuity**. Monogamy refers to a mating system wherein males and females pair bond for life. Gibbons appear to be monogamous. Typically, the adults in monogamous species are similar in size and males appear to invest as much time and effort in offspring as females. Polygyny refers to a arrangements wherein several females reproduce with one male. Gorillas are polygynous. This system is often referred to as a harem. While the females are 'faithful' to a given 'alpha' male while he is in residence with the group he may be usurped and they may repeat the process with a second alpha male. For any given group at a given time the pre-pubescent gorillas are the offspring of the resident alpha and he offers protection to them and the females from other adult males. Polyandry refers to a mating system wherein multiple males reproduce with one female. There isn't a known example of this type of system in the great apes and it is extremely rare in humans. Promiscuity refers to a mating system wherein there are no set pair-bonds and adults copulate freely with one another. Both the common and bonobo chimpanzee are promiscuous. In promiscuous species the paternity of offspring is difficult to ascertain, and in such species females are the primary caregivers and provide the most parental investment.

Which of these systems best describes our mating system? Anthropologists, Darwin amongst them, have recorded examples of all three systems in humans and the debates about the veracity and comparative frequencies of each were under way long before the turn of the twentieth century (Opler, 1943). It has been estimated that *c.* 84 per cent of human societies allow polygyny, *c.* 15 per cent of human societies encourage monogamy, *c.* 1 per cent practise polyandry and *c.* 0.0001 of humans have or do live in genuinely promiscuous cohorts (Brown, 1991). At present, most of the western democracies are orientated toward monogamy in that there are clear social and legal structures designed to facilitate and encourage it. In most of the Muslim world polygyny is permitted and supported by social and legal structures. That we exhibit all four systems may prompt us to wonder if it is worth asking if we have a characteristic mating system given that those mentioned seem adequate. However, it may that there is a fifth system which may be unique to humans as great apes called serial monogamy. Serial monogamy refers to a system whereupon individuals go through a series of more-or-less exclusive pairs bonds through the course of their reproductive life and, indeed, in the human case, beyond.

There are at least two reasons why we might consider serial monogamy to be the system which characterises us. First, our biology licenses such a conclusion, and second, serial monogamy is not new and appears to be becoming more common in populations where social, moral, legal and religious prohibitions do not make it difficult. Let us consider each of these points in turn.

BOX 6.2   SEXUAL DIMORPHISM

'Dimorph' means 'two bodies'. 'Sexual dimorphism' refers to the two distinct body types found in some species. And by 'body type' we mean the body aside from the sex and reproductive organs. Darwin argued that the sexes of species come to be di-morphic in body types courtesy of sexual selection (Darwin, 1871). He also argued that the more di-mophic a species was the less likely it was to be monogamous and that this is true of mammals.

Our anatomy offers up a cue which suggests that humans are not primarily monogamous on a strict definition of that term. When comparing males and females it is apparent that we are a dimorphic species with human males being about 20 per cent heavier than females on average. This situation is to be considered against the fact that the size difference between the sexes is typically close to zero in monogamous species. For unequivocally polygynous species the difference can be 100 per cent or more, with males being twice or thrice the size of females as is the case with gorillas. The fossil record suggests that the dimorphism between the sexes that we see today is less than it has been in our past (see Chapter 3). This implies that we have come from being more-or-less polygynous but the difference that remains implies that we are not strictly monogamous. Sperm production in modern human males points in the same direction. In brief, we produce more sperm that appears to be required where we are polygynous, and less than would be required where we are truly promiscuous (Ridley, 1993).

It is clear that it has been and is common for humans to marry, divorce and remarry when social conditions allow (e.g. Anderson, 1980; Coleman et al., 2000; Fisher, 1989, 1992; Hajnal, 1965; Haley, 2000). Similarly, it is now common for us to cohabit, dissolve the union and recohabit, or to marry, divorce, cohabit, dissolve the union and remarry. In this sense, the practice of having one conjugal partner at a time but more than one over the life course it is a demographic fact. It has been predicted that serial monogamy will become the norm in North America with individuals passing through four forms of family structure: nuclear, extended, matrifocal and blended (Haley, 2000). Traditionally, social and ethnographic surveys do not register serial monogamy as a system (Rubin, 2001), but it is worth noting that there are no known societies that explicitly prohibit serial pair-bonds for all persons under all circumstances. Having gone some way to establishing serial monogamy as at least one of the systems that describes human reproductive patterns let us now look backwards and consider how it may have come about.

WHY SERIAL MONOGAMY?

In the abstract, we can assume that there has been a tension between hominid males and females in that males had greater reproductive potential than did females but females enjoyed certainty of maternity whereas males do not enjoy certainty of paternity. As we have discussed, this tension is explicated in parental investment theory (Trivers, 1973). The predictions that the theory makes are that, all things being equal, for a large slow-breeding mammalian species such as hominids females will exhibit greater levels of parental investment in their offspring than will males because (1) they can be certain that the child is theirs whereas males cannot, and (2) females are incentivised to invest to a greater extent than males by virtue of relatively limited reproductive potential. However, these observations hold for the extant great apes. And we saw earlier in the chapter that their mating systems differ. It follows that differences in reproductive potential and **parental certainty** do not predict the mating system. Let us see how parental investment theory can be used to explain why polygyny and promiscuity work.

Polygyny works for female gorillas because they are fertilised by dominant males, who, by virtue of their dominance over other males, demonstrate the fitness of their genes. The dominance of the male also offers some sort of guarantee of protection for the female from other males. This is important because of infanticide – the tendency of a new dominant male gorilla to kill the offspring he finds in a harem. This protection amounts to parental investment. Of course, polygyny only works for those males who secure a harem, but it does so in a particular way. The dominant male gets exclusive access to two, three, perhaps four females. He enjoys both certainty of paternity and more reproductive success than do the females. A polygynous system is a particular manifestation of the principles of parental investment theory.

In chimpanzees promiscuity works for females in two ways. Like gorillas, pre-pubescent chimpanzees are vulnerable to unrelated males. It is thought that promiscuity in the females causes confusion amongst the males as to whom the father of offspring may be. The logic is that because any number of adult males in the group may have had sex with a given female they may be the father. Accordingly, they behave benevolently toward the offspring (Silk et al., 2005). The second way in which promiscuity works for females is that it spreads her bets in fitness terms. She has reproductive success whoever she mates with but by mating with a number of males she also gets a wider variety of types of offspring. Promiscuity works for male chimpanzees because all, or certainly most (and more than in a polygynous system), get mating opportunities. The trade-off is that there is less chance of enjoying high reproductive success that might be the case in polygynous system and there is no certainty of paternity. Again, a promiscuous system is a particular manifestation of parental investment principles.

How does parental investment theory accommodate the proposal that serial monogamy has evolved in the *Homo* lineage? The answer comes in the form of **encephalisation** and its consequences. Encephalisation refers to the demonstrable trend towards larger brains in hominids in general and the *Homo* genus in particular. Our brains have doubled in size in the last two million years, and a disproportionate amount of the growth has taken place in the last 500,000 years (Striedter, 2005). An outcome of this trend is that *Homo* neonates are profoundly **altricial**. What this means is that they are born in a more vulnerable condition that other primates, and the period of absolute dependence on caregivers has extended. In effect, *Homo* neonates are born premature. However, it is thought that this is necessary due to the anatomy of the female pelvis. Should gestation continue for very many more months then the pelvic girdle would need to be much larger. Aside from the design work needed to bring about such an adaptation, the cost of a larger pelvic girdle would be a loss in bi-pedal efficiency. An outcome of the drift toward altricial offspring is a need for additional caregiving. It is proposed that serial monogamy provides that care (Fisher, 1992). The serial monogamy argument claims that the 'battle of the sexes' – the tension between males and females that arises through the asymmetries in reproductive potential and certainty of maternity – has resolved itself into a mating system whereupon the central tendency is towards a pair-bond that produces one or two offspring, rears them to viability and then dissolves. Accordingly, 'the "seven year itch" – recast as a four year reproductive cycle – may be an evolved phenomena' (Badcock, 2000: 160).

We can frame the serial monogamy hypothesis in a forwards fashion – that is, we can look to see if the proposal works as an adapted outcome to selection pressures in the past. And we can frame it in a backwards fashion – that is, we can take the fact that serial monogamy is common where social and legal conditions allow for it and look to see if it works as an adaptive strategy in the present. For example, it has been reported that in the USA divorce rates peak in the fourth and fifth year of marriage and declining thereafter, that between 1950 and 1989 *c.* 40 per cent of divorces involved childless couples, and that less than 2 per cent of couples with five or more children divorced over the same period (Fisher, 1992). These details license the suggestion that in certain environments we pair bond on a trial basis and if a couple is fecund it stays together for longer than if it is not.

Having discussed mating systems and presented a case for the plausibility of serial monogamy it is now necessary to issue a cautionary note. Analysis of the great apes, reconstruction of the past, and surveys of extant human population suggests that we cannot label our mating patterns in any simple fashion. Accordingly, the term 'family' defies simple definition. We might speak of 'the family' as if there were some sort of unified and identifiable form of human grouping but it is apparent that there is no 'family' but 'families' – each of them distinct. Without wishing to give the impression that serial monogamy leads to the only form of family structure worth discussing, this chapter will further examine now the notion of parental investment courtesy of research conducted on family where one of the resident adults is not the biological parent of one or more of the resident children.

STEP-PARENTS AND THE CINDERELLA SYNDROME

We have seen how theory and evidence give licence to suppose that humans are not inherently and inevitably monogamous. This section will examine some of the consequences of this outcome and look at step-families and step-parents.

The 'Cinderella Syndrome' is a term coined by Daly and Wilson (1998). It refers to the relative paucity of parental investment that step-children may receive from adult caregivers who take or are expected to perform the role of a parent in the knowledge that they are not the biological progenitor of the child.

BOX 6.3 ALLOPARENTING AND COGNITIVE BIASES THAT MAINTAIN RELATIONSHIPS

Sarah Blaffer Hrdy (2009) has argued that cooperative breeding – a strategy also known as alloparenting wherein both parents care for their offspring – preceded the evolution of the very large brains that characterise modern humans. She thinks that alloparenting 'first emerged among upright apes that were only beginning to look like us, and further evolved during the Pleistocene in African *H. erectus* – creatures that did not think or use language to communicate the way we do' (Hrdy, 2009: 24). And she also thinks that alloparenting allowed for a protraction of physical and cognitive development in hominid children: 'bigger brains required care more than caring required big brains' (ibid.).

With a view to being more specific about the function of pair-bonds in humans, and made curious by the fact that single mothers in industrialised societies tend to wean offspring sooner than do those in relationships, Quinlan and Quinlan tested the claim that pair-bonds facilitate breast feeding – this would amount to a form of alloparenting. To do this they looked at the relationship between pair-bond stability, joint parental investment, and cross-cultural trends in lactation (a more technical term for breast feeding) in 58 traditional foraging cultures. They found that robust pair-bonds were associated with significantly later weaning. This association appears to be sound because their data suggests that late weaning is not significantly influenced by women's material status or access to the support of kin. They conclude that stable human pair-bonds may have evolved to support lactation which, itself, is an adaptive strategy because of the benefits it brings to the neonate.

Looking back to Chapter 2 'Evolutionary approaches to thought and behaviour' we might locate Hrdy and Quinlan and Quinlan within the human behavioural ecology tradition whereupon comparative and cross-cultural patterns are understood in term of current adaptive utility. But we can see synergy between human behavioural ecology and evolutionary psychology as we conceived of it in Chapter 2 by looking at three studies conducted more in the latter tradition. Each of them gives us insight into how pair-bonds – and therefore alloparenting – might be maintained by psychological biases.

Peston-Voak et al. (2007) suggest that the idea that some couples see one another through 'rose-tinted glasses' may have an evolutionary basis. In this study romantically attached couples' attitudes towards the quality of their relationship was assessed. Photographs were taken of each couple and the digitised images were then manipulated. Three manipulations increased the attractiveness of the face, and another three decreased its attractiveness. The participants in the study were then asked to say which of seven depictions of their partner was the true representation. It was found that female participants who were positive about the quality of their relationship were more inclined to think that the good-looking manipulations were the true image of their partners. Those who were not positive about the quality of their relationship exhibited the opposite. There are a number of ways in which we might interpret this finding but one that seems reasonable is that the bias in perception facilitates the pair-bond.

Gonzaga et al. (2008) have also produced some evidence to suggest that we have psychological mechanisms that facilitate long term relationships. These researchers supposed that love for a sexual partner acts to suppress interest in other attractive alternative partners. To test this they asked participants to relive emotion in order to trigger feelings of love or sexual desire for a romantic partner and at the same time requested that participants suppress thoughts of an attractive alternative. They found that participants in the love condition reported fewer intrusive thoughts of the attractive alternative and this was corroborated by the fact that they could recall less attractiveness-related details about the attractive alternative than those participants in the sexual desire condition. In other words, it would appear that love rather than sexual desire for a partner acts to diminish the appeal of alternative mates, and it might facilitate commitment. The study by Gonzaga et al. may make some sense of intuition that love and lust may be bedfellows but they are not the same thing.

Picking up on the theme of alloparenting and its benefits, Maner et al. (2008) argue that we may not need to actively suppress thoughts of attractive alternative partners by virtue of that fact that we exhibit 'automatic inattention' in their presence. Support for this claim was elicited from participants whose attention was focused on their feelings towards their partners while being shown images of attractive alternatives. It was found that the ability to attend to details of the images during the very first stages of perception – a cognitive process taken to be automatic and which precedes explicit and conscious attention – was impaired. This impairment was only evident when participants were shown highly attractive images of opposite sex alternatives.

Daly and Wilson argue that, in principle, in species in which parents care for their young, natural selection necessarily favours those who allocate their limited resources in such a way as to promote their own fitness. Humans are an exemplar of such species and, accordingly, the psychology of parental investment and solicitude in humans has evolved to be discriminative. The prediction is that such discrimination manifests itself as preferential treatment of known offspring and this phenomenon is called 'discriminative parental solicitude'. In other words, 'What an evolutionary perspective suggests is that the evolved psychology of parental love, the most nearly selfless love that we know, will not normally be fully activated in stepparents, whose investments will remain restrained in comparison with those of genetic parents' (Daly and Wilson, 1999: 365).

Daly and Wilson argue that defining parental investment in a manner sufficiently precise to be measured is difficult. However, what can be shown more readily are acts of aggression and violence wherein the acts are recorded by police and other authorities. In effect, Daly and Wilson argue that the exceptions demonstrate the rule wherein the greater frequency at which step-parental figures harm step-children shows us that the former are less likely to extend the care and attention – the parental investment – as would biological parents (Daly and Wilson, 1988, 1994).

There is a good deal of evidence which supports Daly and Wilson's position (Harris et al., 2007). Moreover, most of it has not been collected by evolutionary psychologists in the first instance, and it was not originally collected with a view towards demonstrating a particular point. Here are some examples of research work carried out in North America:

- Children in New Zealand hospitalised for wounds intentionally inflicted were twice as likely to have come from a household with a step-parent (Fergusson et al., 1972).
- It has been found that for American children under three years of age and living in a household with a biological parent and a step-parent the risk of physical abuse was 6.9 times greater than for children in a household with both biological parents. The risk factor declines as a function of age but children at 15 are still twice as likely to suffer physical abuse if a step-parent is present (Wilson et al., 1980).

- In 177 Canadian households where police visited to investigate violence against a juvenile, 48 per cent housed a step-parent against a base rate of 11 per cent in the Canadian population as a whole (Daly and Wilson, 1981).
- Of the known in-house abusers of children in Pennsylvania, it was found that the violence was most frequently reserved for step-children (Lightcap et al., 1982).
- In a Canadian sample of 1284 households it was found that children in a home containing a resident step-parent were significantly more likely to be victims of physical abuse than children in other household types even when income was taken into account as a risk factor (Daly and Wilson, 1985).
- Children living with one or more step/substitute parents in the US in 1976 were 100 times more likely to be fatally abused than a child living with both genetic parents (Daly and Wilson, 1988).

Of course, we might wonder if the so-called Cinderella Syndrome is particular to North America and, accordingly, a function of those particular cultures. But the evidence suggests otherwise. Studies showing that children are exposed to excess (i.e. above base rate) risk of maltreatment when being cared for by a step-parent have been conducted in New Zealand (Fergusson et al., 1972) Paraguay (Hill and Kaplan, 1988), New South Wales, Australia (Wallace, 1986), Trinidad (Flinn, 1988), South Korea (Kim and Ko, 1990), Malaysia (Kassim and Kasim, 1995), Finland (Sariola and Uutela, 1996), amongst Aboriginal Australians (Fleming et al., 1997), and in Bogota, Columbia (Klevens et al., 2000).

Daly and Wilson have also reported that where there is lethal violence against a child there are differences in the manner of death when the offender is a step-father. For example, in Canada between 1974 and 1990 stepfathers were 120 times more likely to beat the child to death (or leave it for dead after a sustained assault) than biological fathers and biological fathers were more likely to asphyxiate, poison or shoot the child victim (Daly and Wilson, 1998). They take this information to suggest that step-fathers exhibit a greater degree of malice than do biological fathers. They support this claim by reporting that biological parents in the same Canadian cohort were over 40 times more likely to commit suicide after the homicide than step-fathers. They also report a similar pattern of significant differences for Britain between 1977 and 1990 (Daly and Wilson, 1996).

It is important to pause at this point and be sure of what it is that the foregoing research is being taken to show. It is not being claimed that all step-parents are abusive and violent towards step-children. In fact, far from it. The 'Show-off hypothesis' (Wood and Hill, 2000) – a hypothesis consistent with the claim that we are serial monogamists – suggests that males exhibit high positive regard towards the children of prospective mates as a means of attracting them, and females find males who exhibit positive regard towards babies more attractive (Bleske-Rechek et al., 2006). What is being claimed is that official records of violent abuse show us that adults are less caring and altruistic towards children they know not to be their own, and that, in turn and by inference, this demonstrates kin altruism.

There is some evidence which, it has been argued, suggests that the Cinderella Syndrome is not inevitable (Temrin et al., 2000). Gelles and Harrop (1991) conducted a telephone survey of step- and biological parents in the USA asking questions such as 'after a disagreement

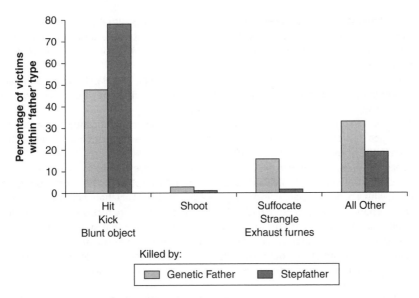

Figure 6.1   Mr Murdstone Syndrome
Source: Figure 1 from Daly, M. and Wilson, M.I. (1994) Some differential attributes of lethal assaults on small children by stepfathers versus genetic fathers. *Ethology and Sociobiology*, 15: 207–217.

or when angry have you slapped/punched/used a knife or gun on your child?' and found no difference between step- and biological parents. However, a partial replication of this study found that when asked if 'discipline' was exercised 'after a disagreement or when angry' – wherein discipline is a less emotive term and does not require the participant to, in effect, admit to physical abuse – there was a difference between step- and biological parents (Hashima and Amato, 1994).

Still, it can be argued that those who actively harm children need to be categorised as different from those who do not. Certainly most legal systems treat such persons as being different and distinct. Harming a child is an action. Failing to extend care towards a child is inaction. Kin selection theory allows us to predict absence of assistance toward non-kin. It does not allow us to predict presence of harm toward non-kin (unless non-kin threaten the well being of kin). A less emotive line of research which is consistent with the inaction prediction that we can derive from kin selection theory is that which shows the comparative neglect of step-parents. Here are some examples of research which focuses on comparative neglect:

- In a Canadian sample it was found that the amount of practical help with homework was a function of sex of step-parent and of the child, with step-parents helping less than biological parents (Downey, 1995).
- In a sample from Albuquerque in the American state of New Mexico self-reports by males on the amount of practical help offered to step as opposed to biological children suggested that the former were assisted less than the latter (Anderson et al., 1999a).

- In a related study conducted in the city of Cape Town in South Africa students from Xhosa High School reported that help with school work, 'quality time' and acts of spontaneous generosity were less frequently experienced by those living with step-parents (Anderson et al., 1999b).

- On a similar note, Marlowe (1999) found that amongst the Hazda peoples in Tanzania, although tolerant of their step-children, men treat them differently from their own children in that they do not play with their step-children.

- Another Canadian study reported that step-fathers were significantly less accurate than biological fathers at knowing or accurately guessing the attitudes and beliefs of the children in the household (Daly et al., 1996).

- Zvoch (1999) reported that in the USA there was a difference in investment in post-compulsory education between biological and step-parent households. Furthermore, young persons living with a biological parent and a step-parent were less likely than their two-genetic-parent counterparts to graduate from high school, to go to college, to receive comparable levels of familial support if they do go to college. It was also found that step-families do not plan ahead and save for children's education to the same extent as do intact families.

- Another American study found that children raised by step-, adoptive, or foster mothers obtain significantly less education, on average, than do the birth children of the same women (Case et al., 2001).

- Tooley et al. (2006) examined cases from the Australian National Coroners' Information System (NCIS). They looked at 32 intentionally and 319 unintentionally occurring fatal injuries in children less than 5 years of age from 2000 to 2003. Tooley et al. found that 'step- children under 5 years of age were found to be at significantly increased risk of unintentional fatal injury of any type, and of drowning in particular . . . children from single parented families were generally not found to be at significantly increased risk of intentional or unintentional fatal injury, while children who lived with neither of their biological parents were at greatest risk overall for fatal injury of any type' (ibid.,: 224).

BOX 6.4   IS STEP-CHILD ABUSE AN ADAPTATION?

We might be tempted to think that the abuse of step-children has been selected for, that it is an adaptation. However, the orthodox view in evolutionary psychology is that this is not so. While infanticide – the killing of infants – is well documented amongst a number of species of mammal and in gorillas, it is not proposed to be 'normal' in humans. As we will see in Chapter 8 'Competition, aggression and violence', lethal violence is thought to be an accidental by-product of an evolved disposition for stringent competition and protection of resources. Similarly, the Cinderella Syndrome is thought to be an accidental by product of nepotism.

It may help us to see this point if we think of step-children as an obstacle to inclusive fitness. Recall that inclusive fitness theory argues that our biological offspring promote a one-sided exchange of time/effort/resources from parent to child just because the child is reproductive success. All other relationships are, or need to be, reciprocal. The one-sided exchange relations that might typify the step-parent/step-child dyad present a drag on the fitness of the step-parent. On this construal, a step-child presents an obstacle: the 'r' factor in Hamilton's formula for kin selection inequality in absent in Br>C. Accordingly, parental solicitude toward a child that is not one's own is inevitably a cost.

Although more difficult to measure and record than lethal assault comparative neglect provides a more mundane and almost certainly more typical demonstration of how parental investment works in step-families. But it is not only step-parents who may feel some ambivalence towards the children they care for. It is also apparent that biological parents harm their children in headline-grabbing and more mundane ways. We can now move on and consider an idea that is, perhaps, amongst the most counter-intuitive that evolutionary theorists proposed.

PARENT–OFFSPRING CONFLICT

Having earlier evoked the imagery that often depicts the dyad of mother and child it is now necessary to temper its resonance of peaceful love and security and introduce the notion of parent–offspring conflict which, like parental investment theory, we owe to Robert Trivers (1973).

Trivers points out that the theory of evolution, based on the central pillars of the selfish gene and inclusive fitness, can be viewed as being about the creation, process and resolution of conflict. The conflicts include species vs. environment, species vs. species and con-specific vs. con-specific. When we see that the conflict is between genes competing for opportunities to replicate it becomes apparent that it extends to parent vs. offspring. Let us see how Trivers unpacks his insight.

The adult human female faces a problem. While the need to reproduce outweighs the massive and life threatening investment required to do so, left open are decisions as to when to reproduce and, in instances where more than one child is produced, which of her offspring she most favours. With a restricted total reproductive potential and a restricted total amount of parental investment, her long-term reproductive success – her inclusive fitness – is dependent on the allocation of her potential and investment. Apart from the perils of gestation, human males too are faced with similar problems.

Trivers reminds us that human reproduction is a long process, involving any number of decisions. Very few humans reach puberty before they are 10 years of age, and 15 is common. As well as making a more-or-less explicit decision to conceive, there are then hourly choices to make with regard to parental investment and the distribution of resources. Parent–offspring conflict theory suggests that at any point in the reproductive process a putative or extant child may or may not represent a rational decision with respect to overall inclusive fitness. Let us now consider a proposed example of parent–offspring conflict of particular interest to psychologist – post-natal depression. Following that we will look at an idea based on the **sexy son hypothesis**.

POST-NATAL DEPRESSION

Sometimes colloquially referred to as the 'baby blues', and also known as post-partum depression, **post-natal depression** is characterised by mild to severe flattening of affect that occurs soon after the birth of a child. While it may be evident before birth, and can last for several months afterwards, there is evidence to suggest that it typically peaks within a week

(Hagen, 1999). More precisely, the symptoms of post-natal depression include a failure to respond to and/or an insensitivity to infant cues (Beck, 1995), ambivalence about and/or a lack of interest in the baby, anxiety about having the ability to care for and love the baby (Campbell and Cohn, 1991), and thoughts about causing accidental or deliberate harm to the baby (Jennings et al., 1999).

Research suggests that the symptoms may be predicted by a number of mutually inclusive events that occur before the birth of the child. These events include pessimism about the financial future, a negative reaction on learning of pregnancy and frequency of thoughts about abortion, the expecting mother being single or in an unstable relationship with the

---

BOX 6.5 PARENT–OFFSPRING CONFLICT DURING GESTATION

There are a number of findings which suggest that tension between the interests of the prospective mother and the prospective offspring are worked out during pregnancy.

Miscarriage (spontaneous abortion)
Perhaps as many as 75 per cent of all human conceptions do not go to term and most spontaneously aborted foetuses have abnormalities. Twins at conception appear to be common but one of the two is usually aborted soon after conception. The reasoning behind miscarriage is that the prospective mother's body terminates the pregnancy because it is not in her interests to proceed.

Maternal diabetes
Before and between pregnancies the glucose levels of most females is moderated in the normal way by courtesy of falling and rising levels of insulin. The typical pattern is that there is ingestion of carbohydrate which leads to rises in blood sugar. This triggers insulin production which enables the liver to store excess glucose as glycogen and leads to falls in levels of blood sugar. However, to a lesser or greater extent during pregnancy sensitivity to insulin decreases causing a rise in insulin levels. This is what we call maternal diabetes. The conflict may be between the mother and foetus wherein the foetus wants higher blood-sugar levels than is ideal for the mother. The foetus manipulates blood-sugar levels by sending chemical signals that decrease the mother's sensitivity to her own insulin. The prospective mother responds by raising her insulin level and when the placenta detects high insulin it ups the signal and disables the mother's 'counter-attack'. The outcome is typically a compromise in insulin sensitivity – after all it is in neither party's interest to go 'zero-sum', but the health of both parties can also be compromised in the long term.

The insulin-like growth factor II
Insulin-like growth factor II (IGF II) is a protein that aids the supply of cell-building resources across the placenta which are vital to foetal growth. It is thought that the foetus carries a paternal IGF II gene which is imprinted with the instruction to express. However, the foetus also carries a maternal gene – IGF IIR – which codes for the production of a receptor that mops up IGF II and so slows delivery of resources across the placenta. Individuals who lack the maternal receptor coding gene are considerably larger than normal (Haig and Graham, 1991). And individual who inherits two copies of paternal IGF II, develop enlarged hearts and

livers and are prone to embryonic tumours – a condition known as Beckwith–Weidermann syndrome. Again, the outcome is typically a compromise between the opposing maternal and paternal genes which keep foetal growth within a normal range.

The foregoing is a particular sort of parent–offspring conflict. We might think of it as an instance of the battle of the sexes *in vitro*. The tension that arises from paternal and maternal genes coding for growth-factor is consistent with the claim that a good deal of biochemical conflict between mother and foetus is triggered by genes on the Y chromosome (i.e. by male genes). What would be the logic? Well, there is a like-lihood that any given embryo may be the one chance for reproduction between any given female with any given female. Accordingly, the female's long-term reproductive health may be of minor interest to the male: his interest is that she carries, bears and raises his child. By contrast, females are concerned with their repro-ductive health across the life-span. Consequently, the male's genes exploit the female's body in the interests of his offspring, while the female's genes counter them in any way that they can in the interest of all offspring.

father, being without a wider network of family and friends, having health difficulties during pregnancy and/or during the delivery, and when the new-born is palpably underweight or ill (Hagen, 1999). These predictions have been supported (Dennis, 2004).

The proposed evolutionary explanation of the link between the symptoms of post-natal depression and the events which appear to presage it is that the period immediately after birth presents an opportunity for the mother to assesses the viability of the child before deciding to commence an extended period of 24/7 parental investment. Thus, worries about the timing of the pregnancy, resources and child-caring, and cues to the health of the child so act as a test of the baby's viability given that post-natal depression, like depression, is characterised by lethargy and inability to act/make decisions that convert into a period of neglect (Badcock, 2000; Daly and Wilson, 1988; Hagen, 1999).

THE OEDIPUS COMPLEX AND THE 'SEXY SON' HYPOTHESIS

For reasons explicable in terms of mating systems, reproductive potential, asymmetrical parental investment and maternal certainty, parent–offspring conflict largely amounts to mother–child conflict. We have seen that the adult human female faces two paradoxes. One is her need to reproduce cast against the massive investment required. The other is which of a number of offspring she most favours. With restricted total reproductive potential and restricted total possible investment her long-term reproductive success is critically dependent on the allocation of her potential and investment.

Meanwhile the newly established genotype – the offspring – has its own problems. The first is to at once secure maximum investment from the mother while maintaining the highly dependent relationship, the second is compete against siblings for more than its fair share of parental resources – something it does, less an overt claim, against the interest of the parent who, in principle, would seek to invest equitably.

In keeping with other attempts to knit together evolutionary psychology and established ideas in psychology in this section we will consider a proposal which seeks to synthesise parent–offspring conflict and the psychoanalytic notion of infantile sexuality. More precisely, we will examine Badcock's claim that the Oedipus complex is explicable in Darwinian terms (Badcock, 1994).

The argument is relatively straightforward. If human mothers have the ability to discriminate when caregiving, and her offspring have to compete for resources against a father and/or siblings, then, it is claimed, the following scenario develops (for the sake of brevity and salience I will illustrate only a mother–son scenario). Male offspring have huge potential reproductive success to offer mothers. This is the males' most powerful card. The male can capitalise on his potential by exhibiting 'sexy son' behaviour. Sexy son behaviour amounts to displays of affection and love toward the mother and hostility toward the primary competitor, the father, who too is after the mother's resources, principally in the form of further offspring. This love and affection is of a sensual nature. It is a demonstration that the son will be a successful reproducer post-puberty. The hostility towards the father demonstrates that the son will compete against other males in order to achieve success. The dramatic and traumatic edge of this process necessary for the depiction to have a proper Freudian import is given by the life or death consequences of the conflict. The profound dependence of the son on the mother and the danger posed by the father and his needs and wants provide this. There is a certain elegance in Badcock's theorising. Sons do carry a potential that should, in principle, appeal to the mother. Using sexuality, or the sexual drive, which will develop into sexuality proper, as a means of soliciting investment is parsimonious and practical.

SUMMARY OF CHAPTER 6

Evolutionary theory and the notion of kin selection theory offer us a number of insights and ways of thinking about families and parenting. *r* and K selection and parental investment theory help us to understand why humans devote so much time and effort to raising children and why females are most often the primary caregivers. We are slow breeding animals, females give birth to of extremely vulnerable young and females can be certain that they are the mother of a given child whereas males cannot.

Mating systems shape the composition of kin groups and parental investment. Humans exhibit a variety of systems, including serial monogamy. The fitness benefits of serial monogamy differ for males and females and it may have come to be a common form of mating system in humans because it goes some way towards providing an adequate amount of parental investment for offspring.

While theory predicts that we are inclined to invest in our offspring it also implies that we are reluctant or unable to invest in offspring that are not biological ours and parent–offspring conflict arises in a number of ways. Post-natal depression and expressed preferences for one offspring over another are compatible with the notion of parent–offspring conflict.

FURTHER READING

Apart from the references in this chapter you may find it interesting and useful to consult one or more of the following:

Barash, D.P. and Lipton, J.E. (2001) *The Myth of Monogamy: Fidelity and Infidelity in Animals and People*. New York, NY: Henry Holt and Company.

Booth, A., Carver, K. and Granger, D.A. (2002) Biosocial perspectives on the family. *Journal of Marriage and Family*, 62: 1018–1034.

Emlen, S.T. (1995) An evolutionary theory of the family. *Proceedings of the National Academy of Sciences*, 92: 8092–8099

Grant, V.J. (1998) *Maternal Personality, Evolution and the Sex Ratio: Do Mothers Control the Sex of the Infant?* London: Routledge.

Hampton, S.J. (2008) Inviting Darwin into the family. *Journal of Gay, Lesbian, Black and Transvestite Family Studies*, 4(1): 37–56.

7 MATE SELECTION

Some of the questions addressed in this chapter:

- How might the mating system shape mate selection?
- What do women want in men?
- What do men want in women?
- What is 'mate value'?
- How is mate value determined?
- How can we accommodate individual differences in mating behaviour?

SOME KEY TERMS AND CONCEPTS

Mate choice; Mating systems and strategies; Parental certainty; Parental investment; r and K selection; Serial monogamy; Sex ratio; Sperm competition.

LEARNING OBJECTIVES

Having studied this chapter you should be better able to:

- Offer an evolutionary analysis of the different values the sexes place on different characteristics.
- Describe the concept of mate value and its role.
- Evaluate the costs and benefits of different mating strategies.

INTRODUCTION

Mating behaviour is of interest to evolutionists not least because it offers up one of the very few unimpeachable certainties about extant members of a sexually reproducing species:

they all descend from an uninterrupted line of ancestors who were motivated and able enough to go through the reproductive cycle. Accordingly, attraction between the sexes and mate selection should be amenable to evolutionary analysis. This may help to explain why there has been and is so much interest in the mating behaviour and mate preferences of humans.

In this chapter we will begin by summing up the main findings about preferences male and females have expressed with regard to potential mates. Having looked at the macroscopic picture we will then drill down to the individual and consider how our **mate value** – that is, how appealing we appear to be to potential mates – might affect our own preferences and behaviour. Following that, we will discuss **mating strategies** and ideas which suggest that we can pursue a mixed strategy wherein we have both short-term and long-term sexual relations interchangeably and coterminously. To set up our discussion of the evolved psychology of mate selection we will begin with some observations on the extent to which we have any real choice over who it is we are attracted to.

Social psychology would appear to confirm the casual observation that in the 'real world' it appears to be the case that we affiliate and exhibit through our behaviour attraction towards others who are similar to us, those with whom we have repeated contact and those who like us. This is known as 'assortative mating' and the idea that 'self seeks like' has gathered the support of at least two evolutionary psychologists (see Alvarez and Jaffe, 2004). We can explain the power of similarity, contact and liking in a number of ways. For example, we are more likely to get along with others who share our values and views: perhaps it appeals to our vanity to have our values and views confirmed by others. We have a greater chance of establishing a common value set with persons we get to know: they become familiar and familiarity brings with it a certain security which is valued in itself. And those who express a positive regard towards us are difficult to dislike: perhaps a person comes to say, 'I like Jane because she is funny and warm . . .' because Jane thinks that that person thinks that she is funny and warm and in the process evokes a positive feeling in Jane about Jane. Mutual liking begins and becomes a virtuous circle wherein both parties bolster one another's self-esteem.

Whatever the validity these sorts of explanations might have there is a point to be made about similarity, contact and liking and it is that there doesn't appear to be a great deal of choosing or selection going on. We cannot choose who is biologically or socially similar to ourselves, we have limited choices over who we do and do not come into contact with (for example, we don't choose who else we study with or who we work with), and, as we have seen, we cannot choose who likes us.

These considerations raise questions as to whether we have choice, whether we select, and who we are romantically attracted to. Think about it. Do you choose to find someone attractive? Can you will yourself to do so? Can you will yourself not to find them sexually attractive? This doesn't mean that you have no choice over what happens next, or what you do about the attraction. But an important event has already occurred over which you may have had no conscious say. It is with this caveat in mind that we will embark upon the material in this chapter and examine the evolved psychology of mate selection.

WHAT WOMEN AND MEN WANT

The last chapter 'Families and parenting' discussed mating systems and in doing so considered the group-level dynamics that determine mating behaviour. This section will consider the characteristics that we deem desirable in prospective partners and how they play a role in the particular strategies that we might adopt toward reproductive opportunities. We will also look at how our particular degree of attractiveness may play a role in the choices open to us and in our actual mating behaviour. To do so we will consider the notion of mate value – the calculation of how attractive any given person is to potential mates. More precisely, we will focus on how any individual might estimate their own mate value, and, having done so, how it might affect their subsequent behaviour.

What do we want from one another? What is it that makes a person attractive? To address these questions we will look to the work of David Buss and collaborators (Buss, 1989, 1990, 1992, 1998, 2000, 2003). This research suggests that there are a large number of things that men and women consider desirable in the opposite sex. In approximate order of importance these include kindness and understanding, intelligence, good looks, outgoing personality, good health, adaptability, creativity, sexual fidelity, the wish for children, being well educated, coming from a healthy family, good financial prospects and cleanliness. We could add many more. For example, loyalty and reliability seem to be important (Buss, 2003).

BOX 7.1   WHAT DO WOMEN WANT IN MEN AND WHAT DO MEN WANT IN WOMEN?

What do women want in men?

1   Kindness and understanding
2   Intelligence
3   Exciting personality
4   Good health
5   Adaptability
6   Physical attractiveness
7   Creativity
8   Earning capacity
9   Graduate
10 Desire for children
11 Good stock
12 Good housekeeper
13 Chastity

What do men want in women?

1   Kindness and understanding
2   Intelligence
3   Physical attractiveness
4   Exciting personality
5   Good health
6   Adaptability
7   Creativity
8   Chastity
9   Desire for children
10 Graduate
11 Good stock
12 Earning capacity
13 Good housekeeper

This is a composite listing of what men and women rank as being the most important qualities and characteristics that they look for in a mate. Notice that many characteristics are seen as being of comparable importance, e.g. kindness, intelligence, creativity and good stock. The key differences between the sexes appear to be the importance and desirability of attractiveness, chastity and earning capacity (see Buss, 1989, 1998).

It was suggested that the lists in Box 7.1 are in approximate order because they represent a fair picture of the ordered preferences expressed by men and women over time and across cultures (Buss, 1989, 2003). However, they do not take note of the differences that have become evident between the sexes. So, while kindness is very important to both men and women, not all characteristics are deemed comparably desirable. The key characteristics on which the sexes differ appear to be on how important good looks are, how important material resources are, and how important sexual history more and fidelity is. The findings suggest that men value good looks more than do women. Men value a 'good' sexual history more than do women. And women value actual and potential resources more than do men.

How are these findings explained in evolutionary terms? Parental investment theory suggests that the sex who invests most in offspring will be most selective in **mate choice**, and the sex who invests the least will be more competitive for sexual access (Trivers, 1972). It is argued that women are attracted to better-off males for two reasons. One, material resources enable a male to give paternal investment. The female pays the biological and metabolic cost of gestation and weaning but the male can facilitate both if he can provide food and shelter. And two, the very fact that the male has resources suggests something about him. It tells the female that he is able, energetic and competitive, and these signal good genes. Similarly, it is argued that men are attracted to attractive, young, chaste females for three reasons. One, youth signals reproductive potential. On the assumption that it had a genetic basis, a preference for females nearing menopause would, in theory, be an evolutionary dead-end. Two, good looks signal good health. The biological and metabolic demands of gestation and weaning are immense and a preference for females in poor physical condition would also be selected against (Buss, 1989, 2003). And three, because males look to trade their material investment for biological investment they value chastity because it signals a solution to the problem of paternal uncertainty. If a male is to tie his own reproductive potential to a female he wants to be certain that the offspring he invests in are his.

With these findings and accompanying rationales in mind let us now consider the notion of mate value.

BOX 7.2   OBJECTIONS TO EVOLUTIONARY PSYCHOLOGY: SEXISM

Is evolutionary psychology sexist? This accusation has long been levelled at evolutionary accounts of human psychology and it has been reiterated by Martha McCaughey in *The Caveman Mystique: Pop-Darwinism and the Debates over Sex, Violence, and Science* (2007).

As we have seen, evolutionary theory predicts, and evolutionary psychology claims to have found differences in the way in which males and females think and behave (Baron-Cohen, 2003; Campbell, 2002). So, if the question 'Is evolutionary psychology sexist?' is taken to mean 'Does evolutionary psychology make a distinction between the sexes?' then the answer is yes.

We have seen that evolutionary psychology takes anatomical differences and the different roles that males and females play in reproduction seriously: i.e. male and female bodies are identical in most ways,

(Cont'd)

profoundly different in some others. For example, male and female hearts are anatomically, physiologically and functionally identical, but testicles are different from ovaries.

The possibility of sex differences is extended to cognition. Cognitive abilities are assumed to be identical in most respects, but to differ fundamentally in certain domains – principally those that underlie mating and parenting (Campbell, 1999b).

However, the assertion of differences does not amount to **sexism** if there is not also an assertion that the differences privilege one sex over the other. In other words, the stipulation of difference does not entail a stipulation of unequal value. For example, for a parent to say that two siblings differ, and to demonstrate the nature of the difference, does not axiomatically embroil that parent in a preference for one sibling over the other. It is worth reiterating that evolutionary theory is agnostic with regard to value. Those who may use the theory to support some or another claim about the relative value of females and males ought not be attributed ownership of the theory itself.

We can often detect questionable intentions when we look at questions that imply or invite an answer that attributes value to one sex or the other. For example, questions such as 'Are ovaries better than testicles?' and 'Are female mating tactics more sophisticated than male tactics?' may betray an intention to ascribe differing values. But in the cold pursuit of information these questions are meaningless in that evolutionary psychology does not ask or seek to answer them.

Sexual selection theory and parental investment theory are most usually appealed to to address questions about sex and gender differences. We have noted that the most pronounced differences relate to mating and parenting. Notice, then, that differences between the sexes are typically understood via reference to the opposite sex. For example, sexual selection theory suggests that psychological properties and behavioural repertoires that are particular to one sex have often come about because of selection pressures exerted by the other sex.

MATE VALUE

It may have occurred to you that we can write wish lists all day long but this does not guarantee that they will be fulfilled. The obverse of the question 'What do I want?' is 'How wanted am I?' To answer this question we need to consider our mate value. The mate value of any given individual is determined by his or her appeal as a sexual partner. As Buller puts it, 'An individual's mate value, or desirability to the opposite sex, is a function of how much an individual can contribute to the reproductive success of members of the opposite sex' (Buller, 2005: 252). Following the logic employed to explain the differeing preferences of men and women outlined in the last section, were we forced to summarise a mate value calculus in a sentence we could say that the mate value (or, in common parlance, the attractiveness) of a male is indexed by his material resources, and the mate value of a female is indexed by her reproductive potential. In practice it is, of course, far more complicated. Any one person's mate value is a weighting of all possible desirable characteristics. We may presume that very few people would score uniformly high on all, very few uniformly low on all. And most of us closer to the average than we might wish to think!

Here we will try to steer a satisfactory middle way through gross oversimplification and the exponential difficulty of weighing very many variables. The focus will be on the key characteristics that affect mate value. There are four core factors: health, age, status and the mating market place in which we operate. We will now consider these factors before look-ing at the role of the media. We will then move on to a discussion of honest and dishonest advertising and the ways in which we might deceive potential mates as to our mate value.

BOX 7.3   CONCEALED OVULATION AND MATE VALUE

While we can think of sexual dimorphism, testes size and sperm production in comparative terms it not so easy to do the same with ovulation. Human females exhibit what is called 'concealed ovulation' – 'concealed' because it is not entirely apparent to human males (or indeed to human females who have had no instruc-tion in reproductive biology). Concealed ovulation is atypical in the great apes. The females amongst our primate cousins clearly exhibit public signs that they are at that part of their estrus cycle wherein they are fertile. It has been suggested that the change from revealed to concealed peak fertility was an outcome of the need for females to secure more paternal investment from males and the desire of males for opportu-nities to copulate (Thornhill, 2007). The idea is that by concealing peak fertility females became sexually appealing to males throughout the cycle and this opened the way for more enduring pair-bonds which would serve both parties well in terms of the successful rearing of offspring.

However, Thornhill (2007) argues that things might not be quite so simple. He claims that human females are most proceptive (i.e. inclined to initiate sex) and receptive (inclined to respond to an invitation of sex) to copulation with high value 'sires' during estrus whether or not a given male is resident. During the remainder of the menstrual cycle human females exhibit 'extended sexuality' which 'evolves in species in which males provide females with nongenetic, material benefits: it functions to obtain these benefits' (Thornhill, 2007: 392).

Certainly there is now evidence which suggests that human males find women in estrus more attractive, that women in estrus may be more flirtatious, and that women may be more receptive to certain forms of language during the estral phase of the cycle. For example, Pipitone and Gallup (2008) found that the appeal of female voices to men varies across the menstrual cycle and it peaks with peak fertility. They sup-posed that voice is an honest signal of fitness and it is affected through sex hormones via the larynx. And it has been found that the tips given by males to female lap dancers also varied across the menstrual cycle and peaked at estrus (Miller et al., 2007). With regard to flirtatious signalling, Schwarz and Hassebrauk (2008) conducted a diary study with a group of German women over the course of one menstral cycle with a view to assessing flirtatiousness the measure of which was clothing style and self-perceived attractiveness as indicated by self-taken photographs and self report. They found that women perceive themselves and are perceived to be more flirtatious during the estral phase of the menstral cycle. And with regard to recep-tivity to mating display, there is some evidence which suggests that females be more receptive during the estral phase. Rosen and Lopez (2009) report that women showed an attentional bias toward what they call 'courtship language' during the fertile phase of their menstrual cycle as measured by error rates on a dichotic listening task. Participants in the fertile phase of the cycle made more shadowing errors (i.e. were more distracted by the courtship distracted message) than did participants at other points in the cycle.

HEALTH

As we have seen, physical condition is considered important by both men and women. To men, the physical condition of women offers cues to fertility and the capacity to gestate, lacate, wean and care. To women, the physical condition of men offers cues to the ability to gain and/or maintain social status and the ability to acquire and protect resources and kin. Accordingly our physical condition powerfully affects our mate value.

AGE

Whereas, albeit for different reasons, health may be of comparable importance to both sexes, the importance of age and status appears to be asymmetrical. The age of females is a critical determinant of her reproductive potential, and the evidence suggests that women's mate value lessens with age. We can expect men's value will also lessen with age. However, because age does not determine the reproductive potential of males nearly so much as it does females it does not affect male mate value so severely. Of course, because there is a relationship between health and age, there is also a point at which the age of any person will impact upon how desirable they are to others.

STATUS

The relationship between social status and mate value inverts the picture we have painted of that between age and mate value. Whereas it is supposed that the social status of women does not significantly impact upon her desirability it is supposed that it does impact on men. This is not to say that a woman's overall appeal is not enhanced if she has power, wealth or fame. Any or all three are likely to be attractive to men as ends in themselves, and any or all may be acquired by a woman courtesy of characteristics deemed desirable such as intelligence, physical attractiveness, an outgoing personality, or creativity. However, the argument is that status is unlikely to confer a high mate value on a female in and of itself. The role that status can play in the mate value of males is different. It is thought that it is attractive to women in its own right as well as signalling other desirable properties such as intelligence, a dominant personality, creativity, ambition and resources. There is evidence to support this view. High-status men remarry more frequently than do high-status women and low-status men, and do so sooner. Wealth and status is not a predictor of females' remarriage frequency, whereas it is for men. And high-status men who do remarry tend to do so with females younger than their former spouse (Lopreato and Crippen, 1999). A recent study claims that when confounds such as women's age, educational attainment, personal wealth, and health are taken into account the wealth – and thereby the status – of her partner predicts sexual satisfaction amongst a sample of Chinese women (Pollet and Nettle, 2009).

THE MARKET PLACE

The very notion of mate value implies a group. To be attractive (or not) implies a judge, and comparison. We can only come to assess our own mate value via the responses of others and in comparison with others. Of course, by definition, the vast majority of us are situated within groups which, taken as a group, are of average attractiveness in much the same way that that we are situated in groups which are of average height. However, we may

	Male (%)	Female (%)	Pearson x^2	p level
Physical attractiveness offered	27.9	39.4	16.96	<.001
Resources offered	38.8	26.1	21.69	<.001
Resources sought	15.8	25.3	15.92	<.001
Commitment sought	44.6	60.8	30.42	<.001

The table above shows the results from a sample of 551 personal advertisements (lonely-hearts ads) placed in a newspaper in Lower Silesian, Poland. As you can see females placed greater emphasis on how attractive they were. Males emphasised their material resources and this seems to match the wants expressed in the female ads. Notice too the discrepancy in the expressed wish for commitment. (Pawlowski and Koziel, 2002)

Figure 7.1   Personal advertisements as indicators of sex differences in mate preferences

Source: Table 1 from B. Pawlowski and S. Koziel (2002) The impact of traits offered in personal advertisements on response rates. *Evolution and Human Behaviour*, 23(2): 139–149.

be situated in non-average groups and, accordingly, be above or under average in terms of mate value in that group. A male with an average resource base in a group of males who are relatively poor would be one example. And a female who is significantly younger than other members of a group would be another.

THE MEDIA

It is all very well to say that both men and women value good looks, but what is it that constitutes 'good looks'? The answer appears to be being distinguishably feminine or masculine in facial appearance, more rather than less symmetric in maxiofacial structure, and in possession of a clear complexion, lustrous hair and good teeth amongst others things which signal good health (Etcoff, 1999). However, the majority of persons on earth are situated within the wider amorphous groups we call cultures or societies and these are exposed to media such as television, cinema and magazines. These media are often populated by persons who, on the definition given above, are unusually good looking. In these worlds of carefully presented beautiful people – people who do not actually exist in the form in which they are seen – our mate values are eroded. As has been remarked, in comparison to these extremely rare and largely fictional people most of us come off worst in comparison (Buss, 2009). Let us pick up on the idea of fictions now and consider how we might advertise our mate value to one another.

HONEST AND DISHONEST ADVERTISING

To frame our consideration of how the sexes may present and advertise themselves to one another and how the ability to do so may be both influenced by and come to have an impact on mate value it will be useful to remind ourselves of inter- and intra-sexual selection.

Intra-sexual selection refers to direct competition between members of the same sex for reproductive access to members of the opposite sex. For example, male gorillas engage in a competition whereupon the winner gains sexual access to one or more females. Where this pattern is thought to be typical of the mating arrangements for a given species we may say that that species is (at least in part) characterised by male rivalry. In such species we expect to see sexual dimorphism between the sexes, with males being decidedly larger than females. The size of males has been selected for because, all things being equal, the bigger the male the greater the likelihood he will succeed in intra-sex competition. Other features that appear to be fitness reducing may also be the result of inter-sexual selection.

Inter-sexual selection refers to indirect competition between members of the same sex that gives for reproductive access to members of the opposite sex. Inter-sexual selection involves a direct appeal from one sex to the other. For example, in humans two males might solicit the attention of and seek to court a female with a view to being her mate choice.

These two ways of looking at sexual selection are not mutually exclusive. One sex can compete amongst itself for access to the other sex but that access is not immediately sexual. Rather, the access involves a further appeal for sexual access which may be denied.

Darwin noted that intra-sexual selection – rivalry and competition between same-sex conspecifics – was typically between males, and that inter-sexual selection typically entailed female choice – that is, males display to females and female are the final arbiter of the decision to copulate or not. Darwin thought that this pattern is especially acute in slow breeding species wherein females typically provide the bulk of parental investment, and he thought that humans fitted the criterion for female choice to be an important consideration. An implication of this that was either lost to his contemporaries or not welcome is that the form that modern humans take is largely a result of female choices over evolutionary time.

It is supposed that inter-sexual selection has given rise to the mate preferences we have discussed (Buss, 1989). For example, kindness as a characteristic has come about because there has been selection pressure to exhibit that trait. Because of its importance we might signal the trait in rather ostentatious ways. For example, it has been proposed that males may express overt care and affection towards the offspring of a potential mate in order to demonstrate kindness (Hill and Kaplan, 1993; Wood and Hill, 2000). It is not that the men are not being kind. It is that they are being overt about their kindness. Such displays are often accommodated by the **handicap principle** (Zahavi and Zahavi, 1997). The handicap principle holds that ostentatious physical features or behavioural repertoires demonstrate that the bearer is in command of his or her environment and can afford such metabolic largess and/or tolerate dangerous risks. Zahavi and Zahavi (1997) have gone so far as to suggest that some traits might be selected for just because they are disadvantageous.

Perhaps you can see what is coming here. If a physical, behavioural or material display is purposely excessive, over-elaborate, designed to capture attention, is it always 'honest'? For example, if a male demonstrates kindness by being generous towards the children of potential mate is the generosity a reliable indicator of his character and future behaviour? In other words, is it honest or dishonest advertising?

Let us think this notion through. We are supposing that we come to know what it is we want in others and what they want in us. However, in order to appear to have more of what it is that is wanted we dishonestly exaggerate or mimic those traits. If we do so successfully, we enhance our mate value – albeit, in some cases, only for a short period.

Taking those characteristics which appear to be most important to men and women, we might expect that we will self-present in certain carefully designed ways, over-exaggerate certain features, or simply lie about them. We might hypothesise that men will exaggerate or mimic actual and/or potential resources, generosity, status and strength. And we might hypothesise that women will exaggerate or mimic fertility via age and/or health cues, chastity and sexual fidelity.

BOX 7.4 NO LAUGHING MATTER

As Greengross (2008) has pointed out, as a ubiquitous feature of human social interaction, laughter and humour (like language – see Chapter 9 – and religion – see Chapter 11) ought to be amenable to evolutionary analysis. However, important exceptions aside (see Freud, 1905/1960) there have been relatively and surprisingly few attempts to develop accounts and theories of this important human behaviour within–psychology and social science as a whole. Martin supposes that the neglect of humour has come about just because it is a positive behaviour springing from positive emotions and interactions and psychology tends to be more interested in the negative and dour (Martin, 2007). Still, there have been some attempts by evolutionary orientated psychologists to make sense of humour.

With a view to formulating a theory of the original function of laughter Polimeni and Reiss (2006) consider a number of possibilities. Candidate explanations include:

- It may be a fixed action pattern triggered by humorous stimuli which engenders positive emotional states which then promotes social activity.
- It may act as a reinforcer to social activity and intimacy.
- It relieves social tension.
- It may have physiological benefits in that it boosts immunological efficiency.

However attractive any of these putative proposals may seem, Polimeni and Reiss acknowledge that laughter carries costs – it is metabolically expensive, can be socially inappropriate and could attract the attention of predators and prey.

Another of Polimeni and Reiss' suggestions is that laughter facilitates sympathy, empathy and intimacy in courtship and might have come about courtesy of sexual selection. Bressler and Balshine (2006) investigated this idea by asking if humour acts to indicate other things about the humorists' personality – the assumption being that being funny is not in itself enough and that the other traits are more important or at least necessary. They found that women more than men found funny prospective partners more attractive. Curiously, Bressler and Balshine (2006) also found that for both men and women 'humorous individuals were seen as less intelligent and trustworthy than their non-humorous counterparts, but as more socially adept' (2006: 29). Perhaps the implication is that we are somewhat suspicious of funny persons just because their humour indicates social skills which may be used for Machiavellian purposes.

Picking up on the observation that a good sense of humour is rated by both sexes as important in a prospective partner, Bressler et al. (2006) explore this line of reasoning and report that there are asymmetries in how the two sexes rate and appreciate humour. They measured the relative importance of production of humour – i.e. being funny – and receptivity to humour – i.e. laughing. They found that men were keener to be seen as funny than they were to be amused, but women valued both equally. However, in a second study they also found that given a forced choice of being with a person who made them laugh or who

(Cont'd)

laughed at them women preferred the former and males the latter. If subsequent research supports these findings we might speculate that humour production is used by women to asses something important about men and by men to assess the interest levels of prospective mates.

Li et al. (2009) do not deny that that the display and appreciation of humour play an important role in romantic relationships, and, indeed, report findings which show that men and women are more likely to initiate humour, laugh more readily in return, and claim a person to be funny if already attracted to them. However, like Polimeni and Reiss, these researchers are also interested in the ultimate origin of humour and they argue that its original function was to initiate, perpetuate, and monitor social relationships more generally. They call this the 'interest indicator model' and it would appear to tally with the more general observation that it is difficult to form any sort of lasting bond with persons who neither find us amusing or amuse us in turn.

MATING STRATEGIES

We have looked at mate selection from the viewpoint of mate preferences, and we have looked at it from the viewpoint of individual mate value. In this section we will look at mate selection from the viewpoint of mating strategies. In particular we will consider the proposal that we adopt long- and short-term mating strategies.

The idea is that humans can pursue a mixed mating strategy. The strategy can be 'long' in that its purpose is to secure an enduring pair-bond or 'short' in that its purpose is secure a delimited number of reproductive opportunities. The strategy adopted at any given time is subject to a range of considerations including mate value and opportunity (Buss, 2003; Buss and Schmitt, 1993).

LONG-TERM STRATEGY

The theory that we are designed to pursue a long-term mating strategy asks us to make some assumptions about our natural history and the environment of evolutionary adaptedness (EEA). If the evidence produced in favour of the theory is to fit with the past and to add evidential weight to a claim that our expressed preferences are evolved dispositions, we need to accept one of two accounts of the past.

One option is to assume that the prevailing mating system that *Homo* inherited from *Australopithecus* was something similar to that which we see in extant chimpanzees and bonobos, both of whom are promiscuous. Under such conditions we add the fact that with the arrival of *Homo* brain size increased and the length of pre-pubescence became extended and the need grew for there to be parental investment from the father (see Hrdy, 2009). In other words, there was selection pressure from the female side towards monogamy. Another option is to assume that the system we inherited was polygyny, or something similar to that which we see in extant gorillas, and that changes in the composition of *Homo* groups included increases in group size and the presence of multiple males. This facilitated direct **female choice** – i.e. females were no longer saddled with the 'winner' of intra-male competition. In both scenarios (and both are plausible) the bottom line was a trade-off between the granting of more or less exclusive reproductive access by females in return for paternal investment from males. Coming from a system characterised by promiscuous behaviour towards something more akin to monogamy, females traded the advantages of paternal uncertainty and the protection against infanticide by males that it may have offered for paternal investment from males. Or, coming from a polygynous system to something akin to monogamy, females traded the advantages of the best-stock of an non-investing alpha male for an investing alloparent. For the males the advantages of ceasing to be openingly promiscuous and becoming more mongamous included some sort of paternal certainty, and coming from the polygynous system it offered reproductive opportunities to those who lost out altogether to dominant males.

As we have discussed, the female preferences that differ most from those of males are seen as more or less conscious expressions of the underlying need to secure material resources from males. To meet this need women need to be able to discern that resources are held or likely to be acquired. This is achieved by looking out for what Daly and Wilson (1988) have called 'fitness tokens'. **Fitness tokens** are reliable physical and/or behavioural indicators of underlying genetic properties and/or behavioural tendencies. The indicators which might signify the properties that females look for in males when exercising mate choice could include a preparedness to invest – this would be signalled by demonstrable generosity and kindness to her and others; an ability to invest – this would be signalled by evidence of wealth or signs of potential wealth; economic fidelity – this would be signalled by evidence of consistency, loyalty and trustworthiness; and an ability to offer protection – this would be signalled by evidence that he has good or high social status, would include good health and physical prowess.

Similarly, male preferences can be seen as more or less conscious expressions of the underlying need to secure the reproductive resources of a fecund female. And, similarly, to satisfy this need men have to be able to discern the reproductive potential of potential mates via reliable indicators of underlying properties. The desired properties and the cues to them could include fertility – this would be signalled by her age since puberty; health – this would be signalled by readily seen features such as skin complexion, hair, teeth, and physical vitality; preparedness to provide maternal care – this would be signalled by evidence of broodiness and empathetic behaviour towards children; and sexual fidelity – this would be signalled by her reputation and sexual history.

SHORT-TERM STRATEGY

The assumptions about the EEA that facilitate the explanation of long-term strategies imply that our mating system is more-or-less monogamous. As we saw in the last chapter 'Families and parenting', the problem is that monogamy can be readily questioned as a best-description of our mating system. In addition, the problem with the claim that we are solely long-term strategists is that there will have been and will always be room for both sexes to cheat on the arrangement. There are a variety of reasons to believe that that temptation is both extant and overwhelming. Let us consider some of them now.

There is evidence which suggests that males crave a variety of sexual partners, and are less choosy as to whom they will have sex with and what they need to know about the person before the act. Perhaps the most vivid demonstration of these points comes in the frequency with which males consume pornography and use prostitutes in comparison to females. For example, pornography as an industry has a greater turnover than the music and film industries put together and 95 per cent of it is consumed by men, and across all cultures that have been studied men have more extramarital affairs and pay for sex 1,000 times more often than do women (Birkhead, 2000).

Other research has focused on the nature of sexual fantasy and the findings support the view that males and females differ in their sexual appetites. Thus, 'The most striking feature of male fantasy is that sex is sheer lust and physical gratification, devoid of encumbering relationships, emotional elaboration, complicated plot lines, flirtation, courtship, and extended foreplay' (Ellis and Symons, 1990: 544). By contrast, Ellis and Symons report that women tend to fantasise about familiar partners, typically someone they are already involved with, and with high emotional/romantic content. This line of research has been supported by a study orchestrated by Schmitt (2003) which found that in a sample of over 16 000 people from 10 regions acroos the entire globe 'sex differences in the desire for sexual variety are culturally universal [and] evident regardless of the measures used to evaluate them' (ibid.,: 85).

Still, there are reasons to think that the short-term picture is more balanced than the evidence we have considered so far may suggest and that women can pursue a short-term strategy. Although we may suppose that females have less incentive to pursue short-term sexual liaisons courtesy of the fact that regardless of how many males a woman has sex with she can only give birth every nine months, there must be some benefit from short-term mating. If there were not, so the argument goes, men would not have retained or evolved a taste for sexual variety.

A cue to the proclivity for females to engage in short-term mating or 'sneak' extra-pair copulations if the circumstances suggest that benefits may be accrued can be discerned in the possibility of **sperm competition** (Baker and Bellis, 1995; Birkhead, 2000; Shackelford et al., 2005). There is some evidence to suggest that the number of sperm ejaculated is proportional to the probability that the female has the semen of another male in her reproductive tract. It is also claimed that males exploit reproductive opportunities by ejaculating more sperm into larger unfamiliar females, and that the volume of sperm produced and retained is greater in extra-pair than in-pair copulations (Baker and Bellis, 1995). The evidence warrants the conclusion that sperm competition could only have evolved if it was common for women to have sex with different males over periods of 0 to 6 days (Shackelford et al., 2005).

A more overtly psychological line of evidence comes in the form of male sexual **jealousy**. It has long been noted that males find the idea of their partners having sex with another more distressing than do females (Buss, 2000; Buss and Haselton, 2005). But but it also appears to be the case that men are prepared to be more aggressive to circumscribe the possibility. It has been argued that a majority of male-on-female violence occurs because the male is sexually jealous (Wilson and Daly, 1992a). For male sexual jealousy to even be at least as common as is female sexual jealousy it must be because sexual suspicion some how 'fits' female behaviour.

Underlying the aggression and violence is a tendency to monitor and coerce females as part of what is called 'mate guarding'. Of course, if it is true to say that males seek a variety of sexual partners then females too ought to mate guard – perhaps more so. To accommodate the difference in the manner of mate guarding male paternal uncertainty is invoked. If cuckolded, males are faced with the evolutionary dead-end of investing in another person's genes. Maternal certainty precludes such a fate for females and they have not developed such extreme strategies to offset a problem that they do not face.

The possibility of having reproductive success without the need to gestate and the possibility of exploiting their reproductive potential tells us why males may seek and capitalise on short-term, or 'sneak', copulations with females. But what advantages does a short-term strategy offer females? Short-term mating and extra-pair copulations cannot raise a female's reproductive potential but both may involve costs. A short–term sexual liaison may come with none or limited paternal investment from the male. And an extra-pair copulation comes with the risk of detection. And both may threaten a woman's reputation because if males value fidelity, cues at variance with this would be a disadvantage. There are a number of proposals at what the benefits for females might be. One is that a woman can secure a limited number of mating opportunities with a partner who is of a higher mate value than her partner. In doing so she secures better genes for the offspring (Gangstead and Thornhill, 1997). A corollary of such a choice is that she also spreads her genetic bets. While she gets half of her genes in the child, the genetic variety offered by the extra-pair partner gives her more genetic variety in her brood. Another proposal is that looking for extra-pair copulations acts as a way of remaining in the mating market. The utility of doing so is that switching mates should the need arise becomes easier (Greiling and Buss, 2000). Notice that support for this hypothesis also supports the serial monogamy argument.

There is also some evidence which suggests that talk of relatively fixed long- or short-term strategies may need to accommodate developmental and life history considerations for both male and females. Koehler and Chisholm (2007) frame extra-pair copulation (EPC) as a form of risk taking – they do so because the term 'extra-pair' implies a pair bond and EPC's jeopardise that bond. They hypothesised that both males and females who had experienced high levels of psychosocial stress during childhood would be more inclined to tolerate the risk and engage in EPC's. Distinguishing between two types of EPC – sex with someone other than one's mate, and sex with another person's mate – Koehler and Chisholm found that males and females who experience high levels psychosocial stress in childhood where most likely to have sex with someone other than their established partner, and men were even more likely to report such behaviour.

Consistent with previous work carried out by Draper and Harpending (1982), Belsky et al. (1991), Chisholm,(1993) and Ellis (2004) who argued that father-absence, insecure attachment, local mortality rates, and paucity of parental investment respectively seems to predict a promiscuous or 'quantitative' reproductive strategy, Koehler and Chisholm conclude that promiscuity may be an adaptive response to environmental and social insecurity. However, they also suggest that the high levels of childhood stress are a product of a risk-prone personality type that exhibits itself in higher levels of EPC in adulthood.

SUMMARY OF CHAPTER 7

'Mate selection' or 'choice' may be misnomers because it is not entirely clear that we actively, consciously choose to find others sexually attractive. This observation gives some licence to the claim that the preferences that we express when asked or exhibit through behaviour may have an evolutionary basis. With respect to the question, 'What do men and women want?' the sexes are similar and characteristics such a kindness and flexibility are highly regarded. However, there is evidence to suggest that men and women differ in the extent to which they value earning capacity, ambition-industriousness, youth, physical attractiveness and chastity. In short, the findings suggest that men value reproductive potential more than do women, and women value material resources more than do men irrespective of cultural background. It has been argued that the explanation for the differences can be attributed to evolved preferences wherein males trade parental investment in the form of material resources for the direct biological and metabolic investment of fecund females who the take to be sexually loyal.

Mate choice is also mediated by mate value. We do not simply choose mates. Potential mates have a choice too and we are as subject to choice as we are choosers. Our mate value is a function of many factors but amongst the most salient are health, age and status. Health is important in both sexes, but the contribution of age to female mate value is higher than it is to male mate value, and status is more important for males than females. Other determinants of mate value include the mate value of others in the group, exemplars set by the media, and our ability to successfully mimic or imply that we have preferred traits or characteristics.

There are reasons to think that humans can adopt long-term and short-term approaches to reproduction as opportunity and mate value allow. Both sexes may benefit from brief relationships and extra-pair infidelity. For example, males can enjoy some of the reproductive potential which their reproductive biology allows for, and females can introduce greater genetic variety into her offspring.

FURTHER READING

Apart from the references in this chapter you may find it interesting and useful to consult one or more of the following:

Barash, D.P. and Lipton, J.E. (2002) *The Myth of Monogamy: Fidelity and Infidelity in Animals and People*. New York, NY: Henry Holt and Company.

Diamond, J. (1997) *Why is Sex Fun? The Evolution of Human Sexuality*. London: Weidenfeld and Nicolson.

Fisher, H.E. (1992) *Anatomy of Love: A Natural History of Adultery, Monogamy and Divorce*. London: Simon and Schuster.

Miller, G. (2001) *The Mating Mind*. New York, NY: Anchor Books.

Ridley, M. (1993) *The Red Queen: Sex and the Evolution of Human Nature*. London: Viking.

8 COMPETITION, AGGRESSION AND VIOLENCE

Some of the questions addressed in this chapter:

- Over what would we expect humans to be most competitive?
- When does competition become aggressive and violent?
- Why are men more violent than women?
- How does competition manifest itself as a function of age?
- How could aggression be adaptive?
- What social factors appear to mediate rates of aggression and violence?

SOME KEY TERMS AND CONCEPTS

Direct and indirect aggression; Future discounting; Intra-sex competition; Jealousy; Marginal strategies; Mate guarding; Risk; Status; Uxoricide.

LEARNING OBJECTIVES

Having studied this chapter you should be better able to:

- Outline arguments which explain sex differences in aggression.
- Identify situations which seems to foster aggression.
- Describe the adaptive value of competitiveness and aggression.

INTRODUCTION

Darwin wrote of a 'struggle for survival' and in doing so explained and predicted an ongoing and endless competition between and within species for resources and reproductive opportunities. Evolutionary approaches to thought and behaviour adopt the view that extant humans are the product of generations of successful competitors and are themselves competitive. An evolutionary view helps us to accommodate the fact that competition is a universal feature of human life. Should you doubt this claim try to think of an aspect of your own life or a walk of life that you have observed that is free from any form of competition. This chapter takes the ubiquity of competition as a given and uses evolutionary theory to make sense of it.

Competition manifests itself in a number of ways. In due course we will be considering what it is men and women compete for and the nature of the competition. To prepare us for that we first need to unpack the notion of competition from an evolutionary standpoint. To operationalise what can be a rather slippery term the chapter will begin by framing competition in terms of aggressive acts, and by taking acts of obvious, overt aggression as a manifestation of competition. Further preparation for the analysis of competition between adults will come in the form of a review of how competition manifests itself in childhood. We will see that the clear sex differences that can be seen in adult behaviour are evident before puberty. The main part of the chapter follows in the form of discussions of male-on-male aggression, male-on-female aggression, female-on-female aggression and female-on-male aggression. We will conclude the chapter with a consideration of some of the social and environmental factors which appear to influence rates of aggression and violence within and between the sexes.

COMPETITION

In Chapter 5 'Cooperation and interdependence' we examined evolutionary solutions to the problem of altruism, and we saw how peaceable and mutually beneficial cooperation between con-specifics can arise because of the selfishness of genes and not in spite of them. In the process we also saw that contemporary evolutionary theory as applied to human social behaviour is built upon the assumption that humans need to cooperate with one another and that good girls and guys can come first. However, our discussion of game theory also showed us that in any population of persons who are disposed to cooperate and invest trust and resources in others there will be room for 'cheats' – those who take benefits without repaying costs.

Cheating occurs because natural selection selects in favour of traits that facilitate the acquisition of resources. Moreover, it is acknowledged that everything comes at a price and it is advantageous to pay less than the going rate if possible. Of course, getting something for less than it may be worth may be achieved by a perfectly cooperative bargain arrangement. A good bargain is to the mutual benefit of both parties. But cheating is something quite different. It involves the acquisition of resources wherein less is paid than demanded, requested or expected. The ability to achieve such outcomes is selected for if its results are undetected and successful. But conflict may come about if the attempted cheating is unsuccessful. Many aspects of both civil and criminal law can be viewed as a societal countermeasure to the ubiquity of cheating and as a more-or-less satisfactory way of resolving the injustice and balancing the losses which arises from it.

Evolutionary theory supposes that not all resources are equally valuable. And evolutionary approaches to human psychology supposes that implcity or explcitly we know this. It assumes that some things are worth more than others in the 'struggle for survival'. The value of a resource can be estimated in two ways. First there is its utility, and the second there is its rarity. Some things are essential but readily acquired. Some things are merely useful but difficult to acquire. Some things are both essential and rare. And some things are all the more valuable just because they are rare. Theory supposes that of greatest value are those resources most directly related to reproduction. And it supposes that competition will be most fierce for such resources. When we come to look at competition between adults we will consider more carefully the value of reputation and resources. Before we do so let us first consider evolutionary analyses of what are taken to be aggressive behaviours in pre-pubescent humans.

DEVELOPMENTAL CONSIDERATIONS

From an adaptationist point of view we can look at psychological and behavioural phenomena which arise during maturation and development in two ways. We can conceive of them as serving immediate on-the-spot purposes. And we can conceive of them as immature manifestations of what will become mature post-pubescent responses to adaptive problems. For example, the most pressing and overarching problem that a pre-pubescent human faces is the need to elicit parental care. Accordingly, this day-to-day problem should have given rise to discernible solutions. Giving parental care is not a day-to-day problem for pre-pubescent humans, but, all thing being equal, it will be. Accordingly, we might expect to be able to discern the first appearance of the caregiving behaviours before puberty.

With the distinction between actual and prospective adaptive problems in mind, and choosing an example apposite to the subject matter of this chapter, it is apparent that mate value is not a day-to-day, real-time issue for pre-pubescent humans whereas resource acquisition is. Therefore, we can expect infants, children and juveniles to compete for resources as immediate and tangible fitness goals. Mate value will become a fitness issue and we may expect to see nascent forms of competitive and cooperative behaviour that are explicable in light of that impending reality (Pelligrini and Archer, 2005).

BOX 8.1   DARWINISM IN DEVELOPMENTAL PSYCHOLOGY

Darwin's influence in developmental psychology is understated but detectable. Few would disagree that Sigmund Freud, Jean Piaget, Frederic Skinner and John Bowlby are amongst the most influential developmental psychologists but the fact that all of them considered themselves to be Darwinians is not so widely noted. For example, Freud thought the Oedipus Complex to be rooted in the need for children to have a trial run at a sexual relationship; Piaget thought that intellectual development in the child mirrored the intellectual development in the species; Skinner thought that individual behaviour, including parenting, was naturally selected in real time just as species typical behavioural repertoires were naturally selected in evolutionary time; and Bowlby thought that attachment behaviour and patterns between caregivers and offspring were adaptive mechanisms to designed to overcome the fact that humans are born altricial and remain acutely dependent on caregiving for many years.

THE APPEARANCE OF AND SEX DIFFERENCES IN AGGRESSIVE BEHAVIOUR

It has been noted that tantrums – noisy displays that imply annoyance – appear in infancy and are usually focused around material objects that are used for play and food (Durkin, 1995). In human toddlers the first exhibitions of aggression towards others emerge in the second year of infancy and usually involve toys. It is also at this time that a sex difference becomes apparent with boys being more aggressive than girls (Campbell et al., 2002; Hay et al., 2000; McGrew, 1972; Sears et al., 1965). During the juvenile period behaviour such as kicking, pushing, slapping and punching is deemed hostile (as opposed to expressive) by both juveniles and adults and becomes more common. While it is observed in both sexes, there is a marked sex difference in the frequency it is exhibited in boys (Bjorkvist et al., 1992). There are a number of reasons why we might expect a sex difference in overt aggression both before and after puberty and these will be discussed in more detail when we consider adult aggression in due course.

There is a form of aggression which may be at least or even more prevalent in pre-pubescent females as it is in males. Researchers refer to it as indirect aggression. Just as with direct, physical aggression, there are debates as to the correct definition of indirect aggression (Bjorkqvist, 1994). Still, there seems to be some agreement that indirect aggression is an act that is intended to harm another but it does not involve direct, physical confrontation. Malicious gossip, the spreading of lies about a person and social ostracism are examples of indirect aggression (Archer, 2004). An instance of any such behaviour could count as a form of indirect aggression simply because it involves non-direct delivery of an unwanted stimulus. The harm comes in the form of breach of confidence, derogation of reputation and/or rupture to friendships.

The study of indirect aggression in children is of some vintage (e.g. Feshbach, 1969), and the subsequent literature has pointed to a sex difference wherein females exhibit it more than do males (Archer, 2004; Bjorkqvist et al., 1992; Hess and Hagen, 2006; Lagerspetz et al., 1988). We might anticipate this finding given that juvenile females coalesce in smaller, more emotionally intimate groups than do males. In such conditions malicious gossip and social ostracism is more readily an option, and it may be an effective form of inflicting harm. It is interesting to note that a relationship between social intelligence and indirect aggression amongst juveniles has been reported with the more socially intelligent being more likely to exhibit indirect aggression (Kaukianen et al., 1999). If this is correct we might also suppose that the form of females' social groupings facilitates social intelligence and social intelligence facilitates indirect aggression.

BOX 8.2   EVOLUTION AND FEMINISM

As we have seen, and the point is made again and again throughout this book, it cannot be denied that evolutionary psychology supposes and stipulates differences between the sexes. Arguing that these differences are played out and worked out in myriad different ways to the mutual benefit of both parties in terms of successful reproduction, does not obviate the temptation for many authors to frame the differences in terms of a 'battle of the sexes'.

Feminists who insist that there are no meaningful biological differences between males and females are unlikely to embrace evolutionary psychology, but feminists who think that women are, in some sense, superior to men might. If there are differences in the way men and women think, then it may be possible to show how and why. For example, if we hold aloft language and the ability to construct theories of others minds as distinct and essentially human achievements, then there may be arguments which suggest that females are, on average, better at them than males.

There are other ways in which evolutionary theory might be of interest to feminists. An enduring concern for feminism is patriarchy – the dominance in families, social groups and societies of males over females. Patriarchy is a demonstrable feature of very many societies through history. Smuts (1995) has presented a rationale as to why patriarchy came about and persists. She argues that, at bottom, the male subjugation of women is a response to paternal uncertainty. On this analysis patriarchy is a product of the asymmetry in power between male and females with regard to certainty of paternity and a demonstration of their weakness.

And the attention of feminism might also be drawn to Darwin's notion of female choice. Darwin argued that the females of species, especially mammals, are in practice the 'gate-keepers' of the sexual act. While there is sexual coercion and rape, sex is almost always consensual but females control the process of consent. On this analysis males are as they are because they have been shaped by female choice. Maleness owes itself to females rather than vice versa.

THE ROLE OF PLAY IN THE DEVELOPMENT OF COMPETITION AND AGGRESSION

For some time it has been thought that play of infants and children functions as a way of imagining, modelling and manipulating the physical and social world, and that it is sex-typed (Piaget, 1955). It is evident that once beyond infancy children express a preference toward play with members of the same sex (Harris, 1998; Maccoby, 1998), but that this may reflect a preference for masculine or feminine play styles rather than a preference for sex of play-mate (Alexander and Hines, 1994).

Play takes a variety of forms that map (approximately) onto age and these forms appear in a sequence. As humans emerge from infancy into childhood 'the literature on children's pretend play is unequivocal in documenting sex differences in themes enacted in fantasy' (Pellegrini and Archer, 2005: 231). A review of this literature documents a difference between the 'social dramatic' character of girls play from about two years of age wherein the play is orientated around mothering, family and consensual narrative, and the 'thematic fantasy' character of boys play wherein it is orientated around machinery, battle and adventure narratives (Power, 2000). These differences extend into the school years of childhood.

BOX 8.3   SEX AND THE GENDERED CONVENTIONS OF PLAY

There is an obvious and customary criticism of the view that the differences in play styles that we observe reflect something innate: the differences are imposed through socialisation rather than spontaneously expressed through biology. This criticism almost certainly has virtue. After all, children do not have complete control over the objects with which they play, and adults approve of and thus condition and reinforce, certain types of play depending on the sex of the child. However, the very fact that we can gender play-style implies that there are different forms of play, and evidence has been presented which suggests that infants as young as nine months can discern a difference and express a preference (Campbell et al., 2000). Also, the criticism that play styles are imposed upon children does not dispel the proposal that sex-typed play styles are risk-free dress rehearsals for adaptive problems to come. And it leaves open the question as to why parents and other caregivers promote sex-typed play in their efforts to prepare children for adulthood.

As females and males travel through the juvenile period from about eight years of age through to puberty, the onset of adolescence play becomes more socially cooperative and peer orientated, more clearly rule governed, but also more competitive (Power, 2000).

A clear difference in play emerges between the sexes during the juvenile period. Observation suggests that boys enjoy more games that involve more physical contact than do girls (Boulton, 1992; Loeber and Hay, 1997), expend more energy during play (Pelligrini et al., 1998), and take winning and losing more seriously as indicted by physical threats of force against competitors (Savin-Williams, 1987; Schlegel, 1995). The suggestion is that aggressive games condition boys physically and prepare them psychologically for intra-sex dominance competition that they will face after puberty.

This supposes that children's and juveniles' competition is a prelude to the 'real thing'. It is now time to turn to adults and the more dramatic and serious aggression that they exhibit compared with children and juveniles. Before doing so it is necessary to do a little more theoretical work and unpack the claim that aggression is a manifestation of competition over key resources.

BOX 8.4   HOMICIDE AS A MANIFESTATION OF COMPETITION AND AGGRESSION

Martin Daly and Margo Wilson's volume *Homicide* is one of the canonical texts of contemporary evolutionary psychology (Daly and Wilson, 1988). Daly and Wilson's objective is to explicate the evolutionary logic of aggression and it uses homicide data as a vehicle. The book comprises three analyses. One of them covers male-on-male homicide, one covers male-on-female homicide and another covers adult-on-child homicide. The focus is on homicide, or murder, because while most of us have a visceral sense of what sorts of behaviour constitute aggression, a clean, clear and unambiguous definition of aggression is difficult to stipulate. To illustrate this difficulty, consider the following scenarios while asking which of them constitutes an act of aggression:

- A husband defends his wife's honour by pushing to the ground a man who insulted her.
- A parent smacks his disobedient six-year-old child.
- A woman gouges the eyes of a would-be assailant.
- A wife shouts obscenities at her husband when he returns home late and intoxicated.
- A female employee passes on rumours at work about a rival's sex life.
- Out of spite, a man tells his girlfriend that her make-up and clothing are 'a real mess'.
- As a 'joke', two students write rude graffiti on the door of a friend's room.

An argument can be made in favour of labelling all of these cases as examples of aggressive acts should we adopt a widely used definition of aggression as being an act whereupon harm is intentionally inflicted upon another person who did not wish to be so afflicted (Geen, 1990). Consideration of each case shows us that we can identify an intention to harm and a victim who would rather not be the recipient of the harm. While we might accept the legitimacy of the actions of the husband, the parent, the woman who is attacked, the wife and, even perhaps the employee, the boyfriend and the students, we are bound to concede that harm – albeit it more or less – is directed at what we may take as an unwilling recipient. However, different definitions of aggression would yield a different set of judgements, and there is no universally accepted definition of aggression.

Daly and Wilson seek to circumvent problems that arise from the nature of intention, the nature of the harm and the participation of the 'victim' and semantic debates about the meaning of 'aggression'. To do so they decided to concentrate on homicide because they take it to be as good as an unequivocal example of aggression. Also, with a view to collecting data, homicide statistics offer a measure of aggression and interpersonal conflict which are not so encumbered by legal and bureaucratic noise as are non-lethal assaults. Looked at as a tip of an iceberg, Daly and Wilson use homicide data as a way of measuring and analysing interpersonal conflict in general. In particular they see it as a way of assessing who aggresses most and against whom, and of determining the precedents of aggression.

WHO AGGRESSES AGAINST WHOM UNDER WHICH CIRCUMSTANCES?

Males are markedly more physically aggressive and overtly violent than females (Archer, 2004; Hyde, 2005). The evidence suggests that males physically aggress against one another more than they do against females; that males physically aggress against females more often than do females against males; and that females physically aggress against one another least often (Geen, 2001). To explain these patterns evolutionary psychology argues that competition and aggression arises over those resources and relationships that matter most to Darwinian fitness. We saw in Chapter 7 'Mate selection' that there are four broad categories of things that relate closely to Darwinian fitness: mate value (i.e. status and beauty), reproductive opportunity (i.e. copulation), kin (i.e. inclusive fitness) and material resources. The four are in continual interplay. For example, mate value is partly determined by material resources, and inclusive fitness is partly determined by copulation. However, it is possible to see how one or another shows itself as most salient in certain situations.

We will now look at evolutionary explanations of male-on-male aggression, male-on-female aggression, female-on-female aggression and female-on-male aggression. The research base which supports these explanations – just as is almost all which focuses on human aggression and physical violence – comprises post-hoc analyses of known events and is essentially observational. The reason for this is simple. It is deemed unethical to conduct experiments that trigger or evoke aggression in humans. Accordingly, in the scheme presented in Chapter 2 'Evolutionary approaches to thought and behaviour' the discussion can be characterised as being of a piece with the 'backward approach'. This is because it is establishing facts that pertain in the present, it is stipulating frequencies and patterns and proposing adaptive benefits, and it is then hypothesising the behaviours as arising from selection pressures in the past.

Table 8.1   Which sex kills which other most often?

		Sex of offender:	
		Male	**Female**
Sex of victim:	Male	68%	10%
	Female	20%	2%

The percentages exhibited above represent the typical pattern of homicides as a function of sex of offender and victim where records exist. Male-on-male homicide is by far the most common type and female-on-female by far the least common type. At the broadest level of explanation these findings are explained by higher rates of intra-sexual competition between males for females.

MALE-ON-MALE AGGRESSION

Data generated by criminal justice systems in the US America and Canada, and historical data from a variety of other countries where records exist, suggest that male-on-male homicide accounts for aproximately nine out of every ten homicides and that this pattern is stable across cultures and over time (Daly and Wilson, 1988; Ghiglieri, 1999). Furthermore, in approximately eight of out ten cases of male-on-male homicide the aggressor and the victim are under thirty years of age (Wilson and Daly, 1997).

The reason for this large sex difference is attributed with extent and nature of intra-sexual competition between males in comparison with that between females. Consistent with Darwin's theory of female choice (Darwin, 1871) and Trivers' theory of parental investment (Trivers, 1972), the argument is that males – most especially younger males – compete with one another for status and resources in order to boost mate value. Increased mate value then increases access to reproductive opportunities and, ultimately, to the resource of maternal investment.

It is proposed that humans, like other mammalian and primate species, are concerned with **dominance hierarchies** and status. Daly and Wilson appeal to the protracted nature of the struggle for dominance and status amongst males into adulthood to account for the frequency of male–male homicide in younger men (Daly and Wilson, 2003).

The desire for social dominance is selected for because it confers a number of advantages. One of these are the rewards which may be accrued courtesy of **effective polygyny**. As you may recall, polygyny refers to a mating system wherein some males get access to more than one female. Effective polygyny refers to a situation wherein while there are no legal or cultural prescriptions that allow for polygyny as a formal system, some males enjoy appreciably more reproductive encounters than do others. If this results in appreciably more off-spring then that amounts to effective polygyny. This plays out in the possibility that for any given group of males the variance of paternity is greater than is the variance of maternity. In other words, in a population wherein the average number of children is, say, four per adult over the life span, we can expect that average to encompass the majority of females with a minority having fewer and more than the average. But we can also expect that the average encompasses a smaller majority of males with a larger minority having no children and a larger minority having more than the average. The competition to be amongst the latter minority courtesy of dominance and status amongst other males is fought out amongst younger males with the result being high rates of homicides amongst them. This reasoning is supported by research which suggests that males embrace risks to their physical well-being more readily than do females (Kruger and Nesse, 2004; Wilson and Daly, 1985). It is claimed that the male psyche has evolved to be more risk accepting in competitive situations than is the female psyche because greater fitness variance selects for greater risk acceptance in pursuit of scarce means which enhance reproductive success (Baker and Maner, 2008; Pawlowski et al., 2008).

That's the theory, and what we know of the precursors to male-on-male aggression appears to support it. There is evidence which suggests that the catalyst for most male-on-male aggression is threats to reputation and status. It has been noted that what ends up as lethal fights begin as altercations over trivial matters such as small sums of money, verbal insults and jostling in queues (Fessler, 2006; Tedeschi and Felson, 1994; Wolfgang, 1958) An evolutionary analysis employing the concept of dominance hierarchies suggests that such incidents are important because of the effects they have on the status of the males involved within in-groups and the wider community (Daly and Wilson, 1985, 1988, 2003).

A second precursor to male-on-male aggression also relates to reputation but affects groups of males and appears to have a resources dimension in the form of territory and how the control of it opens up the possibility of making money. For example, at the time of writing police in London are questioning four males aged between 15 and 17 years of age in connection with the murder of a 40-year-old father of two children. The victim appears to have affronted the group by asking them to modify their behaviour and vacate a territory that they considered to be their 'patch' or 'manor'.

MALE-ON-FEMALE AGGRESSION

Second to the rates seen for male-on-male homicide are those seen for male-on-female homicide and uxoricide (the killing of a wife, or, functional equivalent) is the most common form (Archer 2000; 2004; Wilson and Daly, 1992b). If we are to locate the motive for such acts in our categories of status, reproduction, kin and resources it appears to be the case that reproduction and resources are the most likely.

The concept of **mate guarding** applies to both sexes and the constituent words may render the term self-explanatory. In zoological parlance, to mate guard is to shield one's mate from competitors. It is behaviour which protects what is seen as a reproductive resource from others who seek the resource. Taken as a measure of coercive behaviour, the frequency of male-to-female aggression and violence within the confines of a pair-bond can be interpreted as a form of pre-emptive and retributive mate guarding (Campbell, 2005; Daly and Wilson, 1988; Wilson and Daly, 1992a).

Pre-emptive coercion can be seen as adaptive in that the control by a male of his partner's behaviour may prevent exposure to other males. This may take the form of he being insistent that she gives notice, reports on and is required to explain absences from his company that are atypical from conventional work-a-day arrangements. The coercion may take the form of implied threat to withdraw from the pair-bond (see below 'female-on-male aggression'), or withdrawal of resources such as financial cooperation, domestic labour or child care. It may take the form of attacks on self-esteem or insistence on certain forms of dress or future time-keeping. Or it may be a threat of or actual acts of violence (Wilson and Daly, 1992a).

Retribution may be seen as a response to a perceived failure to control the behaviour of the partner or as an attempt to coerce her into remaining within the bond in light of temptation to engage in sneak copulations, actual extra-pair copulations, or the wish to terminate the bond. Violent retribution is a form of risky behaviour that is designed to retain the reproductive resource. At the least it is risky because it may invite retaliation from kin literal and virtual, and it may accelerate her desire to leave the relationship because of its threat to her fitness. Still, by physically damaging the female the male is damaging the mate value of his partner, he is signalling a preparedness to be violent to competitors and he is threatening to further erode her fitness.

These considerations notwithstanding, the obvious problem with evolutionary explanations of uxoricide and sub-lethal aggression that seriously impairs the health of woman is that it is difficult to see how such behaviour can be fitness enhancing for the male. If we allow ourselves to see the female as a hard-won reproductive resource, damage to or destruction of that resource must be fitness reducing. As we will see in Chapter 10 'Evolution and abnormal psychology', there are various ways in which fitness reducing, or negative, behaviours can be accommodated within an evolutionary framework, but we may only need to invoke the notion of **scruffy engineering** (Hampton, 2004a) to see how an adaptive strategy can go wrong. At its simplest, scruffy engineering refers to the sub-optimal design that we may expect any mature adaptation to exhibit due to a cascade of genetic and developmental events that occur during its formation. With regard to uxoricide, scruffy engineering exhibits itself in a disjunction between intended and actual outcome. The male threatens and executes a violent act with the intention of coercing his partner's behaviour but the outcome may be an unintended fatality.

BOX 8.5   THE BLINDNESS OF VIOLENCE

There are other ways of accommodating violence towards partners and others within an adaptationist framework. It has been suggested that hostile aggression has its root in the 'flash of anger' (Fessler, 2006). The anger is evoked – and in using this term no moral justification is intended – by what is perceived to be a transgression of an individual's self-interest and results in the delivery of a noxious stimulus to the perceived transgressor. Ordinarily, we take a response that can be categorised as violent as an over- reaction whereupon we mean that the 'punishment' received by the transgressor is disproportionate to the offence committed. However, a disproportionate response can be functional if the long-term outcome is to permanently deter the immediate transgressor and other potential transgressors from repeating the offence (Fessler, 2006; McGuire and Troisi, 1990). The proposal is that the very 'blindness' of anger, hallmarked by an absence of control, is designed to overcome our tendency to defer costs from the immediate presence to the vagaries of the future. Anger and the aggressive and violent behaviour which it precipitates allows us to take a risk that most often pays off in terms of reducing the likelihood that we will suffer further transgressions (Fessler, 2006).

FEMALE-ON-MALE AGGRESSION

If we work on the assumption that a workable and equitable mating strategy for both males and females is a more-or-less long-term pair bond, then it is apparent that males are also a valuable source of parental investment (Hrdy, 2009). Accordingly, if males are a reproductive resource to females as are females to males, it may occur to us that the factors which give rise to male coercion of females hold for females. That is, we should expect females to exhibit pre-emptive and retributive coercion too. Campbell (1995) cites data in the form of a relationship between frequency of female-on-male homicide and the age of the female at the time which may go some way towards supporting this expectation: Females may be more likely to kill their partner or other females when older and past peak fecundity because as her mate value declines the value of the pair bond rises. Under this scheme, we can interpret mariticide (a term used to describe the killing of a husband by a wife and here used more loosely to describe the killing of a male by the female in a pair-bond) as a misbegotten attempt by the female to defend and retain their mate through violence. However, homicide data across place and time suggests otherwise because female-on-male homicide is very much less frequent than the obverse (Archer, 2000, 2004). In addition, an orthodox interpretation of the data is that when females do kill their male partners it is often in self-defence (Daly and Wilson, 1988).

Still, should we wish to maintain the suppositions above we could argue that in the female-on-male case using homicide as an indication of rates and frequency of sub-lethal aggression may be less useful because females use other, less direct, forms of coercion and aggression against their partners just as they do against other females. Further research into female-on-male coercion may come to settle the matter but there are other reasons why the disparity in rates of inter-sex violence may be expected.

First, we can return to the idea that while females are under pressure to compete for, and retain resources, the costs of doing so via physical aggression outweigh the benefits. When we add the consideration that males are typically about 20 per cent larger than females and, all things being equal, are likely to be able to defend themselves and successfully retaliate against an attack by a woman, we have grounds to explain the sex difference in the frequency of opposite sex violence.

Second, we need to think again about the implication of paternal uncertainty. As has been explained and illustrated (see Chapter 7 'Mate selection'), a profound asymmetry in the reproductive landscape is that between the near certainty that females have in their confidence of maternity and the practical uncertainty that males have in their confidence of paternity. While the likelihood of a female mistakenly investing in a child that she thinks is hers are near zero the likelihood of a male doing the same is real. Maternal uncertainty is not a fitness problem for females. Paternal uncertainty is a problem for males. And the consequences of failing to solve it are high. In light of these considerations it has been proposed that males have evolved anti-cuckoldry strategies (Buss, 2000; Daly and Wilson, 1988; Wilson and Daly, 1992 a and b). It is claimed that this can be discerned in the manner in which romantic and sexual jealousy differs between the sexes, one of the differences being that jealousy and the concomitant anxiety is produces is more readily evoked in males than it is in females when they are faced with the prospect of their mate having extra-relationship sex (Buss, 2000; Townsend, 1995). Another strategy is coercion, and this can lead to aggression and lethal violence. Between them, sexual dimorphism and paternal uncertainty may account for the different patterns of homicide and sub-lethal aggression that are observed between the sexes.

FEMALE-ON-FEMALE AGGRESSION

Crime statistics which show that male-on-male homicide is most common also show that female-on-females homicide is least common. Taking homicide as a cue to sub-lethal acts of same sex aggression, we may expect to find that females assault one another less frequently than do males and this is indeed the case (Campbell, 1999b). It has been argued that the reason for the relative rarity of female-on-female assault when such behaviour is taken to be related to dominance and status is due to the relative paucity of a pay-off in terms of reproductive success (Campbell, 1995). As was suggested in Chapter 7 'Mate selection', female mate value is not so sensitive to status as is that of males. Furthermore, the impact on mate value of physical damage is greater for females than it is to males because of its impact on a females' appearance and the ability to gestate and raise a child.

The foregoing considerations open up the intriguing possibility that social intelligence has evolved, in part, in response to the need to compete but to do so via means that minimise the risk of physical damage. If, as appears to be the case, indirect aggression is exclusive to humans, and that it is a more sophisticated form of aggression than direct aggression, it may be that females are as aggressive as males but also more sophisticated in their tactics. We saw when looking at the development of aggression through the juvenile period that there is evidence to suggest that females use indirect aggression against one another more frequently than do males, and the sex differences may persist into adulthood (Archer, 2004; Bjorkvist et al., 1992). It may be that females use indirect aggression more than do males as adults because they have the underlying **theory of mind** skills that allow for it (Baron-Cohen, 2003).

BOX 8.6   OBJECTIONS TO EVOLUTIONARY PSYCHOLOGY: AGENCY AND RESPONSIBILITY

A concomitant of the suggestion that evolutionary approaches to thought and behaviour entail **determinism** is the fear that determinism entails a diminution or lack of agency. In turn, this raises the problem of **moral responsibility**: if we are not free to make choices in what sense are we responsible for our behaviours? Or, in terms particular to evolutionary theory, does a subscription to an evolutionary point of view commit us to the claim that we are not responsible for our actions because our genes make us do things?

The reply to this question is no. You and your genes are not separable – you are your genes and your genes are you. To deny this claim we need to consider what sense it makes to suppose that we are somehow separate from our genes; that in the act of 'them' making 'us' do something they are an external or outside agency. It seems apparent that any such suggestion is untenable. Our genes are no more separate from us than are any other parts of our body. Indeed, they are more integral to us than are, say, our fingers and toes, or hands and feet, even our hearts and kidneys because there is no possibility of us surviving their removal or of them being transplanted. To see how the assertion that you are your genes and your genes are you plays out in an ordinary day-to-day setting imagine trying to explain away an immoral act by telling, say, your boss (or your partner or your parents) that your genes made you do it.

Still, while evolutionary psychology does not argue that we are unable to make decisions, it does say that certain sorts of issue are of greater salience than others and that we may be inclined to pursue certain sorts of outcome over others. Nevertheless, most of us (here excluding those of diminished responsibility) possesses the ability understand, obey or disobey moral injunctions. In addition, and as we have seen at various points, there are a number of plausible arguments which suggest that we are moral because of our genes, not in spite of them, and that morality is product of our genes (see Dennett, 2003).

SOCIAL AND ENVIRONMENTAL FACTORS AND RATES OF AGGRESSION

In this final section of the chapter we will consider social and economic variables which appear to affect the rates at which people aggress against one another. For both male and female adults, the critical factor appears to be income inequality and the effect that this has on males' ability to gain status. Following the precedent in this chapter, let us consider income in equality and male-on-male aggression first.

We have already considered the prospect that outside of coercive moral and legal systems which successfully legislate against it humans live in conditions of effective polygyny. Pellegrini and Archer (2005) argue that male-on-male competition during development is calibrated according to the predominant mating system and nutritional resource base in which males are reared. A polygynous system in a nutrition-rich environment encourages more competition between males than does a monogamous system in a nutrition-poor environment. The macro-mapping of development behaviour to contours of the social and ecological conditions is mirrored in the tendency for males to adjust and moderate their competitive behaviour when mixing with juvenile females (Maccoby, 1998; Pellegrini, 1992).

This analysis can be extend to adult males and used to account for differing rates of homicide, aggression and the underlying competition that they point towards. Data from the United States and Canada suggests that homicide rates are sensitive to local income inequality between neighbouring groups in cities and regions. It is argued that awareness of apparently inaccessible resources heightens the desire to acquire resources and status and in doing so intensifies competition within less well off groups (Daly et al., 2001). Hiraiwa-Hasegawa (2005) has presented data for Japan. Actual or perceived income inequality triggers '**future discounting**' wherein the risks that males – typically younger men under the age of 25 – will take to secure what they see as positive outcomes related to resource acquisition and status become greater and greater. The outcome is an increased rate of homicide.

BOX 8.7   RISK, THE FUTURE AND IMMEDIATE GRATIFICATION

The term 'future discounting' encompasses the idea that persons who engage in high-risk behaviours, including criminal activity such as violence and theft, show a tendency towards immediate as opposed to delayed gratification. In other words, they show an apparent disregard for the long-term consequences of their actions in the interests of obtaining short-term outcomes. Characterised as being impulsive, impatient, lacking self-control and exhibiting a myopic concentration on short-term goals, we may ask how such mind-sets could be adaptive given the life-long problem of survival and reproduction?

Wilson and Daly (1997) suggest that the steep discounting of the future costs of immediate gratification may be seen as a rational response to social and environmental cues which indicate a low probability of surviving to reap delayed benefits. Apparently reckless risk taking could be a sound strategy if the anticipated benefits outweigh those which are unlikely to be gained from a less risky alternative.

Future discounting maps surprising neatly onto the sociological concept of relative deprivation. Used to analyse the problem of growing crime rates in affluent societies by Runciman (1966), relative deprivation refers to disparities in wealth and opportunity between individuals and groups. It is said to occur where there is an actual or perceived imbalance between opportunities and or outcomes and ability. The result of relative deprivation is an increase in inter-group hostility and a disregard for rules and laws seen to be set by the advantaged group.

An analogous and complementary picture can be painted for rates of female-on-female aggression. It has been shown that the ages at which we see heightened same-sex aggression is similar for males and females – that is, young females tend to be more aggressive than older females just as younger males are more aggressive than older males. Campbell (1995) is of the view that this is in need of explanation and has proposed the 'few good men' hypothesis which is based on two assumptions. First, while it may be the case that humans are not a strictly monogamous, pair-bond-for-life species, it does appear to be the case that many couples do pair bond for protracted periods that encompass gestation and the rearing of the infant. And, second, that there is intra-sexual competition between females for what are deemed to be the most desirable males.

Campbell points out that the default assumption tends to be that females express their intra-sexual competition via 'epigamic display' – that is, by advertising their attractiveness to males (see Etcoff, 1999; Symons, 1979) – but argues that the picture is rather more complicated, especially when the number of desirable good-quality males is perceived to be few. Campbell's idea can be linked to Pellegrini and Archer's (2005) suggestion that levels of aggression in juvenile males is sensitive to cues to the competitiveness of the local adult mating system in that she supposes that females will also be sensitive. If the local system is quasi-monogamous then the intensity of female competition will rise as will acts of aggression. The competition inherent for mates in a quasi-monogamous system can be compounded by an actual or perceived paucity of desirable males.

SUMMARY OF CHAPTER 8

Cooperation pays. But it is also the case that competition for resources and mating opportunities is an inherent and inevitable aspect of the evolutionary process and a feature of human natural history. Competition entails winners and losers but not necessarily physical harm. However, competition can lead to aggression, aggression to violence and violence to lethal harm. Homicide has been used by evolutionists to estimate rates, reasons and patterns of competition and aggression amongst humans. Males are more aggressive than females – a finding that can be seen during childhood. Adult males harm one another more frequently than they do females. This is attributed to more intense intra-sexual competition between males for access to females. Males also harm females more often than do females. This is attributed to mate guarding and the protection and retention of females as a reproductive resource. Females harm one another more often than they do males. This difference is explained by supposing that while they are a more valuable resource than makes, some males are of greater value than other and females will aggressively compete for the better of them. That there are fairly stable patterns of female-on-female physical aggression supports the view that males are a reproductive resource worth using force to retain. Comparatively low rates of female-on-female physical aggression may mask us to the possibility that there are higher rates of indirect aggression between females. Evolutionary psychologists do not suppose that lethal aggression is necessarily adaptive. Rather it can be seen as an unintended by-product of the need to compete, protect status and retain resources. The desire for status and resources in groups which are actually or apparently denied access to them may also explain differing rates of aggression between groups. Income inequality may produce conditions wherein males take greater risk to secure status and resources in the absence of safer and long-term strategies. Similarly, in the absence of a wide choice of high-status, well-resourced males, females may take greater risk to access and retain the few who have status and resources.

FURTHER READING

Apart from the references in this chapter you may find it interesting and useful to consult one or more of the following:

Chagnon, N. (1988) Life histories, blood revenge, and warfare in a tribal population. *Science*, 239: 985–992.

Keeley, L.H. (1996) *War Before Civilization: The Myth of the Peaceful Savage*. New York, NY: Oxford University Press.

Thornhill, R. and Palmer, C.T. (2000) *A Natural History of Rape: Biological Bases of Sexual Coercion*. Cambridge, MA: Massachusetts Institute of Technology Press.

Wilson, E.O. (1978) *On Human Nature*. Cambridge, MA: Harvard University Press – see Chapter 5 'Aggression'.

Wrangham, R. and Peterson, D. (1996) *Demonic Males: Apes and the Origins of Human Violence*. London: Houghton Mifflin.

9 EVOLUTION AND LANGUAGE

Some of the questions addressed in this chapter:

- What is language?
- Is human language a unique form of communication in the animal world?
- Is language an evolved adaptation?
- When did language evolve?
- What is the function of language?
- Should we anticipate sex differences in the use of language?

SOME KEY TERMS AND CONCEPTS

Broca's aphasia; **Cognitive niche**; Gossip hypothesis; Language competence and language performance; Mating mind hypothesis; Poverty of the stimulus; Universal grammar; Wernicke's aphasia.

LEARNING OBJECTIVES

Having studied this chapter you should be better able to:

- Outline the characteristics of language.
- Evaluate arguments which claim that language is an adaptation.
- Outline different hypotheses as to why it may have evolved.

INTRODUCTION

Human beings are different from all other species. This much is obvious, and true by taxonomic definition. What is not obvious and true by definition is whether the difference is trivial or of fundamental importance to psychology and the social sciences: should we emphasise our continuity with other species or focus on those phenomenon which suggest discontinuity? As has been pointed out, the issue of continuity vs. discontinuity between humans and other species has often focused on the phenomenon of communication and language (Corballis and Lea, 1999a). On the one hand, we might insist that language as it is exhibited by humans is unique to humans and that we cannot trace its **phylogeny** through other species. On the other hand, we might go with the suggestion that the phylogeny of human language can be discerned in either what certain species do naturally or in what they can be taught to do. The position adopted by most evolutionary psychologists is that language as exhibited by humans is only exhibited by humans but that it is an adaptation and as such has been selected.

The status of language as a uniquely human phenomenon is important to those who favour an evolutionary approach. As our 'crowning glory' and something so characteristic of modern humans, if language cannot be accounted for in evolutionary terms then the wider enterprise is jeopardised. However, if language can be accommodated in adaptationist terms – especially if this can be achieved without a dependency on comparative evidence and the concomitant critique of **anthropomorphism** – then the enterprise is strengthened.

This chapter's discussion of language and evolution will begin with a consideration of what is meant by the term 'language'. It will then work through some of the reasons that warrant the conclusion that language has been selected for; in particular, we examine the claim that language is an innate ability underpinned by specific parts of the brain. Working on the assumption that it is an evolved adaptation, we will then consider some of the theories that have been proposed in order to explain when and why it came about.

WHAT IS LANGUAGE?

Language is a form of communication. But not all forms of communication are language. Most animals communicate with con-specifics via sound and through gesture – think of the growl of a dog, the posture of a frightened cat. It has been proposed that the critical difference between language proper and communication more generally is that the language exhibits 'contextual freedom' and communication comprises 'fixed signals' (Oller and Griebel, 2005).

To illustrate the distinction between 'contextual freedom' and 'fixed signals' we can consider one of the many interesting attempts to teach great apes to speak – the case of the chimpanzee 'Nim Chimpsky'. Nim was raised under the tutelage of Herbert Terrace at Columbia University from the mid-1970s until Nim died at the age of 26 in 2000. 'Project Nim' was an attempt to teach a chimpanzee language. It ended when Terrace and his co-workers came to the conclusion that although Nim had learned to use many three- and four-word combinations that made sense (e.g. 'apple me eat' and 'tickle me Nim play'), he had not and it was deemed to be unlikely that he would exhibit anything nearly so sophisticated as human language. In Oller and Griebel's terms, his ability to sound and sign communications were 'fixed signals' because they were restricted to expressions that he had learned and which mapped onto immediate needs or wants. Amongst other things, in order for Nim to have exhibited 'contextual freedom' he would have needed to be able to express ideas detached from present needs or wants, and use sounds or signals in the absence of the objects referred to (Oller and Griebel, 2005).

The contextual freedom exhibited by human language is made possible because language is a rule-governed system which combines sounds into words and words into sentences which allow us to represent our thoughts, feelings and ideas. That is, we use rules of grammar to combine sounds into (potentially indefinitely long) sequences which depict actual or supposed states of affairs. Another way of defining language is to say that it comprises sounds that are uttered according to the precepts of a grammar in order for them to have meaning. Importantly, a limited number of basic sounds known as phonemes can be ordered by rules known as syntax in order to represent anything actual or imagined. What this system allows for is an ability to communicate about physical entities, sequences of physical events and arrangements of physical entities. It allows for communication about other people, sequences of social and mental events, social arrangements and scenarios. Additionally, all of the possibilities can be talked about in past, present or future tenses (Pinker, 2003).

There is, of course, very much more that could be said in a definition of language. Indeed, the more said the more it is apparent that as impressive as, say, whale-song, birdsong, the waggle-dance of bees and the alarm calls that various monkeys issue to one another may be, set against the representational range of human speech they are impoverished and do not withstand comparison to it.

BOX 9.1 WHAT IS LANGUAGE 'MADE' OF?

By convention, linguists break language up into components, each of which forms an area of interest and study.

Phonemes
Phonemes are the sounds that comprise a language. There are about 40 such sounds in English with more or less in other languages. Examples of phonemes in English include the 'b' sound, 'ugh', 'k', 'f', and so on.

Morphemes
Morphemes are blocks of phonemes that comprise words. For example, the word cat is comprised of 'ca' and 't'.

Syntax
Syntax refers to the rules that govern admissible strings of morphemes. You will have come across syntax as grammar wherein the right and proper order of words is stipulated.

Semantics
Semantics is the study of what words refer to and what sentences mean. The study of meaning is much more open and philosophical because of how we can be creative with combinations of phonemes, into morphemes and morphemes into admissible strings.

Pragmatics
Pragmatics refers to the study of how social and cultural rules and conventions govern what can be said and when and by whom and in what order.

LANGUAGE AS AN ADAPTATION

In Chapter 2 we considered some of the criteria that have been stipulated if we are to say with some confidence that a given behaviour is adaptive, or is the product of an adaptation. As we have seen, it is easy to be rather casual with the term 'psychological adaptation' and it is easier to offer abstract definitions than it is to provide concrete examples. To answer the question 'Is language an adaptation?' in the following sections we will consider if it is innate and if it is modular.

THE INNATENESS OF LANGUAGE

On of the most famous and influential papers in psychology and linguistics is Noam Chomsky's 'A review of B.F. Skinner's "Verbal Behaviour"' (Chomsky, 1959). A standard bearer of behaviorism and proponent of the view that almost all goal-directed, organised behaviour in man and animals is learned, Skinner had argued that humans learn their language entirely from the linguistic environments in which they are reared. Skinner argued that we learn language in much the same way as we learn what works and how to achieve thing through trial and error. According to this view, we come to say something such as 'the cat sat on the mat' because we learn the speech sound that equates to 'cat', 'sat' and 'mat', and we learn the speech sound that equates to the relation 'on'. We then try the sentence 'the cat sat on the mat' and the responses of others confirms that it is correct (or not) as an intelligible statement, observation or comment (Skinner, 1957). Chomsky thought otherwise. His crucial insight is the '**poverty of the stimulus**' argument which claims that the **language performance** exhibited by children cannot be explained in a trial and error manner because children show an ability to understand and produce sentences which they have never before heard. He suggests that humans share an unlearned or native '**universal grammar**' which enables us to acquire a language or languages as we mature, and that the language environment in which we are reared simply shapes the language or languages that we come to speak (Chomsky, 1986). In short, Skinner and behaviourism holds that language is learned entirely from linguistic environment and depends on no innate knowledge whereas Chomsky and nativism holds that language is acquired during development wherein the linguistic environment provides stimulus for the realisation of innate potential.

The idea of an innate **language acquisition device** governed by the principles of a universal grammar is supported by the species typical sequence we show as we become proficient in using language. The outline of the sequences provided below appears to be robust regardless of the actual language environment into which we are born.

The finding is that although responses are varied we often find that children say that they see 'two wugs' and complete the sentence with the reply 'wugs'. This finding is taken to show that children can create intelligible language and deploy grammatical rules that they could not possibly have learned. (Adapted from Gleason, 1958).

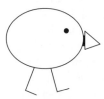

Child participants are shown the image above and told that, 'This is a "wug"'. They are then shown the image below and asked the question, 'What do you see?' or asked to complete a sentence such as, 'Now there are two . . . '

The finding is that although responses are varied we often find that children say that they see 'two wugs' and complete the sentence with the reply 'wugs'. This finding is taken to show that children can create intelligible language and deploy grammatical rules that they could not possibly have learned. (Adapted from Gleason, 1958.)

Figure 9.1   The wug test

BOX 9.2   UNIVERSAL GRAMMAR

Chomsky makes a distinction between language competence and language performance wherein competence = innate knowledge and performance = language use. He argued that nativist linguistics should be concerned with the study of competence. Competence can be studied courtesy of syntax, and Chomsky thinks that the study of the different sorts of syntax exhibited in different languages implies that there is such a thing as a 'universal grammar' because all languages of the world are realisations at the surface level of a universal grammar. How so?

Complete sentences in all natural languages appear to share a common phrase structure. What this means is that all ordinary declarative statements – sentences that make a claim about the world – comprise noun phrases and verb phrases. For example, 'the cat sat' comprises the noun phrase 'the cat' and the verb phrase 'sat'. We add complexity and further information by adding an adjective phrase as in 'the lazy cat sat' wherein the adjective is 'lazy'. We can add further information by adding a second noun phrase as it 'the lazy cat sat on the mat' wherein 'the mat' is the second noun phrase. 'The quick brown fox jumped over the lazy dogs' is a sentence which uses every letter in the English alphabet but it can be readily analysed in term of noun, verb and adjective phrases. While the surface grammar of different languages places the phrases in characteristically difference sequences, the underlying structure remains the same.

We are without any sort of organised speech our first nine months. Up to about six months we communicate but do so only via crying which is a signal of discomfort and smiling which is a signal of pleasure. At about six months we begin to babble. This may include vocalisations with hints of intonation. A typical first word that we recognise is our own name as cued by a tendency to respond to it by the turning of head and eyes towards the source of the utterance. At around nine months we typically enter what is known as the **holophrastic phase** wherein we use single words in an ostensive manner by pointing to objects and naming them. This may be done as a way of issuing an instruction such as 'drink!' or 'look!' Such is our ability to enunciate, perhaps only those most familiar with the child will be able to recognise what is being uttered. Our usage of single words is also characterised by **over-** and **under-extension**. An example of the former would be the application of the term 'daddy' to a number of males, and an example of the latter would be the use of 'cat' for only the family cat. What appears to be happening here is a muddling of names and nouns. In the examples given, 'daddy' is taken as the noun 'man' and 'cat' is taken as a name (Carroll, 2004; Ingram, 1999).

Around the first birthday we understand simple instructions such as 'no', 'hold' and 'sit'. Babbling becomes more complex and exhibits the formation of a wider range of phonemes. The holophrastic stage is soon augmented by **telegraphic speech** wherein we put together nouns and verbs such as 'mummy play' and 'daddy sit'. This stage is open ended in that even as adults we resort to telegraphic speech to convey messages in certain circumstances. Our vocabulary at about 18 months may be as large as 50 words, most of which are nouns and names. Around our second birthday we begin to have some command of prepositions such as 'on', 'under' and 'in' and our vocabulary is expanding weekly. The pronouns 'I', 'me' and 'you' may be used and later so are 'my' and 'mine' (Carroll, 2004; Ingram, 1999).

At three years of age the ability to understand language is far in advance of the ability to produce it. For example, we are typically able to respond to instruction such as 'point to your nose' but are unable to generate or mimic a sentence of that complexity. However, our sentence construction soon reaches that sort of standard. Our use of pronouns such as 'I' and 'you' are consistently correct and we can generate plurals although these may be grammatically incorrect. For example, we may say that 'we goed park' instead of 'we go to the park' or 'we went to the park'. Our vocabulary may now be upwards of 800 words with a richer variety of verbs to complement the noun and name base. A rudimentary understanding of self may be exhibited in the ability to say what our name is, how old we are and if we are a boy or a girl (Carroll, 2004; Ingram, 1999).

At four years of age we are nearing the ability to construct complete sentences that stipulate subjects, nouns and verbs. It is around about now that our ability to understand and generate completely novel sentences, including instructions, commands and questions gives rise to the poverty of the stimulus argument. The suggestion is that the rules of grammar are now understood to the extent that they are used in the comprehension and production of speech (Carroll, 2004; Ingram, 1999).

The size of our vocabulary and our use of grammar continues to mature until, at around the age of eight, we near adult-level competency. Of course, ordinarily, at eight we have a limited set of experiences, and a limited number of interests to talk about and so 'competency' must not be confused with content or theme.

The sequence outlined above appears to be invariant. That is, it is step-wise with each stage seeming to be a necessary pre-condition for its successor. There are individual differences in the timing at which each stage is reached but not a change in order. These considerations invite us to think of language as a maturational process as much as it is a developmental process. In other words, our ability to comprehend and produce language is inevitable provided we are neurologically intact and in a more-or-less normal language environment (Carroll, 2004; Ingram, 1999).

That language acquisition is inevitable and, therefore, innate, is further evidenced by the phenomenon of **pidgins** and **creoles** (Pinker, 2003). Pidgins are rudimentary languages which arise when persons who do not share a common language develop one of their own. Pidgins may be compared to the grammar-impoverished speech we produce as three- and four-year-olds. Creoles are developments of pidgins and do exhibit complex grammar. Children have been observed to generate their own creole in the absence of adult tuition and cultural transmission (Bickerton, 1981). This has been taken to mean that children will spontaneously generate a language (Pinker, 2003).

BOX 9.3 OBJECTIONS TO EVOLUTIONARY PSYCHOLOGY: LEARNING

One consequence of the idea that our thought and behaviour is determined is that we cannot and do not learn wherein 'learn' means acquire information which then influences our thought and behaviour. The rejoinders to the claim that evolutionary psychology is deterministic aside, we might still ask, 'Do evolutionary approaches suggest that we cannot and do not acquire information through experience which then shapes our behaviour?' The answer to this question is no.

On the contrary, the fact that we are a long-lived species, that we have a protracted period of life before we are able to reproduce, and that we need to acclimatise to the fluidity of the physical and social environment all suggest that we must be flexible learners. What evolutionary approaches do argue is that what we can learn is both aided and constrained by our native psychological endowment. For example, we readily acquire language if we are neurologically intact and immersed in a language environment. But it is also apparent that learning to read and write is considerably more difficult. A particular spoken language is relatively easy to learn because we are equipped with specific adaptations which facilitate acquisition. Written language is relatively difficult to learn because we do not have a specific adaptation which facilitates that particular skill.

The learning objection may also be taken to mean 'Do evolutionary approaches argue that we are not flexible, plastic or malleable?' Again, the answer is no. Following Tooby and Cosmides (1992), we might refrain from taking such terms as 'flexible', 'plastic' and 'malleable' seriously if their precise meaning is not specified in the context of psychology. The following explains why. Let us say that plasticine is 'flexible', or 'malleable'. But let us also say that so too is, say, bamboo 'flexible' or 'malleable'. Or that lead is flexible and malleable. A modicum of further thought shows us that while it may be true to say that plasticine, lead and bamboo are flexible and malleable the three substances are not equivalently flexible and malleable. Plasticine is not flexible in the same sense and for the same reasons as is, say, lead, or bamboo. In order to add some precision to the terms 'flexible' and 'malleable' in this context we need to concede that to understanding flexibility of anything we must understand something more fundamental. For example, the flexibility of plasticine is a product of its particular physical properties. The flexibility of lead is a product of its particular but different physical properties. Ditto bamboo. Analogously, the flexibility and malleability of human thought and behaviour is a product of the physical properties of our nervous system and how it is organised. Flexibility in thought and behaviour occurs by virtue of out neurophysiology not in spite of it. And what flexibility we have is as specific to us as it that of a lump of plasticine. We are flexible learners as a result of selection pressures in the past (Tooby and Cosmides, 1992).

THE MODULARITY OF LANGUAGE

You may recall our discussion of **modularity** from Chapter 2 'Evolutionary approaches to thought and behaviour'. To say that something is modular is to say that it is discrete in form, function or both. In biology that which is said to be modular is discrete in that we can pick out the anatomy and physiology of a part of the body and specify its function. This sort of analysis can also be applied to the human brain. For example, it very much appears to be the case that the occipital lobe at the rear of the brain is specialised for vision. In cognitive psychology that which is said to be modular is discrete in that we can pick out a cognitive ability which is specific in its function. For example, it appears to be the case that we have a more-or-less discrete ability to store visual information for short periods of time. In specifying a particular function we are not saying that the modular component is not a necessary part of the whole, but we are saying that it can be treated as discrete for the purpose of analysis. With our understanding of the term modularity refreshed, we can consider the proposal that language is modular.

Clinicians recognise a number of selective cognitive impairments or pathologies wherein persons show an inability to perform certain 'ordinary' tasks but a normal ability to perform others. Selective impairments frequently exhibit **double disassociation**. For example, moving and seeing can be doubly disassociated in that a person could be unable to see courtesy of damage to one part of her brain (the occipital lobe) but able to execute a normal range of bodily movements courtesy of the fact that another part of her brain (the parietal lobe) is intact. And another person could be able to see but unable to execute movements. Sight and movement are said to be double disassociated because impairments to one of those abilities do not directly affect the other. Selective or disassociated patholo-gies suggest neural and cognitive modularity. Speech and language research suggests that we can be competent in other cognitive domains but not in language and competent in language when other cognitive abilities are impaired. Furthermore, our overall language performance appears to fit the criteria of modularity also because damage to brain areas can result in impairment of only particular linguistic abilities.

There seem to be two parts of the human brain that are particularly important for lan-guage and their identification supports the view that language is a modular system. Both were discovered in the nineteenth century. The first to be detailed is known as Broca's area and the second, Wernicke's area. Damage to either of these areas of the brain results in aphasia which is the label used to refer to a loss or impairment in the ability to communi-cate through language.

Broca's aphasia is also known as 'production aphasia' and it refers to a demonstrable inability to speak normally. Those suffering from it – usually because of damage to the inferior left frontal lobe (the part of your brain just rearward of your left temple) – cannot produce fluent speech. Their speech is slow, laboured, hesitant and often produced one syllable at a time. Sentence construction is simple in that it is made up of elementary propositions and said to be 'telegrammatic' in that it hinges on nouns and is devoid of gram-matical construction. **Wernicke's aphasia**, on the other hand, and by contrast, is known as 'comprehension aphasia' and it refers to an inability to understand normal speech. Again those who suffer from it and have been studied usually have damage to the left side of the brain but the damage is to the superior temporal gyrus (the part of your brain just rearward of your left ear). These patients speak fluently and their grammar is sound, but there does appear to be some problem is the usage of nouns. As result of this is that it is not clear what it is they are talking about and their speech is filled with made-up nonsense words and, overall, what is said makes no sense especially in light of what they have been asked to talk about or the question being answered.

Our account of these two interesting and important pathologies is hugely simplified from a clinical point of view. But it is sound enough to go some way towards showing that specific parts of our brains are largely if not entirely devoted to performing particular language tasks – the production and comprehension of speech – and that they may fit the modularity criterion set out by evolutionary psychologists.

PHYLOGENY OF LANGUAGE: WHEN DID IT COME ABOUT?

As we saw when we encountered Tinbergen's '**four whys**' in Chapter 2, there are a different sorts of question that we can ask of any phenomenon that we take to be a product of natural selection, and we can do the same with language. To some extent we have already considered its development (or ontogeny), and we have considered proximate mechanisms that underlie language, i.e. the parts of the brain that produce and comprehend language. That we have done so should give us confidence that Tinbergen's other two 'whys' can be addressed, namely the natural history (or phylogeny) of language and its ultimate adaptive function. In this section we will look at the first of these questions before going on to the latter.

The concession that language proper is exclusive to humans makes the question as to when it came about particularly difficult to address because we cannot discern its natural history via comparative evidence. To illustrate this point let us think back to our previous discussion of human mating systems. In Chapter 6 'Families and parenting' we were able to look to the mating systems exhibited by the great apes, to consider which of them may be our closest living relative, and then to work through the more-or-less plausible alternative mating systems that may best fit humans. Strictly speaking that was not an exercise in comparative psychology but in phylogeny: we were looking to extant apes with a view to seeing which of them may best represent a prior state of our lineage. The point is that such an exercise is difficult to perform with regard to language: because we can draw no comparisons we cannot use other species to construct a phylogeny.

Furthermore, in assuming that language is exclusive to humans we face the problem of intermediate forms: the absence of extant predecessors (in this case one or more of our hominid ancestors) leaves us with no concrete starting point when asking when language came about in our lineage. The problem is compounded by the inherent limits that fossil evidence might offer up when considering language. Fossils may provide some clues as to brain anatomy via endocranial casts and larynx position, but the soft tissues that generate utterances do not fossilise and, of course, neither does sound.

Nevertheless, a variety of theories as to how language evolved have been proposed. Included amongst them are early, intermediate and late theories which, respectively, argue that it appeared with the genus *Homo* c. two million years ago, it appeared with the species *Homo sapien c.* 150,000 years ago and it appeared when we began to produce art *c.* 60,000 years ago. The 'early' theory supposes that the utterances and gesticulations of apes constitute the grounds from which language proper evolved and it did so very gradually (Pinker and Bloom, 1990). The 'intermediate' theory emphasises changes in the central nervous system and the brain that characterise *Homo sapien.* On the one hand, it has been suggested that the unusual degree to which human brains are asymmetric shows that language evolved as (typically) a left-sided modular specialism relatively independently of other cognitive abilities (Corballis, 1991). And on the other, it has been suggested that the unusual degree to which human brains (especially the neo-cortex) have increased in sized shows how language evolved as a more general unifying cognitive ability (Mithen, 1996). The 'late' theory is essentially dismissive of phylogenetic explanation arguing that language is a fortuitous though accidental by-product of increased brain size (Lieberman, 1998). While the late theory may lack credibility in adaptationist terms, it does map its account of the appearance of language to the archeological record which gives us firm evidence of symbolic thought and representation.

With some idea of the variety of views about when language appeared in mind, let us consider one in a little more detail. Picking up on accounts such as that of Corballis (1991) which suggests that the earliest forms of language emerged from elaborations of ape gesticulation and vocalisation, and that of Bickerton (1990) which suggests that a precursor to grammatically structured language is the 'protolanguage' which we see in human two-year-olds and pidgins, Donald's 'mimetic' theory of language evolution proposes that a further precondition for the evolution of language is rehearsal of motor skills (Donald, 1991, 1999). Key to Donald's thesis is the notion of mime, or kinematic imagination, allied to consciously controlled rehearsal. Donald argues that an ability to imagine and practise movements, including gesticulation, is a necessary precursor to the production of fully articulated speech. He supposes that we must stipulate precursor skills if we are to avoid a punctuated account wherein language suddenly appears and with no intermediate forms. Also, the precursor skills would have been functional in their own right. It is claimed that they would have facilitated more elaborate cultural transmission within groups and engendered more complex social dependencies that language proper presupposes. Donald's theory is of a piece with Darwin's account of the evolution of facial expressions of emotional states as a form of communication (Darwin, 1871), it is consistent with the idea that language arises from the ability to develop a theory of mind and it is consistent with theories which suppose that spoken language is an elaboration of gesture. And the model of memory that Donald's idea requires is not obviously inconsistent with contemporary evidence which supports the tripartite division of working memory into a phonological loop, audio-visual sketch pad and a central executive (Baddeley, 2003). With regard to when language came about, Donald's account claims that its root lies in ape gesticulation, it was augmented by mimesis in hominids, protolanguage emerged with *Homo*, and grammar completed the picture with *Homo sapiens.*

Having considered some of the ideas which seek to establish when language emerged let us now move on to a consideration of why it was that language evolved.

THE ADAPTIVE FUNCTION OF LANGUAGE: WHY DID IT COME ABOUT?

In this section we will look at three theories which try to answer the question as to why language came about. First, we will consider the 'survivalist' account – the idea that it came about in order to solve problems related to resource acquisition. Next we will consider the '**gossip hypothesis**' – the idea that it evolved to solve social problems. And lastly we will consider the '**mating mind hypothesis**' – the idea that language is a product of sexual selection. Having looked at each of the ideas we will see that they are not mutually exclusive. Language has a number of adaptive advantages and all three theories have merit.

THE SURVIVALIST ACCOUNT

As we saw in Chapter 3 'The natural history of humans', evolutionary psychology places considerable emphasis on using hunter-gatherer peoples as a model for humanity in the past. This approach is, perhaps, bound to encourage the thought that the form of subsistence was the driving force behind the evolution of language. The core of the idea is that a shift from a scavenger-gather mode of subsistence to a hunter-gather mode was both facilitated by and facilitated the evolution of language (Tooby and Devore, 1987). The intuitive appeal of the survivalist account of language evolution may be easier to appreciate when we look at some of the component abilities that underpin hunter-gathering.

First, there is the need for cooperation between and within groups. The between group cooperation exists between those who hunt and those who gather. The within group cooperation exists within the two groups. The hunting and trapping of animals by a group requires complex communication with regard to division of labour and roles. It also requires some sort of theory of the prey's behaviour or mind, where the prey might be, and when. And it requires the communication of updates to the agreed plan if the hunt is protracted. Furthermore, if hunting involves tool use this too implies a sharing of information as to tool manufacture. Still, as appealing as the survivalist account is it can be questioned.

First, a variety of large carnivorous mammals demonstrate the hunting can be successful in packs without language. Groups of chimpanzees have been observed trapping smaller primates without it. Another characteristic of successful trapping is that the final stages of the hunt are performed in silence. Second, contemporary pedagogy suggests that skill acquisition is easier when the tutelage is via practical demonstration than it is via verbal instruction: we learn to do by doing rather than by description. It is reasonable to assume that this would have held for tool manufacture and the act of trapping and butchering prey. However, even if we accept these criticisms of the survivalist account, we are still left with the opportunities and problems that hunter-gathering offers and poses in terms of social organisation. The act of hunting may not have required speech but its arrangements may have. This leads us to Dunbar's gossip hypothesis (1996).

THE GOSSIP HYPOTHESIS

Dunbar has put forward the theory that the function of language is to exchange information about other con-specifics (Dunbar, 1996). Language is presented as an adaptation to the need to know about the biography, personality and intentions of others – thus the epithet 'the gossip hypothesis'. It is important to be mindful of the connotations that the term 'gossip' may have. We may be inclined to suppose that it signifies something rather trivial and therefore unimportant and to allow such thoughts to colour our view of Dunbar's idea. This would be an error, for the gossip hypothesis is well constructed and attested. Let us look at it in more detail.

Most primates live in groups (a notable exception being the orangutan) and the benefits of doing so include protection from predation and varied reproductive opportunities. A characteristic of primate social behaviour is 'grooming'. This involves protracted one-to-one interactions wherein individuals remove parasites from one another's bodies. In large primate groups, such as chimpanzees, grooming cliques are formed. What this means is that individuals selectively groom others and vice versa. Dunbar argues that grooming cliques form coalitions of individuals which amount to in-groups within the larger group. If we allow ourselves to anthropomorphise for a moment, we may say that grooming facilitates reciprocation, trust and loyalty between members of the coalition. The proximate mechanism which provides positive reinforcement for grooming is elevated opiate levels which trigger the phenomenological experience of pleasure.

In principle, grooming cliques cannot be too large in the sense that one cannot have too many allies. However, grooming is time-costly. To survive and reproduce there are other problems to solve, and one-to-one grooming imposes a constraint on the size of any given coalition. For example, baboons and chimpanzees live in groups of about 50 individuals. While grooming has benefits, Dunbar suggests that to spend more than about 20 per cent of waking time grooming would begin to compromise an individual's ability to solve other adaptive problems.

BOX 9.4 THE MAGIC NUMBER 150

Neocortex ratio refers to the ratio between the size of the neocortex, or the frontal lobes and the rest of the brain. Located above the eyes and immediately behind the forehead, the neocortex is that part of the brain which is unusually large in primates, great apes and humans in comparison to other mammals. For any given primate species, the neocortex ratio can be plotted against the group size that we see a species form. The neocortex ratio for humans is approximately 4:1 and it predicts a group size of approximately 150. This prediction wins support from a range of observations about the size spontaneous or natural human groups:

- Modern hunter-gatherer societies often comprise variable groupings, temporary bonds. Consistent groupings, 'clans' average almost exactly 150.
- The villages of modern horticulturists in Indonesia, the Philippines and South America typically number 150 individuals.
- The Hutterites (a people who have pursued a fundamentalist Christian way of life) have communes of just over 100 because as soon as they exceed 150 they divide in two.
- After years of 'evolution' in military strategy, during the Second World War, the average size for a company (the smallest functioning unit) comprised 170 members.
- 'Small world' research suggests that adults have access to knowledge about 130 persons through actual interpersonal relations.

There is evidence to suggest that 'natural' cohesive human groups comprise about 150 individuals (Dunbar, 1996). Were it the case that physical grooming was our basic social glue the time devoted to it would need to be near 50 per cent of our waking time. Physical contact is, of course, common amongst humans, especially between adults and their infants and romantic partners. But it is atypical to find persons in physical contact with others for four, five or six hours per day. What is common is to find that people are in verbal contact with others about 20 per cent of the time. The inference is that *Homo* has solved the grooming problem by using gossip as a form of grooming.

To add weight to the argument we can specify a number of advantages that gossip has over physical grooming. One, gossip it is not inherently dyadic and it can be done in a group. This allows any given individual to groom two, three, four, five or even more others at once. It has been suggested that spontaneous conversational groups typically number three or four members (Henzi et al., 2007). When they become larger than that they tend to split into two. This observation maps neatly onto the fact that a gossip group of 1:3/4 is about three times as efficient at a grooming group of 1:1 and that human groups are about three times the size of chimpanzees. Two, the object–subject relations facility of language permits much richer information exchange about both present and absent members of the group as well as recollection of past information and speculation about future behaviour. Seen as a form of reciprocation, information exchange in groups permits reciprocal obligations to be met *en masse*, and it allows for relatively risk-free assessment as to the likely fecundity of reciprocal alliances as well as exchange of information about possible cheats. In support of the hypothesis, Dunbar has shown that gossip – exchange of socially relevant information about others – is the single most common use of language amongst humans (Dunbar et al., 1997).

The gossip hypothesis is not without its problems – for example, it is not obvious that gossip and physical grooming are equivalent activities – and an alterative view about the social nature of the selection pressures behind the evolution of language has been proposed. It is to an alternative that we now turn.

BOX 9.5   THE FUNCTIONS OF MALE VOICE PITCH

In accord with Miller's mating mind hypothesis and the claim that language can be used as a form of display and an indicator of intelligence (Miller, 2000), Rosenberg and Tunney (2008) found that men, but not women, 'used more low frequency words after an imaginary romantic encounter with a young female shown in a photograph relative to when they viewed photographs of older females' (2008: 538). It may be the case that the size and range of a person vocabulary is at least in part determined by biology. But it is also the case that vocabulary can be learned and it may not be a honest signal of underlying heritable traits.

Another line of research concerning the fitness implications of language has focused on male voice pitch and the results invite us to consider at least two possible functions that it has.

It has been established that there is a relationship between higher testosterone levels and low voice pitch (what amounts to what we ordinarily call a 'deep voice') in males but not females (Dabbs and Mallinger, 1999). Why? Well, 'One explanation is physiological, in which testosterone changes the bulk, length, or tension of the vocal folds. The other is psychological, in which testosterone affects the vocal style that an individual uses as part of a social interaction strategy' (ibid.,: 801). What needs to be noted here is that the social interactions that are correlated with elevated testosterone include assertiveness, aggression, and dominance (ibid.).

The apparent relationship between voice pitch and social dominance led Puts et al. (2006) to hypothesise that 'male intrasexual competition was a salient selection pressure on the voices of ancestral males and contributed to human voice sexual dimorphism' (ibid.,: 283). To support this claim these researchers looked the relationship between how voice pitch influenced the judgements of male listeners and self reports of sexual behaviour. The experiment involved the manipulation of males voices whereupon pitch was lower or made higher. The voices where then rated by participants. The findings suggest that low-pitched voices indicate physical dominance and, to a lesser extent, social dominance, and that men manipulate pitch according to the situation: they lower it if they take themselves to be dominate over the interlocutor and do the opposite if they take themselves to be subservient. So far as the male intersexual competition hypothesis is concerned the key finding was that pitch did not predict more mating success.

Further research has also provided support for the male intersexual competition hypothesis. Puts et al. (2007) found that when pulled apart by manipulation both the fundamental frequency of male voices – i.e. pitch – and format frequency – i.e. timbre – influenced how dominant the speaker was perceived to be: 'Recordings lowered in either F_0 [pitch] or D_f [timbre] were perceived as being produced by more dominant men than were the respective raised recordings. D_f had a greater effect than did F_0, and both D_f and F_0 tended to affect physical dominance more than social dominance, although this difference was significant only for D_f' (Puts et al., 2007: 340).

However, there is also some evidence that male voice pitch influences how attractive a male is to women and that it may has a intersexual function. Also focusing on fundamental frequency, and working on the hypothesis that female choice for high quality males is mediated by voice pitch, Puts et al. (2005) found 'that low VP is preferred mainly in short-term mating contexts rather than in long-term, committed ones, and this mating context effect is greatest when women are in the fertile phase of their ovulatory cycles' (ibid.,: 388). Puts et al. also found that males with lower pitch did report having more sexual partners.

As is so often the case, there is probably merit in both positions. If voice pitch is effected by higher testosterone, and testosterone promotes an assertive behavioural style which often enough leads to dominance we can think of it as a intrasexual phenomenon. However, we also have some evidence which suggests that females are attracted to socially dominant males (see Chapter 7 'Mate selection') which means that we can also think of voice pitch as an intersexual phenomenon.

THE MATING-MIND HYPOTHESIS

Of the time spent on social topics in single-sex conversation groups, approximately two-thirds is spent discussing social issues surrounding the behaviour of non-members and about one-third concerning members' behaviour. In addition to the evidence which suggest that we are natural-born gossips, a sex difference has been reported wherein males devote 63.1 per cent of conversation time to social topics whereas females devote 69.8 per cent (Dunbar et al., 1997). Also, when mixed-sex conversation groups are considered there may be a significant difference in what it is that males and females offer as topics for discussion. It has been found that in mixed groups males spend more time on abstract or intellectual topics such as art, literature, science and politics (Dunbar et al., 1997). These differences provide us with a way into a consideration of Miller's mating-mind hypothesis of language evolution. In short, Miller suggests that the evolution of language has been driven by the need for males to advertise themselves to females and for both sexes to reveal and explore one another's biographies before committing to a pair-bond (Miller, 2000).

Miller employs sexual selection to account for the evolution of language. He argues that it is the best thought through and attested mechanism that can bring about speedy and dramatic evolutionary change. He argues that the sex differences that have been observed may be explained if we assume that social information is of greater importance to females, and males use conversation to compete with other males and to attract females. On the one hand, being the choosier sex, females can use mixed-sex conversation groups to gather information about males, and, on the other hand, mixed-sex conversation groups offer males an opportunity to advertise themselves to females.

The suggestion is that the gossip hypothesis describes a form of reciprocal altruism. Gossip facilitates the exchange of valuable information about others in the group. Miller reckons that seen as a form of exchange the gossip hypothesis fails to fully account for the nature of our language. For example, Chapter 5 'Cooperation and interdependence' surveyed some of the arguments and evidence which underpins the claim that we should expect humans to be social and cooperative. But we also saw that the for-best-results strategy was a somewhat conservative 'tit-for-tat' approach which gives and takes in a measured and proportional manner. If language is a form of reciprocal altruism we might expect that we would obey the old dictum 'two ears and one month – use them in proportion'. That is, we should be inclined to be listeners more than we are talkers. But our anatomy suggests otherwise. Our auditory systems are not dissimilar to the great apes, and as a proportion of our cortex that devoted to audition is only about 10–20 per cent larger than would be predicted in comparison with other primates. In terms of our anatomy, it is that which is specialised for speech which marks us out. Not only is it the case that this apparatus must have been selected for and carries some metabolic cost, it also carries a very direct fitness cost – because of the way in which our larynx is organised we are the only species that can choke.

Citing the work of Ogden and Richards (Ogden, 1940), who claim that English needs to be comprised of more than 850 words, Miller points out that natural languages have far greater vocabularies than necessary. The implication is that language is, in essence, ornamental.

Our verbosity is akin to plumage. But unlike the plumage of the peacock or bird of paradise, the excesses of language indicate intelligence rather than physical fitness. Miller suggests elaborate linguistic performances in the form of rich vocabularies leads to higher social status and that social status leads to increased mate value.

Of course, females must necessarily be at least equal in linguistic competence to judge the verbal display of males. The key sex difference is that male performance exceeds that of females. The claim is that males are more likely to perform linguistically in public and to use opportunities to speak about themselves – in mixed-sex conversation groups males devote two-thirds of social conversation to issues concerning themselves. And they use the opportunity to demonstrate worldly knowledge. In single-sex conversation groups, males devote about 5 per cent of conversation time to subjects like art, literature and politics, whereas in mixed-sex conversation it rises to about 15–20 per cent.

As previously intimated, each of the preceding accounts of language evolution could be correct. More than one selection pressure can be responsible for any given trait or ability. It may be that the ability to send an receive information verbally began as an adjunct to hunting, that it developed as a form of reciprocal altruism through the exchange of socially relevant information and that as an exhibition of intelligence it was favoured by sexual selection. Selection pressures can operate consecutively and simultaneously.

SUMMARY OF CHAPTER 9

The one common and obvious ability that distinguishes humans from other species and from other primates is language. This presents a problem for evolutionary psychology in that language is difficult to study via comparison. Whereas we may be able to look at, say, human parental investment and draw comparisons with other species in order to illuminate the phenomenon and consider its phylogeny, it is very much more difficult to do this with language. Nevertheless, the very universality of language encourages us to consider it from an evolutionary point of view. It appears to have a distinct biological basis as evidenced the anatomy of our brain and vocal tract. And it appears to be innate as evidenced by the manner in which it matures and develops in infants and children. The problem facing us when we consider when language may have some about may be intractable because the soft tissues that generate it and the phenomenon itself does not fossilise. Perhaps the safest assumption is that it came about relatively recently in *Homo* evolution and is, in the form we see it exhibited today, unique to *Homo sapiens*. As to why it came about there are a number of plausible and mutually consistent accounts. It may have evolved as an adjunct to hunting and gathering. It may have evolved because of the need to share information about one another. It may have evolved as a form of epigamic display. Or it have evolved for all three reasons. Language is so useful and flexible that it is hard to see how it would ever pay *not* to be able to communicate information and ideas about the past, present and future.

FURTHER READING

Apart from the references in this chapter you may find it interesting and useful to consult one or more of the following:

Aitchison, J. (2007) *The Articulate Mammal: An Introduction to Psycholinguistics* (5th edn). London: Routledge.

Corballis, M. (2002) *From Hand to Mouth: The Origins of Language.* Cambridge, MA: Princeton University Press.

Jackendoff, R. (2002) *Foundations of Language: Brain, Meaning, Grammar, Evolution.* Oxford: Oxford University Press.

Kenneally, C. (2007) *The First Word: The Search for the Origins of Language.* New York, NY: Viking.

McManus, C. (1999) Handedness, cerebral lateralization, and the evolution of language. In Corballis, M.C. and Lea, S.E.G. (eds) *The Descent of Mind: Psychological Perspectives on Hominid Evolution.* New York, NY: Oxford University Press.

Pinker, S. (1994) *The Language Instinct.* New York, NY: HarperCollins.

10 EVOLUTION AND ABNORMAL PSYCHOLOGY

Some of the questions addressed in this chapter:

- Why can't we use evolutionary theory to make precise predictions about our behaviour?
- How can patterns of thought and behaviours that negatively impact on adaptive functioning be accommodated within an evolutionary framework?
- What does it mean to say that certain psychopathologies and disorders are 'natural'?
- What is 'domain mismatch' and how does it anticipate maladaptive beheviour?
- What is 'scruffy engineering' and how does it anticipate individual differences in mental health?
- Is modern life driving us mad?

SOME KEY TERMS AND CONCEPTS

Actual and proper domain; Anorexia nervosa; Anxiety; Autism; Domain mismatch; Frequency dependent selection and strategies; Psychopathy; Sociopathy; Theory of mind.

LEARNING OBJECTIVES

Having studied this chapter you should be better able to:

- Describe some of the different ways that the evolutionary process generates individual differences.
- Outline the tenets of 'evolutionary psychiatry' and some of the ways that it seeks to explain abnormal mind-sets and behaviour.
- Offer and evaluate a evolutionary explanations of some common psychiatric conditions.

INTRODUCTION

Evolutionary psychology claims that our minds are comprised of adaptations which have been winnowed, shifted and shaped by natural and sexual selection such that we can successfully function in the world. Our minds have been designed by the forces of evolution to make us good at solving the problems our species need to solve. If this is true, we may ask how evolutionary psychologists accommodate the fact that many of us go through more-or-less protracted periods wherein we think and behave in a **maladaptive** manner? How can patterns of thought and subsequent behaviours that negatively impact on adaptive functioning, but are also sufficiently common to be amenable to (more-or-less precise) classification, be accommodated within an evolutionary framework? To put it another way, how can the adaptationist viewpoint explain maladaptive behaviour? Answering these questions is the aim of this chapter.

We will begin with a consideration of the ways in which evolutionary approaches to thought and behaviour accommodate individual differences. We will see that an analysis of individual differences is the key to explaining many maladative and abnormal behaviours. We will also see that an implication of the fact that individuals differ – that some people will behave in ways taken to be unusual or odd – is that it is not possible to predict how individuals think and behave with absolute precision. Following that, we will look at **evolutionary psychiatry** (Nesse, 1994, 2005; Troisi, 2008) and consider some of the different ways it conceptualises and types abnormal behaviours and psychiatric conditions. To illustrate how evolutionary psychiatry might work we will look at a series of examples of how it explains mental illnesses such as **anxiety disorder**, **anorexia nervosa**, **autism** and **psychopathy**.

Before we begin it needs to be noted that this chapter does not seek to emulate a clinical text or provide a detailed description or aetiology of psychiatric conditions. The central aim of this chapter is to introduce ways of thinking about maladative behaviour and abnormal psychology that are derived from the insights provided by evolutionary theory.

INDIVIDUAL DIFFERENCES AND THE IMPRECISION OF PREDICTIONS

As you may have noticed, predictions derived from evolutionary theory are typically tempered, either explicitly or implicitly, by recourse to the caveat 'all things being equal'. For example, in Chapter 6 'Families and parenting' we saw that should inclusive fitness theory be seen as a theory of nepotism, then, all things being equal, we should expect to see heightened positive regard and preferential treatment given to and by individuals who are (or are under the impression that they are) biologically related. In other words, we expect most family members to treat one another favourably most of the time. Similarly, should we have confidence in the claim that humans are serial monogamists – a claim we also examined in Chapter 6 – then, all things being equal, we will predict that individuals will engage in two or more (more-or-less) sexually exclusive pair-bonds over the life course. Again, in other words, we would expect it to be common to for people to have more than one deep and meaningful romantic relationship. The 'all things being equal' clause enables us to acknowledge and accommodate individual differences in thought and behaviour which appear to be exceptions to our rules and predictions. As we are using the term here 'all things being equal' can be taken to mean 'most people, most of the time, but not all people at all times' because not all people respond in the same way in all circumstances.

However, while recourse to the caveat 'all things being equal' enables us to accommodate the fact that people vary, doing so also weakens our theories of human psychology and behaviour because the hypotheses we derive from them are always probabilistic. What this means is that in saying that 'x will occur all thing being equal' we are saying that 'it is *likely* that x will occur'. Such an approach is vulnerable to the accusation that it builds in a get-out clause for any given case that does not fit the prediction. To counter the accusation that we are trying to explain away cases that fail to conform to theory we need to explicate the nature of the 'all things being equal' qualification and show how it is given licence by and is consistent with evolutionary theory. In actuality, there are at least three interrelated reasons why we ought to temper our predictions and expect to find variations from a supposed norm.

The first reason why individual differences in thought and behaviour will inevitably arise is due to variations of form in genotypes that come about through **sexual recombination** and mutation. The second is that we can expect the behaviour of individuals (and groups) to exhibit variations from a theoretical template derived from depictions of past selection pressures due to **domain mismatches** between the environments which selected for adaptations and the environments in which those adaptations now operate. And the third reason is derived from game theory which suggests that any population of humans will be comprised of a variety of different **frequency dependent strategies** of behaviour. Let us look at each of these reasons why we should expect to see individual differences in more detail.

VARIATIONS OF FORM

As we saw in Chapter 1 'Darwin's argument and three problems', the engine of evolutionary change is variation of form and function. Because we can anticipate that sexual reproduction will produce individuals that vary both from their progenitors and their peers our predictions about how people in general will think and behave are inherently probabilistic rather than strictly deterministic. What this means is that while we can suppose that a 'typical' person will think and/or act in a certain way in certain circumstances it is only ever going to be more-or-less likely that an actual person thinks and/or behaves that way because there is no 'typical' person in actuality. For any given morphological characteristic, behaviour pattern or psychological trait said to be typical of a species we will have a picture, or description, of what we mean by typical, but we also work on the assumption that in any given individual the characteristic, pattern or trait will be a variation of the species typical form. Accordingly, while we expect any random member of a species to exhibit a characteristic, behaviour pattern or trait we can also expect individual differences in the actual exhibition of the characteristic, behaviour pattern or trait.

BOX10.1 VARIATION OF FORM AND PREDICTIONS OF BEHAVIOUR

TRY IT THIS WAY . . .

I am fond of spaghetti carbonara. In saying this I am saying that there is a particular sort of identifiable dish that I like eating. But I have never had any two plates of carbonara that are the same – not *exactly* the same. While almost all recipes for the dish include pancetta (or some sort of bacon), egg, garlic, parmesan (or some sort of hard cheese), olive oil and black pepper, they vary from cook to cook, chef to chef. Also, of course, you can't eat two plates of food that contain *exactly* the same ingredients. So, carbonara is a particular type of dish but no two examples are the same. Accordingly, if I had to predict that I will or will not enjoy the next carbonara that I eat I can only say for sure that I will *probably* enjoy it.

DOMAIN MISMATCHES

The term 'domain mismatch' was introduced by Sperber (1994) and is used to accommodate atypical and fitness-reducing behaviours within an evolutionary framework. Domain mismatch refers to any differences between the physical and social niche(s) that modern humans evolved in and are adapted to – the '**natural domain**' or, simply, the past – and the physical and social niche(s) we now occupy – the '**actual domain**' or, simply, the present. As we saw in Chapter 3 'The natural history of humans', the EEA is said to have been our natural domain but our past is not so easy to characterised as we might wish. Still, we have also seen that we know enough about it to be able to stipulate with some confidence some mismatches between the natural and actual domains, between the past and the present. For example, liberal estimates for the advent of agriculture are that it is 20,000 years old (and, of course, it is yet to be adopted by a number of extant cultures). Accordingly, agriculture is 'new' in terms of natural history and, it follows, so are concomitants of agriculatural economies such as trans-generational wealth and land ownership. Anything that is pervasive now and at the same time novel in terms of our natural history presents us with the possibility of a mismatch between the past and the present.

For current purposes, the importance of domain mismatches comes in the problem they create when we try to predict thought and behaviour. Because evolutionary psychology uses models of the past to explain the presence and operation of psychological adaptations, mismatches between the past and present may confound those predictions. Indeed, as we will see in due course, novel environments may invoke novel behaviours some of which vary so far from what is typical that they are considered abnormal.

BOX 10.2 DOMAIN MISMATCHES AND PREDICTIONS OF BEHAVIOUR

TRY IT THIS WAY …

Whenever I consider buying a car I check out the estimated fuel consumption. Manufacturers are obliged to provide figures which offer an average in urban and motorway conditions and a mixture of the two in order to give us, the consumer, as good an estimate of the cars performance as possible. However, I find that the numbers never quite work out in practice. The reason for this is due to the fact that the conditions under which a vehicle is tested for fuel consumption are not repeated when it is in use. Manufacturers use test tracks and rolling roads. I have access to neither of these and neither would take me to work, the supermarket or the beach. I drive in a range of weather conditions and temperatures, with one, two, three or four people in the car with or without baggage or goods. Sometimes I am in a hurry, other times not. Sometimes my windows are open, sometimes closed. I don't check my tyres as often as I should … The point is that while the car I drive is of the same design as that tested by the maker the conditions in which it operates are not and so the manner in which it behaves is both different and, to a certain extent, unpredictable. And the same holds true for other cars of the same design. The mismatch between the two sets of conditions acts to confound precise predictions.

FREQUENCY DEPENDENT STRATEGIES

The concept of frequency dependent strategies gives us a third reason to invoke the 'all things being equal' caveat when making predictions about thought and behaviour. Recall that in Chapter 5 'Cooperation and interdependence' we looked at **evolutionary stable strategies**. We saw that within a population of cooperators – reciprocating individuals who played the cooperative game unless defected against and given reason to withhold their cooperation – a minority of cheaters can exist and flourish. Such a strategy is an example of a frequency dependent strategy. The success and persistence of a cheater strategy towards reciprocal material exchange is dependent upon it being relatively rare. Indeed, we could look at a cooperative strategy as frequency dependent too, only with cooperation it depends on the strategy being common. The game theory approach shows us that it is theoretically plausible to assume that different humans can deploy different strategies in the pursuit of reproductive success. So, again, while our accounts of kin and reciprocal altruism licenses the supposition that most people will offer and repay favours most of the time the existence and persistence of different 'takes' on the rules of reciprocation means that we cannot be certain that all people will repay favours all of the time.

BOX 10.3 FREQUENCY-DEPENDENT STRATEGIES AND PREDICTIONS OF BEHAVIOUR

TRY IT THIS WAY …

How do you get yourself noticed in a crowd? Do different! Any crowd of people can be said to be a crowd (as opposed to a completely accidental and random conglomeration of people) by virtue of some or another characteristic behaviour, motive for being in the same place at the same time, tastes and/or attire. For example, let us say that at a sporting event the persons present are bound into being a crowd by virtue of them observing the play. The common behaviour renders the group a crowd and in doing so renders the individuals that comprise the crowd anonymous. In such a circumstance doing different and standing out might be achieved by *not* watching the game. As a strategy for getting noticed in this instance, in this crowd of watchers not watching the game works only if you are the only one adopting it. As the strategy catches on it works less and less well. So it is with certain behaviours in evolution. They work just because they are unusual and will cease to work when they are usual. Accordingly, while we can make predictions about how people will behave in certain circumstances because the behaviour works, such predictions can be undone by different sorts of behaviours that also work just because they exploit what is typical.

With these ways of accommodating difference from the norm in mind we can now move on to look at a number of ideas which may allow us to accommodate abnormal behaviours within an evolutionary framework.

EVOLUTIONARY PSYCHIATRY

The notion of abnormality depends upon a depiction of what is normal. One only knows that something is other-than-normal if one knows what normal is, or what 'normal' means, in a given context for a given phenomenon. Accordingly, one of the tasks of psychology is to furnish psychiatry with a description of 'normal' or ordinary psychological functioning in order to set the parameters of what constitutes 'abnormal' psychological functioning (Andershed et al., 2002). As a part of this project it is argued that evolutionary psychology can furnish psychiatry/clinical psychology with a normative account of mental functions and their distribution in populations (Abed, 2000; Dubrovsky, 2002: McGuire and Troisi, 1998). Thus:

> The greatest contribution an evolutionary perspective can offer to psychiatry is to show how the functions of psychological traits can be scientifically studied, and thus to begin to provide, for psychiatry, what physiology provides for the rest of medicine ... The physiologist demarcates the respiratory, circulatory, and immune systems, not by their anatomy but by their functions. The surgeon knows the functions of the gallbladder, and therefore the consequences of removing it.... The psychiatrist has, however, no comparable body of knowledge. The psychiatrist does not know the normal functions of the systems disrupted by mental disorders ... For example, when a patient presents with depression, the psychiatrist does not know the normal functions of the capacity for mood and therefore has difficulty in distinguishing between normal and pathological sadness. (Nesse, 1991: 24)

With this rationale in mind we can use evolutionary theory to generate different ways of thinking about and classifying psychological disorders into one of four types. These types can be called 'distributed abnormalities', 'mismatch abnormalities', 'ontogenetic abnormalities' and 'frequency dependent abnormalities'. Let us look at each of these ways of classifying disorders in more detail.

DISTRIBUTED ABNORMALITIES

In theory, **distributed abnormalities** refer to states of mind and behaviours that are under- or over-amplified manifestations of normal or ordinary expressions of adaptive states. The validity of this idea is derived from the observation that all evolved adaptations vary both in biological form and function, in genotype and phenotype. For all things that we can identify and measure we expect them to vary around a typical characterisation. In other words, we expect individual instances of the phenomenon of interest to be distributed around a mean. The example to which we will pay most attention is anxiety. On the assumption that we can accept that humans are naturally or inherently fearful of certain phenomenon, and on the assumption that the extent and expression of the fear varies from individual to individual, then we may conclude that some individual's propensity to exhibit fear is 'abnormal' wherein 'abnormal' means fitness reducing against an established or theoretical norm.

MISMATCH ABNORMALITIES

Mismatch abnormalities refer to thoughts and/or behaviours that are, or would have been, adaptive and functional in the proper environment – that is, the environment to which the thoughts or behaviour was originally selected for – but abnormal (wherein abnormal means fitness reducing) in certain new or novel environments. The validity of this idea is derived from the claim that we are designed to function in a certain type or set of environments and not others. For example, it is apparent that we are not adapted to submarine environments. However, it is also apparent that we can operate and reproduce in a range of environments other than that depicted by the EEA. Mismatch abnormalities are said to arise when the differences between the proper domain and the actual domain are not catastrophic in terms of survival but they do detrimentally impinge on certain functions. In due course we will analyse anorexia nervosa as a mismatch abnormality.

ONTOGENETIC ABNORMALITIES

Ontogenetic abnormalities refer to states of mind and behaviours that are the result of problems during the development and maturation of the some or another part of the central nervous system (such problems are sometimes referred to as 'epigenetic failure'). The validity of this idea is derived from the claim that the ontogeny of certain characteristics more-or-less recapitulates phylogeny – that the actual development and maturation of the psychology of extant humans mirrors the development of psychological traits in the species. Any characteristic that is expected to develop but fails to do so courtesy of an epigenetic abnormality would provide an example. To illustrate the concept we will be looking at autism and the proposal that it is a problem with the ordinary development of theory of mind. We will examine the claim that the ability to read the minds of others that humans exhibit is not one shared by those classed as autistic.

FREQUENCY DEPENDENT ABNORMALITIES

Frequency dependent abnormalities may be the result of frequency selection for certain characteristics or social conditions that elicit **marginal strategies**. The validity of this idea is derived from game theory and the observation that different environmental conditions trigger different patterns of ongoing behaviour. The conditions can be very long standing or relatively local. If the conditions are long-standing, more-or-less fixed features of the physical and/or social environment then the behaviour they trigger may be inflexible. If the conditions are local and/or temporary then the behaviours triggered may be changed in response to changes in conditions. Frequency-dependent abnormalities differ somewhat from the others we have considered in that while they appear odd or atypical they can, nevertheless, be fitness enhancing. We will be considering the possibility that **anti-social personality disorder** (or psychopathy, or **sociopathy**) is a frequency-dependent abnormality.

It is now time to piece the ideas we have been discussing together and use them to consider some common abnormal psychological conditions.

ANXIETY DISORDERS

BOX 10.4   WHY WORRY?

Why do we worry about things? Of course, there are real things to worry about – how to get to lectures, deadlines, the health of friends and family we know to be ill, and so on. But why worry about the unforeseen, the improbable, even the imaginary as so many of us appear to do? The affect of undue worry is not pleasant and in that sense has a cost, but what is the benefit? Can you envisage getting through life and achieving things if you quite literally never worried about a thing?

Let us begin by being clear as to what the term 'anxiety' refers to. An orthodox definition of anxiety is one wherein it refers to a vague, unpleasant emotional state characterised by apprehension, dread and unfocused distress. The definition can be sharpened somewhat when compared to definitions of fear and phobia. Fear is a form of anxiety characterised by being identifiably attached to a person, place or circumstance; that is, it is focussed on someone or something. And phobia, the etymology of which is the Greek term for fear, is characterised by the caveat that the fear is persistent and irrational wherein the reasoning offered by the person experiencing the fear is not obviously coherent or appears to be illogical to others.

An evolutionary analysis of anxiety, fears and phobias is enabled in the first instance by the assumption that fear is a more-or-less adaptive response to threatening and/or dangerous stimuli, and acute anxiety and phobic disorders are more-or-less maladaptive responses to objects and situations which are not obviously threatening or dangerous, or are not as threatening or dangerous as they are perceived to be. To help us to see how fear makes sense in evolutionary terms we can think about it in comparison to pain and physical disease and note that many unpleasant physical states are adaptive responses to environmental slights. For example, high body temperature, coughing and vomiting can be normal responses to threats to function that come about through bacterial infection. While unpleasant, each is an adaptive response in certain circumstances. To say that fear, as unpleasant as it is to experience (and to witness), has a function is to say that it is adaptive. In other words, fear makes sense in evolutionary terms just because it is elicited by objects or situations that could be or are detrimental to well-being. In contrast, anxiety, in its ordinary mundane, day-to-day form it may be viewed as a form of worry wherein a concern about a perceived problem or issue is exaggerated and persistent. Acute or disordered anxiety and phobia do not make sense in evolutionary terms just because they do not map onto objects or situations that threaten well being to the extent that the anxiety suggests.

In order to get an evolutionary grip on anxiety disorder, it will help to re-employ error management theory (Green and Swets, 1966). As you may recall, error management theory suggests that when we are faced with a situation or stimuli that might be fitness reducing it is better to err on the side of a false positive than a false negative. What this means is that it is better to interpret something quite harmless as harmful and take action to avoid it than it is to interpret something harmful as harmless and take no action to avoid it. In the first instance we might experience unnecessary psychological discomfort such as fear or acute anxiety and incur an unnecessary metabolic cost in an attempt to avoid or escape the situation. However, in the second instance, we may experience a non-reversible cost to fitness. As popular wisdom has, it is better to be safe than sorry.

If it is the case that we are inclined to interpret events, including the intentions of others, as being threatening, harmful or dangerous before we have experience or evidence to the contrary we might expect to find that humans are prone to anxiety. This may help to explain general or 'background anxiety' – a persistent unfocussed sense of pessimism about the future and scepticism about others (Heimberg et al., 2004).

An evolutionary approach suggests that general or background anxiety has evolved to deal with general uncertainty about the stability of the physical and social environment (Nesse and Williams, 1995). Notice that error management theory is not particularly concerned about the accuracy or validity of the interpretation of events which gives rise to the anxiety. Rather, it claims that the predilection pays for itself in the long run. To accommodate anxiety levels that are so consuming of time and paralysing of action we may only need to show that the general tendency differs from individual to individual and that some individuals exhibit it or experience it to an extent that is fitness reducing.

With regard to phobias, it has been noted that many which are common in the West map onto proposed sources of actual danger that existed during our evolution (Brown, 1991). Common phobias include those that centre on snakes, spiders, heights, darkness, blood, strangers, social scrutiny, separation, leaving home, open spaces, closed spaces and social rejection. The suggestion is that most phobias are exaggerations of the basic anxiety that each of the foregoing produces, and each of them is explicable in evolutionary terms (Marks and Nesse, 1994). For example, snakes and spiders have been a problem for our ancestors and we are motivated to avoid them. And a certain trepidation about strangers has been an adaptive response to the potential threat that they have carried. Support for an innate basis for fear and phobic responses and the 'non-associative' theory of fear which supposes that we inherit a limited set of relevent dispositions to develop a fear response has been offered by Poulton and Menzies (2002). Following a review of available evidence they argue that 'Recent retrospective and longitudinal studies have tested predictions from the non-associative model. In general, findings support the non-associative hypotheses, and are difficult to reconcile with neo-conditioning explanations of fear acquisition' (ibid.,: 127).

Physiologically the phobic response has a set of consistent biological markers each of which serves a function. The markers include increased heartbeat – this increases blood flow to muscles; increased respiration – this increases the oxygen content in blood; muscle contractions – these act as a natural warm-up in preparation for energetic movement; increased catabolism wherein the endocrine system speeds up the break down of complex molecules resulting in increased blood-sugar levels – this facilitates energetic movement. Additionally, the phobic stimulus triggers a psychological fixation on avoidance wherein thinking is wholly focussed on escaping from the stimulus. In short, anxieties are designed to facilitate escape from life-threatening dangers, and phobias are the result of an imagined excess of the anxiety-provoking stimuli. The perceived persistence and ubiquity of the anxiety provoking stimuli can lead to the anxiety being permanently 'on' and attached to a salient example of the stimuli.

ANOREXIA NERVOSA

BOX 10.5   WHY BE CONCERNED ABOUT BODY SHAPE?

Why do so many of us – be we under-, over- or of normal weight – care so much about our body shape? Insofar as our weight pertains to our health it seems to be understandable to be concerned with weight, but what about body shape? Do you think that your body shape and that of others tells them something about you and you something about them? If so, what is in a silhouette?

As a psychological disorder anorexia nervosa is characterised by an intense fear focussed on becoming 'fat' or obese. This fear may be realised courtesy of a distorted self-image which suggests to the sufferer that they are overweight in the absence of any measures or objective evidence which supports such a belief. Suffers exhibit a persistent unwillingness to eat which results in severe weight loss. The weight loss is deemed a desirable outcome, and it may also be achieved by excessive exercise and self-induced vomiting. Outcomes include a variety of negative affects associated with malnutrition, including death. Most of those who suffer anorexia nervosa (or the associated illness bulimia or **bulimia nervosa**) are young women. Here we will consider two alternative ideas that attempt to explain anorexia and bulimia in evolutionary terms. The first is the **social uncertainty hypothesis**, and the second is the female intra-sexual competition hypothesis. The social uncertainty hypothesis is the more general of the two and the competition hypothesis makes more specific predictions. Both assume that eating disorders have their roots in an assessment of social environments in relation to mate value and reproductive strategy. While different, the two are not necessarily in competition and both could be valid.

The social uncertainty hypothesis is the product of a number of authors (Anderson and Crawford, 1992; Juda et al., 2004; Wasser and Barash, 1983, 1986). The key fact that drives the idea is ovulation in human females (and a variety of other mammals) is sensitive to the proportion of body mass that is fat. It is assumed that because insufficient fat reserves at the onset of pregnancy significantly reduces the chances of a successful pregnancy, and, later, a positive outcome for mother and child in term of the long-term health of both, ovulation is delayed and/or suspended if fat reserves are in sufficient. It is also reasonable to assume that inconsistency and paucity of food resources in ancestral conditions may be taken to have been a frequent occurrence – just as it is today in certain places.

To these considerations the social uncertainty hypothesis adds the idea that weight manipulation is a reliable way of turning off menstruation and is used when the reproductive future looks uncertain. Accordingly, the manipulation of fat reserves has come to be an optional strategy for females who do not want not conceive (Salmon et al., 2008). We might think of it as an archaic form of contraception. This strategy is deployed by females when the reproductive future looks uncertain.

The social uncertainty hypothesis predicts that any perceived rupture to ancestrally normal or favourable social conditions required for a successful outcome to pregnancy and rearing to puberty could trigger desire for weight loss. These ruptures could include low self-esteem which acts to disrupt the ability to confidently calculate mate value and thereby make reproductive decisions with confidence. A second possibility is an inability to confidently estimate male intentions and, therefore, likely parental investment. It has been suggested that such a lack of confidence could itself be triggered by sexual abuse and that this is consistent with the frequency with which a history of abuse if found in suffers of anorexia (Mealy, 2005). And a third possibility is actual, or perceived, inadequacy of social relations with same sex peers. The outcome this could result in a collapse in confidence that there is sufficient social capital available to augment maternal investment. Related to this is anxiety and pessimism about the stability of the social environment.

The basic idea underlying the intra-sexual competition hypothesis is that young females adjust their weight to match or undercut a local norm and this norm has steadily decreased over the twentieth century pushing females into anorexia/bulimia (Abed, 1998). The local norm is matched or undercut because body weight affects body shape and body shape offers cues to age and fecundity. Change in the social environment triggers the condition and locates anorexia as a mismatch abnormality.

In addition, Abed (1998) argues that the size and distribution of fat deposits around the hips and waist in females alters with the number of offspring that she has. Accordingly, fat deposits act as a cue to her reproductive status and history. Consistent with Buss' (1989) claim that what males find attractive ultimately boils down to fecundity, and Singh's (1993a, 1993b, 2000) work on waist to hip ratio preferences, the sexual competition hypothesis claims that in ancestral conditions females would seek to retain or enhance body shape as an indicator of nubility against a local norm – that is, against cues from same sex con-specifics in their group. Of course, this implies that food resources are sufficiently abundant for such decisions to be an option.

Supposing that females are designed to monitor local norms for body shape with a view to retaining one which cues potential mates to their nubility assumes that such thought and behaviour was adaptive. Abed argues that two further conditions are needed to render it maladaptive. The first is intensified female competition for mates and the other is a change in the local norm. The first condition is met in western populations courtesy of modern contraceptive techniques and demographic changes which lead to delayed first birth. And the second condition is met courtesy of a shift in the norm for body shape being set by idealised imagery of the female form in the media, advertising, fashion magazines and the cinema. The idolised role model of attractiveness for western females is no longer an older sister, or another group member who is seen to be attractive to males, but film and pop stars and fashion models. Indeed, the particulars of their body shape and how it is achieved is more accessible due to detailed imagery and information about diet. The effect of intensified female competition and a resetting of the desired body shape norm leads to four predictions. One, that those who suffer from anorexia and bulimia will be most concerned or obsessed with body shape, especially the torso and midrift – research by Crisp (1980), Kerr et al. (1991) and Birkeland et al. (2005) supports this prediction. Two, that anorexia and bulimia should be most prevalent in societies where nubile body shapes are retained by virtue of low birth rates – research by Raphael and Lacey (1992) supports this prediction. Three, that anorexia and bulimia should be most prevalent in societies where nubile body shapes are presented as ideal – research by Tiggemann and Pickering (1996), Tiggemann (2003) and Vaughan and Fouts (2003) supports this prediction. And, four, that because nubility is a sex-typed predictor of reproductive value, eating disorders should be most prevalent amongst females. In support of this prediction it has been reported that anorexia, seen as a clinical issue, represents the most lopsided sex ration known to psychiatry with approximately 9.5 female sufferers to every 1 male sufferer (Woodside and Kennedy, 1995).

Abed's hypothesis illustrates the way in which evolved psychological mechanisms may meshed with novel environmental cues to provide explanations of thought and behaviour. What it lacks is an explanation as to why an individual would pursue such a strategy, literally, to death.

AUTISM

BOX 10.6   WHAT AM I THINKING?

Do you know what those familiar to you are thinking? I do not mean right now and in detail. I mean most of the time while you are with them. Perhaps you do not know if you know what they are thinking. To show yourself that you do, try to think of how often it is that you are outright flabbergasted, genuinely and utterly surprised, at something they say or do. My guess is that it is not that often. But what if it was often. What if just about everything those around did and said came as an utter surprise? And, vice versa – you were a mystery to them too. Do you think that you could develop friendships in such circumstances?

Autism has been explained in evolutionary terms most lucidly by Baron-Cohen (2004). As a condition, autism manifests itself in a number of ways. Just as schizophrenia is said to comprise positive and negative symptoms wherein positive symptoms refer to a groups of behaviours that *are* exhibited present but ought not be such as formal thought disorder, disorganised speech, delusions, hallucinations, thought insertion and thought control, and negative symptoms refers to a group of behaviours that *are not exhibited* should be (such as care about hygiene, social withdrawal, alogia, avolition and blunted emotional affect), autism may be thought of as having 'positive' and 'negative' aspects. Behaviours which characterise autism and which should not be exhibited include excessive preoccupation with certain objects or forms of information and repetitive behaviours. Ordinary behaviours which ought to be evident include emotional attachment to caregivers, lack of eye contact, poor facial recognition, poor or no use or understanding of metaphorical language, inability to recognise a speaker's communicative intention or intended meaning, and the ability to sympathise and empathise with others.

The observation that the autistic is unable to sympathise and empathise with others is at the heart of the evolutionary account of autism. Known as the 'theory theory' of autism, the claim is that the human capacity to build theories of one another's mind is phylogenetically novel. That is, our particular ability to have an elaborated theory of other people is unique to us. The autistic does not develop this phylogenetically new and novel skill. The inability to build theories of others is responsible for the suit of socially peculiar behaviours that autistics exhibit. The 'theory theory' maintains that the autistic individual cannot form normal social relations because he/she does not understand that others have mental states.

In support of this position research suggests that autistics do not understand that others have mental states wherein a fact is both comprehended and an attitude is adopted towards that fact. Mental states (also known as 'intentional states') have the property of being about something – they have content, and attached to the content is an attitude toward it – it is liked/desired/disliked/unwelcome. For example, one can have a mental state whereupon one understands/cognises that it is raining and hold an attitude about the fact.

At bottom, to have a theory of another's mind we need to understand that others have attitudes about facts. So, to have a theory of another we need to have a mental state about the mental state of another. For example, to have a theory of Joshmo we need to understand that it is raining, that Joshmo understands that it is raining and that he is unhappy about the fact. Such ascriptions of mental states are both how we understand and predict the behaviour of others. Accordingly, Joshmo's act of running to a shop doorway is explicable in terms of his understanding that it is raining and his unhappiness about the fact. In other words, our theory of Joshmo's action is a product of establishing a fact, and establishing his attitude towards the fact. Our theory of his behaviour is a product of seeing the circumstances from his point of view.

We can complicate this simplified picture. One important way of doing so is to suppose that mental states in others can be about others. For example, we can suppose that Joshmo holds a certain attitude toward Shmojo. In this case our theory of Joshmo is a theory about his attitude towards another person. Let us suppose that Joshmo thinks that Shmojo is cool. This may explain why Joshmo seeks Shmojo's company. We can further complicate the picture by supposing that Joshmo thinks that Shmojo thinks that Joshmo is cool. In this case we are building a theory of what Joshmo's theory of Shmojo is. Our theory of Joshmo includes his theory of Shmojo. And so it goes on. For example, we can have a theory of Joshmo wherein we think that he thinks that Shmojo thinks that that Dayglo thinks Shmojo is aggressive. Here our theory of Joshmo is about his theory of Shmojo's theory of Dayglo's attitude towards Shmojo.

The ability to build a theory of other minds typically appears between three and four years of age (Baron-Cohen, 2003). For example, ask a three-year-old what a Smarties tube contains and they will say 'Smarties'. Show them that it actually contains a pencil and they will correctly revise their view if you ask them again. However, next ask them what they think their friend/mum/dad will think regarding the contents of the tube and they will say 'pencil'. They do not appear to understand until about a year later that others are not privy to their information (Perner et al., 1989).

The point about autism is that those who suffer from it do not appear to be able to form theories of other minds via sequences of intentional states. Baron-Cohen (2003) calls this 'mind blindness'. The reason we might class autism – if the condition does develop from a basic inability to model the minds/intentional states of others – as a 'phylogentic' disorder is because the condition is **atavistic**.

ANTISOCIAL PERSONALITY DISORDER

BOX 10.7 HOW WOULD YOU BEHAVE IF YOU KNEW YOU COULDN'T BE PUNISHED?

If you could take or steal something you wanted you without fear of the police getting involved, would you do so? If not, why not? What stops you from being a thief or a con-artist? Is it just not having the know-how or the opportunity? Why don't you exploit the many opportunities to take, steal and cheat that present themselves if you only cared to look? Is it because you are not ruthless, callous, careless, selfish and greedy? Think now of some of the very successful and wealthy people you know of. To what extent do you think that a certain ruthlessness, callousness, carelessness, selfishness and greed has been instrumental in their success and ability to accumulate wealth? It may be true that crime does not pay, but it may also be true that some of the characteristics that we associate with criminality does.

Antisocial personality disorder appears to be becoming the preferred term to label a condition that has been and is also referred to as psychopathy and as sociopathy. In the 1960s and 1970s the term sociopathy came to be preferred over psychopathy because constraint regarding the use of the terms 'psychopathy' and 'psychopath' had been lost and usage became somewhat colloquial. Also, 'sociopathy' reflected the 'social turn' in psychiatry prompted by the anti-psychiatry movement in the 1960s when the work of Laing (1960) and Szasz (1970) gained currency. What is important to note is that all three terms refer to a personality disorder which is characterised by disturbed social relationships and anti-social behaviours (Andrade, 2008).

Here we will retain the earlier term 'psychopathy' for reasons to be explicated shortly. And we will follow a distinction between primary and secondary psychopathy (see Coyne and Thomas, 2008) wherein primary psychopathy is proposed to be a pattern of thought and behaviour which has its roots in features of the genome whereas secondary psychopathy is elicited by environmental conditions (Burt and Mikolajewski, 2008). The proposal is that primary psychopaths carry a key genotypic similarity and behave similarly despite different developmental and ongoing environments, and secondary psychopaths demonstrate a behaviour strategy that could, in principle, be typical of humans in certain circumstances.

Thought of as an inclusive 'in-group', behavioural similarities between primary and secondary psychopaths include apparent absence of socially specific emotions such as remorse, shame, guilt, sympathy, empathy, profound egocentrism manifesting itself as unreliable and irresponsible social behaviour, and impulsivity (Andrade, 2008; Book and Quinsey, 2004). It has also been noted that psychopaths are marked out by a diminished or an apparent absence of fear of social opprobrium and isolation, and they are less responsive to fear of social exclusion as a conditioning tool (Birbaumer et al., 2005), and that this imay be especially true for males (Blair et al., 2005). These characteristics result in an inability to form lasting, equitable social bonds and relationships and reluctance in others to pursue them (Babiak and Hare, 2006). Contrary to some cinematic and literary depictions, primary and secondary psychopaths exhibit normal IQ and normal theory of mind (Blair et al., 1995, 1996). The ability to exploit others may be enhanced by a capacity to think clearly about social situations which offer the prospect of exploitation because moral reasoning is not cluttered by considerations about the effect and affect on others. This may also enhance the psychopath's ability to decieve and manipulate others (Andrew et al., 2008; Austin et al., 2007; Lykken, 1995).

If the distinction between primary and secondary psychopaths is valid a number of predictions arise. First of all, we might expect to find that the proportion of primary psychopaths in different populations should not vary as a function of cultural differences and socio-economic conditions. Consistent with this prediction is the report that baseline frequency appears to be constant over time and place, and that primary psychopaths are equally likely to come from all socio-economic backgrounds as a proportion of the total population (Mealy, 1995; Skeem et al., 2004; Sullivan and Kosson, 2005; Walsh and Kosson, 2007). Also, we should expect to find that the behavioural markers are robust against rehabilitation and Lykken (1995), Caldwell et al. (2006, 2007) and Douglas et al. (2005) suggest that this may well be the case.

The distinction also yields a number of predictions about the secondary psychopaths. Research suggests that developmental and environmental factors which may trigger the strategy include a disrupted family life wherein a child receives inconsistent feedback about the morality of its actions, poor pro-social behavioural models and father absence (Barr and Quinsey, 2004). Poverty and poor housing also appears to be important. The anti-social behaviour is tied to age, hormone levels and competitive status. The secondary psychopath exhibits frequent but not emotionless cheating – he or she is susceptible to the stabilising effect of an affection/equitable bond (Caldwell et al., 2006, 2007; Douglas et al., 2005).

These considerations explain cultural/temporal differences in rates of sociopathy as indicated by certain types of crime. And it may explain the finding that sociopathy shows a kin effect due to inter-generational transmission of response to competitive disadvantage. It has been reported that the proportion of secondary psychopaths varies in relation to socio-economic status (Mealy, 1995). The likelihood of the strategy appearing is said to be sensitive to chances of it being successful as a means of acquiring resources.

SUMMARY OF CHAPTER 10

Evolutionary psychology assumes that our minds have been shaped such that we are successful survivors and reproducers. This implies that we should think and behave in an adaptive manner. It follows that maladaptive thought and behaviours present a problem for evolutionary psychologists. Evolutionary psychiatry attempts to solve this problem by first providing a normative analysis of human thought and behaviour derived from an analysis of what are minds are for in adaptationist terms. And it presents a scheme wherein we can render maladaptive or abnormal persons explicable in evolutionary terms. One way of doing so is to acknowledge that people vary. This means that each of us will be more-or-less good at solving the problems of survival and reproduction, and some of us will be unusual – so unusual that we might be described as being abnormal. Such abnormalities can be called 'distributed abnormalities' and we have to consider anxiety disorders to be a candidate condition. Another way of dealing with maladaptive behaviour is to invoke the notion of domain mismatch wherein differences between the environments we evolved in and those we occupy now creates difficulties for psychological functioning. Anorexia nervosa was considered as a possible result of domain mismatch. Autism was also considered but as an example of an ontogenetic abnormality – a failure of maturation and development of our ability to formulate theories of others' minds. And, finally, we looked at the idea of frequency-dependent abnormalities. We saw that under certain conditions unusual ways of thinking and behaving can be adaptive responses, and we took psychopathy and sociopathy as potential examples.

FURTHER READING

Apart from the references in this chapter you may find it interesting and useful to consult one or more of the following:

Baron-Cohen, S. (ed.) (1996) *The Maladapted Mind: Classic Readings in Evolutionary Psychopathology.* Hove and Cambridge, MA: Psychology Press.

Baron-Cohen, S. (2003) *The Essential Difference: Men, Women, and the Extreme Male Brain.* Harmondsworth: Penguin/Allen Lane.

Fábrega, H. (2002). *Origins of Psychopathology: The Phylogenetic and Cultural Basis of Mental Illness.* New Brunswick, NJ: Rutgers University Press.

Horrobin, D. (2001) *The Madness of Adam and Eve: How Schizophrenia Shaped Humanity.* London: Bantam Press.

Stevens, A. and Price, J. (2000) *Evolutionary Psychiatry: A New Beginning* (2nd edn). London: Routledge.

11 EVOLUTION AND CULTURE

Some of the questions addressed in this chapter:

- Should we to be able to 'see' natural and sexual selection in culture?
- Does natural history predict culture?
- How does evolutionary theory accommodate cultural phenomena?
- Are cultures adaptations?
- Do the social sciences need evolutionary theory?
- Is evolutionary theory a cultural phenomenon?

SOME KEY TERMS AND CONCEPTS

Epidemiological culture; Evoked culture; Genetic leash; Metaculture; Memes; Standard social science model.

LEARNING OBJECTIVES

Having studied this chapter you should be better able to:

- Evaluate the claim that psychology and the social sciences have been dominated by the standard social science model.
- Present the general argument that evolution has shaped culture.
- Develop your own views on the need for the social sciences to adopt evolutionary theory.

INTRODUCTION

It will not have escaped your attention that those who use evolutionary theory to explain thought and behaviour frequently frame their analysis within a depiction of the physical and social context. Let us refresh our memory with some examples. In Chapter 2

'Evolutionary approaches to thought and behaviour', we saw that evolutionary psychology relies upon an account of past selection pressures, and in Chapter 3 'The natural history of humans' we looked at what they might have been and saw that there is some agreement that some of the most important selection pressures have arisen from our means of food acquisition and our mating behaviour. The profound importance of others was the focus of Chapter 5 'Cooperation and interdependence' where the claim that we are adapted to be cooperative was examined. In Chapter 7 'Mate selection', we saw how attractiveness is not absolute but comparative. We do not decide our own mate value. Others do that, and they do so in a wider social climate. While Chapter 8 'Competition, aggression and violence' began with a series of claims about why males are typically more aggressive than females, the frequency of aggression is contingent on social and economic conditions was also discussed. Chapter 9 looked at language and made a distinction between **language competence** and language performance. Competence refers to our innate ability to acquire language, and performance refers to the actual language we speak. All evolutionary theories of language are interactive accounts involving the biology of the central nervous system and the social milieu in which it finds itself. The importance of the physical and social environment is, perhaps, never more salient than when we think about abnormal thought and behaviour as shown in Chapter 10 'Evolution and abnormal psychology'. The notion of domain mismatch demands a comparative analysis of environments old and new to facilitate explanations of fitness-reducing behaviours. An understanding of how ancient adaptations fail to mesh with the modern world can only be achieved via a nuanced depiction of which aspects of new environments create problems.

The aim of this chapter is to consider in more detail the relationship between evolution, culture and social science, and to introduce a variety of ways of thinking about culture that have been inspired by Darwinism. We will begin by looking again at 'the standard social science model' – an account of the history of the psychological and social sciences that was introduced in Chapter 2 – and consider the conceptual bridge that an evolutionary approach needs to cross if it is to become part of the theoretical tool kit used by the social sciences and scholars of culture. Following that we will review a tripartite proposal that has been made with a view to establishing an evolutionary account of culture. Using it as a framework, other evolutionary analyses of culture will be introduced. More specifically we will consider the notion that genes constrain culture, that cultures are adaptive and that ideas can be conceived of as 'memes' and can be seen as analogous to genes. Our consideration of evolution and culture will close after a disscussion of the prospects of evolutionary social science and the proposal that evolutionary theory as a component of culture is itself amenable to sociological analysis.

Before we get on with our task it ought to be noted that there is much that this chapter does not include. There are numerous theories which look to accommodate and explain culture in Darwinian. One of the first was proposed as long ago as 1908 by William McDougall (1908), and there is a growing number of more recent attempts (see Cochran and Harpending, 2009; McDonald, 2009; Sanderson, 2001; Tomasello, 1999; Wilson, 2002). Among the more influential are Durham's (1991) and Boyd and Richerson's (1985; Richerson and Boyd, 2005) co-evolutionary theories which posit culture – or, more precisely, certain components of of culture such as food and codified forms of cooperation – as an intergral part of evolution. In these accounts genes are not the only selective forces at play. However, as important as these theorists are they are not the focus of this chapter.

THE STANDARD SOCIAL SCIENCE MODEL OF MIND AND CULTURE

As we saw in Chapter 2 'Evolutionary approaches to thought and behaviour', the standard social science model thesis is a component of evolutionary psychology in that it is a depiction of what evolutionary psychology is not. The standard model is what evolutionary psychology is up against. It is a model of how *not* to do social science (Tooby and Cosmides, 1992). It is argued that the social sciences, and in particular social anthropology and sociology for the best part of the twentieth century, failed to make meaningful progress because of the manner in which psychology and culture and the relationship between the two have been conceptualised. On the one hand, there has been a depiction of mind as being a *tabula rasa* – a blank slate. On the other hand, there is the depiction of culture as being the source of information and the scripts that are written onto the blank slate. Dealing first with mind, and then with culture, and with a view towards establishing what is thought to be wrong with it, let us look at the standard model thesis in more detail.

The standard model is said to subscribe to the 'psychic unity' of human kind (Tooby and Cosmides, 1992). Humans are more similar in terms of biological endowment than they are dissimilar. Psychological variation in humans begins at birth. Nature in the raw form of the newborn is overridden and overwritten by the social forces we call 'culture'. That nature is overridden demonstrates that human biological and genetic endowment is insignificant. Individuals, undirected by cultural rules, would be feral and we do not spontaneously exhibit organised behaviour or recognisable emotions. It follows that patterns of within-group similarity and between-group differences show culture to be the causal agent. These considerations lead to the conclusion that human nature – insofar as there can be said to be such a thing – is defined by its capacity to be enculturated. Its most salient feature is that it is malleable (Levy, 2004; Pinker, 2002; Tooby and Cosmides, 1992).

Because culture is said to be the source of organised psychological content, it is to culture that we should turn to understand thought and behaviour. However, specifying what is meant by 'culture' has shown itself to be difficult. A conservative definition might say that culture refers to all that is learned, shared and understood about the world, and how to behave towards and respond to it by a group of persons. But many theorists would want to add detail to that sketch (Geertz, 2000; Kroeber and Kluckhohn, 1952). What is important so far as the standard model is concerned is the power of culture as a causal agent. Following on from the claim that we are born a blank slate and our minds are shaped by a ready-organised social world, the cause of organised behaviour and mental content is without and not within the individual. Culture is said to be self-sustaining and perpetuating. Cultural 'facts' as consequences, or effects, are invariably preceded by cultural antecedents, or causes. Given this relation, culture is (at the very least from a methodological point of view) independent of human nature. Social science is said to subscribe to the conclusion that because culture is the cause of behaviour and mental content, it is culture that must be studied if an account is to be given of its effects (Levy, 2004; Pinker, 2002; Tooby and Cosmides, 1992).

BOX 11.1 OBJECTIONS TO EVOLUTIONARY PSYCHOLOGY: REDUCTIONISM

All complex, multifaceted problems or questions need to be atomised in order to be addressed. That is, we need to decompose, or deconstruct, the overall problem or question, into tractable component problems or questions in order to begin the process of addressing the whole problem or question. In fact, it may be the case that the very nature or scope of the overall problem only becomes apparent when the number and nature of the component problems are discerned. If this way of tackling problems is **reductionism** then evolutionary psychology is reductionistic. More precisely, it subscribes to the view that if you want to know something – even if that something is everything – you have to start somewhere. In the attempt to provide a paradigm for the social sciences, evolutionary approaches make the assumption that the modern human mind preceded modern societies and that the latter would not exist without the former and does not exist independently of the former. So, the starting point is the thing between our ears. If evolutionary psychology is reductionistic it is so only in the sense that what it is that is between your ears is complex but not mysterious and complexity is made up of elements/parts that are less complex than the whole.

While always open to the accusation that it is simplistic, this process can be seen at work in the way in which the psychological and social sciences array themselves into fields such as social psychology, cultural anthropology, economics and many others. In turn, each field factures again into sub-fields. One consequence of this process is that the fields and sub-fields become antagonistic toward one another (Good, 2000). The broadest division of all is that between the fields that prioritise 'nature' and those that prioritise 'nurture'. One version of the claim that evolutionary psychology is reductionist suggests that it denies that factors other than evolved adaptations are irrelevant and that social and cultural considerations are unimportant. We have seen that this is not the case. Human minds are embedded in a changing flux of social conditions and relations, and changing information. How they respond and what they do is dependent on what is outside of them in much the same way as how, say, a given metal 'behaves' and is dependent on ambient temperature. Moreover, evolutionary psychologists argue that the conditions in which minds function have been created by other minds. For example, the profusion of attractive foods to be found in supermarkets that appeal to our evolved tastes are the expression of comparable tastes in other minds.

GENES, BRAINS AND CULTURE

Evolutionary psychology subscribes to some of these claims. It agrees that human nature is the same everywhere. But it does not agree that we come into the world blank. Evolutionary psychologists agree that culture has effects on thought and behaviour. But it does not agree that culture is an independent system. Evolutionary psychologists claim that the ready-organised adaptations that comprise the human mind create culture and to understand culture we need to understand the nature of psychological adaptations (Tooby and Cosmides, 1992; Salmon, 2008). The general argument of evolutionary psychology is that because our brains are coded for by our genes (i.e. that nothing other than genes build brains), and that thought is dependent on and a product of our brains (that nothing other than brains think), it follows that a relationship exists between genes and thought. Furthermore, because natural and sexual selection works at the level of genes (i.e. it is alleles that are selected for not the bodies they build), it follows that natural and sexual selection should be discernible in thought and behaviour (Salmon, 2008). For example, if we accept Hamilton's solution to the problem of altruism we should expect selection for genes that code for brains that think and promote acts of nepotism (Gangested, 2008).

We can extend this reasoning to build a general argument for an evolutionary account of culture. Beginning with the claim that natural and sexual selection should be discernible in thought and behaviour, we add the proposition that culture is a product of thought and behaviour (i.e. where there is no thought there is no culture) and arrive at the claim that the tastes and dispositions selected for by natural and sexual selection should be discernible in culture which, on the whole, should reflect what is important from an evolutionary point of view. For example, if we accept Hamilton's solution to the problem of altruism we should expect selection for genes that code for brains that think and act nepotistically, and we should also expect kinship to be a recurrent matter of high salience and importance in all human cultures both past and present – which it is (Finkler, 2001). On this reasoning, kinship will be a component of culture – be the component rules and rituals of conduct and organisation, stories, myths and histories, or artefacts in celebration of kinship – and it is rooted in human biology.

Having considered the broad critique of and the solution to the bifurcation of mind and culture we can now consider how the leading exponents of evolutionary psychology have developed a preliminary theory of evolution and culture. The focus will be on the tripartite cleaving of the term 'culture' introduced by Tooby and Cosmides (1992). Although the discussion will be led by their terms 'metaculture', 'evoked culture' and 'epidemiological culture', we will consider other ways of using evolutionary theory to explicate and understand each.

BOX 11.2   OBJECTIONS TO EVOLUTIONARY PSYCHOLOGY: HISTORICAL DETERMINISM

Historical determinism refers to a suite of philosophies which argue that humanity is on some sort of unstoppable trajectory towards some final state. Probably the most influential example of historical determinism is that espoused by Karl Marx in a variety of works including *Das Kapital* (McLellan, 1978). Marx argued that humanity had passed through a number of stages or historical epochs and that an analysis of these showed that we were heading for a final stage called socialism or communism.

Evolutionary accounts of historical events and processes might be taken as being a form of historical determinism in that they assume or suppose that some sort of final outcome/state of humanity (good or bad) is inevitable. It would, however, be an error to think that evolutionary psychology makes any such assumption. From Darwin onwards, evolutionists eschew the idea that evolution is a process of progress toward perfection or that we are on some sort of inevitable upward trajectory towards a better state. Similarly it eschews the notion that that we are on some sort of trajectory towards a worse state. Evolutionary theory is agnostic about the moral or ethical 'value' of the past, present and the future. We need to remind ourselves that evolution is 'blind' and without intention. It is a process which cannot see the future or anticipate change. For these reasons evolution is not going anywhere in particular and is certainly not driven or determined by any form of purpose.

METACULTURE

Metaculture refers to those aspects of societies that reflect the enduring dispositions and goals of *Homo sapiens* (Tooby and Cosmides, 1992). The prevalence of concern about kinship and biological relations provides an example. Preoccupation with sex and food are others. We could add to this power, status, appearance, material resources – indeed anything that equates to problems of survival and reproduction because metaculture may be seen as consisting of the broad set of problems that human have solve to reproduce. As an observable phenomenon metaculture is made up of the day-to-day behaviours that humans have engaged in to solve reproductive problems.

While these behaviours can take myriad forms we can utilise the notion of a '**genetic leash**' to understand and predict which forms have and may persist (Lumsden and Wilson, 1981; Wilson, 1998). The basic claim is that genes constrain culture. Just as the general argument for an evolutionary account of culture outlined above suggests, genes enable culture and cultural forms and practices. The forms and practises that facilitate the replication of the genes that underpin them will proliferate and persist. Those that do not will not. Genes are said to prescribe epigenetic rules. This refers to the process by which genetic information in concert with the environment results in behaviour. Some of these behaviours enhance the fitness of those who practise them. Some are fitness-neutral. Others reduce the fitness of those that practise them and will, axiomatically and over time, die out. Accordingly, metaculture comes about and is held back by it fitness consequences.

EVOKED CULTURE

Evoked culture refers to what happens when a mind that is adapted to the specific environments and problem that comprised the past finds itself in different and variable contexts. Tooby and Cosmides illustrate evoked culture thus:

> Imagine that extraterrestrials replaced each human being on earth with a state-of-the-art compact disc jukebox that has thousands of songs in its repertoire. Each jukebox is identical. Moreover, each is equipped with a clock, an automated navigational device that measures its latitude and longitude, and a circuit that selects what song will play on the basis of its location, the time, and the date. What our extraterrestrials would observe would be the same kind of pattern of within-group similarities and between-group differences observable among humans: In Rio, every jukebox would be playing the same song, which would be different from the song that every jukebox was playing in Beijing, and so on, around the world. (Tooby and Cosmides, 1992: 115–116)

The songs in this thought experiment represent the repertoire of all possible behaviours that we could exhibit. Tooby and Cosmides suggest that as time moved on so to would the songs played. And if we moved the jukeboxes from place to place they would play the tunes triggered by the characteristics of each place. The notion of evoked culture accommodates cultural differences within the framework of metaculture. While we expect to see the same and persistent problems beneath, on the surface differences in cultural practices and forms in different environments explain within group similarities and between group differences. An example of evoked culture would the differing patterns of female-on-female aggression we discussed in Chapter 8 'Competition, aggression and violence'. You may recall that Campbell (1995) explains differing rates of female-on-female aggression as a function of the paucity of good-quality males. When young females sense that market for high status, high investing males is tight they employ riskier competitive strategies. In other words, aggressive competition in females is evoked by social conditions.

As we saw when discussing the adaptive mind approach in Chapter 2, human behavioural ecology supposes that variations between groups may be explained by assuming that humans seek to maximise their reproductive potential and in doing so come across or invent subsistence practices that fit with environmental and social conditions. This line of reasoning gives rise to the suggestion that cultures and the practices that comprise them are adaptive (Cziko, 1995). This view asserts that widespread cultural 'habits' serve a function which has fitness-effects for all who practice and promulgate the habits. The fitness-effect can be positive, negative or neutral. With relatively few exceptions, widespread and persistent habits are introduced and adopted because, *prima facie*, they seem to offer the chance of longevity and/or fecundity. Habits get altered because they do not have these effects, because the disadvantaged reject them or because the environment alters (Kenrick et al., 2003). We adopt them because the tried and tested is less expensive to learn than trial and error. Cultural innovations and novelties are introduced by few and copied by many.

EPIDEMIOLOGICAL CULTURE

So, if metaculture explains the enduring preoccupations of humans, and evoked culture explains how these preoccupations take the particular forms that they do from place to place and over time, what remains in need of explanation is why we have culture, how we engage with it and why it changes. These questions must be addressed when we consider the insistence that culture is not independent of mind but a product of it: why did the adapted mind create culture, how does it interact with cultural rules and artefacts and how does it alter these rules and artefacts?

The proposed answer comes in the form of '**epidemiological culture**' (Tooby and Cosmides, 1992). The term 'epidemiology' is borrowed from medicine and it refers to the study of the causes, transmission and distribution of disease. In the current context, it is used to refer to the beginning, spread and fate of the ideas and behaviours that comprise cultures. The claim is that cultures can come about because humans can learn and transmitt to others what has been learned. What we can learn and what we are motivated to learn is shaped by selection, but we can discover new solutions to the problems posed by the physical and social environments. As cultural anthropology and sociology suggest, we come into a ready-made cultural world and we interact with it. We come to understand through childhood what the rules of the culture are and what purposes they serve – or are supposed to serve. Language, symbolism and imitation are the ways through which culture is transmitted from person to person across place and time. And cultures change for the same reasons that they begin: decomposed into constituent parts and seen as solutions, new solutions replace the old. In sum, cultures are the shared understandings of how to interact with the physical and social world that we adopt, modify and retain or discard.

An interesting and influential way of thinking about the transmission of the flotsam and jetsam of more-or-less transient ideas that comprise epidemiological culture is via the concept of memes (Dawkins, 1976). 'Meme' is derived from the Greek word for imitation and the term refers to units of information. It is intentional that the word sounds like 'gene', and the proposal is that ideas spread in a manner analogous to genes. Just as genes are seen as selfish replicators, memes also replicate as they spread from person to person. Memes replicate and spread by virtue of them being more-or-less contagious. Their contagion depends upon their fitness relevance, how easily they are to memorise, how well they map onto existing ideas and how well they appear to make sense of the environment of the holder (Dawkins, 1976). There has been much discussion as to how closely the analogy with genes proper should be (Blackmore 1999; Dennet 1995; Shennan, 2002). The consensus appears to be that there is a comparison to be made between genetic and memetic evolution but the mechanisms are not identical. Certain memes, so-called 'viruses of the mind', may enhance the fitness of those hold them. Memes vary and they can be passed on 'clean' or in a mutated form. But they can blend and are Lamarkian in that they can be acquired through experience and passed from generation to generation. The real utility of the meme concept is that it can offer an more-or-less organised way for us to think about imitation and the 'rules' of epidemiological culture. We will return to the topic of memes in the latter part of this chapter.

THE ADAPTATIONIST EXPLANATION OF ART

Of course, not all cultural innovations are solutions to problems, and even broad definitions of culture include the set of artefacts that we commonly call art. We might point to the transient nature, exhibition of innovation and novelty that characterises art as a way of untying the tether between psychological adaptations and culture. However, one way of accommodating art as culture within the adaptationist framework is to suppose that what is new is, underneath, old and that 'beneath new culture is old psychology' (Barkow, 1992: 627). Let us consider soap operas, narratives and pictorial art to illustrate this claim.

Soap operas are open-ended stories about the lives, loves, hatreds, rivalries and fortunes of a bounded but changing community of people. A phenomenon mostly of television (but also radio) they appear to be popular wherever available. Barkow argues that the appeal of soap operas can be understood in terms of their being a form of gossip (Barkow, 1992). You may recollect from Chapter 9 'Evolution and language' the discussion of the claim that language may have evolved in order for humans to exchange biographical information about one another. Called the gossip hypothesis, the prediction that can derived from it is that most of our oral communication is about absent others and our relationships with them (Dunbar et al., 1997). Gossip is functional in that we collect potentially useful and important information about others. Its functionality also makes it pleasurable to engage in. The idea is that soap operas mimic gossip and similarly are a source of pleasure. However, unlike in real life the soap viewer gets to know all the gossip in the virtual community. Soaps give us what we would like to have in real life – complete knowledge of the social scene in which we embedded. The viewer is privy to all twists, turns, deceptions, plots and plans whereas the virtual actors are not. This God-like omniscience is itself a source of enjoyment. Mapping soaps onto the evolution of gossip gives us what most evolutionary accounts of known behaviours do – it offers an explanation of an established phenomenon by telling us why something happens.

Pinker suggests that we can view other art forms in a similar way. He argues that the most popular novels and films are centred on five narrative forms, these being love, sex, social threat, revenge and money (Pinker, 2002). These themes recur and are often intertwined because we can empathise with each as a motive for action. We can understand, say, the romantic comedy wherein mutual attraction is potentially thwarted because we understand the underlying narrative as a 'fitness narrative'. That is, within the story line there are embedded fitness consequences for the actors and it is these that we understand and become emotionally involved with. So productive is the approach ouitlined by Pinker it has given rise to what Carroll (2004, 2005) calls adaptationist or Darwinian literary study.

The appeal of pictorial art can be dealt with in a comparable manner (Solso, 2004). Those forms which are popular and persist can be decomposed into cues which resonate with adaptations which are designed to attend to 'fitness tokens' (Daly and Wilson, 1988). It is apparent that much of the most popular and acclaimed pictorial art depicts safe, open landscape which are warmly coloured . Many still-life paintings are of food and flowers which cues us to a bounty of natural resources and fertility. Art is pleasing (when it is pleasing) because it mimics the colours, shapes and scenes that would have triggered a positive response in the EEA (Solso, 2004).

BOX 11.3   EVOLUTION AND RELIGIOUS BELIEF

It is fairly unusual for an edited volume of essays focused on a field of specialist interest that does not claim to be an encyclopaedia or handbook to be comprised of fifty separate entries. Bulbulia et al.'s *The Evolution of Religion: Studies, Theories, and Critiques* is just such a volume, and its publication shows how acute is the interest in the relationship between evolution and religion, and how evolutionary theory might facilitate our understanding of religious belief (Bulbulia et al., 2008). There is also a pressing need for an evolutionary account of religion because as Atran points out: 'all known human societies – past or present – bear the very substantial costs of religion's material, emotional, and cognitive commitments to factually impossible, counter intuitive worlds' (2008: 477).

Tinbergen's 'four whys' (see Chapter 2) heuristic can be fruitfully applied to religious and spiritual belief. For example, we can ask what appears to trigger spiritual belief – might it be an awareness of our

(Cont'd)

own mortality? Or we can ask how religious belief has developed through history – how and when did it become institutionalised? However, the literature that has emerged recently has tended to focus on two of Tinbergen's 'why's': What is the function, or adaptive value, of religion (if any)? And what is the ontogeny of the cognitive skills that allow us to entertain belief in metaphysical entities? To give us a sense of how these questions have been tackled we can look at some examples of answers to each of these questions.

Wilson et al. (2008) suppose that religions are adaptive. The purpose they serve is to bind individuals into stable and cohesive groups that persist over extended periods and that such groups can win in between-group competition for resources. While accepting that what they call 'methodological individualism' – i.e. the selfish gene approach – has been the orthodox view they argue that 'natural selection is now know to operate at multiple levels of the biological hierarchy [and] when between-group selection dominates within-group selection, a major evolutionary transition occurs and the group becomes a new, higher level organism' (Wilson et al., 2008: 6). Wilson (2002) has argued that order this transition actually took place some time ago and one of the vehicles for it were religious groups.

A rather more modest claim has been put forward by Weeden et al. who suggest that 'a central function of religious attendance in the contemporary United States is to support a high-fertility, monogamous mating strategy' (Weeden et al., 2008: 327). In support of this claim they present evidence from the United States General Social Survey and a sample of over 21 000 respondents which show that attitudes towards sexual behaviour was the single strongest predictor of religious observance and church attendance. A second study using nearly 1 000 undergraduate students were taken to demonstrate that the moral position of the participants towards sex and positive attitude toward monogamy were the best predictors of religious observance.

Concerning the ontogeny of the cognitive basis of religious belief and belief in metaphysical entities Bering and Parker (2006) investigated children's attributions of intentions to an invisible agent. Working with children aged from 3 to 9 years of age these researchers looked at how the participants responded to the claim that an invisible agent called Princess Alice would let them know when n they made an incorrect choice in a forced choice game. The results suggest that only at about 7 years of age do children begin to read into unanticipated events the intention of an unseen agent and then only when they have been primed to the idea. In other words, we may be incapable of religious belief proper until we are seven or more and have a range of cognitive abilities that most would accept far exceed other mammals including primates.

In accord with Bering and Parker's findings, and, contrary to others scholars, working on the assumption that religious beliefs appear to entails costs that are not outweighed by obvious benefits Beck and Forstmeier (2007) argue that superstition and concomitant religious belief is a by product of what they call 'associate learning'. Their proposal is that we need to tell the difference between events that are patterned and those that are random. If we seen patterns where there are none we make an error whereupon we believe something that is not true. On the other hand, if we see a pattern when the events are, in fact, random coincidences then we make another type of error. Their point is that there is a trade-off between types of error and evolution favours the second type of mistake. This reasoning encourages Beck and Forstmeier to conclude that 'superstitious beliefs [are] an inevitable consequence of an organism's ability to learn from observation of coincidence [and that] humans have evolved a unique ability to judge from experiences whether a candidate subject has the power to mechanistically cause the observed effect' (2007: 35). The adaptive value of this ability comes in a capacity to read the environment courtesy of suppositions about abstract entities and unseen causes. Accordingly, 'assuming that natural selection has favored individuals that learn quicker and more successfully than others owing to (1) active search to detect patterns and (2) the desire to explain these patterns mechanistically, we suggest that superstition has evolved as a by-product of the first, and that belief has evolved as a by-product of the second' (ibid.,: 35).

DO THE SOCIAL SCIENCES NEED EVOLUTION?

The examples in the last section, and many others throughout this book, illustrate how evolutionary explanations of human thought and behaviour already accommodate 'social facts'. What this means is that, at least implicitly, we already have a body of work which we might call 'evolutionary social science' wherein evolutionary theory provides a rationale as to why things happen at group and cultural levels. As we have seen, evolutionary psychologists have not been reluctant to promote their paradigm to the other social sciences. It has been suggested that some sociologists and other social scientists are 'missing the revolution' (Barkow, 2006).

There are very many reasons why social scientists and others interested in human thought and behaviour criticise Darwinism, and we will be looking at some of them in detail in Chapter 12 'Some problems with evolutionary approaches'. But we might speculate somewhat and say that, at bottom, evolution and the social sciences (with the exception, perhaps, of anthroplogy) are in two irreconcilable businesses. Evolutionary theory is used to try and establish a theory of unchanging human nature. Most of the social sciences are interested in the analysis of change and the alleviation of prejudice, inequality and disadvantage. The problem arises when these two enterprises are seen as being at odds with one another. For example, if we are to say that step-parents are by biological decree unlikely to invest as much time, effort and emotion in their step-children as do biological parents (see Chapter 6 'Families and parenting') then those who see such an outcome as a problem (or morally wrong) appear to be duty-bound to reject the theory behind the claim. In short, those driven by the ideals of equality through change must reject claims to unchanging truth when the supposed truth is taken to be an obstacle to justice.

While it cannot be denied that some within the social sciences remain deeply resistant to Darwinism (Jackson and Rees, 2007), the qualifier 'some' must be stressed. The American Sociological Association now has a division called 'Evolution and Sociology', and the European Sociological Association is following suit. These moves follow the suggestion that, in particluar, sociology is in a crisis and it must embrace evolutionary theory if it is to remain credible and survive (Lopreato and Crippen, 1999). Part of the problem seems to be that there is a lay acceptance of Darwinian ideas and evolutionary ways of talking about and seeing human thought and behaviour which has marginalised sociological and other forms of social explanation (Jackson and Rees, 2007). For example, evolutionary ideas are now used in literary studies (Carroll, 2004; Zipes, 2006), history (Schrepfer and Scranton, 2003) economics (Hodgson, 1993, 2004), law (Jones, 2005), and political science (Kanazawa, 2009). The probable solution is for the social sciences to embrace and articulate with biology and evolution, to use the theories and findings, and in the process demonstrate that they are open to ideas.

Thus we come to face the prospect of having something called 'evolutionary social science' just as we have evolutionary psychology. However, the fear is that such an enterprise would actually lead to a colonisation of the social sciences (Rose, 2000), and that evolutionary ideas would come to dominate the social sciences in a manner comparable to the way evolutionary ideas dominate the psychologists who call themselves evolutionary psychologists. Also, for there to be evolutionary social scientists implies that there are non-evolutionary social scientists, those who do belong, and those who do not. Divisions based on labels have been called 'boundary disputes' and they lead to disharmony rather than harmony within the wider disciple (Good, 2000).

Perhaps the way around the problem is to embrace the term 'evolution and social science' or 'social science and evolution'. It implies an independence of the two constituent terms via the disjunction imposed by 'and', and it can also imply a reciprocal arrangement wherein the parties enrich one another. The disjunction allows us to foreground social forms of explanation and include evolution as well as vice versa. We can see this at work if we think about some of the studies that have been discussed in this book and mentioned in the introduction to this chapter. Yes, evolutionary psychology accommodates social facts, but it also relies upon them to generate hypotheses. For example, were we to attempt to predict rates of violent aggression amongst young males we would need a nuanced account of the social and economic conditions in which they live. We would also need an account of the attitudes and ideas they have about the sorts of aggression deemed permissible and functional within their group. In other words, evolutionary psychology needs to embrace sociology in a more explicit way that it does at present if it is to make progress by way of detailed predictions about human behaviour in variable contexts.

BOX 11.4   DO THE SOCIAL SCIENCES NEED A PARADIGM?

Do we need a monolithic theory which explicates the rules and purpose of 'evolutionary social science'? Perhaps not. There are a number of ways of using evolutionary ideas to illuminate sociological level phenomenon, and a number of ways of using sociological phenomenon to examine evolutionary hypotheses. We can:

- Think about social and political history in evolutionary terms by seeing history as analogous to natural selection.
- Conceive of religious, political and scientific ideologies as memeplexes by looking at cultures as assemblages of what are taken as readily understood beliefs.
- Take material cultures as adaptations to the problems of survival by thinking of tool technologies as means to meet biological ends.
- View in-and out-group formations within communities and societies in terms of 'virtual' kin altruism wherein our social identities act as a proxy which facilities cooperation.
- Suppose that gender is an ideological and material playing out of sex differences wherein our folk-theories of femaleness and maleness, femininity and masculinity act as reference points which facilitate problem solving.

EVOLUTIONARY PSYCHOLOGY AS A MEME

In Chapter 2 'Evolutionary approaches to thought and behaviour' we noted that evolutionary theory has been a persistent strain within academic psychology since the late nineteenth century. Indeed, such has been its persistence that we might argue that Darwin's wish that psychology be founded on his ideas has been fulfilled insofar as any number of authors have tried to see it realised, and any adequate history of psychology needs to accommodate document those attempts.

We might also argue that, at least in part, Darwinism is considered to be a major player is psychology so far as the wider public is concerned. It is noteworthy that many of the landmark and often cited texts in evolutionary psychology have proved to be popular beyond academe and that the market for explicitly popular books offering evolutionary explanations of human behaviour is unusually large when compared to popular expositions of other branches of science. There is no better example of this than the *Origin of the Species* itself. It was aimed at a lay audience and it was a resounding commercial success, as were Darwin's other major works (Desmond and Moore, 1991). Arguably the first textbook in social psychology was William McDougall's *Social Psychology* of 1908. It was explicitly Darwinian and went to 18 editions before the last was published in 1923. Other popular expositions of what we might loosely think of as evolutionary psychology before the term was formalised and used as label to describe a particular approach was Robert Ardrey's *African Genesis* (1967) and Desmand Morris' *The Naked Ape* (1967). The latter has been reprinted, the latest print being in 1994, and it was also made into a film in 1974. Richard Dawkins' *The Selfish Gene* (1976) was amongst the best-selling science books of the twentieth century, it is in a second edition and its thirtieth anniversary was celebrated with an event at the London School of Economics. In the 1990s and into the twenty-first century the popular thirst for lay-analyses of our thought and behaviour through an evolutionary lens appears to be unquenched. Even were we to assume that these expositions are true – and that is not plausibly the case for them all – the veracity of the general idea cannot explain their popularity. There are many sound expositions of ideas and applications of most branches of the natural and social sciences that are not nearly so popular. There seems to be something about the idea of human evolution that gives it an extraordinary appeal. The appeal and adoption of the idea is itself a cultural phenomenon. How are we to understand this? Are evolutionary theory and evolutionary psychology memes?

To address this question it is useful to place evolutionary explanations of human behaviour alongside other origin 'stories' or myths. Most of the established religions begin with and are facilitated by an account of human origin. Evolutionary ideas have largely come from societies that are of a Christian orientation and, therefore, powerfully coloured by the notion of genesis. While their stars may be waning somewhat, the ideas of Karl Marx and Sigmund Freud were of unsurpassed influence during most of the twentieth century, and an account of our origin, or natural state, was integral to both of their theories.

Whereas Darwin was relatively restrained in the detail of his depiction of our origins and was what we might call atopian with regard to the moral and political status of the past, Marx and Freud were more forthcoming with detail. Marx's vision was utopian while Freud's was dystopian. Marx looked at the past as a peaceful, happy place since distorted for the worse by historical forces. Freud looked at it as a crude and brutal place since alleviated by the power of rationalism and science. What is important for current purposes is that the three great secular thinkers of the nineteenth century shared with religion a story of our origin.

In addition to the parallel that can be drawn between the narrative structure of various origin stories it has also been suggested that leading exponents of evolutionary theory exhibit a quasi-religious zeal in their accounts how the theory has influenced them and the manner of their proselytising (Nelkin, 2000). As we have seen, evolutionary psychologists want to integrate the human sciences with evolutionary theory acting as the over-arching paradigm (Tooby and Cosmides, 1992). And the forcefulness with which alternative viewpoints are sometimes dismissed implies intolerance which may also serve to alienate (Hampton, 2004c).

These two factors invite us to consider the prospect that evolutionary theory and its general account of the origin and nature of the human mind and behaviour is itself a meme. Moreover, if we take it to be a meme we can see that it works and replicates for the same reasons as do religious ideas. In introducing memes Dawkins chose to present the idea of God as an example. This is how he accounts for its ' "survival value" [as a] meme in the meme pool' (Dawkins, 1976: 193):

> What is it about the idea of gods that gives it its stability and penetrance in the cultural environment? The survival value of the god meme in the meme pool results from its great psychological appeal. It provides a superficially plausible answer to deep and troubling questions about existence. (ibid.).

We might say the same of the 'Darwin meme' in a secularised world. Recall that the ability of a meme to replicate and persist is said to depend upon its fitness relevance, how memorable it is, how it well it maps onto existing ideas and how much apparent sense it makes of the world. In simplified form at least, we might suggest that evolutionary psychology fits the bill. Its fitness value is difficult to determine but it is not obviously fitness reducing, the basics of the theory are relatively simple, it maps onto origin narratives that almost all citizens in the west are exposed to from childhood onwards, and it offers plausible accounts of salient behaviours such as aggression and attraction. Finally, it is behaving like a successful meme in that it is spreading (Hampton, 2006).

A word of warning is needed here. To suggest that evolutionary psychology fits the criterion of being a meme in manner analogous to that of religious ideas does not entail that it has the same status historically, philosophically or culturally. Nor does it imply that the two share the same epistemological status or the same truth value. To say that an evolutionary psychology – or any other idea – is a meme says nothing about its veracity or truth.

SUMMARY OF CHAPTER 11

This chapter considered the relationship between evolutionary theory, culture and sociology. It showed that many evolutionary psychologists see their enterprise as one which has been marginalised in psychology and the social sciences to the detriment of the latter. The so-called standard social science model is an account of the history of the psychological and social sciences. It is also said to be a dominant paradigm that privileges theories of learning and accounts of the cultural prescriptions and norms that are learned.

There have been a number of attempts to develop theories which might act as a conceptual bridge between those who work with evolutionary theory and those who study culture. Amongst the most influential and well articulated of these theories is that proposed by John Tooby and Leda Cosmides. They make a distinction between metaculture, evoked culture and epidemiological culture. Metaculture refers to the goal-driven behaviours which all peoples exhibit such as mating, parenting and the acquisition of essential resources. The notion of metaculture can be seen as a variant of the idea that genes hold culture on a leash and our genetic make-up shapes the sort of cultures that we have and could develop. Evoked culture refers to the ways that particular physical and social environments elicit from groups certain ways of dealing with the problems of survival and reproduction. The notion of evoked culture is not entirely different from that which sees cultures and the myriad social patterns that comprise them as being adaptive responses in given contexts. And epidemiological culture, the third component in Tooby and Cosmides explanation of the psychological foundations of culture, refers to the way in which the ideas and beliefs that comprise a culture are spread and passed from one generation to the next. Epidemiological culture may be compared to another idea that has been inspired by evolutionary theory and used to make sense of culture – memes. Memes are said to be ideas that can be compared to genes in the way that they replicate and survive – or not.

It is noticeable that the attempts to reconcile evolutionary theory and the study of culture have been rather one-sided in that they have tended to come from evolutionists. This tempts us into thinking that cultural theorists and sociologist do not want integration. We can ask if sociology needs biology and evolutionary theory. And a sensible reply is to say why not? Without it being dominated by evolutionary theory, sociology can use the framework in various ways which may provide it with interesting and novel insights while it retains its status as a discipline. Among the phenomena that require a sociological analysis is the very popularity of evolutionary explanations of human thought and behaviour and their role in how we see ourselves and others.

FURTHER READING

Apart from the references in this chapter you may find it interesting and useful to consult one or more of the following:

Janicki, M.G. and Krebs, D.L. (1998) Evolutionary approaches to culture. In Crawford, C.B. and Krebs, D.L. (eds) *Handbook of Evolutionary Psychology: Ideas, Issues and Applications*. Mahwah, NJ: Lawrence Erlbaum Associates.

Midgley, M. (2000) Why Memes? In Rose, H. and Rose, S. (eds) *Alas, Poor Darwin: Arguments Against Evolutionary Psychology*. London: Jonathan Cape.

Orians, G.H. and Heerwagen, J.H. (1992) Evolved responses to landscapes. In Barkow, J., Cosmides, L. and Tooby, J. (eds) *The Adapted Mind: Evolutionary Psychology and the Generation of Culture*. Oxford: Oxford University Press.

Saad, G. (2003) Evolution and political marketing. In Somit, A. and Peterson, S.A. (eds) *Human Nature and Public Policy: An Evolutionary Approach*. London: Palgrave.

Somit, A. and Peterson, S.A. (2003) From human nature to public policy: evolutionary theory challenges the 'Standard Model'. In Somit, A. and Peterson, S.A. (eds) *Human Nature and Public Policy: An Evolutionary Approach*. London: Palgrave.

Stone, L. and Lurquin, P.F. (2007) *Genes, Culture and Human Evolution: A Synthesis*. Oxford: Blackwell.

12 SOME PROBLEMS WITH EVOLUTIONARY APPROACHES

Some of the questions addressed in this chapter:

- What limits does evidence about the past place on evolutionary psychology?
- Why is it thought that social selection pressures have been important in human evolution?
- On what grounds might we be sceptical about the utility of supposing that our psychology is underpinned by psychological adaptations?
- What are the lessons that contemporary approaches can learn from previous forms of Darwinian psychology?
- What substantive difference does it make to our explanations of behaviour to say that any given one of them is adaptive?
- What are some of the issues that need to be resolved if evolutionary psychology is to become part of the fabric of psychology in the future?

SOME KEY TERMS AND CONCEPTS

Circularity; Encephalisation; Environment of evolutionary adaptedness; Evolutionary arms race; Habit; Instinct; Psychological adaptation; Runaway selection.

LEARNING OBJECTIVES

Having studied this chapter you should be better able to:

- Develop a critique of the EEA concept.
- Develop a critique of the concept of psychological adaptations.
- Formulate a view on the future of contemporary evolutionary approaches to thought and behaviour.

INTRODUCTION

At the outset of this book it was suggested that most psychological and social scientists subscribe to the view that human beings are an evolved species and that the selection pressures which brought us about can be discerned in our gross anatomy and physiology, including the central nervous system. And it was suggested that most also agree that the central nervous system is the seat of thought and behaviour. The point in making these observations is that if we are to go so far as to accept them to be valid then it becomes difficult to avoid the conclusion that evolutionary processes have shaped the way in which we think, feel and behave. In other words, and using the term loosely, we are all now evolutionary psychologists.

To illustrate this line of reasoning, let us consider the common, species-typical, pan-human phenomenon of sleep. No one argues that sleep does not have a biological basis, and that it does not perform a biological function. And noone argues that sleep is a purely social convention – which is not to say that that it is not wrapped in certain historical and geographically shaped social conventions. On the face of it then, sleep – probably the most ubiquitous single form of behaviour in which humans engage – shows us that the claim that 'The significance of Darwinian theory lies not so much in whether it is right or wrong as in its power' (Dunbar, 1988: 161) is correct. In short, the proper question we should be asking about human psychology and behaviour in light of modern evolutionary theory is not whether the evolutionary principles can aid explanation but to what extent. That is the position that has been adopted in this book. Our working assumption has been that since evolutionary theory is the best account we have of how and why life forms appears in the form they do and persist over time, it must have something interesting and important to say about the products of the process of natural selection, including modern humans.

In one form or another this assumption has been the starting point for very many scholars and researchers since Darwin's time. It has shaped a number of different approaches to human thought and behaviour, and it will shape new approaches. Accordingly, evolutionary psychology, broadly conceived, has a future, and it has a future because the assumptions are sound and evolutionary theory is not going to go away. However, the approaches that dominate Darwinian psychology today are not without problems, and it is to some of them that this chapter turns.

We will begin by revisiting the past and the concept of the environment of evolutionary adaptedness (EEA). We will see that the devil does indeed lurk in the details. Much of the past was in the minds of our ancestors and ours brains are probably as they are because of selection pressures that we will never be able to evidence via fossils because they were social. One way of getting around this problem is to minimise the differences between now and then. However, this tactic invites other problems, not least the prospect that evolutionary approaches cease to be really evolutionary.

We will then move on to look at a problem which impacts upon evolutionary psychology to a greater extent than it does human behavioural ecology because it centres on the notion of psychological adaptations. In short, the problem is that the way psychological adaptations have been described may make them impossible to find. Following that we will consider a question which may impact more on human behavioural ecology. The question is promoted by a consideration of the fate of the instinct concept and asks what value an appeal to adaptations adds to our thinking and explanations.

This book's final word concerns the future of evolutionary psychology and it also draws upon the history of psychology. If there is one lesson to be learned from human evolution is that it pays to cooperate. Competition and antagonism can pay but not so well as cooperation – not in the long run. Perhaps evolutionary approaches should take heed if, in due course, the term 'evolutionary' will be dropped and we will all just be psychologists again.

THE ENVIRONMENT OF EVOLUTIONARY ADAPTATION REVISITED

Some of the detail of our natural history was examined in Chapter 3 'The natural history of humans', and its role in evolutionary approaches was discussed in Chapter 2. We saw that evolutionary psychology subscribes to the idea that 'the past explains the present', and, in keeping with the injunction that disciplines should be conceptually integrated, evolutionary psychology needs to take careful note of the findings from palaeontology. We also saw in Chapter 3 that human behavioural ecology and sociobiology also depend upon depictions of the past, albeit must less explicitly. They use the past to legitimise the claim that the patterns of behaviour that they observe have an evolutionary basis.

In this section we will further consider the EEA concept and see that a number of difficulties arise for researchers who depend on knowledge of our natural history. However, there are profound and potentially insuperable difficulties in recovering the details of the past. The difficulties are compounded when we make a distinction between physical selection pressures and social selection pressures. We will see that evolutionary psychology tends to underestimate the difficulty of ascertaining the natural history that their programme demands. If Darwinian approaches are to have the future envisioned for them the fossil record must not be overlooked when generating hypotheses about the present or making inferences from the present about the past.

THE PHYSICAL AND THE SOCIAL EEA

The variety of *Homo* lineages that have existed promotes a distinction between two construals of the EEA, the physical and the social (Hampton, 2004a). This follows from the fact that similar physical environments produced distinct outcomes because if climate, fauna and flora were at times and places similar then speciation must have been influenced by other features of the world that *Homo* lineages occupied. The dominant proposal is that the other features were social. This raises the question as to whether the many of the most important and interesting features of the past can ever be discovered.

BOX 12.1   THE SOCIALITY ACCOUNT OF HUMAN BRAIN SIZE

The modern human brain has come about with relative speed in evolutionary terms (Corballis and Lea, 1999b), and its size and physical organisation is unique (Beran et al., 1999). Based on an examination of more than 100 hominid skulls, including fossils taken to be representative of *Homo habilis*, *Homo ergaster*, *Homo erectus*, *Homo heidelbergensis*, *Homo neanderthalensis*, and archaic *Homo sapiens* and covering a period of at 2 million years, it has been argued that 'a significant and substantial proportion of variation in brain size may be related to changes in temperature' (Ash and Gallup, 2007: 109). Nevertheless, there is near consensus on the view that our large brains are the product of the degree and manner of our sociality (e.g. Baron-Cohen, 1999; Byrne, 1999; Corballis, 1991; Dunbar, 1988, 1996, 2007; Flinn and Alexander, 2007; Haslam, 1997; Humphrey 1976, 1992; Miller, 2007; Whiten, 1999; Whiten and Byrne, 1988). The theme of the argument is that the need to live in and negotiate larger social groups is the most significant selection pressure which led to the elaboration and enlargement of our neo-cortex – a phenomenon known as encephalisation. Pinker explains the reasoning thus:

> There's only so much brain power you need to subdue a plant or a rock, the argument goes, but the other guy is about as smart as you are and may use that intelligence against your interests. You had better think about what he is thinking about what you are thinking he is thinking. As far as brain power goes, there's no end to keeping up with the Joneses. (Pinker, 1997: 193)

To understand how sociality could have had a particularly strong influence in our evolution we need to keep in mind the fact that there is no evolution if there is no selection pressure (less genetic drift). Unchanging environments tend to select against change in species. Also, discrete selection pressures differ in the size of their effects. The rapid growth in brain size give us grounds to suppose an **evolutionary arms race** where one complex adaptation is pitted against another and the outcome is runaway selection (e.g. Sigmund, 1993).

If the sociality account of brain growth is correct, the arms race could have come about courtesy of a number of different problems which flowed from increased social interdependence. Flinn and Alexander (2007) call this runaway social selection. The trigger in the arms race for larger brains – the problem requiring better and better and more reliable solutions – could have been the need to develop theories of others intentions (Baron-Cohen, 1996; Dunbar, 2007). It could have been the need to understand and communicate ideas pertinent to survival (Pinker and Bloom, 1992). It could have been the need to negotiate social hierchies while avoiding physical harm (Cummins, 2005). It could have been the need to engage in tactical deception (Byrne and Whiten, 1988; Duntley, 2005). It could have been the need to attract and retain desirable mates (Miller, 2007). It could all of the above and others (Kaplan et al., 2007). The key point is that if we are to attribute the evolution of brain growth to the nature of the social setting then the selection pressures were psychological and exerted by con-specifics. With this point in mind, consider the following passage:

> They have set out early, this band of six purposeful individuals, striding across rolling, grassy terrain punctuated here and there by flat-topped acacia trees. The sky hovered between gray and pink as the sun rose close to breaking the line of hills in the east, on the other side of the vast lake … Everyone had heard the sabre-toothed cats during the night, repeated choruses of throaty moans, a sure sign of a hunt in progress. Even though the band felt itself relatively safe at its riverside camp a mile from the lake, there was always tension when sabre-toothed cats were near. Only a year ago a child had been attacked when he strayed from the watchful eyes of his mother and her companions. Returning hunters, the same group of men who were setting out this day, arrived just in time to drive the predator away. But the boy had died some days later from the loss of blood and the kind of rampant infection that can be so deadly in the tropics. Not surprisingly, this morning's discussions urged extra care on the women and their offspring, gathering tubers and nuts near the camp, and the men on their hunt. These men too were predators. (Leakey and Lewin, 1992: 3–4)

This is an imaginary scene, and the authors accept that it is scientific fiction. It is part of the prelude to a book about what the evidence can tell us about our ancestors. It may be taken as a wish-list of palaeoanthropology and the detail it would like to be able to go into if it had the evidence. And it betrays what is not yet empirically established. There are many assumptions embedded in this passage. For example, it is assumed that we know:

- That the hunting party took place in a specific place, at a specific time by a specific species of hominid.
- What the attitude towards specific other species was.
- What the home-range was.
- The nature of intra-sexual selection and the nature of inter-sexual competition.
- The nature of parental investment together with kin and reciprocal strategies towards that end.
- The development path of children, including sex differences.
- The length of puberty for both sexes.
- The occurrence and length of menopause.
- The size and constitution of the group.
- That this species had an aesthetic sensibility.
- That this species had language and used it for specific purposes.

The point is that these are *assumptions*. Some are better attested than others. For example, the anatomy of the hominids in question and the fauna and flora around them is fairly well established. But those which speak of social organisation and cognitive abilities are not.

This presents a problem for evolutionary psychology and human behavioural ecology. If evolutionary psychologists cannot specify the adaptive problem it cannot specify the psychological solution that solves it. And if human behavioural ecology cannot specify the problem it cannot say with confidence which current ways of solving the problems of survival and reproduction have an evolutionary basis.

CONFUSING THE PAST AS THE PRESENT AND THE PRESENT AS THE PAST

In Chapter 3 we discussed ethology and one of the most important and useful tools that the discipline produced, the 'four whys' heuristic (Tinbergen, 1963). The four whys give us a way of sorting our questions into types. We can look into the natural history of a trait or characteristic – why did it come about? We can ask about the function of a trait or characteristics – what problem does it solve? We can look at how a trait or characteristic matures and develops in an individual organism – what is its ontogeny? And we can examine how a trait or characteristics works – what is its mechanism? Evolutionary approaches interested in human thought and behaviour often collapse these four ways of addressing traits and characteristics into two by simplifying the situation and asking ultimate questions – questions about the selection pressures that brought a given trait of characteristic about, and proximate questions – questions about how the trait solves the selection problems in the here and now. Here we see again the distinction between the past and the present. The past comprises ultimate questions and a set of causes for the present, and the present comprises proximate questions and set of causes for how we think and behave.

Making a clear distinction between ultimate and proximate causes wherein the former bring about the latter and the latter bring about current behaviours is said to distinguish evolutionary psychology from human behavioural ecology (Badcock, 2000; Sherman and Reeve, 1997; Symons, 1990; Tooby and Cosmides, 1990). Adherence to the distinction enables evolutionary psychology to escapes the problem of **circularity** which is said to beset human behavioural ecology which looks to current behaviours that are fitter than others (in that they generate more reproductive success), supposes that they were selected for in the past, and then supposes that there are adaptations underlying these behaviours in the present. A criticism of this way of thinking is that it generates a cause from an effect (Barkow, 1992; Symons, 1992).

BOX 12.2   CIRCULAR ARGUMENTS

A circular argument is an argument wherein one (or more) of the premises used to deduce the conclusion is itself supported by the conclusion. There is an example which reveals the structure of circular arguments:

- Let us say that X is an extant human mind.
- All extant features of X are adaptations.
- All adaptations are products of the past.
- All adaptations can be discerned in the present.

These premises promotes two conclusions:

- If something is a feature of the past then it is a feature of the present,
- If something is a feature of the present it is a feature of the past.

The criticism is that the conclusions say nothing more than the premises used in their support.

It is not denied that there is some utility in what we have called the backwards approach (see Chapter 3 and Caporael, 2001; Smith et al., 2001). But the argument is that evolutionary psychology can escape any suggestion of circularity via an explicit appeal to the past wherein we search for adaptive features of non-extant organisms rather than not for adaptive features of extant organisms. In other words, traits and characteristics should not be categorised according to their current effect on survival and reproduction (Crawford, 2007). What we should do is take the past as a cause and assess the effect in the present rather than take the present as an effect into the past to determine its cause.

If the distinctions between and the mutual roles of the past and the present are beginning to get you a little confused then you are in good company. Consider the following:

> ... the size of intimate human groups has changed little across evolutionary time ... The absence of genetic kin is probably the greatest difference between the [typical academic] department's social organization and that of a hunter-gatherer tribe ... In terms of the sociality of the situation, the way kinship, reciprocity, group size, resource distribution, and so on impact on social organization of a typical group, the sociality of a modern academic department may differ little from that of our Pleistocene ancestors. (Crawford, 1998: 287)

To begin with, we might find it remarkable to so casually dismiss the fact that a hunter-gatherer tribe and a modern academic department differ only on the dimension of their constitution of kin given the importance of inclusive fitness theory to contemporary evolutionary theory. But we might also find it remarkable that pretty much all else is more-or-less the same. The author is saying that the problems of specifying and differentiating between the ultimate and the proximate, the past and the present dissolves if we assume that the past and the present are more-or-less identical. Crawford argues that 'the most plausible hypothesis about the EEA current environment differences is that ancestral and current environments do not differ vis-à-vis any particular adaptation, and that the proper course of action is to make a null hypothesis' (Crawford, 1998: 285). In taking this view Crawford seems to be arguing that the past explains the present because the past just is the present and the present just is the past, and he endorses this view as a methodological assumption.

There are apparent virtues in this approach. For example, we overcome the difficulties of trying to reconstruct the past in the type of detail discussed in the previous section. But it has a number of weaknesses. First, conflating the past and present means that evolutionary approaches cease to be truly evolutionary and they become a sort of comparative history as opposed to an exercise that draws upon natural history. Second, there is no non-question begging means of sorting out the past and the present. Humans clearly exhibit a diversity of living arrangements, means of subsistence, technologies and social systems, and we cannot say which of them is 'natural' without importing evidence which pre-dates *Homo sapien* (see Foley, 1996). Should we choose to emphasise certain features which we exhibit (e.g. monogamy) we simply continue doing what psychologists and social scientists have long done and hypothesise variations rather than types (Foley, 1996). In such circumstances evolutionary approaches amount to a form of the Standard Model. They differ from the Standard Model in that causes are pushed back into an unseen history as opposed to the immediate past and present. Evolutionary approaches are in much the same position as many other branches of psychological and behavioural science which search for human universals (see Daly and Wilson, 1988). What they add are some general statements to the end that humans want to eat, have sex, form families, form friendships, and so on, because of evolution.

What do these observations about the EEA concept and appeals to the natural history of humans tell us about the outlook for evolutionary approaches? There is a need for those who rely upon depictions of our natural history to treat the evidence with great care. While we may assume that the archaeological evidence expresses only a fraction of what our ancestor was psychologically and behaviourally capable of, we must constrain our assumptions. And most of all we not fill gaps in knowledge by ignoring them. Material evidence must be taken as the final arbiter with regard to which assumptions are reasonable and which are not. Accordingly,

> Because modern hunter-gatherers are often presumed to provide a reasonable picture of early human foragers, and living apes are closely related to modern humans, studies of these two groups might provide an insight into early hominid life. Such field studies are no doubt significant, but any more specific inferences about the behaviour and ecology of early hominids must rely on material evidence from the geological record. (Potts, 1992: 326)

Ultimately, we must insist that evolutionary psychology be in possession of evidence as to what the precise problems were in the past before we are asked to accept the solutions. And human behavioural ecology must do likewise before we are asked to take solutions as being of evolutionary origin.

BOX 12.3 OBJECTIONS TO EVOLUTIONARY PSYCHOLOGY: IS OUR THOUGHT CONSTRAINED BY BIOLOGY?

Evolutionary psychologists readily accept that which is obvious: humans learn new and novel ways of thinking and behaving. However, they also argue that we are malleable and plastic within prescribed parameters and that our ability to learn is framed by our adaptations (see Box 9.3 'Objections to evolutionary psychology: learning' on p. 151). This proposal opens space for the claim that evolutionary psychology supposes that there is a limit on what we can think or conceive of. In other words, to say that there are only certain sorts of things that we can readily learn entails subscription to the claim that there are only certain sorts of things that we can think. For example, if we take the view that, ultimately, what we can think of is limited by what we can perceive then evolution places upon us an intellectual constraint. To grasp this point, consider this: we know that many breeds of dog have a wider hearing register than we do. It follows that, in some sense, they are open to at least one form of sensory experience that appears to be closed to us. Comparable claims can be made for many other species, e.g. the vision of eagles or the olfaction of sharks. If perception is the food of thought then other species are dinning at a different table. We have no means of knowing of course, but because we do not have the same sensory experience as, say, a bat we have no sense of and can make no existential sense of the life of a bat (Nagel, 1974).

Insofar as the intellectual constraint objection is an objection to evolutionary psychology as opposed to a problem in the philosophy of epistemology, evolutionary psychologists must concede that at least insofar as technological innovation goes, history suggests that we are not so constrained. In order to accommodate the objection and the profusion of new ideas that marks out our recorded history we could point to the fact that inevitability of variation of forms of human minds courtesy of sexual reproduction suggests that there will always be novelty of thought.

PSYCHOLOGICAL ADAPTATIONS AND IDEALISATIONS

One of the reasons why the concept of instinct was dropped from much academic psychology from about 1930 onwards is because theorists could not disambiguate mental states that appeared to be candidates for the designation of 'instinct' and those that were not (Bernard, 1924). In part, the problem arose because the definition of the term became more and more abstract as the debate about its proper definition developed (Hampton, 2006).

Notwithstanding past failures, for evolutionary psychologists it seems to have become more obvious than ever that distinct and species-typical anatomical features of organisms are 'for' something, and this analysis can be extended to human psychology (Hagen, 2005). Accordingly, psychology should be about psychological adaptations – the 'essence of evolutionary psychology' according to Crawford (2007) – because they are universal features of humans. But the term 'universal' presents a problem. People do not all think and behave in the same way. We discussed ways around the problem in Chapter 10 'Evolution and abnormal psychology'. This section will address another way around it and a consequence for those who want to build a theory of psychology based on the idea of universal psychological adaptations. We will see that the price of universal psychological adaptations in light of individual differences is that psychological adaptations become abstractions decoupled from thought and behaviour. To begin, we need to consider the notion of universality and species-typicality in more detail.

How universal is species typicality? There are two approaches to this question. The first says that we must take heed of the term 'typical'. It means that there is no strict equivalence between individuals. Because of sexual reproduction we are all unique. The second says that it is not a sensible or meaningful question. Any trait or characteristic said to be typical is universal for all organisms properly classed as a type. Those who place psychological adaptations at the centre of their endeavours prefer to see species-typicality in this second way and tend to reject the first. Let us consider their reasoning.

That which is said to be species typical and universal is a property of the human genome wherein the genome is conceived of as a design and the design is overwhelmingly more important than examples of its variable instantiation. Thus,

> Nearly all of population genetics consists of the elaboration of a mathematics to describe the varieties of genetic change and ongoing selection … In population genetics, designs show up purely as some allele or combination of alleles, that is, as part of some system of genetic variation. As alleles become fixed they tend to disappear from the analysis, leaving the accumulated uniformity of the evolving organism's complex design invisible to these tools of mathematical analysis. (Tooby and Cosmides, 1990: 380)

The important distinction here is that between fixed alleles and variable genes. It is being argued that too close an interest in actual genotypes leads to a misleading concentration on variations. And it is argued that a consequence of this is that:

> … empirical studies tended to focus on related phenomena that were observable: the distribution of genetic variation; the relationship between genetic variation and phenotypic variation; the patterns of variability within and between populations; fitness differentials between individuals … For this reason, there are many studies of such phenomena as environmental gradients associated with genetic or phenotypic gradients. But when a gene reaches fixation it no longer creates heritable differences between individuals; at that point it disappears from the analytic scope of the study of variation. Consequently, present variation in design and ongoing selection was visible to these methods, whereas the uniform design reflecting already completed selection was invisible. Unfortunately, the vast preponderance of organic design representing the accumulated effects of four billion years of selection reflects completed rather than ongoing selection. To study variation is to bypass most of the structure of complex functional design. (ibid.,: 380–381)

The point is that we cannot see species-typical adaptations in differences between genotypes because:

> An adaptation is more than a mere collection of phenotypic properties which, in a particular individual, happen to have the effect of enhancing reproduction … An adaptation is a recurrent design that reappears across generations and across individuals … This means that the phenotype of an individual organism must be carefully distinguished from the design of the phenotype – fitness should be assigned to designs, not to individuals. (ibid.,: 394)

Evolutionary psychology takes up this reasoning and claims that it is necessary to describe that which is variable in terms of that which is recurrent and stable: 'Thus, individual phenotypes are instances of designs, not designs themselves … to recover adaptive design out of behavioural or morphological observations, one needs to determine what is variable and what is invariant across individuals' (ibid.,: 395). In other words, we should more-or-less ignore actual properties of actual organisms in favour of hypothesised invariant properties. This approach is said to allow us to suppose psychological adaptations in the absence of enough consistent evidence which would allow us to infer its existence. In short, the price we pay for subscribing to the idea of universal features are abstract, idealised psychological adaptations.

It is for you to decide if the price is too high. On the one hand, framing psychological adaptations as abstractions accommodates variations in behavioural output or performance because we can say that the proposed adaptation is subject to different input conditions. However, we do not need to treat them as if they actually exist. Framing psychological adaptations as abstract designs renders them somewhat immune from evidence gathered from behaviour and that is unlikely to suit those who take themselves to be behavioural scientists.

ADAPTATIONS AND ADDED VALUE

What happened to the concept of instinct? One answer to the question is that it was rejected by behaviourism and replaced by the concept of habit. Another is that it never went away. On the one hand, it was adopted by ethologists, and in psychology beyond behaviourism it was replaced by other comparable terms (see Box 12.3). And a third answer is that it ceased to become clear what value the term added to findings which suggested that certain persons or groups behaved in a characteristic manner in response to certain stimuli or situations. We can ask a similar question: what value does it add to an explanation to say that a given behaviour has an adaptive basis?

BOX 12.4 CAN INSTINCTS BE GIVEN UP IN PSYCHOLOGY?

This is the title of a paper by Edward Tolman published in 1922. In it Tolman tried to show how impoverished psychology would become should it reject instinct theory – and with it evolutionary theory – altogether. Tolman suggested that the more modest term 'driving adjustment' take the place of instinct. Others were to follow. The following is a list (it is not exhaustive) of terms that were used to replace instinct. It conveys something of what happened to the concept of instinct in psychology during the twenties, thirties and forties.

'Fundamental desires' – Dunlap, *Elements of Scientific Psychology* (1922)
'Unit of reaction' – Kuo, *Psychology without Heredity* (1924)
'Human proponent reflexes' – Allport, *Social Psychology* (1924)
'Native impulses' – Ellwood, *The Psychology of Human Society* (1925)
'Primary desires' – Dunlap, *Civilized Life* (1934)
'Motives' – Gurnee, Elements of Social Psychology (1936)
'Dependable motives' – Woodworth, *Psychology* (1929) and Klinberg, *Social Psychology* (1940, 1953)
'Drives' – Murphy, Murphy and Newcomb, *Experimental Social Psychology* (1937)
'Viscerogenic and psychogenic needs' – Murray, *Explorations in Personality* (1939)

To tackle this question let us consider the myriad ways in which humans reproduce and form groups. Like evolutionary psychologists, behavioural ecologists are very much interested in reproduction. However, they tend to focus on family structures to a greater extent than on certain characteristics in members of the opposite sex (Voland, 2007). As you may recall from Chapter 3, behavioural ecologists prefer to emphasise the adaptive nature of behaviour rather than the adapted nature of the mind. Accordingly, families are seen as adaptive strategies and different forms are as seen as being more-or-less adaptive in response to the physical and social niche in which they form. Obviously, evidence gathered about family forms is gathered from extant human populations and are, in the first instance, descriptive. For example, Leonetti et al. (2007) found that the nature of paternal investment differed within and between to two ethnic groups – the Khasi and Bengali in northeast India. To go beyond a description we need some theory. We need to try and give an account of the findings; to say how the observed phenomenon comes about and why it comes about. In this instance the researchers employed the idea that types and patterns of parental investment alters as a function of the need to ensure that children develop certain sorts of skill given the context and reproductive outlook (Kaplan, 1996). As it turns out the theory that inspired the research is given partial support by the evidence collected.

Now look again at the last sentence and consider the terms 'inspired' and 'support'. On the one hand, without the theory the researchers would not have been inspired to look for what they did. It provided them with a 'way of seeing', a way of thinking about what was already there. On the other hand, they did not see quite what the theory predicted. This kind of outcome is very common. Perhaps the theory needs to be modified. Perhaps the method needs to be refined.

What we need to do is ask what the purpose of the research was. In this case it was to search for a biological basis for parenting behaviour. It is at this point that we might stop and ask in what way is the original finding enhanced, what else do we know if we did say that the phenomenon is a result of an adaptation? This is especially pressing given that we do not really know what a psychological adaptation is. Perhaps it would be more parsimonious if we did not invoke the concept of psychological adaptations and simply say that the Khasi and Bengali are in the habit of rearing their children in a certain manner and that the habits change over time in response to changing circumstances. That way we can minimise our assumptions, and include in our explanatory system causes which we can specify as being present.

BOX 12.5   INSTINCTS AND HABITS: THE INNATE AND THE LEARNED

The behaviourists considered themselves to be good Darwinians. Behaviourism concentrated on a pragmatic view of learning and it brokered no principled distinction between species. John Watson clearly took himself to be true to Darwin: 'The behaviorist … recognizes no dividing line between man and brute' (Watson, 1913: 158). Skinner too thought he was true to Darwin: 'You have precisely the same problems with operant behaviour that Darwin faced with evolution. Natural selection and operant conditioning are very similar. Both move purpose from before to after. This explains origination' (Skinner in Cohen, 1977: 280).

Behaviourism looked to replace the study of instinct with the study of habit and its formation and took Darwin himself to have issued the license:

> How unconsciously many habitual actions are performed, indeed not rarely in direct opposition to our conscious will! ... Habits become easily associated with other habits, with certain periods of time, and states of the body. When once acquired, they often remain constant throughout life. Several other points of resemblance between instincts and habits could also be pointed out. As in repeating a well known song, so in instincts, one action follows another by a sort of rhythm; if a person be interrupted in a song, or in repeating anything by rote, he is generally forced to go back to recover the habitual train of thought. (Darwin, 1859: 192)

For Darwin the distinction between habit and instinct was not to be discerned in behaviour – 'the resemblance between what was originally a habit and an instinct becomes so close as not to be distinguished' (ibid.,: 192) – but in their origin. In Darwin's view, 'slight variations of instinct might be profitable to a species' (ibid.,: 192). He viewed habits as a form of functional adjustment bounded by the problems and needs faced by an organism in the course of its lifetime. An implication of this seized upon by behaviourists is that while variations in the behaviour of organisms of a species may be a result of natural selection, it is as likely to be the result of environmental factors extrinsic to organisms.

The behaviourist Knight Dunlap attempted to pick apart how one might be able to distinguish between instincts and habits:

> I can see no way of distinguishing usefully between instinct and habit ... All reactions are instinctive: all are acquired ... Practically, we use the term instinctive reaction to designate any reaction whose antecedents we do not care, at the time, to inquire into; by acquired reaction, on the other hand, we mean those reactions for whose antecedents we intend to give some account. (Dunlap, 1919: 92)

What is noteworthy in this passage is the classification of the issue into theoretical and practical components. Dunlap suggested that any insistence on the pursuit of instinctive designations was, in effect, a resignation of the pursuit of cause.

The wider point to be made about the value of invoking adaptations is that it is not always obvious that we are in possession of some sort of distinct or definite knowledge, that we know something over and above, something extra or more if we attach tags such as 'evolution' or 'Darwinian' to results. The danger is that such tags are used to legitimise or add weight to otherwise ordinary, day-to-day, research. Generating hypotheses coloured by an overt allegiance to evolutionary theory does not guarantee their quality. The truth value of evolutionary theory does not transfer to appended propositions. We must judge each piece of research on its own merits because the brand name of Darwin does not legitimise or rescue questionable methods or results.

BORING'S TRAP

To bring this chapter to a close we will draw upon the thoughts of the historian of psychology, Edwin Boring.

Boring was the president of the American Psychological Association in 1928 and his presidential address was titled *The Psychology of Controversy*. In the address and the paper that followed it Boring examined the way in which psychology is constituted by controversy, and, as the title suggests, the psychological basis of controversy (Boring, 1929). He wanted to make the point that competing schools of academic thought have characteristics that can be compared to the persons behind them. He was also wanting understand psychological research as part of the wider enterprise of scientific inquiry in order to show that psychology was rooted in and driven by controversy, just as were the 'exact sciences'.

> … I have come reluctantly to the conclusion that scientific truth, like juristic truth, must come about by controversy… It seems to me that scientific truth must transcend the individual, that the best hope of science lies in its greatest minds being often brilliantly and determinedly wrong, but in opposition, with some third, eclectically minded, middle-of-the-road nonentity seizing the prize while the great fight for it, running off with it, and sticking it in a textbook for sophomores written from no point of view and in defence of nothing whatsoever. (Boring, 1929: 98)

Taking what he took to be the 'verdict of the history', Boring substantiated his claim by reference to the history of psychology. And he went to some lengths to show how vitriolic were some of the personal criticisms and how acute the personal antipathy between the protagonists.

Boring also discussed what he called the 'negativism of progress'.

> With respect to scientific movements there seems to exist something like Newton's third law of motion: action equals reaction. You cannot move – in the sense of starting a movement – unless you have something to push against … Science can actually, by the empirical method … lift itself by its own bootstraps, but the result is not what we call a 'movement' because motion can be defined only with respect to a frame of reference. A movement must move with respect to something, and progress must move away from something, if the movement is to command observational attention. It is therefore the business of the founders of new schools, the promoters and propagandists, to call persistent attention to what they are not … (ibid.,: 108)

Boring gave a series of examples and highlighted the what was then an old controversy between functionalists – broadly speaking, those who seek to understand the purpose of psychological phenomenon, and structuralists – broadly speaking, those who seek to understand how idea relate to one another.

> In those days the opposite of functionalism was structuralism, but nobody – except perhaps some graduate students – ever called himself a 'structuralist'. Titchener adopted the phrase 'structural psychology' and abandoned it long before it went out of use. No, the functionalist had to have something definite to push against, and it was only they who talked about 'structuralists'. (ibid.,: 110)

Boring thought that apparent controversies are, in fact, 'often one sided because directed against no particular opposition' and that 'fights' in psychology are, in fact, against 'windmills' (ibid.).

The psychological and behavioural sciences have long been immersed in how to deal with and accommodate Darwinism and its implications (Degler, 1991; Hampton, 2004b; Plotkin, 2004; Richards, 1987). It is historically incorrect to say otherwise. Also, while it may be true that 'respect for parents may be laudable and yet hinder the free development of youth', subscription to the Standard Model thesis and an insistence on division only invites neglect of an extensive literature which has tried to work out many of the theoretical and empirical problems faced by evolutionary approaches.

Reading *The Psychology of Controversy* today cannot but put us in mind of evolutionary psychology – 'the new science of the mind' – and its detractors. What was going on in Boring's time seems to be going on now. In opposing so much of what has gone before evolutionary approaches have promoted antagonism in psychology and social science. Boring teaches us that evolutionary approaches to human thought and behaviour have embroiled themselves in a controversy of their own making and they need to extricate themselves from it if the future is not to continue in the same vein as the past. Evolutionary approaches can escape Boring's trap if they embrace the history of psychology. If they do not, they may become part of it. Using Boring's phrase we might suggest that evolutionary psychology 'is past its prime as a movement because movements exist upon protest and it no longer needs to protest' (Boring, 1929: 111).

SUMMARY OF CHAPTER 12

There is a choice of ways in which to think about and frame it but no real alternative to the Darwinian perspective for those who seek a biological foundation for explanations of human thought and behaviour. This claim assures us that evolutionary approaches have a future as well as a past. However, the approaches that comprise the present have problems to consider and negotiate if they are going to continue to thrive.

One of these problems concerns the proper treatment of the evidence we have that humans have evolved. The fossil record tells us much, but it also tells us very little about the particulars of how we lived, and what happened to bring us about in our current form. We cannot recover the thoughts, beliefs, desires and intentions that made up much of the EEA, and we must be careful not to allow assumptions about the past slip by as known truths. We must allow guard against casual assumptions that the past and the present were much the same. The present is greatly varied cultural myopia may make us turn the past into that which we each experience.

The search for accurate description of the programmes that govern out thought and behaviour is the driving goal of evolutionary psychology. These programmes are conceived of as psychological adaptations and these adaptations are said to be universal and species typical features of humans. But framing them as such makes them abstractions or idealisation that appear to be decoupled from evidence. The danger is that the idea of psychological adaptations is held onto regardless of how people behave. There is also a danger that psychologists and social scientists become transfixed by the idea of adaptations and the apparent power of evolutionary theory. We need to remain mindful of what the notion of adaptation adds to our theorising and explanations. To say that a given behaviour is the result of evolution of an adaptation does not necessarily explain it but simply labels it. Although the theory of evolution by natural selection is remarkably elegant, parsimonious and really quite simple it does not follow that it is similarly elegant, parsimonious and simple to attribute the cause of behaviour to our natural history when cause might also be located in the present.

Our final word on the future of the contemporary approaches that dominate Darwinian psychology and social science draws upon the history of the arts and sciences which can be seen as one long debate. Sometimes these debates are productive, sometimes not. It has been argued that they are least productive when positions are taken against positions that do not actually exist. Evolutionary approaches may be guilty of this. They are certainly guilty of claiming to be new and novel when this is not really true. The danger is that energy is spent making enemies and noise instead of real progress. If there is one lesson to be learned from human evolution is that it pays to cooperate. Competition and antagonism can pay but not so well as cooperation – not in the long run. Perhaps evolutionary approaches should take heed if, in due course and as envisioned, the term 'evolutionary' will be dropped and we will all just be psychologists again. Otherwise it may be that evolutionary psychology becomes an idea with a great future behind it.

FURTHER READING

Apart from the references in this chapter you may find it interesting and useful to consult one or more of the following:

Brown, A. (1999) *The Darwin Wars: The Scientific Battle for the Soul of Man.* London: Simon and Schuster – see Chapter 4 'Marxists at the Museum' and/or Chapter 6 'Primitive Combat'.

Buller, D.J. (2005) *Adapting Minds: Evolutionary Psychology and the Persistent Quest for Human Nature.* Cambridge, MA: MIT Press.

Buss, D.M., Haselton, M.G., Shackleford, T.K., Bleske, A.L. and Wakefield, J.C. (1998) Adaptations, exaptations, and spandrels. *American Psychologist*, 53: 533–548.

Hampton, S.J. (2004) Domain mismatches, scruffy engineering, exaptations and spandrels. *Theory and Psychology*, 14(2): 147–166.

Laland, K.N. and Brown, G.R. (2002) *Sense and Nonsense: Evolutionary Perspective on Human Behaviour.* Oxford: Oxford University Press.

Rose, S. (2000) Escaping evolutionary psychology. In Rose, H. and Rose, S. (eds). *Alas, Poor Darwin: Arguments Against Evolutionary Psychology.* London: Jonathan Cape.

GLOSSARY

actual domain   The current physical and social environment in which evolved adaptations operate. To be compared to *natural domain.*

adaptation   Any more or less discrete physical, physiological or psychological characteristic that has arisen through natural or sexual selection in order to solve a problem more-or-less related to development, survival or reproduction. For example, your eyes are an evolved adaptation to the problem of negotiating yourself through space and identifying objects and persons as you do so.

adapted mind   Often associated with evolutionary psychology, the view that the human mind comprises a suite of more-or-less inflexible adaptations to past environments.

adaptive mind   Often associated with human behavioural ecology, the view that the human mind is a more-or-less flexible computational device orientated towards the maximisation of inclusive fitness.

African Eve   See **out of Africa hypothesis.**

allele   Refers to a form of a gene which can be identified by its location on a specific chromosome. The total set of alleles comprises all forms of a gene which are thought to code for a particular process or characteristic.

altricial   Refers to the state of development or maturity of an animal at the point of birth. Human neonates are profoundly altricial in comparison to other mammals and primates. It has been suggested that we do not catch up to something like the altricial norm for primates until we are about six months old.

altruism   It is notoriously difficult to provide an example of true altruism wherein something is given and absolutely nothing is gained – not even a private sense of satisfaction that one has been of assistance to another. Accordingly, for present purposes the definition is given as a behaviour that is selfless in that the net cost is greater than the net gain.

anisogamy   Reproduction initiated by the union or fusion of two sex cells which are markedly different in size and/or form.

anorexia nervosa   A clinical term referring to disordered thought and behaviours which focus on an obsessive fear of gaining weight.

anthropomorphism   The tendency to impute human characteristics, feelings and/or dispositions on non-human animals, plants or objects. For example (and at the risk of offending the reader) you may know persons who describe their pet as being human-like in terms of its personality, emotions, likes and dislikes.

antisocial personality disorder   A clinical condition characterised by deceit, manipulation of others for selfish purposes, and a persistent disregard and violation of what would be considered to be the rights of others in the context. See **psychopathy** and **sociopathy**.

anxiety disorder   An unpleasant emotional state characterised by apprehension which is not specifically focussed on a person(s), social setting(s) or object(s).

apoptosis   Also known as programmed cell death (PCD), this is part of the developmental and maturation process for most animals species and it involves cell death which is controlled by the cell itself. This feature has encouraged the notion that during apoptosis cells commit suicide.

atavistic   The Latin root of this term is ancestor and it refers to a psychological or behavioural state that is said to be archaic and/or an exemplification of a previous form. Comparable to the notion of 'regression' wherein we might as adults behave as we did as children, we are atavistic when as *Homo sapiens* we behave as we would have as a prior evolutionary form.

Australopithecus   A genus of the family Hominidae. Including the species *Australopithecus afarensis, africanus* and *boisei,* this is the genus which is thought to be that which evolved from something akin to extant chimpanzees and into the superfamily *Homo.*

autism   A spectrum of psychological and behavioural disorders characterised by impairments in social interaction, verbal communication and repetitive behavior, all of which tend to be exhibited before a child is three years of age.

B

background anxiety   Refers to persistent unfocussed worry which impacts on the ability to engage with and participate in whatever would seem to the sufferer as ordinary and desirable behaviour and interaction.

behaviourism A movement in psychology prompted by Ivan Pavlov (1849–1936), promoted by John Watson (1878–1958), promulgated by Frederic Skinner (1904–1990), and underpinned by the conviction that behaviour can be scientifically measured whereas thought cannot, that prior experience determines current response, and that behaviour can be controlled and shaped by various forms of conditioning via rewards and punishments.

biological determinism A doctrine which supposes that biological objects can be accounted for in scientific cause-and-effect terms and as biological objects this is true of humans and their thought and behaviour. One difficulty with doctrine is that it is not clear that any well-established school of thought in psychology subscribes to it in bald terms. See also **determinism**.

bottle-neck theory Refers to the idea that modern humans came about courtesy of a significant reduction in the population of our immediate predecessors wherein a relatively small number survived some or another catastrophic event and the possibility of evolution came about because new advantageous mutation could come to fixation in a small population.

Broca's aphasia Also known as non-fluent or production aphasia, those who suffer from this condition exhibit produce meaningful speech but it is produced slowly and the grammar is truncated.

bulimia nervosa An eating disorder wherein a person eats excessively and then seeks to purge themselves of the food via vomiting and/or the use of laxatives because they are fearful of weight gain and obsessed with their body shape.

C

chromosome A string of DNA which can be divided into genes. In humans the nucleus is most cells contain 23 three pairs of such strings.

Cinderella Syndrome Refers to the claim that step-parents offer or provide relatively limited parental care.

circularity This term refers to particular type of argument whereupon the conclusion reached is presupposed by one or more of the proposition or statements deployed to support it.

classical cascade A way of deconstructing the general enterprise of cognitive psychology into three more tractable and mutually compatible problems or tasks. Resting on the assumption that the mind is instantiated in the brain, the three tasks are the problem the mind/brain needs to solve, the algorithmic procedure that solves the problem and the nature of the machine or device that can run the algorithmic procedure.

cognitive niche   Used most often in discussions about the evolution of language and the claim that language is an adaptation this term refers to the mental environment that amounted to an adaptive problem for our ancestors wherein they needed to respond in an organised manner to the thought of the social group.

competitive replacement   The process wherein one (or more) species are ousted from an ecological niche by another species which is better at exploiting the resources in the environment.

computational metaphor   The idea that thought is akin to a programme such as those we design and use with digital computers. The metaphor holds that the thought is like a programme and brain is like a digital computer.

conceptual integration   A project aimed towards making physical, biological, psychological and social sciences consistent with one another. See **reductionism**.

creole   A grammatically sophisticated language which is a hybrid of two or more languages of a grammatically sophisticated development of a *pidgin* language.

D

Darwinian fitness   The total direct reproductive success of an organism as measured by the number of offspring produced in comparison to the local average. The concept can also been explained as being the number of genes from a given genotype present in the next generation in comparison to the local average. To illustrate, you may wish to consider how many children a group of persons have, calculate an average, and then compare each member of the group to the average in order to assess their Darwinian fitness.

Darwinism   The body of theory and evidence which licenses the claim that all life forms are a product of evolution and nothing else.

design stance   The view that any given organism, or part therein, can be analysed in terms of what it is for and what its purpose is. Taken as a whole, evolutionary theory tells us that any given organism is designed to reproduce and in the process clone its DNA. Seen in parts, the design stance tells us to explain how any given component of the whole facilitates the general enterprise.

determinism   A doctrine which supposes that if everything has a particular cause (i.e. there are necessary and sufficient conditions that bring about any given event) then provided the conditions that comprise the cause hold then the effect is inevitable.

direct aggression   Delivery of a stimuli which has fitness negative consequences from one person to another.

distributed abnormalities   Behaviours and/or patterns of thought that are selected for and adaptive when present in normal amounts or expressed in normal ways but also vary in their expression from individual to individual. If a given adaptive response is rarer than the norm or more common then either may result in fitness reducing outcomes.

domain mismatch   A disjunction between the environment to which a trait or characteristic is adapted and that which it now operates.

dominance hierarchies   Describes the ranking system in a social group wherein each organism has a place and this place (or rank) goes some way towards determining its access to resources needed by and available to the group. While the establishment of a hierarchy may entail aggression it is also thought that once settled a hierarchy also prevents aggressive competition.

dominant gene   Refers to alleles that are expressed in the phenotype. Examples of dominant alleles in humans include those that code for brown eyes, dark hair, curly hair, dimples and freckles.

double aspect theory   Claims that the mental and the physical are two parts of the whole that we call a person or a personality.

double dissociation   Refers to a situation wherein it is supposed and can be shown that two functions are independent of one another. To show this one must be able to stipulate that of two functions one can remain in tact while the other is impaired and vice versa.

E

effective polygyny   A situation whereupon the variance in reproductive success is greater for one sex – almost always the males – than for the other.

eliminative materialism   (Also known as eliminativism) argues that our intuitions about mind and its nature (especially those endorsed by dualism) are wrong and that we need to replace mental-speak and terminology with a technical lexicon that is derived from and consistent with neurology and cognitive neuroscience.

encephalisation   Refers to growth in human brain size over the past *c.* two million years.

Environment of Evolutionary Adaptation (EEA)   All of the past selection pressures which have brought about the adaptations of which we are currently comprised.

epidemiological culture   The socially acquired set of practices and patterns of thought that distinguish groups of persons as being of a particular society.

epigenetic failure   Abnormalities or disorders of a physical or behavioural nature that arise through the dependence of genes on environments.

error management theory   Refers to the idea that when faced with making decisions we are biased towards the option which would reduce the likelihood of negative fitness consequences. The theory predicts that we choose a cautious option if the cost of getting a decision wrong is high. On the other hand, we might choose an ambitious option if the cost of getting the decision wrong is low. In both instance we manage the cost of error.

ethology   The observational study of animals in their natural setting.

evoked culture   The environmentally contingent set of practices and patterns of thought that distinguish groups of persons as being of a particular society.

evolutionary arms race   Circumstances wherein adaptations which serve to exploit conspecifics or other species trigger an adaptive response designed to offset the advantage. Dimorphism in body size between the sexes illustrates the idea of an arms race. For example, human males do not need to be about 20 per cent larger than human females for any reasons directly associated with development, maturation, reproduction and survival: the fact that females can get by demonstrates this. It must be the case that human males are as large as they are because being big pays – very probably in terms of direct physical aggression against same sex rivals. The logic is that being bigger begets itself because it is self selecting.

evolutionary psychiatry   An approach to mental illness and clinical disorders which seeks to establish a normative depiction of mental functioning by asking what mind and mental states – including those we often take to be abnormal and in need of remedy – are for in evolutionary terms.

evolutionary psychology   Generally speaking, explanations of thought and behaviour which frame humans as animals shaped by natural selection and motivated to reproduce. More precisely, the term refers to a combination of evolutionary theory and cognitive psychology which sees the human brain as an information-processing machine which solves the problems of survival and reproduction faced by our ancestors over the past six million years.

evolutionary stable strategy   Abbreviated as EES, this term arises from game theory and refers to a way of behaving and/or a behavioural tactic which is robust against invasion from another strategy. For example, 'tit-for-tat' is a strategy for reciprocal exchange wherein the policy is to return favours given but not engage in exchanges with those who have not returned favours in the past. Tit-for-tat is said to be stable against others strategies and, accordingly, it could offer us a model of reciprocal altruism.

F

female choice   Refers to the observation that in most species, and typically in mammals, females are the gatekeepers of the sexual act and signal to a willing males that copulation is available.

fitness   The total reproductive success of an organism.

fitness tokens   In line with the idea that the general problem of reproduction break up into tens, hundreds, even thousands of smaller problem's which, if solved, will result in reproductive success, fitness tokens can be seen as problems solved and points scored towards the overall goal. Examples of fitness tokens could be good-quality food, a reciprocal alliance and a safe haven.

fixed action pattern   Refers to a functional sequence of behaviours which is typical of a species and is triggered by a specific stimulus.

four whys   An analysis heuristic used by biologists wherein physical and behavioural phenomena (e.g. the eye, or species typical attachment exhibitions) are considered in four different ways, each of which answers a particular sort of 'how?' or 'why?' question.

- Phylogenetic questions — how has the behaviour/physiological system/phenomenon developed through natural history?
- Ontogenetic questions — how does the behaviour/physiological system/phenomenon develop/mature through the life span?
- Functional questions — what is the purpose of the behaviour/physiological system/phenomenon?
- Mechanistic questions — how does the behaviour/physiological system/phenomenon work?

frequency dependent abnormalities   Seemingly maladaptive mindsets and/or behaviours which are rare but may be stable in terms of relative numbers of sufferers in a population. See *frequency dependent selection* and *frequency dependent strategies*.

frequency dependent selection   The process whereupon a given characteristic or behaviour is favoured by natural or sexual selection by virtue of it being atypical.

frequency dependent strategies   Fitness-enhancing patterns of thought and/or behaviour that work as a function of their relative rarity in comparison to all other patterns of thought and behaviour in the population.

function   The purpose of the characteristic in question

future discounting   The proposal that under certain circumstances the adoption of what appears to be a myopic, or short-sighted, short-term, strategy may be the rational option in overall fitness terms.

G

game theory   This involves the formal and abstract modelling of behaviours which are then set against one another in some form of competition. The idea is to examine which patterns of action would do best against other patterns of action over time and multiple iterations.

gamete   Refers to a sex cell which carries a random half of the alleles from the donor. Human male gametes are sperm. Human female gametes are ovum.

genes   Stretches of DNA comprising instruction for the neucleotide sequence for a single protein.

genetic leash   The idea that our genes constrain the types and form of culture we are able to create and sustain.

genotype   The set of genes carried by an organism, arranged on chromosomes, following meiotic recombination.

gossip hypothesis   The claim that the root function of human language is to exchange information about salient and pertinent other in our social groups.

group selection   A theory which supposes that the unit of selection is a breeding population. This supposition carries the implication that members of the group will behaviour in accordance with what is best for the group as a whole.

H

handicap principle   Sexual selection theory (see **sexual selection**) tells us that physical and/or behavioural characteristics that appear to mitigate against survival may facilitate reproduction (e.g. the peacock's tail). The handicap principle goes a little further and claims that some physical and/or behavioural characteristics are selected for because they advertise the fact that the bearer can survive the negative impact and that this is itself appealing to the opposite sex. Excessive and apparently pointless risk taking in young males may be just such an example.

heritability   When a characteristic is said to be subject to inter-generational transmission.

Holocene   A period in geological and natural history which began about 12,000 years ago and continues through to the present time. In anthropological term it is sometimes referred to in order to mark out the beginning of agriculture.

holophrastic phase   Refers to the use of a single word to convey complex meaning, intention, or desire. For example, a child may say 'me' when pointing at an object. What the child means is 'I want that', or 'Give that to me', or 'That belongs to me'.

hominid   Refers to any organism which we typically call a 'great apes'. The great apes include extant orangutans, gorillas, chimpanzees, and all extinct humans forms as well as ourselves.

Homo   Meaning 'human' this term encompasses the bipedal species that appeared about two million years ago in eastern Africa.

human behavioural ecology   Working from the assumption that human seek to optimise their reproductive success this discipline, or approach within the Darwinian tradition, favours a comparison of models of how the goals of reproductive success might be achieved in particular physical and social environments and observed behaviours.

humaneering   The idea that the psychological and social sciences ought to be able to provide theory and information geared towards improving human lives.

hunter-gatherer   A labelled applied to groups whose means of subsistence involves a combination of capturing animals and gathering vegetable foodstuffs (see also **scavenger-gatherer**).

I

identity theory   Refers to the claim that the mind and the brain are one and the same thing. On this account anything that can be said to be true of one is true of the other.

imprinting   Refers to a form of learning which is sensitive to the state of maturation and development of the organism. The proposal is that a certain sort of stimulus need to be present, or a certain type of event needs to take place at a certain point in the organisms maturation for a cognitive ability of behaviour to develop normally.

in-group   A collective of persons who as part of their sense of self and self-identity shared component.

inclusive fitness   Refers to total reproductive success of an organism as measured by the number of offspring directly produced and indirectly produced by related others. The concept can also been explained as being the number of genes that are identical to a given genotype present in the next generation in comparison to the local average. To illustrate, you can calculate your own inclusive fitness by adding up how many offspring you, your parents, your siblings, your cousins, your grandchildren and, indeed, anyone who you know you share genetic material with have.

indirect aggression   Refers to a harmful act precipitated by one onto one or more others wherein the act is delivery via oblique means and, in the current context, has negative fitness consequences for the victim. Examples of indirect aggression is include malicious gossip and social ostracism.

inheritance   The passing of something from one generation to its successor. In biology that which is passed are genes through sexual reproduction.

inheritance of acquired characteristics   See **Lamarckism**.

instinct debate   Collection of views centred on an attempt to ground psychology in Darwinism which persisted from about 1890 to about 1930. The enterprise attempted to establish a widely accepted definition of the term 'instinct', and an attempt to list the instincts of humans.

intentional stance   A way of explaining and predicting the behaviour of animate objects and animals which is facilitated by assuming that behaviour is driven by beliefs about the world and desires about goal states.

intentionality   An irreducible property of thought and certain designed objects wherein the thought (or mental state) or object is about something other than itself: the thought or object is orientated and configured in the way that it is because it represents something outside or other than itself.

inter-sex selection   Preferences expressed by one sex for members of the other. Iteration of such preferences over time leads to selection for the desired characteristics or traits.

intra-sex competition   Rivalry amongst same-sex members of a group for resources such as mating opportunities.

J

jealousy   A state of mental discomfort or pain centred on a suspicion, fear or knowledge that another has something one coverts.

K

kin selection theory   Also known as kin altruism, refers to the claim that related organisms (i.e. those that share genetic material) may behave in a more-or-less selfless manner toward one another wherein the cost to direct Darwinian fitness is balanced by the reward of indirect inclusive fitness.

L

Lamarckism   Refers to a theory of evolution by acquired characteristics. The idea is that the frequency of use of a limb, muscle and/or organ impacts not only on its own characteristics but also on the nature of the muscle and/or organ in an organisms offspring. On this view change in species over time occurs because offspring can inherit physical, behavioural and psychological characteristics acquired by their progenitors during the course of their lifetime. The suggestion with respect to giraffes, for example, is that because they can only survive by eating leaves high up in trees they stretch their necks to access leaves and the resultant stretched neck is bequeathed to subsequent offspring.

language acquisition device   This is said to be neurological machinery which allows humans to hear, identify, comprehend and produce language.

language competence   This term refers to knowledge of the rules (or syntax) and the words (lexicon) that govern and comprise a linguistic or communicative system.

language performance   This term refers to the actual production of speech. It give an indication of but does not necessarily provide a reliable guide to language competence.

law of dominance   Also known as Mendel's first law of inheritance, this states that in a hybrid union between sexual reproducing organisms of the two alleles only one will be expressed in the phenotype. The expressed allele is called dominant. That which is not expressed is called recessive. It needs to be noted that while dominance can been seen at work in many traits, in many species there are cases where dominance is incomplete or absent.

law of independent assortment   States that in a hybrid union between sexual reproducing organisms pairs of alleles separate independently when gametes are formed and that his applies to both sexes. The outcome is that the traits transmitted to offspring are independent of one another.

law of segregation   States that in a hybrid union between sexual reproducing organisms pairs of alleles randomly separate or segregate when gametes are formed and that this applies to both sexes. The outcome is a random half of all the alleles of both parents unite at fertilisation in the new embryo.

life history theory   A way of looking at what fitness issues face organisms over the life course.

M

maladaptive   Any behaviour that reduces inclusive fitness (see **inclusive fitness**).

marginal strategies   see **frequency dependent strategies**.

mate choice   The decision an organism makes with regard to reproductive partner(s). Sexual selection theory suggests that in mammalian species, including our own, females have greater control of such decisions than do males.

mate guarding   Behaviour which shields and/or protects a reproductive partner from conspecifics who seek mating opportunities with him/her.

mate value   The overall appeal of an organism as a reproductive partner to members of the opposite sex in a breeding population.

materialism   The view that there is nothing over and above physical matter and energy in the world and the universe. In psychology this view lead to the claim that there is not anything called 'mind' if such a term implies something other than physical matter.

maternal certainty   The implicit or explicit knowledge that a female has concerning whether she is or is not the biological progenitor of any given organism.

mating mind hypothesis   The claim that sexual selection is responsible for those seemingly unique properties of human psychology such as language, artistic creative or narrative imagination.

mating strategies   The patterns of behaviour that comprise the mating system for a species. Typically, males and females exhibit different patterns, and each sex may exhibit a different pattern over the life course.

mating systems   This term refers to the ways in which sexual reproducing species are organised in terms of the patterns of interaction between males and females. A given mating system indicates which males mate with what females in which way (see **mating strategies**).

metaculture   Refers to the goal-orientated practices exhibited by all peoples and groups.

meta-theory   A theory which spawns and may comprise a number of sub- or more particular theories. For example, we can think of Marxism as a meta-theory of historical change from which any number of more specific theories can be derived to explain particular phases of history in particular locations. We can see evolutionary theory as a meta-theory which explains how life forms reproduce and change and from this theory we can derive more specific theories to explain the behaviour of particular species, and particular aspects of their reproductive behaviour.

memes   Ideas or units of information as exemplified by axioms, maxims, musical tunes, designs and instructions that can be transmitted from person to person and can mutate, vary and compete in a manner analogous to genes.

metaculture   This term refers to the trans-historical and geographical constituents of human cultures; the habits, preoccupations and phenomenan of interest to all known cultures.

mind–body problem   The problem concerns the relationship and manner or interaction between thought and the brain given that it is clear that there is a dependency of one upon the other.

mismatch abnormalities   Abnormal mindsets and/or behaviours which arise from a disjunction between the environment which selected for a psychological adaptation or trait and the environment in which the adaptation or trait now operates.

modularity   The claim that the human mind comprises discrete parts which perform discrete functions.

monogamy   A mating system wherein the sexes form a single life-long pair bond.

moral responsibility   If we are free to choose how to behave, and if we are able to discern what is right and what is wrong with regard to the welfare and rights of others, then we can be held to account for our actions and judged according to their consequences. If we are not free to choose because our behaviour is determined by forces beyond ourselves then we cannot be held to account.

multi-regional hypothesis   A claim supported by a minority of scholars and researchers which suggests that extant modern humans evolved not from a single common stock but from geographically isolated groups of a predecessor species.

mutation   Refers to a change in the DNA sequence of a gene which results in a change to the protein coded for by that gene.

N

natural domain   The physical and social environment to which we are adapted. To be compared to the **actual domain** as part of **domain mismatch** theory.

natural selection   The process which brings about and shapes species courtesy of some organisms exhibiting features which better enable it to survive and reproduce, and pass those features onto succeeding generations.

nepotism   Preferential treatment afforded or a positively biased assessment of family members.

O

ontogenetic abnormalities   Within the confines of *evolutionary psychiatry* this term refers to maladaptive ways of thinking and/or behaving that result from problems during the maturation and development of the brain. The abnormality is said to be explicable in evolutionary terms because that which fail to mature and develop is part of the normal cognitive repertoire for humans.

ontogeny   The process and pattern of maturation and development typical of any organism of a species following conception.

out of Africa hypothesis   Refers to the claim that modern humans are the descendants of *Homo sapiens* which evolved in, and subsequently migrated out of, Africa and colonised the globe. Also known as the African Eve, Mitochondrial Eve and African Replacement hypothesis.

over-extension   A characteristic of children's speech wherein one word is used to refer to all things that share a single property. For example, the use of the word 'car' to refer to all four-wheeled vehicles.

P

palaeoanthropology   See **palaeontology**.

palaeontology   Archaeological and geological science which studies the fossil remains of organisms and related artefacts. In the context of this book the fossils of interest are those of organisms thought to be the near and far ancestors or modern humans which indicate how those ancestors behaved and what their cognitive abilities might have been.

paradigm   The set of supposed 'truths' that comprise the knowledge base in a given discipline and govern how research is conducted. For example, in psychology and the social science psychoanalysis, behaviourism, structuralism and functionalism may be thought of as paradigms in that they are ways of seeing and interpreting though and behaviour. The erm was made common and popular in the history, philosophy and sociology of science in the 1960s and 1970s following the publication of Thomas Kuhn's *The Structure of Scientific Revolutions* (1962, University of Chicago Press, London and Chicago) wherein Kuhn argued that the history of science can be characterised as being a series of changes in prevailing belief systems. More latterly the term paradigm has been used to refer to more modest sets of belief or practice. For example, very particular techniques such as grounded theory in qualitative research, or particular theories of memory such as the three-stage model (wherein we are said to have sensory, short-term and long-term memory stores) may be referred to as paradigms.

parent–offspring conflict   Explicit or implicit antagonism between progenitor and progeny which results from differing fitness interests. For example, a child might seek to secure more of its parents' attention in its own interests than parents wish to give given their own reproductive interests.

parental certainty   The knowledge (presumed to be implicit in species other than humans and explicit in humans) that any given member of the same species is one's offspring. Human females are said to enjoy *maternal certainty* by virtue of the birthing process. Human males are said to suffer paternal uncertainty for the same reason.

parental investment   Any time or resources that an organism devotes to the care of an offspring that it could otherwise devote to activity related to reproductive success.

phenotype   The expression of the **genotype**. The physical make-up coded for by dominant genes in the environment in which the coding takes place.

phylogeny   The evolutionary history of a species and its adaptations.

physical stance   The view that any given object, or part therein, can be analysed in terms of it physical make-up and properties, and that an understanding of its make-up and properties will allow us to explain and predict its behaviour.

pidgin   A grammatically simple language which comes about when persons speaking distinct languages develop a system of rudimentary communication or a grammatically simple language invented by children. Pidgins form the basis for *creole* languages.

pleistocene   A period in geological and natural history which began about two million years ago and ended about 12,000 years ago when superseded by the Holocene period. For current purposes its importance comes in relation to its mapping onto the appearance of the genus *Homo* and the advent of hunter-gathering.

pliocene   A period in geological and natural history which began about five million years ago and ended about two million years ago when superseded by the *Pleistocene*. For current purposes its importance comes in relation to its mapping onto the appearance of the genus *Australopithecus* at one end and the appearance of the genus *Homo* at the other.

polyandry   A mating system wherein one female forms a mating bond with two or more males who do not form a mating bond with other females.

polygyny   A mating system wherein one male forms a mating bond with two or more females who do not form a mating bond with other males.

post-natal depression   A form of depression suffered by new mothers and characterised by flattered emotional affect, lethargy, anxiety, low self-esteem and a sense of powerlessness which appears to be triggered by the birth of the child.

poverty of the stimulus   A rejoinder to the claims of behaviourism which argues that any and all behaviours can be learned courtesy of sensory information provided by the environment. Instead, it is claim that certain cognitive abilities and behaviours – notably language – exhibit a sophistication and novelty that goes beyond what could have been derived from sensory information.

promiscuity   A mating system wherein no ongoing pair-bonds are formed between mating couples.

proper domain   (In contrast to *actual domain*) this term refers to the physical and social environment for which and to which an adaptation has been selected.

protolanguage   The known or supposed predecessor of a known language or set of related languages. In this context, it is supposed that the innumerable fully fledged languages exhibited by humans through history developed from a less sophisticated form of language that may be thought of as a prototype.

psychopathy   Often and informally used interchangeably with **sociopathy** and **anti-social personality disorder**, in this volume the term has been used to refer to a psychological condition wherein a person exhibits selfish cheating in social relations and this behaviour pattern may be an example of a frequency dependent strategy at the level of the gene.

R

r **and K selection**   Refers to a way of conceiving of and placing in comparison the amount of *parental investment* that different species, sexes within species, or even different organisms of the same species and sex exhibit. *r* selected species provide little or no investment in offspring. K selected species provide lots. *r* selection is about quantity. *r* selected organisms produce multiple offspring, few of which survive. K selection is about quality. K selected species produce few offspring, many more of whom survive in comparison. In species that are K selected offspring are relatively immature and vulnerable at birth, and, undergo a long period before puberty. Consequently, the more K selected a species is the more there is a need for parental investment.

racism   The belief that there are pronounced and demonstrable biological differences among human races.

recessive gene   Refers to alleles that will be not be expressed in the phenotype if the allele it is paired with is dominant. Examples of recessive alleles in humans include those that code for blue and green eyes, blond, red and straight hair, and thin lips.

reciprocal altruism   A form of exchange wherein two actors swap favours that amount to a cost to one and a benefit to the other in terms of reproductive success. Iterations of such exchanges are mutually beneficial over time.

reductionism   Subscription to the view that any given phenomenon could and should be explained in terms of its constituent parts, and that these constituent parts, treated as phenomena, can themselves be explained in terms of their constituent parts, and so on until all is explained in as atomistic a level of detail as possible.

releasing mechanism   A term largely restricted to ethology which refers to a hypothetical psychological property which when presented with a particular stimulus triggers a particular behavioural sequence. See **fixed action pattern**.

reproductive success   All and any behaviour which results in the genes that comprise an individual replicated. The most obvious a direct form of such replication is in the form of direct descendants (i.e. offspring), but it can also come in the form of indirect descendants such as nephews, nieces and grandchildren.

runaway selection   Refers to a process wherein sexual selection is at work and is used to explain exceptional instances of characteristics which militate against survival or appear to be unnecessarily elaborate or metabolically costly. The notion of 'runaway' is invoked to illustrate how once inter- or intra-sex selection comes into play a characteristic which effectively and directly aids reproductive success can become grotesquely exaggerated over time.

S

scavenger-gatherer   A labelled applied to groups whose means of subsistence involved a combination of secondary foraging for animal carcasses killed by other species and gathering vegetable foodstuffs – see **hunter-gatherer**.

scruffy engineering   It is tempting to suppose that the evolutionary process producers optimally designed adaptations. However, evolution works on a 'good enough' basis and produces adaptations which are more-or-less well designed for purpose. Accordingly, a functional analysis of a given adaptation ought not to expect it to exhibit flawless construction or performance.

serial monogamy   A mating system wherein the sexes form two or more sexually exclusive pair-bonds over the life course.

sex ratio   The percentage of males to females in any given breeding population.

sexism   The belief that there are pronounced and demonstrable psychological and biological differences between males and females.

sexual dimorphism   Refers to typical and characteristic differences in the morphology of the sexes of a species other than those which directly pertain to copulation and gestation.

sexual recombination   The process whereby a new set of genes – a *genotype* – is formed courtesy of conception.

sexual selection   Refers to a process wherein organisms evolve particular characteristics that are not obviously related to survival but to reproduction. The process can be driven by mate choice wherein the different sexes of a species evolve into distinct forms because one of the sexes selects mates with particular features. This we call **inter-sex selection**. The process can be driven by competition for reproductive opportunities among members of one sex. This we call **intra-sex competition**. It may also be the case that both processes have been at work to produce characteristics. For example, the reason why human males are, on average, significantly larger than females may be down to intra-sex competition between males for access to females and to female preference for larger males.

sexy son hypothesis   This term refers to the idea that females may be motivated to preferentially choose to have and/or invest in male offspring because male offspring may be able to enchance their Darwinian fitness to a greater extent than can female offspring, courtesy of their greater reproductive potential.

social identity theory   The claim that we derive at least some part of our sense of self and self-esteem courtesy of the groups to which we belong. The formation and existence of groups of persons who derive a sense of self and self-esteem from such groups are known as in-groups and in-groups entail out-groups, i.e. groups of persons whose sense of self and self-esteem is derived from a different milieu.

social uncertainty hypothesis   With a view to explaining anorexia nervosa this idea claims that anxiety about the stability of the social environment and the prospects for successful child rearing leads to an attempt to control weight which, in turn, can control the menstrual cycle.

sociobiology   A variety of neo-Darwinian thought that arose in the 1970's and which sought to analyse the behaviour of species in terms of **inclusive fitness theory**.

sociopathy   Often and informally used interchangeably with **psychopathy** and **anti-social personality disorder**, in this volume the term has been used to refer to a psychological condition wherein a person exhibits selfish cheating in social relations and this behaviour pattern may be an example of a frequency dependent strategy which is elicited by social conditions. It is said to 'work' as a behavioural strategy in certain environments wherein models of and opportunities for ongoing mutually beneficial cooperation are few or non-existent.

sperm competition   Refers to circumstances wherein the sex cells of two or more males are alive in the reproductive tract of a female and are seeking to fertilise an ova.

standard social science model (SSSM)   A conceptual label used by some evolutionary psychologists to refer to twentieth-century psychology and social science which was said to be betrothed to the assumption that cultures shape human minds and not vice versa.

T

taxonomy   Refers to the science and practice of classifying species as types which bare relationships typically within hierarchies.

telegraphic speech   Also known as the 'two-word' stage of language acquisition, this term refers to the use of conjoined terms to convey complex meaning, intention, or desire. For example, with gesticulating a child might say 'got toy' meaning 'I have a toy', 'give toy' meaning 'get toy' meaning 'Go and get the toy'.

theory of mind   It has been suggested that the reason why humans have such large brains is because we need to develop workable and reasonably accurate explanations of why others think, feel and behave as they do.

tragic vision   An adjunct to the claim and implications that human nature is 'red in tooth and claw', this term is used to exemplify the supposed pessimism about humans and the prospects for the race said to be inherent in biological and evolutionary accounts of human nature.

U

under-extension   A characteristic of children's speech wherein a word or term is used to refer to only one item or thing rather than all such items or things which share the same property. For example, the use of the word 'car' to refer to only the family vehicle.

universal grammar   The claim that underlying the different combinations of sounds that comprise different languages there are a set of principles that they share.

Upper-Palaeolithic transition   Also known as the Middle-Upper Palaeolithic transition, this terms refers to the archeological record from *c.* 60,000 to *c.* 40,000 years ago which points towards the emergence of new tool technologies, the production of decorative personal ornamentation, symbolic art and land use which is taken to characterise the behaviour of modern pre-agricultural humans.

V

variation   The differing forms that any thing of a given class of things can and do take. For example, identifiable languages share a common stock of words. But all languages also have accents wherein the common stock of words are said or enunciated slightly differently from place to place. The differing enunciations are variations of a common form. Similarly, each of us exhibits physical and behavioural characteristics which are variations of a common form.

W

Wernicke's aphasia   Also known as comprehension aphasia, those who suffer from this condition produce non-meaningful speech which is fluent in that it is produced quickly but it exhibits over-elaborated grammar and the inclusion of redundant phrases and clauses.

Y

young-male syndrome   Evidence suggests that males between puberty and approximate ten years thereafter are more aggressive and accepting of risk to health than they are themselves at early and later ages and than females. The robustness of this finding promotes the claim that being between puberty and about ten years older is a risk to self for males and other in their vicinity.

Z

zero-sum game   A competition for or circumstance involving the allocation of resources wherein the winner takes all.

zygote   The root of this term is 'join' and it refers to the joining of two sex cells (the technical term being haploid cells) courtesy of fertilisation.

REFERENCES

Abed, R.T. (1998) The sexual competition hypothesis for eating disorders. *British Journal of Medical Psychology*, 71(4): 525–547.

Abed, R.T. (2000) Psychiatry and Darwinism: time to reconsider? *British Journal of Psychiatry*, 77: 1–3.

Aiello, L.C. (1992) Human body size and energy. In, Jones, S., Martin, R. and Pilbeam, D. (eds) *The Cambridge Encyclopedia of Human Evolution*. Cambridge: Cambridge University Press. pp. 44–45.

Alexander, G.M. and Hines, M. (1994) Gender labels and play styles: their relative contribution to children's selection of playmates. *Child Development*, 65: 869–879.

Alled, W.C., Emerson, A.E., Park, O., Park, T. and Schmidt, K.P. (1949) *Principles of Animal Ecology*. Philadelphia, PA: W.B. Saunders.

Allport, F. (1924) *Social Psychology*. Boston, MA: Houghton–Mifflin.

Alvarez, L. and Jaffe, K. (2004) Narcissism guides mate selection: humans mate assortatively, as revealed by facial resemblance, following an algorithm of 'self seeking like'. *Evolutionary Psychology*, 2: 177–194.

Andershed, H., Kerr, M., and Stattin, H. (2002) Understanding the abnormal by studying the normal. *Acta Psychiatrica Scandinavica*, 106(Suppl. 412): 75–80.

Anderson, J.L. and Crawford, C.B. (1992) Modelling the costs and benefits of reproductive suppression. *Human Nature*, 3: 299–334.

Anderson, K.G., Kaplan, H. and Lancaster, J. (1999a) Paternal care by genetic fathers and stepfathers I: reports from Albuquerque men. *Evolution and Human Behavior*, 20: 405–431.

Anderson, K.G., Kaplan, H. and Lancaster, J. (1999b) Paternal care by genetic fathers and stepfathers II: reports by Xhosa high school students. *Evolution and Human Behavior*, 20: 433–451.

Anderson, M. (1980) *Approaches to the History of the Western Family*. Cambridge: Cambridge University Press.

Andrade, J. (2008) The inclusion of antisocial behavior in the construct of psychopathy: a review of the research. *Aggression and Violent Behavior*, 13(4): 328–335.

Andrew, J., Cooke, M. and Muncer, S.J. (2008) The relationship between empathy and Machiavellianism: an alternative to empathizing–systemizing theory. *Personality and Individual Differences*, 44(5): 1203–1211.

Angell, J. R. (1906) *Psychology: An Introductory Study of the Structure and Function of Human Consciousness* (3rd edn). New York, NY: Henry Holt and Co.

Angell, J.R. (1907) The province of functional psychology. *Psychological* Review, 14: 61–91.

Archer, J. (2000) Sex difference in aggression between heterosexual partners: a meta-analysis. *Psychological Bulletin*, 126: 651–680.

Archer, J. (2004) Sex differences in aggression in real-world settings: a meta-analytic review. *Review of General Psychology*, 8(4): 291–322.

Ardrey, R. (1967) *African Genesis: A Personal Investigation into the Animal Origins and Nature of Man.* London: Collins.

Ash, J. and Gallup, G.G. (2007) Paleoclimatic variation and brain expansion during human evolution. *Human Nature*, 18(2):109–124.

Atran, S. (2008) The evolutionary psychology of religion. In Crawford, C.B. and Krebs, D. (eds), *Foundations of Evolutionary Psychology*. Hillsdale, NJ: Erlbaum. pp. 477–498.

Augoustinos, M. and Walker, I. (1995) *Social Cognition: An Integrated Introduction*. London: Sage.

Austin, E.J., Farrelly, D., Black, C. and Moore, H. (2007) Emotional intelligence, Machiavellianism and emotional manipulation: does EI have a dark side. *Personality and Individual Differences*, 43(1): 179–189.

Axelrod, R. (1984) *The Evolution of Cooperation*. New York, NY: Basic Books.

Babiak, P., and Hare, R. D. (2006) *Snakes in Suits: When Psychopaths Go To Work*. New York, NY: Regan Books.

Badcock, C. (1994) *PsychoDarwinism: A New Synthesis of Darwin and Freud*. London: HarperCollins.

Badcock, C. (2000) *Evolutionary Psychology: A Critical Introduction*. Cambridge: Polity Press.

Baddeley, A.D. (2003) Working memory and language: an overview. *Journal of Communication Disorders*, 36(3): 189–208.

Baddeley, A.D. (2007) *Working Memory, Thought and Action*. Oxford: Oxford University Press.

Baker, R.R. and Bellis, M.A. (1995) *Human Sperm Competition*. London: Chapman and Hall.

Baker, M.D. and Maner, J.K. (2008) Risk-taking as a situationally sensitive male mating strategy. *Evolution and Human Behavior*, 29(6): 384–390.

Barkow, J.H. (1992) Beneath new culture is old psychology: gossip and social stratification. In Barkow, J.H., Cosmides, C. and Tooby, J. (eds) *The Adapted Mind: Evolutionary Psychology and the Generation of Culture*. Oxford: Oxford University Press. pp. 627–638.

Barkow, J.H. (2006) *Missing the Revolution: Evolutionary Psychology for Social Scientists*. Oxford: Oxford University Press.

Barkow, J.H., Cosmides, L. and Tooby, J. *The Adapted Mind: Evolutionary Psychology and the Generation of Culture*. Oxford: Oxford University Press.

Baron-Cohen, S. (1996) *The Maladapted Mind: Classic Readings in Evolutionary Psychopathology*. Hove and Cambridge, MA: Psychology Press.

Baron-Cohen, S. (1999) Evolution of a theory of mind? In Corbalis, M. and Lea, S. (eds) *The Descent of Mind: Psychological Perspectives on Hominid Evolution*. Oxford: Oxford University Press. pp. 261–277.

Baron-Cohen, S. (2003) *The Essential Difference: Men, Women and the Extreme Male Brain*. Harmondsworth: Penguin/Allen Lane.

Barr, K. N. and Quinsey, V. L. (2004) Is psychopathy a pathology or a life strategy? Implications for social policy. In Crawford, C.B. and Salmon, C. (eds) *Evolutionary Psychology, Public Policy, and Personal Decisions*. Hillsdale, NJ: Erlbaum. pp. 293–317.

Beach, F.A. (1955) The descent of instinct. *Psychological Review*, 62: 401–410.

Beck, C.T. (1995) The effects of postpartum depression on maternal–infant interaction: a meta-analysis. *Nursing Research*, 44: 298–304.

Beck, J. and Forstmeier, W. (2007) Superstition and belief as inevitable by-products of an adaptive learning strategy. *Human Nature*, 18(1): 35–46.

Beckwith, J. (1981) The political use of sociobiology in the United States and Europe. *The Philosophical Forum*, 13(2/3): 311–321.

Belsky, J., Steinberg, L., and Draper, P. (1991) Childhood experience, interpersonal development, and reproductive strategy: an evolutionary theory of socialization. *Child Development*, 62: 647–670.

Beran, M.J., Gibson, K.R. and Rumbaugh, D.M. (1999) Predicting hominid intelligence from brain size. In Corballis, M.C. and Lea, S.E.G. (eds) *The Descent of Mind: Psychological Perspectives on Hominid Evolution*. New York, NY: Oxford University Press. pp. 88–97.

Bering, J. M., and Parker, B. D. (2006) Children's attributions of intentions to an invisible agent. *Developmental Psychology*, 42: 253–262.

Bernard, L.L. (1924) *Instinct: A Study in Social Psychology*. London: George Allen and Unwin.

Bickerton, D. (1981) *Roots of Language*. Ann Arbor, MI: Karoma.

Bickerton, D. (1990) *Language and Species*. Chicago: University of Chicago Press.

Binford, L. (1985) Human ancestors: changing views of their behaviour. *Journal of Anthropological Archaeology*, 4: 292–327.

Birbaumer, N., Veit, R., Lotze, M., Erb, M., Hermann, C., Grodd, W., and Flor, H. (2005) Deficient fear conditioning in psychopathy: a functional magnetic resonance imaging study. *Archives of General Psychiatry*, 62(7): 799–805.

Birkeland, R. Thompson, K.J., Herbozo, S., Roehrig, M., Cafri, G. and van den Berg, P. (2005) Media exposure, mood, and body image dissatisfaction: an experimental test of person versus product priming. *Body Image*, 4: 137–145.

Birkhead, T. (2000) Promiscuity: *An Evolutionary History of Sperm Competition and Sexual Conflict*. London: Faber and Faber.

Björkqvist, K. (1994) Sex differences in physical, verbal, and indirect aggression: a review of recent research. *Sex Roles*, 30(3/4): 177–188.

Björkqvist, K. Lagerspetz, K.M.J. and Kaukainen, A. (1992) Do girls manipulate and boys fight? Developmental trends in regard to direct and indirect aggression. *Aggressive Behaviour*, 18: 117–127.

Björkqvist, K., Osterman, K. and Kaukiainen, A. (1992) The development of direct and indirect aggressive strategies in males and females. In Bjorkqvist, K. and Niemela, P. (eds) *Of Mice and Women: Aspects of Female Aggression*. San Diego, CA: Academic Press. pp. 51–64.

Björkqvist, K. Osterman, K. and Lagerspetz, K.M. (1994) Sex differences in covert aggression among adults. *Aggressive Behavior*, 20: 27–33.

Blacker, C.P. (1952) *Eugenics: Galton and After*. London: Duckworth.

Blackmore, S. (1999) *The Meme Machine*. Oxford: Oxford University Press.

Blair, R.J.R., Budhani, S., Colledge, E., and Scott, S. (2005) Deafness to fear in boys with psychopathic tendencies. *Journal of Child Psychology and Psychiatry*, 46(3): 327–336.

Blair, R.J.R., Sellars, C., Strickland, I., Clark, F., Williams, A., Smith, M., and Jones, L. (1995) Emotion attributions in the psychopath. *Personality and Individual Differences*, 19(4): 431–437.

Blair, R.J.R., Sellars, C., Strickland, I., Clark, F., Williams, A., Smith, M., and Jones, L. (1996) Theory of mind in the psychopath. *Journal of Forensic Psychiatry*, 7(1): 15–25.

Bleske-Rechek, A., Eau Claire, C. Remiker, M.R., Swanson, M.R. and Zeug, N.M. (2006) Women more than men attend to indicators of good character: two experimental demonstrations. *Evolutionary Psychology*, 4: 248–261.

Book, A. and Quinsey, V.L. (2004) Psychopaths: cheaters or warrior-hawks? *Personality and Individual Differences*, 36(1): 33–45.

Boring, E. (1929) The psychology of controversy. *Psychological Review*, 36: 97–121.

Boulton, M.J. (1992) Rough physical play in adolescents: does it serve a dominance function? *Early Education and Development*, 3: 312–333.

Bowlby, J. (1969) *Attachment* (vol. 1 of *Attachment and Loss*). London: Howarth Press.

Boyd, R. and Richerson, P.J. (1985) *Culture and the Evolutionary Process.* Chicago, IL: University of Chicago Press.

Bressler, E.R. and Balshine, S. (2006) The influence of humor on desirability. *Evolution and Human Behaviour*, 27(1): 29–39.

Bressler, E.R., Martin, R.A. and Balshine, S. (2006) Production and appreciation of humour as sexually selected traits. *Evolution and Human Behavior*, 27(2): 121–130.

Brosnan, S.F. (2006) Nonhuman species' reactions to inequity and their implications for fairness. *Journal of Social Justice*, 19: 153–185.

Brown, D. (1991) *Human Universals.* New York, NY: McGraw Hill.

Brown, R. (2000) Social identity theory: past achievements, current problems and future challenges. *European Journal of Social Psychology*, 30: 745–778.

Bulbulia, J., Sosis, R., Genet, C., Harris, E. and Wyman, K. (eds) (2008) *The Evolution of Religion: Studies, Theories, and Critiques.* Santa Margarita, CA: Collins Foundation Press.

Buller, D.J. (2005) *Adapting Minds: Evolutionary Psychology and the Persistent Quest for Human Nature.* Cambridge, MA: Massachusetts Institute of Technology Press.

Burt, S. A., and Mikolajewski, A.J. (2008) Preliminary evidence that specific candidate genes are associated with adolescent-onset antisocial behavior. *Aggressive Behavior*, 34: 437–445.

Buss, D.M. (1989) Sex differences in human mate preferences: evolutionary hypotheses tested in 37 cultures. *Behavioural and Brain Sciences*, 12: 1–49.

Buss, D.M. (1990) International preferences in selecting mates: a study of 37 societies. *Journal of Cross-Cultural Psychology*, 21: 5–47.

Buss, D.M. (1992) Mate preference mechanisms: consequences for partner choice and intra-sexual competition. In Barkow, J.H., Cosmides, L. and Tooby, J. (eds) *The Adapted Mind: Evolutionary Psychology and the Generation of Culture.* Oxford: Oxford University Press. pp. 249–266.

Buss, D.M. (1995) Evolutionary psychology: a new paradigm for psychological science. *Psychological Inquiry*, 6(1): 1–30.

Buss, D.M. (1998) The psychology of human mate selection: exploring the complexity of the strategic repertoire. In Crawford, C. and Krebs, D.L. (eds) *Handbook of Evolutionary Psychology: Ideas, Issues and Applications.* Mahwah, NJ: Lawrence Erlbaum Associates. pp. 405–430.

Buss, D.M. (2000) *The Dangerous Passion: Why Jealousy is as Necessary as Love and Sex.* New York, NY: Free Press.

Buss, D.M. (2003) *The Evolution of Desire: Strategies of Human Mating* (2nd edn). New York, NY: Basic Books.

Buss, D.M. (2005) Foundation of evolutionary psychology. In Buss, D.M. (ed.) *The Handbook of Evolutionary Psychology.* Hoboken, NJ: John Wiley & Sons. pp. 1–3.

Buss, D.M. (2009) *Evolutionary Psychology: The New Science of the Mind* (3rd edn). Boston: Pearson Education.

Buss, D.M. and Hasleton, M. (2005) The evolution of jealousy. *Trends in Cognitive Sciences*, 9(11): 506–507.

Buss, D.M. and Schmitt, D.P. (1993) Sexual strategies theory: an evolutionary perspective on human mating. *Psychological Review*, 100: 204–232.

Byrne, R.W. (1999) Human cognitive evolution. In Corballis, M.C. and Lea, S.E.G. (eds) *The Descent of Mind: Psychological Perspectives on Hominid Evolution.* New York, NY: Oxford University Press. pp. 71–87.

Byrne, R.W. and Whiten, A. (1988) *Machiavellian Intelligence: Social Expertise and the Evolution of Intellect in Monkeys, Apes and Humans.* Oxford: Clarendon.

Caldwell, M.F., McCormick, D.J., Umstead, D., and Van Rybroek, G.J. (2007) Evidence of treatment progress and therapeutic outcomes among adolescents with psychopathic features. *Criminal Justice and Behavior,* 34(5): 573–587.

Caldwell, M.F., Skeem, J., Salekin, R., and Van Rybroek, G. (2006) Treatment response of adolescent offenders with psychopathy features: a 2-year follow-up. *Criminal Justice and Behavior,* 33(5): 571–596.

Campbell, A.C. (1995) A few good men: evolutionary psychology and female adolescent aggression. *Ethology and Sociobiology,* 16: 99–123.

Campbell, A.C. (1999a) Gender, evolution and psychology: nine feminist concerns addressed. *Psychology, Evolution and Gender,* 1(1): 57–80.

Campbell, A.C. (1999b) Staying alive: evolution, culture and women's intra-sexual aggression. *Behavioural and Brain Sciences,* 22: 203–214.

Campbell, A.C. (2002) *A Mind of Her Own: the Evolutionary Psychology of Women.* Oxford: Oxford University Press.

Campbell, A.C. (2005) Aggression. In Buss, D.M. (ed) *The Handbook of Evolutionary Psychology.* Hoboken, NJ: John Wiley & Sons. pp. 628–652.

Campbell, A.C., Shirley, L. and Cargill, L. (2002) Sex-typed preferences in three domains: do 2-year-olds need cognitive variables? *British Journal of Psychology,* 93: 203–217.

Campbell, A.C., Shirley, L., Heywood, C. and Crook, C. (2000) Infants' visual preference for sex congruent babies, children, toys and activities: a longitudinal study. *British Journal of Developmental Psychology,* 18: 479–498.

Campbell, S.B., and Cohn, J.F. (1991) Prevalence and correlates of postpartum depression in first-time mothers. *Journal of Abnormal Psychology,* 100(4): 594–599.

Cann, R.L., Stoneking, M. and Wilson, A.C. (1987) Mitochondrial DNA and human evolution. *Nature,* 325: 31–36.

Caporael, L. (2001) Evolutionary psychology: toward a unifying theory and a hybrid science. *Annual Review of Anthropology,* 52: 607–628.

Carroll, D.W. (2004) *Psychology of Language* (4th edn). Belmont, CA: Thompson Wadsworth.

Carroll, J. (2004) *Literary Darwinism: Evolution, Human Nature, and Literature.* London: Routledge.

Carroll, J. (2005) Literature and evolutionary psychology. In Buss, D.M. (ed) *The Handbook of Evolutionary Psychology.* Hoboken, NJ: John Wiley & Sons. pp. 931–952.

Case, A., Lin, I.-F. and McLanahan, S. (2000) How hungry is the selfish gene? *Economic Journal,* 110: 781–804.

Case, A., Lin, I.-F. and McLanahan, S. (2001) Educational attainment of siblings in stepfamilies. *Evolution and Human Behaviour,* 22: 269–289.

Chalmers, A.F. (1999) *What Is This Thing Called Science?* (3rd edn). Buckingham: Open University Press.

Chisholm, J.S. (1993) Death, hope, and sex: life-history theory and the development of reproductive strategies. *Current Anthropology,* 34: 1–24.

Chomsky, N. (1959) A review of B.F. Skinner's 'Verbal Behaviour'. *Language,* 35: 26–58.

Chomsky, N. (1986) *Knowledge of Language: Its Nature, Origin and Use.* New York, NY: Praeger.

Churchland, P.M. (1981) Eliminative materialism and the propositional attitudes. *Journal of Philosophy,* 78(2): 67–90.

Cochran, G. and Harpending, H. (2009) *The 10,000 Year Explosion: How Civilization Accelerated Human Evolution.* New York, NY: Basic Books.

Cohen, D. (1977) *Psychologists on Psychology.* London: Routledge, Kegan and Paul.

Coleman, M., Ganong L.H. and Fine, M. (2000) Reinvestigating remarriage: another decade of progress. *Journal of Marriage and Family*, 62: 1288–1307.

Corballis, M.C. (1991) *The Lopsided Ape: Evolution of the Generative Mind.* Oxford: Oxford University Press.

Corballis, M.C. and Lea, S.E.G. (1999a) Are humans special: a history of psychological perspectives. In Corballis, M.C. and Lea, S.E.G. (eds) *The Descent of Mind: Psychological Perspectives on Hominid Evolution.* New York, NY: Oxford University Press. pp. 1–15.

Corballis, M.C. and Lea, S.E.G. (1999b) Preface. In Corballis, M.C. and Lea, S.E.G. (eds) *The Descent of Mind: Psychological Perspectives on Hominid Evolution.* New York, NY: Oxford University Press. pp. v–vii.

Cosmides, L. (1989) The logic of social exchange: has natural selection shaped how humans reason? Studies with the Wason Selection Task. *Cognition*, 31: 187–276.

Cosmides, L., Tooby, J. and Barkow, J.H. (1992) Evolutionary psychology and conceptual integration. In Barkow, J. Cosmides, L. and Tooby, J. (eds), *The Adapted Mind: Evolutionary Psychology and the Generation of Culture.* Oxford: Oxford University Press. pp. 3–18.

Coyne, S.M. and Thomas, T.J. (2008) Psychopathy, aggression, and cheating behavior: a test of the Cheater–Hawk hypothesis. *Personality and Individual Differences*, 44(5): 1105–1115.

Crawford, C.B. (2007) Reproductive success: then and now. In Gangestad, S.W. and Simpson, J.A. (eds) *The Evolution of Mind: Fundamental Questions and Controversies.* New York, NY: Guilford Press. pp. 69–77.

Crawford, C.B. (1998) Environments and adaptations: then and now. In Crawford, C. and Krebs, D.L. (eds) *Handbook of Evolutionary Psychology: Ideas, Issues and Applications.* Mahwah, NJ: Lawrence Erlbaum Associates. pp. 275–302.

Crisp, A.H. (1980) *Anorexia Nervosa: Let Me Be.* London: Academic Press Inc.

Crossman, A. and Neary, D. (2005) *Neuroanatomy* (3rd edn). Edinburgh: Elsevier/Churchill Livingstone.

Cummins, D. (2005) Dominance, status, and social hierarchies. In Buss, D.M. (ed) *The Handbook of Evolutionary Psychology.* Hoboken, NJ: John Wiley & Sons. pp. 676–697.

Cziko, G. (1995) *Without Miracles.* Cambridge, MA: Massachusetts Institute of Technology Press.

Dabbs Jr., J.M. and Mallinger, A. (1999) High testosterone levels predict low voice pitch among men. *Personality and Individual Differences*, 27(4): 801–804.

Daly, M. and Wilson, M. (1981) Child maltreatment from a sociobiological perspective. *New Directions for Child Development*, 11: 93–112.

Daly, M. and Wilson, M. (1985) Child abuse and other risks of not living with both parents. *Ethology and Sociobiology*, 6: 197–210.

Daly, M. and Wilson, M. (1988) *Homicide.* New York, NY: Aldine de Gruyter.

Daly, M. and Wilson, M. (1994) Some differential attributes of lethal assaults on small children by stepfathers versus genetic fathers. *Ethology and Sociobiology*, 15: 207–217.

Daly, M. and Wilson, M. (1996) Violence against step-children. *Current Directions in Psychological Science*, 5: 77–81.

Daly, M. and Wilson, M. (1998) *The Truth about Cinderella: A Darwinian View of Parental Love.* London: Weidenfeld and Nicholson.

Daly, M. and Wilson, M. (1999) Special issue: step-parental investment. *Evolution and Human Behavior*, 20: 365–366.

Daly, M. and Wilson, M. (2003) Evolutionary psychology of lethal interpersonal violence. In Heitmeyer, W. and Hagan, J (eds) *Handbook of Research on Violence.* New York, NY: Westview. pp. 709–734.

Daly, M., McConnell, C. and Glugosh, T. (1996) Parents' knowledge of students' beliefs and attitudes: an indirect assay of parental solicitude? *Ethology and Sociobiology*, 17: 201–210.

Daly, M., Wilson, M. and Vasdev, S. (2001) Income inequality and homicide rates in Canada and the United States. *Canadian Journal of Criminology*, 43: 219–236.

Dart, R, and Craig, D. (1959) *Adventures with the Missing Link*. New York, NY: Harper and Brothers.

Darwin, C. (1859) *On the Origin of Species by Means of Natural Selection, or the Preservation of Favoured Races in the Struggle for Life*. London: John Murray.

Darwin, C. (1871) *The Descent of Man and Selection in Relation to Sex*. London: John Murray.

Dawkins, R. (1979) Twelve misunderstandings of kin selection. *Zeitschrift f r Tierpsychologie*, 51: 184–200.

Degler, C. (1991) *In Search of Human Nature: The Decline and Revival of Darwinism in American Social Thought*. New York, NY: Oxford University Press.

Dennett, D.C. (1978) *Brainstorms*. Montgomery, VT: Bradford Books.

Dennett, D.C. (1987a) Intentionality. In Gregory, R.L. (ed.) *The Oxford Companion to the Mind*. Oxford: Oxford University Press. pp. 383–386.

Dennett, D.C. (1987b) *The Intentional Stance*. Cambridge, MA: Bradford Books/Massachusetts Institute of Technology Press.

Dennett, D.C. (1991) *Consciousness Explained*. New York, NY: Little Brown.

Dennett, D.C. (1995) *Darwin's Dangerous Idea: Evolution and the Meanings of Life*. London: Allen Lane.

Dennett, D.C. (2003) *Freedom Evolves*. Harmondsworth: Penguin.

Dennis, C.L. (2004) Can we identify mothers at risk for postpartum depression in the immediate postpartum period using the Edinburgh Postnatal Depression Scale? *Journal of Affective Disorders*, 78(2): 163–169.

Desmond, A. and Moore, J. (1991) *Darwin*. Harmondsworth: Penguin.

Dewey, J. (1896) The reflex are concept in psychology. *Psychological Review*, 3: 357–370.

Dewey, J. (1930) *Human Nature and Conduct: An Introduction to Social Psychology*. New York, NY: Random House.

Donald, M. (1991) *Origins of the Modern Mind: Three Stages in the Evolution of Culture and Cognition*. Cambridge, MA: Harvard University Press.

Donald, M. (1999) Preconditions for the evolution of protolanguages. In Corballis, M.C. and Lea, S.E.G. (eds) *The Descent of Mind: Psychological Perspectives on Hominid Evolution*. New York, NY: pp. 138–154.

Douglas, K.S., Vincent, G.M., and Edens, J.E. (2005) Risk for criminal recidivism: the role of psychopathy. In Patrick, C.J. (ed.), *Handbook of Psychopathy*. New York, NY: Guilford. pp. 533–554.

Downey, D.B. (1995) Understanding academic achievement among children in step-households: the role of parental resources, sex of step-parent, and sex of child. *Social Forces*, 73: 875–894.

Draper, P., and Harpending, H. (1982) Father absence and reproductive strategy: an evolutionary perspective. *Journal of Anthropological Research*, 38: 255–273.

Drever, J. (1917) *Instinct in Man*. Cambridge: Cambridge University Press.

Dubrovsky B. (2002) Evolutionary psychiatry: adaptationist and nonadaptationist conceptualizations. *Progress in Neuropsychopharmacology and Biological Psychiatry*, 26(1): 1–19.

Dunbar, R.I.M. (1988) Darwinising man: a commentary. In Betzig, L., Borgerhoff-Mulder, M. and Turke, P. (eds) *Human Reproductive Behaviour: A Darwinian Perspective*. Cambridge: Cambridge University Press. pp. 161–169.

Dunbar, R.I.M. (1996) *Grooming, Gossip and the Evolution of Language*. London: Faber and Faber.

Dunbar, R.I.M. (2007) Evolution of the social brain. In Gangestad, S.W. and Simpson, J.A. (eds) *The Evolution of Mind: Fundamental Questions and Controversies*. New York, NY: Guilford Press. pp. 280–286.

Dunbar, R.I.M., Duncan, N.D.C. and Marriot, A. (1997) Human conversational behaviour. *Human Nature*, 8: 231–245.

Dunlap, K. (1919) Are there any instincts? *Journal of Abnormal Psychology*, 14: 307–311.

Dunlap, K. (1922) The identity of instinct and habit. *The Journal of Philosophy*, 19(4): 85–94.

Dunlap, K. (1932) *Habits – Their Making and Unmaking*. New York, NY: Liveright.

Duntley, J.D. (2005) Adaptations to dangers from humans. In Buss, D.M. (ed) *The Handbook of Evolutionary Psychology*. Hoboken, NJ: John Wiley & Sons. pp. 224–249.

Durham, W. (1991) *Coevolution: Genes, Culture and Human Diversity*. Stanford, CA: Stanford University Press.

Durkin, K. (1995) *Developmental Social Psychology: From Infancy to Old Age*. Oxford: Blackwell.

Edelman, G.M. (1987) *Neural Darwinism: The Theory of Neuronal. Selection*. New York, NY: Basic Books.

Ellis, B.J. (2004) Timing of pubertal maturation in girls: an integrated life history approach. *Psychological Bulletin*, 130: 920–958.

Ellis, B.J. and Bjorklund, D.F. (eds) (2005) *Origins of the Social Mind: Evolutionary Psychology and Child Development*. New York, NY: Guilford Press. pp. 219–244.

Ellis, B.J. and Symons, D. (1990) Sex differences in sexual fantasy: an evolutionary approach. *Journal of Sex Research*, 27(4): 527–555.

Etcoff, N. (1999) *The Survival of the Prettiest*. London: Little Brown.

Falk, D. (1992) *Braindance*. New York, NY: Henry Holt and Co.

Farr, R.M. (1985) Some reflections on the historical development of psychology as an experimental and social science (Inaugural professorial lecture). London: LSE Publications.

Feder, K. and Park, M. (1997) *Human Antiquity: An Introduction to Physical Anthropology and Archeology*. Boston: McGraw-Hill.

Fergusson, D.M., Fleming, J. and O'Neill, D.P. (1972) *Child Abuse in New Zealand*. Wellington: Government of New Zealand Printer.

Feshbach, N. (1969) Sex differences in children's modes of aggressive responses towards outsiders. *Merill-Palmer Quarterly*, 15: 249–258.

Fessler, D.M.T. (2006) The male flash of anger: violent response to transgression as an example of the intersection of evolved psychology and culture. In Barkow, J.H. (ed.) *Missing the Revolution: Darwinism for Social Scientists*. Oxford: Oxford University Press. pp. 101–118.

Finkler, K. (2001) The kin in the gene: the medicalization of family and kinship. *Current Anthropology*, 42(2): 235–263.

Fisher, H.E. (1989) Evolution of human serial pairbonding. *American Journal of Physical Anthropology*, 78: 331–354.

Fisher, H.E. (1992) *Anatomy of Love: A Natural History of Adultery, Monogamy and Divorce*. London: Simon and Schuster.

Fisher, R.A. (1930) *The Genetical Theory of Natural Selection*. Oxford: Oxford University Press.

Fleming, J., Mullen, P. and Bammer, G. (1997) A study of potential risk factors for sex abuse in childhood. *Child Abuse and Neglect*, 21: 41–58.

Flinn, M. and Alexander, R. (2007) Runaway social selection in human evolution. In Gangestad, S.W. and Simpson, J.A. (eds) *The Evolution of Mind: Fundamental Questions and Controversies*. New York, NY: Guilford Press. pp. 249–255.

Flinn, M.V. (1988) Step and genetic parent/offspring relationships in a Caribbean village. *Ethology and Sociobiology*, 9: 335–369.

Foley, R.A. (1987) *Another Unique Species: Patterns in Human Evolutionary Ecology*. Harlow: Longman.

Foley, R.A. (1988) Hominds, humans and hunter-gatherers: an evolutionary perspective. In Ingold, T., Riches, D. and Woodburn, J. (eds) *Hunters and Gatherers 1*. New York, NY: St Martin's Press. pp. 207–221.

Foley, R.A. (1996) The adaptive legacy of human evolution: a search for the environment of evolutionary adaptedness. *Evolutionary Anthropology*, 4(2): 194–203.

Franks, B. (1995) On explanation in the cognitive sciences: competence, idealisation, and the failure of the Classical Cascade. *British Journal for the Philosophy of Science*, 46(4): 475–502.

Freud, S. (1905/1960) *Jokes and Their Relation to the Unconscious*. (J. Strachey, Trans.) New York, NY: W.W. Norton.

Galton, F. (1979) *Hereditary Genius. An Inquiry into its Laws and Consequences*. London: Julian Friedman.

Gangested, S.W. (2008) Biological adaptations and human behaviour. In Crawford, C.B. and Krebs, D. (eds) *Foundations of Evolutionary Psychology*. New York, NY: Lawrence Erlbaum Associates. pp. 153–172.

Gangstead, S.W. and Thornhill, R. (1997) The evolutionary psychology of extra-pair sex: the role of fluctuating asymmetry. *Evolution and Human Behavior*, 18: 69–88.

Geen, R.G. (2001) *Human Aggression* (2nd edn). Buckingham: Open University Press.

Geertz, C. (2000) *The Interpretation of Cultures: Selected Essays*. New York, NY: Basic Books.

Gelles, R.J. and Harrop, J.W. (1991) The risk of abusive violence among children with non-genetic caretakers. *Family Relations*, 40: 78–83.

Ghiglieri, M.P. (1999) *The Dark Side of Man: Tracing the Origins of Male Violence*. Reading, MA: Perseus Books.

Gintis, H., Bowles, S., Boyd, R. and Fehr, E. (2007) Gene-culture coevolution and the emergence of altruistic behaviour in humans. In Crawford, C.B. and Krebs, D. (eds) *Foundations of Evolutionary Psychology*. New York, NY: Lawrence Erlbaum Associates. pp. 313–329.

Gleason, J.B. (1958) The child's learning of English morphology. *Word*, 14: 150–177.

Gonzaga, G.C., Hasleton, M.G., Smurda, J. Davies, M, M. and Poore, J.C. (2008) Love, desire, and the suppression of thoughts of romantic alternatives. *Evolution and Human Behaviour*, 29(2): 119–126.

Good, J.M.M. (2000) Disciplining social psychology: a case study of boundary relations in the history of the human sciences. *Journal of the History of the Behavioural Sciences*, 36(4): 383–403.

Green, D.M. and Swets, J.A. (1966) *Signal Detection and Psychophysics*. New York, NY: John Wiley.

Greengross, G. (2008) Survival of the funniest: a review of Rod Martin's 'Psychology of Humor: An Integrative Approach'. *Evolutionary Psychology*, 6(1): 90–95.

Greiling, H. and Buss, D. (2000) Women's sexual strategies: the hidden dimension of short-term extra-pair mating. *Personality and Individual Differences*, 28: 807–963.

Hagen, E.H. (1999) The function of postpartum depression. *Evolution and Human Behavior*, 20: 325–359.

Hagen, E.H. (2005) Controversial issues in evolutionary psychology. In Buss, D.M. (ed) *The Handbook of Evolutionary Psychology*. Hoboken, NJ: John Wiley & Sons. pp. 145–173.

Haig, D. and Graham, C. (1991) Genomic imprinting and the strange case of the insulin-like growth factor-II receptor. *Cell*, 64: 1045–1046.

Hajnal, J. (1965) European marriage patterns in perspective. In Glass, D.V. and Eversley, D.E.C. (eds) *Population in History*. London: Edward Arnold. pp. 101–143.

Haley, S. (2000) The future of the family in North America. *Futures*, 32: 777–782.

Hamilton, W.D. (1964a) The genetical evolution of social behaviour. *Journal of Theoretical Biology*, 7: 1–16.

Hamilton, W.D. (1964b) The genetical evolution of social behaviour. *Journal of Theoretical Biology*, 7: 17–52.

Hampton, S.J. (2004a) Domain mismatches, scruffy engineering, exaptations and spandrels. *Theory and Psychology*, 14(2): 147–166.

Hampton, S.J. (2004b) Adaptations for nothing in particular. *Journal for the Theory of Social Behaviour*, 34(1): 35–54.

Hampton, S.J. (2004c) The instinct debate and the standard social science model. *Sexualities, Evolution and Gender*, 6(1): 15–44.

Hampton, S.J. (2005a) Darwinian psychology old and new. In, Mulberger, A. and Gomez-Zuniga, B. (ed.) *Recent Contributions to the History of the Human Sciences*. Munich: Profil Verlag. pp. 228–244.

Hampton, S.J. (2005b) Family eugenics. *Disability and Society*, 20(5): 553–562.

Hampton, S.J. (2006) Can evolutionary psychology learn from the instinct debate? *History of the Human Sciences*, 19(4): 57–74.

Hardin, G. (1968) The tragedy of the commons. *Science*, 162: 1243–1248.

Harris, G., Hilton, N., Rice, M., and Eke, A. (2007) Children killed by genetic parents versus stepparents *Evolution & Human Behavior*, 28(2): 85–95.

Harris, J.R. (1998) *The Nurture Assumption: Why Children Turn Out the Way they Do*. London: Bloomsbury.

Hashima, P. and Amato, P. (1994) Poverty, social support, and parental behavior. *Child Development*, 65: 394–403.

Haslam, N. (1997) Four grammars for primate social relations. In Simpson, J.A. and Kenrick, D.T. (eds) *Evolutionary Social Psychology*. Mahwah, NJ: Lawrence Erlbaum Associates. pp. 297–316.

Hay, D.F., Castle, J. and Davies, L. (2000) Toddlers' use of force against familiar peers: A precursor of serious aggression? *Child Development*, 71(2): 457–467.

Heimberg, R.G., Turk, C.L. and Mennin, D.S. (2004) *Generalised Anxiety Disorder: Advances in Research and Practise*. New York, NY: Guilford Press.

Henzi, S.P., de Sousa Pereira, L.F., Hawker-Bond, D., Stiller, J., Dunbar, R.I.M. and Barrett, L. (2007) Look who's talking: developmental trends in the size of conversational cliques. *Evolution and Human Behavior*, 28(1): 66–74.

Hess, N. and Hagen, E.H. (2006) Psychological adaptations for assessing gossip veracity. *Human Nature*, 17(3) 337–354.

Hess, N.H. and Hagen, E.H. (2006) Sex differences in direct aggression: Psychological evidence from young adults. *Evolution and Human Behaviour*, 27(3): 231–245.

Hill, K. and Kaplan, H. (1988) Tradeoffs in male and female reproductive strategies among the Ache, part 2. In Betzig, L., Borgerhoff Mulder, M. and Turke, P. (eds) *Human Reproductive Behavior*. Cambridge: Cambridge University Press. pp. 291–305.

Hill, K. and Kaplan, H. (1993) Why do male foragers hunt and share food? *Current Anthropology*, 34: 701–706.

Hiraiwa-Hasegawa, M. (2005) Homicide by men in Japan, and its relationship to age, resources and risk taking. *Evolution and Human Behavior*, 26(4): 332–343.

Hobbes, T. (1996/1651) *Leviathan, or the Matter, Forme, and Power of a Common Wealth Ecclesiasticall and Civil*. Oxford: Oxford University Press.

Hobhouse, L.T. (1901) *Mind in Evolution*. London: Meuthen.

Hodgson, G.M. (1993) *Economics and Evolution: Bringing Life Back into Economics*. Cambridge: Polity Press and University of Michigan Press.

Hodgson, G.M. (2004) *The Evolution of Institutional Economics: Agency, Structure and Darwinism in American Institutionalism*. London: Routledge.

Hrdy, S.B. (2009) Meet the Alloparents: shared child care may be the secret of human evolutionary success. *Natural History*, 118(3): 24–29.

Hume, D. (1739/1978) *A Treatise of Human Nature; Book 1: Of the Understanding.* Oxford: Clarendon Press.

Humphrey, N. (1976) The social function of intellect. In Bateson, P.P. and Hinde, R.A. (eds) *Growing Points in Ethology.* Cambridge: Cambridge University Press. pp. 303–318.

Humphrey, N. (1992) *A History of the Mind.* London: Chatto and Windus.

Hyde, J.S. (2005) The gender similarities hypothesis. *American Psychologist*, 60(6): 581–592.

Ingram, D. (1999) *First Language Acquisition.* Cambridge: Cambridge University Press.

Isaac, G.L. (1977) The food sharing behaviour of proto-humans. *Scientific American*, 238: 90–108.

Isaac, G.L. (1978) Food sharing and human evolution: archaeological evidence from the Plio-Pleistocene of East Africa. *Journal of Anthropological Research*, 34: 311–324.

Jablonka, E. and Lamb, M. (2006) *Evolution in Four Dimensions.* Cambridge, MA: Massachusetts Institute of Technology Press.

Jackson, S. and Rees, A. (2007) The appalling appeal of nature: the popular influence of evolutionary psychology as a problem for sociology. *Sociology.* 41: 917–930.

James, W. (1890) *Principles of Psychology* (Vols. I and II). New York, NY: Washington Square Press.

Jennings, K.D., Ross, S., Popper, S. and Elmore, M. (1999) Thoughts of harming infants in depressed and non–depressed mothers. *Journal of Affective Disorders*, 54(1/2): 21–28.

Johanson, D., and B. Edgar (1996) *From Lucy to Language.* New York, NY: Simon and Schuster.

Jones, G. (1998) Theoretical foundations of eugenics. In Peel, R. (ed.) *Essays in the History of Eugenics.* London: The Galton Institute.

Jones, O.D. (2005) Evolutionary psychology and the law. In Buss, D.M. (ed) *The Handbook of Evolutionary Psychology.* Hoboken, NJ: John Wiley & Sons. pp. 953–974.

Juda, M.N., Campbell, L. and Crawford, C.B. (2004) Dieting symptomatology in women and perceptions of social support: an evolutionary approach. *Evolution and Human Behaviour*, 25(3): 200–208.

Kanazawa, S. (2009) Evolutionary psychological foundations of civil wars. *The Journal of Politics*, 71(1): 25–34.

Kaplan, H. (1996) A theory of fertility and parental investment in traditional and modern societies. *Yearbook of Physical Anthropology*, 39: 91–135.

Kaplan, H.S. and Gangestad, S.W. (2005) Life history theory and evolutionary psychology. In Buss, D.M. (ed) *The Handbook of Evolutionary Psychology.* Hoboken, NJ: John Wiley & Sons. pp. 68–95.

Kaplan, H.S., Gurven, M. and Lancaster, J.B. (2007) Brain evolution and the human adaptive complex: an ecological and social theory. In Gangestad, S.W. and Simpson, J.A. (eds) *The Evolution of Mind: Fundamental Questions and Controversies.* New York, NY: Guilford Press. pp. 269–279.

Kassim, K. and Kasim, M.S. (1995) Child sex abuse: psychosocial aspects of 101 cases seen in an urban Malaysian setting. *Child Abuse and Neglect*, 19: 793–799.

Kaukianen, A., Bjorkqvist, K., Lagerspetz, K.M.J., Osterman, K., Salmivalli, C. and Rotheberg, S. (1999) The relationship between social intelligence, empathy, and three types of aggression. *Aggressive Behaviour*, 25: 81–89.

Kenny, A. (1968) *Descartes: A Study of His Philosophy.* New York, NY: Random House.

Kenrick, D.T., Li, N.P. and Butner, J. (2003) Dynamical evolutionary psychology: individual decision rules and emergent social norms. *Psychological Review*, 100: 3–28.

Kerr, J.F., Wyllie, A.H., and Currie, A.R. (1972) Apoptosis: a basic biological phenomenon with wide-ranging implications in tissue kinetics. *British Journal of Cancer*, 26(4): 239–257.

Kerr, J.K., Skok, R. and McLaughlin, T.F. (1991) Characteristics common to females who exhibit anorexic or bulimic behaviour: a review of current literature. *Journal of Clinical Psychology*, 47(6): 846–853.

Kim, K. and Ko, B. (1990) An incidence survey of battered children two elementary schools in Seoul. *Child Abuse and Neglect*, 14: 273–276.

King, W. (1864) The reputed fossil man of the Neanderthal. *Quarterly Review of Science*, 1: 88–97.

Kitcher, P. (1987) *Vaulting Ambition: Sociobiology and the Quest for Human Nature*. Cambridge, MA: Massachusetts Institute of Technology.

Klevens, J., Bayón, M.C. and Sierra, M. (2000) Risk factors and context of men who physically abuse in Bogotá, Colombia. *Child Abuse and Neglect*, 24: 323–332.

Koehler, N. and Chisholm, J.S. (2007) Early psychological stress predicts extra-pair copulations. *Evolutionary Psychology*, 5(1): 184–201.

Kohn, M. (1999) *As We Know It: Coming to Terms with an Evolved Mind*. London: Granta.

Kroeber, A. and Kluckhohn, C. (1952) *Culture: A Critical Review of Concepts and Definitions*. New York, NY: Meridian Books.

Kruger, D.J., and Nesse, R.M. (2004) Sexual selection and the male:female mortality ratio. *Evolutionary Psychology*, 2: 66–85.

Lagerspetz, K.M.J., Bjorkvist, K. and Peltonen, T. (1988) Is indirect aggression typical of females? Gender differences in 11 to 12 year old children. *Aggressive Behaviour*, 4: 403–414.

Laing, R.D. (1960) *The Divided Self: An Existential Study in Sanity and Madness*. Harmondsworth: Penguin.

Laland, K.N. and Brown, G.R. (2002) *Sense and Nonsense: Evolutionary Perpepctives on Human Behaviour*. Oxford: Oxford University Press.

Leakey, R. (1994) *The Origin of Humankind*. London: Weidenfeld and Nicholson.

Leakey, R.E. and Lewin, R. (1992) *Origins Reconsidered: In Search of What Makes Us Human*. New York, NY: Random House.

Lee, R.B. and DeVore, I. (eds) (1968) *Man the Hunter*. Chicago, IL: Aldine–Atherton.

Leonetti, D.L., Nath, D.C and Hemam, N.S. (2007) The behavioral ecology of family planning: two ethnic groups in northeast India. *Human Nature*, 18(3): 225–241.

Levy, N. (2004) Evolutionary psychology, human universals, and the standard social science model. *Biology and Philosophy*. 19(3): 459–472.

Lewis, D. (1966) An argument for the identity theory. *Journal of Philosophy*, 63: 17–25.

Li, N.P., Griskevicius, V., Durante, K.M., Jonason, P.K., Pasisz, D.J. and Aumer, K. (2009) An evolutionary perspective on humor: sexual selection or interest indication? *Personality and Social Psychology Bulletin*, 35(7): 923–936.

Libert, B. (2003) Timing of conscious experience: Reply to the 2002 commentaries on Libert's findings. *Consciousness and Cognition*, 12: 321–31.

Libert, B. (2004) *Mind Time: The Temporal Factor in Consciousness*. Cambridge, MA: Harvard University Press.

Lieberman, P. (1998) *Eve Spoke: Human Language and Human Evolution*. Berkeley, CA: University of California Press.

Lightcap, J.L., Kurland, J.A. and Burgess, R.L. (1982) Child abuse: a test of some predictions from evolutionary theory. *Ethology and Sociobiology*, 6: 61–67.

Linz, B., Balloux, F., Moodley, Y., Manica, A., Liu, H., Roumagnac, P., Falush, D., Stamer, C., Prugnolle, F., van der Merwe, S.W., Yamaoka, Y., Graham, D.Y., Perez-Trallero, E., Wadstrom, T., Suerbaum, S. and Achtman, M. (2007) An African origin for the intimate association between humans and *Helicobacter pylori*. *Nature*, 445: 915–918.

Lloyd-Morgan, C. (1894) *Introduction to Comparative Psychology*. London: Walter Scott.

Loeber, R. and Hay, D. (1997) Key issues in the development of aggression and violence from childhood to early adulthood. *Annual Review of Psychology*, 48: 371–410.

Lopreato, J. and Crippen. T. (1999) *Crisis in Sociology: The Need for Darwin*. New Brunswick, NJ: Transaction Publishers.

Lorenz, K. (1966) *On Aggression*. New York, NY: Harcourt and Brace.

Lorenz, K. (1981) *The Foundations of Ethology*. New York, NY: Springer-Verlag.

Lumsden, C.J. and Wilson, E.O. (1981) *Genes, Mind and Culture: The Co-evolutionary Process*. Cambridge, MA: Harvard University Press.

Lykken, D.T. (1995) *The Anitsocial Personalities*. Hillsdale, NJ: Lawrence Erlbaum Associates.

Maccoby, E.E. (1998) *The Two Sexes: Growing Up Apart, Coming Together*. Cambridge, MA and London: Belknap.

Malthus, R. (1798) *An Essay on the Principle of Population: Or a View of its Past and Present Effects on Human Happiness*. London: J. Johnson.

Maner, J.K., Rouby, D.A. and Gonzaga, G.C. (2008) Automatic inattention to attractive alternatives: the evolved psychology of relationship maintenance. *Evolution and Human Behavior*, 29(5): 343–349.

Marks, I. and Nesse, R.M. (1994) Fear and fitness: An evolutionary analysis of anxiety disorders. *Ethology and Sociobiology* 15(5–6): 247–261.

Marlowe, F. (1999) Showoffs or providers? The parenting effort of Hadza men. *Evolution and Human Behavior*, 20: 391–404.

Marr, D. (1980) *Vision: A Computational Investigation into the Human Representation and Processing of Visual Information*. San Francisco, CA: Freeman.

Martin, R. (2007) *Psychology of Humor: An Integrative Approach*. Burlington, MA: Elsevier Academic Press.

Maynard-Smith, J. (1982) *Evolution and the Theory of Games*. Cambridge: Cambridge University Press.

McCaughey, M. (2007) *The Caveman Mystique: Pop-Darwinism and the Debates over Sex, Violence, and Science*. New York, NY: Routledge.

McCullough, M. E., Kimeldorf, M.B. and Cohen, A.D. (2008) An adaptation for altruism? The social causes, social effects, and social evolution of gratitude. *Current Directions in Psychological Science*, 17(4): 281–285.

McDonald, K. (2009) Evolution, psychology, and a conflict theory of culture. *Evolutionary Psychology*, 7(2): 208–233.

McDougall, W.D. (1908) *An Introduction to Social Psychology*. London: Methuen.

McDougall, W.D. (1923) *An Introduction to Social Psychology* (18th edn). London: Methuen.

McGrew, W.C. (1972) *The Ethological Study of Children's Behaviour*. New York, NY: Academic Press.

McGuire, M. and Troisi, A. (eds) (1998) *Darwinian Psychiatry*. Oxford: Oxford University Press.

McGuire, M.T. and Troisi, A. (1990) Anger: an evolutionary view. In Plutchik, R. and Kellerman, H. (eds) *Emotion, Psychopathology and Psychotherapy*. San Diego, CA: Academic Press. pp. 43–57.

McLellan, D. (1978) *Karl Marx: His Life and Thought*. London: HarperCollins.

Mead, G.H. (1934) *Mind, Self and Society*. Chicago, IL: University of Chicago Press.

Mealey, L. (1995) The sociobiology of sociopathy: an integrated evolutionary model. *Behavioural and Brain Sciences*, 18(3): 523–599.

Mealey, L. (2005) Evolutionary psychopathology and abnormal development. In Burgess, R.L. and MacDonald, K. (eds) *Evolutionary Perspectives on Human Development* (2nd edn). Thousand Oaks, CA: Sage. pp. 381–405.

Mellars, P. (1990) *The Emergence of Modern Humans: An Archaeological Perspective.* Edinburgh: Edinburgh University Press.

Mellars, P. (1996) The emergence of biologically modern populations in Europe: a social and cognitive revolution? In Runciman, G., Maynard-Smith, J. and Dunbar, R.M.I. (eds) *The Evolution of Social Behaviour Patterns in Primates and Man.* Oxford: Oxford University Press for the British Academy. pp. 179–201.

Miller, G.F. (2001) *The Mating Mind.* London: Heinemann.

Miller, G.F. (2007) Brain evolution. In Gangestad, S.W. and Simpson, J.A. (eds) *The Evolution of Mind: Fundamental Questions and Controversies.* New York NY: Guilford Press. pp. 287–293.

Miller, G., Taylor, J.M. and Jordan, B.D. (2007) Ovulatory cycle effects on tip earnings by lap dancers: economic evidence for human estrus? *Evolution and Human Behavior,* 28(6): 375–381.

Miller, J.M.A. (2000) Cranialfacial variation in *Homo habilis*: an analysis of the evidence for multiple species. *American Journal of Physical Anthropology,* 112: 103–128.

Miller, L.C. and Fishkin, S.A. (1997) On the dynamics of human bonding and reproductive success: seeking windows on the adapted-for human-environment interface. In Simpson, J.A. and Kenrick, D.T. (eds) *Evolutionary Social Psychology.* Mahwah, NJ: Lawrence Erlbaum Associates. pp. 197–235.

Mitchell, R. and Myles, F. (2006) *Second Language Learning Theories* (2nd edn). London: Hodder Arnold.

Mithen, S. (1996) *The Prehistory of the Mind.* London: Thames and Hudson.

Morris, D. (1967) *The Naked Ape: A Zoologist's Study of the Human Animal.* London: Jonathan Cape.

Nagel, T. (1974) What is it like to be a bat? *The Philosophical Review,* 83(4): 435–450.

Nelkin, D. (2000) Less sacred than selfish? Genes and the religious impulse in evolutionary psychology. In Rose, H. and Rose, S. (eds) *Alas, Poor Darwin: Arguments Against Evolutionary Psychology.* London: Jonathan Cape. pp. 14–27.

Nesse, R.M. (1991) Psychiatry. In Maxwell, M. (ed.) *The Sociobiological Imagination.* New York, NY: Suny Press. pp. 23–40.

Nesse, R.M. (1994) An evolutionary perspective on psychiatry. *Comparative Psychiatry,* 25: 575–580.

Nesse, R.M. (2005) Evolutionary psychology and mental health. In Buss, D.M. (ed) *The Handbook of Evolutionary Psychology.* Hoboken, NJ: John Wiley & Sons. pp. 903–927.

Nesse, R.M. and Williams, G.C. (1995) *Evolution and Healing: The New Science of Darwinian Medicine.* London: Weidenfield and Nicholson.

Ogden, C.K. (1940) *General Basic English Dictionary.* London: Evans Brothers Limited.

Oller, D.K. and Griebel, U. (2005) Contextual freedom in human infant vocalization and the evolution of language. In Burgess, R.L. and MacDonald, K. (eds) *Evolutionary Perspectives on Human Development* (2nd edn). Thousand Oaks, CA: Sage. pp. 135–166.

Opler, M.K. (1943) Woman's social status and the forms of marriage. *The American Journal of Sociology,* 49(2): 125–148.

Patterson, S. (1998) Competence and the classical cascade: a reply to Franks. *British Journal for the Philosophy of Science,* 49(4): 625–636.

Pawlowski, B. and Koziel, S. (2002) The impact of traits offered in personal advertisements on response rates. *Evolution and Human Behaviour,* 23(2): 139–149.

Pawlowski, B., Atwal, R. and Dunbar, R.I.M. (2008) Sex differences in everyday risk-taking behaviour in humans. *Evolutionary Psychology,* 6(1): 29–42.

Pelligrini, A.D. (1992) Preference for outdoor play during early adolescence. *Journal of Adolescence,* 15: 241–254.

Pellegrini, A.D. (2004) Perceptions and possible functions of play and real fighting in early adolescence. *Child Development,* 74: 1459–1470.

Pellegrini, A.D. and Archer, J. (2005) Sex difference in competitive and aggressive behaviour: a view from sexual selection theory. In Ellis, B.J. and Bjorklund, D.F. (eds) *Origins of the Social Mind: Evolutionary Psychology and Child Development.* New York, NY: Guilford Press. pp. 219–244.

Pelligrini, A.D., Horvat, M. and Huberty, P.D. (1998) The relative cost of children's physical activity play. *Animal Behaviour,* 55: 1053–1061.

Perner, J., Leekham, S.R., and Wimmer, H. (1989) Three-year-oldsdifficulty with false belief. *British Journal of Developmental Psychology,* 5: 125–137.

Peston-Voak, I.S, Rowe, A.C. and Williams, J. (2007) Through rose-tinted glasses: relationship satisfaction and representations of partners' facial attractiveness. *Journal of Evolutionary Psychology,* 5: 169–181.

Piaget, J. (1955) *The Child's Construction of Reality.* London: Routledge and Kegan Paul.

Piazza, J and Bering, J.N. (2008) Concerns about reputation via gossip promote generous allocations in an economic game. *Evolution and Human Behavior,* 29(3): 172–178.

Pilbeam, D.R. (1986) The origin of *Homo sapiens:* the fossil evidence. In Wood, B.A., Martin, L. and Andrews, P. (eds) *Major Topics in Primate and Human Evolution.* Cambridge: Cambridge University Press. pp. 98–118.

Pinker, S. (1997) *How the Mind Works.* Harmondsworth: Penguin.

Pinker, S. (2002) *The Blank Slate: The Modern Denial of Human Nature.* London: Allen Lane/Penguin Press.

Pinker, S. (2003) Language as an adaptation to the cognitive niche. In Christiansen, M. and Kirby, S. (eds) *Language Evolution: States of the Art.* New York, NY: Oxford University Press. pp. 16–37.

Pinker, S. and Bloom, P. (1990) Natural language and natural selection. *Behavioral and Brain Sciences* 13(4): 707–784.

Pinker, S. and Bloom, P. (1992) Natural language and natural selection. In Barkow, J.H., Cosmides, C. and Tooby, J. (eds) *The Adapted Mind: Evolutionary Psychology and the Generation of Culture.* Oxford: Oxford University Press. pp. 451–494.

Pipitone, R.N. and Gallup, G.G. (2008) Women's voice attractiveness varies across the menstrual cycle. *Evolution and Human Behavior,* 29(4): 268–274.

Plotkin, H.C. (2002) *The Imagined World Made Real: Towards a Natural Science of Culture.* London: Allen Lane/Penguin.

Plotkin, H.C. (2004) *Evolutionary Thought in Psychology: A Brief History.* Oxford: Blackwell.

Polimeni, J. and Reiss, J.P. (2006) The first joke: exploring the evolutionary origins of humor. *Evolutionary Psychology,* 4: 347–366.

Pollet, T.V. and Nettle, D. (2009) Partner wealth predicts self-reported orgasm frequency in a sample of. *Evolution and Human Behavior,* 30(2): 146–151.

Potts, R. (1992) The hominid way of life. In Jones, S., Martin, R. and Pilbeam, D. (eds) *The Cambridge Encyclopedia of Human Evolution.* Cambridge: Cambridge University Press. pp. 325–334.

Poulton, R. and Menzies, R.G. (2002) Non-associative fear acquisition: a review of the evidence from retrospective and longitudinal research. *Behaviour Research and Therapy,* 40(2): 127–149.

Power, T.G. (2000) *Play and Exploration in Children and Animals.* Mahwah, NJ: Lawrence Erlbaum Associates.

Purves, D. (1994) *Neural Activity and the Growth of the Brain.* Cambridge: Cambridge University Press.

Puts, D.A. (2005) Mating context and menstrual phase affect women's preferences for male voice pitch. *Evolution and Human Behavior,* 26(5): 388–397.

Puts, D.A., Gaulin, S.J.C. and Verdolini, K. (2006) Dominance and the evolution of sexual dimorphism in human voice pitch. *Evolution and Human Behavior,* 27(4): 283–296.

Puts, D.A., Hodges, C.R., Cárdenas, R.A. and Gaulin, S.J.C. (2007) Men's voices as dominance signals: vocal fundamental and formant frequencies influence dominance attributions among men. *Evolution and Human Behavior*, 28(5): 340–344.

Quinlan, R. and Quinlan, M. (2008) Human lactation, pair-bonds, and alloparents: a cross-cultural analysis. *Human Nature*, 19(1): 87–102.

Raphael, F.J. and Lacey J.H. (1992) Sociocultural factors in eating disorders. *Annals of Medicine*, 24: 293–296.

Reeve, H.K. and Sherman, P.W. (2007) Why measuring reproductive success in current populations is valuable. In Gangestad, S.W. and Simpson, J.A. (eds) *The Evolution of Mind: Fundamental Questions and Controversies*. New York, NY: Guilford Press. pp. 86–94.

Relethford, J.H. (2003) *The Human Species: An Introduction to Biological Anthropology* (5th edn). Boston: McGraw Hill.

Richards, G. (2005) Ideological meanings and uses of instincts. In Mulberger, A. and Gomez-Zuniga, B. (eds) *Recent Contributions to the History of the Human Sciences*. Munich: Profil Verlag. pp. 194–204.

Richards, R.J. (1987) *Darwin and the Emergence of Evolutionary Theories of Mind*. Chicago, IL: University of Chicago Press.

Richerson, P.J. and Boyd, R. (2005) *Not By Genes Alone: How Culture Transformed Human Evolution*. Chicago, Ill: University of Chicago Press.

Richmond, B.G. and Strait, S.S. (2000) Evidence that humans evolved from a knuckle walking ancestor. *Nature*, 404: 382–385.

Ridley, M. (1993) *The Red Queen: Sex and the Evolution of Human Nature*. London: Viking.

Roberts, M. (1999) *Boxgrove: A Middle Pleistocene Hominid Site at Eartham Quarry, Boxgrove, West Sussex*. London: English Heritage.

Robinson, D. (1981) *An Intellectual History of Psychology* (2nd edn). Madison, WI: Macmillan.

Rocca, M.D. (1996) *Representation and the Mind–Body Problem in Spinoza*. Oxford: Oxford University Press.

Rose, H. (2000) Colonising the social sciences?. In Rose, H. and Rose, S. (eds) *Alas, Poor Darwin: Arguments Against Evolutionary Psychology*. London: Jonathan Cape. pp. 106–128.

Rose, H. and Rose, S. (2000) Introduction. In Rose, H. and Rose, S. (eds) *Alas, Poor Darwin: Arguments Against Evolutionary Psychology*. London: Jonathan Cape. pp. 1–13.

Rosen, M.L. and Lopez, H.H. (2009) Menstrual cycle shifts in attentional bias for courtship language. *Evolution and Human Behaviour*, 30(2): 131–140.

Rosenberg, J. and Tunney, R.J. (2008) Human Vocabulary use as display. *Evolutionary Psychology*, 6 (3): 538–549.

Rubin, R.H. (2001) Alternative lifestyles revisited, or whatever happened to swingers, group marriages, and communes? *Journal of Family Issues*, 22(6): 711–727.

Runciman, W.G. (1966) *Relative Deprivation and Social Justice*. London: Routledge and Kegan Paul.

Ruvolo, M. (1997) Genetic diversity in hominoid primates. *Annual Review of Anthropology*, 26: 515–540.

Ryle, G. (1949) *The Concept of Mind*. Harmondsworth: Penguin.

Salmon, C. (2008) Heroes and hos: reflections of male and females natures. In Crawford, C.B. and Krebs, D. (eds) *Foundations of Evolutionary Psychology*. New York, NY: Lawrence Erlbaum Associates. pp. 281–290.

Salmon, C., Crawford, C., Dane, L. and Zuberbier, O. (2008) Ancestral mechanisms in modern environments: impact of competition and stressors on body image and dieting behavior. *Human Nature*, 19(1): 103–117.

Sanderson, S. (2001) *The Evolution of Human Sociality: A Darwinian Conflict Perspective*. Boulder, CO: Rowman & Littlefield.

Sariola, H. and Uutela, A. (1996) The prevalence and context of incest abuse in Finland. *Child Abuse and Neglect*, 20: 843–850.

Savin-Williams, R.C. (1987) *Adolescence: An Ethological Perspective*. New York, NY: Springer-Verlag.

Schlegel, A. (1995) A cross cultural approach to adolescence. *Ethos*, 23: 15–32.

Schmitt, D.P. (2003) Universal sex differences in the desire for sexual variety: tests from 52 nations, 6 continents, and 13 islands. *Journal of Personality and Social Psychology*, 85(1): 85–104.

Schrepfer, S. and Scranton P. (2003) *Industrializing Organisms: Introducing Evolutionary History*. London: Routledge.

Schwarz. S. and Hassebrauck, M. (2008) Self-perceived and observed variations in women's attractiveness throughout the menstrual cycle – a diary study. *Evolution and Human Behavior*, 29(4): 282–288.

Sears, R.R., Rau, L. and Albert, R. (1965) *Identification and Childrearing*. Palo Alto, CA: Stanford University Press.

Shackelford, T.K., Pound, N., Goetz, A.T. and Lamunyon, C.W. (2005) Female infidelity and sperm competition. In Buss, D.M. (ed) *The Handbook of Evolutionary Psychology*. Hoboken, NJ: John Wiley & Sons. pp. 372–418.

Shennan, S. (2002) *Genes, Memes and Human History: Darwinian Archaeology and Cultural Evolution*. London: Thames and Hudson.

Sherman, P. and Reeve, K. (1997) Forward and backward: alternative approaches to studying human social evolution. In Betzig, L. (ed.) *Human Nature: A Critical Reader*. New York, NY: Oxford University Press.

Sigmund, K. (1993) *Games of life: Explorations in Ecology, Evolution and Behaviour*. Oxford: Oxford University Press.

Silk, J. B., Brosnan, S.F., Vonk, J., Henrich, J., Povinelli, D., Richardson, L., Susan, A., Mascaro, J. and Schapiro, S. (2005) Chimpanzees are indifferent to the welfare of unrelated group members. *Nature*, 437: 1357–1359.

Singer, P. (1999) *A Darwinian Left: Politics, Evolution and Cooperation*. New Haven, CT: Yale University Press.

Singh, D. (1993a) Adaptive significance of waist-to-hip ratio and female physical attractiveness. *Journal of Personality and Social Psychology*, 65: 293–307.

Singh, D. (1993b) Body shape and female attractiveness: the critical role of waist-to-hip ratio (WHR). *Human Nature*, 4: 297–321.

Singh, D. (2000) Waist-to-hip ratio: an indicator of females mate value. *International Research Centre for Japanese Studies, International Symposium*, 16: 79–99.

Skeem, J.L., Edens, J.F., Camp, J. and Colwell, L.H. (2004) Are there ethnic differences in levels of psychopathy? A meta-analysis. *Law and Human Behavior*, 28: 505–527.

Skinner, B.F. (1957) *Verbal Behaviour*. New York, NY: Appleton-Century-Crofts.

Smith, E.A., Borgerhoff Mulder, M. and Hill, K. (2001) Controversies in the evolutionary social sciences: a guide for the perplexed. *Trends in Ecology and Evolution*, 16(3): 128–135.

Smith, F.H. (1991) The Neanderthals: evolutionary dead ends or ancestors of modern people? *Journal of Anthropological Research*, 47(2): 219–238.

Smuts, B. (1995) The evolutionary origins of patriarchy. *Human Nature*, 6: 1–32.

Solso, R. (2004) *The Psychology of Art and the Evolution of the Conscious Brain*. Cambridge, MA: MIT Press.

Soltis, J., Boyd, R. and Richerson, P.J. (1995) Can group functional behaviours evolve by cultural group selection? An empirical test. *Current Anthropology*, 36(3): 473–494.

Sperber, D. (1994) The modularity of thought and the epidemiology of representations. In Hirschfield, H. and Gelman, S. (eds) *Mapping the Mind: Domain Specificity in Cognition and Culture.* Cambridge: Cambridge University Press. pp. 39–67.

Stack, C.B. (1974) *All Our Kin: Strategies for Survival in a Black Community.* New York, NY: Harper and Row.

Stainton Rogers, R., Stenner, P, Gleeson, K. and Stainton Rogers, W. (1995) *Social Psychology: A Critical Agenda.* Cambridge: Polity Press.

Strawson, P.F. (1959) *Individuals: An Essay in Descriptive Metaphysics.* London: Methuen.

Striedter, G.F. (2005) *Principles of Brain Evolution.* Sunderland, MA: Sinauer Associates.

Stringer, C. (1992) Evolution of early humans. In Jones, S., Martin, R. and Pilbeam, D. (eds) *The Cambridge Encyclopedia of Human Evolution.* Cambridge: Cambridge University Press. pp. 241–254.

Stringer, C.B. and Andrews, P. (2005) *The Complete World of Human Evolution.* London: Thames and Hudson.

Stringer, C.B. and Gamble, C. (1993) *In Search of the Neanderthals: Solving the Puzzle of Human Origins.* New York, NY: Thames and Hudson.

Stringer, C.B. and Grün, R. (1991) Time for the last Neanderthals. *Nature,* 35: 701–702.

Sullivan, E., and Kosson, D.S. (2005) Ethnic and cultural variations in psychopathy. In Patrick, C.J. (ed) *Handbook of psychopathy.* New York, NY: Guilford. pp. 437–458.

Symons, D. (1979) *The Evolution of Human Sexuality.* New York, NY: Oxford University Press.

Symons, D. (1990) Adaptiveness and adaptation. *Ethology and Sociobiology,* 11(4–5): 427–444.

Symons, D. (1992) On the use and misuse of Darwinism in the study of human behaviour. In Barkow, J. Cosmides, L. and Tooby, J. (eds) *The Adapted Mind: Evolutionary Psychology and the Generation of Culture.* Oxford: Oxford University Press.

Szasz, T. (1970) *The Manufacture of Madness: A Comparative Study of the Inquisition and the Mental Health Movement.* London: Routledge and Kegan Paul.

Tajfel, H. (1970) Experiments in intergroup discrimination. *Scientific American,* 223(5): 96–105.

Tajfel, H. (1981) *Human Groups and Social Categories.* Cambridge: Cambridge University Press.

Tattersall, I. (1995) *The Fossil Trail.* New York, NY: Oxford University Press.

Tattersall, I. (1997) Out of Africa again . . . and again? *Scientific American,* April: 60–70.

Tattersall, I. and Schwartz, J. (2000) *Extinct Humans.* Boulder, CO: Westview Press.

Tedeschi, J.T. and Felson, R.B. (1994) *Violence, Aggression and Coercive Actions.* Washington, DC: American Psychological Association.

Temrin, H., Buchmayer, S. and Enquist, M. (2000) Stepparents and infanticide: new data contradict evolutionary predictions. *Proceedings of the Royal Society of London,* 267: 943–945.

Thorndike, E.L. (1911) *Animal Intelligence.* New York, NY: Hafner Publishing Co.

Thornhill, R. (2007) The evolution of women's estrus, extended sexuality, and concealed ovulation, and the their implications for human sexuality research. In, Gangstead, S.W. and Simpson, J.A. (eds) *The Evolution of Mind: Fundamental Questions and Controversies.* New York, NY: Guilford. pp. 391–396.

Thornhill, R. and Fincher, C.L. (2007) What is the relevance of attachment and life history to political values? *Evolution and Human Behavior,* 28(4): 215–222.

Titchener, E.B. (1914) On psychology as the behaviourist views it. *Proceedings of the American Philosophical Society,* 53: 1–17.

Tiggemann, M. (2003) Media exposure, body dissatisfaction and disordered eating: television and magazines are not the same! *European Eating Disorders Review,* 5(11): 418–430.

Tiggemann, M. and Pickering, A.S. (1996) Role of television in adolescent women's body dissatisfaction and drive towards thinness. *International Journal of Eating Disorders,* 20(2): 199–203.

Tinbergen, N. (1951) *The Study of Instinct.* Oxford: Clarendon Press.

Tinbergen, N. (1963) On aims and methods in ethology. *Zeitschrift für Tierpsychologie*, 20: 410–433.

Tolman, E.C. (1922) Can instincts be given up in psychology? *Journal of Abnormal Psychology*, 17: 139–152.

Tolman, E.C. (1923) The nature of instinct. *Psychological Bulletin*, 20: 200–218.

Tolman, E.C. (1932) *Purposive Behaviour in Animals and Men*. Los Angeles, CA: University of California Press.

Tomasello, M. (1999) *The Cultural Orgins of Human Cognition*. Cambridge, MA: Havard University Press.

Tooby, J. and Cosmides, L. (1988) *The Evolution of War and Its Cognitive Foundations*. Institute for Evolutionary Studies Technical Report 88–1. Palo Alto, CA.

Tooby, J. and Cosmides, L. (1989) Evolutionary psychology and the generation of culture: part I, theoretical considerations. *Ethology and Sociobiology*, 10: 29–49.

Tooby, J. and Cosmides, L. (1990) The past explains the present: emotional adaptations and the structure of ancestral environments. *Ethology and Sociobiology*, 16: 375–424.

Tooby, J. and Cosmides, L. (1992) The psychological foundations of culture. In Barkow, J.H., Cosmides, C. and Tooby, J. (eds) *The Adapted Mind: Evolutionary Psychology and the Generation of Culture*. Oxford: Oxford University Press. pp. 18–136.

Tooby, J. and Cosmides, L. (1996) Friendship and the banker's paradox: other pathways to the evolution of adaptations for altruism. *Proceedings of the British Academy*, 88: 119–143.

Tooby, J. and Cosmides, L. (2005) Conceptual foundations of evolutionary psychology. In Buss, D.M. (ed) *The Handbook of Evolutionary Psychology*. Hoboken, NJ: John Wiley & Sons. pp. 5–67.

Tooby, J., and DeVore, I. (1987) The reconstruction of hominid behavioral evolution through strategic modeling. In Kinsey, W.G. (ed) *The Evolution of Human Behavior: Primate Models*. Albany, NY: Suny Press.

Tooley, GA., Karakis, M., Stokes, M. and Ozanne-Smith J. (2006) Generalising the Cinderella effect to unintentional childhood fatalities. *Evolution and Human behaviour* 27(3), 224–230.

Townsend, J.M. (1995) Sex without emotional investment: an evolutionary interpretation of differences. *Archives of Sexual Behaviour*, 24: 173–206.

Trinkaus, E. and Shipman, P. (1992) *The Neanderthals: Changing the Image of Mankind*. New York, NY: Knopf.

Trivers, R.L. (1971) The evolution of reciprocal altruism. *Quarterly Review of Biology*, 46: 35–57.

Trivers, R.L. (1972) Parental investment and sexual selection. In Campbell B. (ed.) *Sexual Selection and the Descent of Man, 1871–1971*. Chicago, IL: Aldine de Gruyter. pp. 136–179.

Trivers, R.L. (1973) Parent–offspring conflict. *American Zoologist*, 10: 249–264.

Trivers, R.L. (1983) *The Evolution of a Sense of Fairness*. New York, NY: International Cultural Foundation Press.

Trivers, R.L. (1985) *Social Evolution*. Menlo Park, CA: Benjamin Cummings.

Troisi, A. (2008) Psychopathology and mental illness. In Crawford, C.B. and Krebs, D. (eds) *Foundations of Evolutionary Psychology*. New York, NY: Lawrence Erlbaum Associates. pp. 453–474.

Tybur, J.M., Miller, G.F and Gangestad, S.W. (2008) Testing the controversy: an empirical examination of adaptationists' attitudes toward politics and science. *Human Nature*, 18(4): 313–328.

Vaughan, K. and Fouts, G. (2003) Changes in television and magazine exposure and eating disorder symptomatology. *Sex Roles*, 49(7/8): 313–320.

Voland, E. (2007) Evolutionary psychology meets history: insights into human nature through family reconstitution studies. In Dunbar, R.I.M. and Barrett, L. (eds) *The Oxford Handbook of Evolutionary Psychology*. Oxford: Oxford University Press. pp. 415–432.

Wallace, A. (1986) *Homicide: The Social Reality*. Sydney: New South Wales Bureau of Crime Statistics and Research.

Walsh, Z. and Kosson, D. S. (2007) Psychopathy and violent crime: a prospective study of the influence of the socioeconomic status and ethnicity. *Law and Human Behavior*, 31: 209–229.

Wasser, S.K. and Barash, D.P. (1983) Reproductive suppression among females mammals. Implications for biomedicine and sexual selection theory. *Quarterly Review of Biology*, 58: 513–538.

Wasser, S.K. and Barash, D.P. (1986) Reprodcutive failure among women. Pathology or adaptation? *Journal of Psychosomatic Obstetrics and Gynaecology*, 5: 153–175.

Watson, J.B. (1913) Psychology as the behaviourist views it. *Psychological Review*, 20: 158–177.

Watson, J.B. (1919) *Psychology from the Standpoint of a Behaviourist*. Philadelphia and London: J.B. Lippincott.

Watson, J.B. (1930) *Behaviorism*. Chigaco, IL: University of Chicago Press.

Watson, J.B. (1931) *Behaviourism*. London: Kegan Paul, Trench, Trubner and Co.

Weeden, J., Cohen, A.B. and Kenrick, D.T. (2008) Religious attendance as reproductive support. *Evolution and Human Behaviour*, 29(5): 327–334.

Whiten, A. (1999) The evolution of deep social mind in humans. In Corballis, M.C. and Lea, S.E.G. (eds) *The Descent of Mind: Psychological Perspectives on Hominid Evolution*. New York, NY: Oxford University Press. pp. 173–193.

Whiten, A and Byrne, R.W. (1988) Tactical deception in primates. *Behavioural and Brain Sciences*, 11: 233–273.

Wilm, E.C. (1925) *The Theories of Instinct: A Study in the History of Psychology*. New Haven, CT: Yale University Press.

Wilson, A.C. and Cann, R.L. (1992) The recent African genesis of humans. *Scientific American*, April: 22–27.

Wilson, D.S. (2002) *Darwin's Cathedral: Evolution, Religion, and the Nature of Society*. Chicago, IL: University of Chicago Press.

Wilson, D.S. and Sober, E. (1994) Reintroducing group selection to the human behavioral sciences. *Behavioral and Brain Sciences*, 17(4): 585–654.

Wilson, D.S., Van Vugt, M. and O'Gorman, R. (2008) Multilevel selection theory and major evolutionary transitions: implications for psychological science. *Current Directions in Psychological Science*, 17(1): 6–9.

Wilson, E.O. (1975) *Sociobiology: The New Synthesis*. Cambridge, MA: Belknap Press.

Wilson, E.O. (1994) *Naturalist*. Washington, DC: Island Press.

Wilson, E.O. (1998) *Consilience: The Unity of Knowledge*. New York, NY: Knopf.

Wilson, M. and Daly, M. (1985) Competitiveness, risk taking, and violence: the young male syndrome. *Ethology and Sociobiology*, 6: 59–73.

Wilson, M. and Daly, M. (1992a) The man who mistook his wife for a chattel. In Barkow, J.H., Cosmides, C. and Tooby, J. (eds) *The Adapted Mind: Evolutionary Psychology and the Generation of Culture*. Oxford: Oxford University Press. pp. 289–322.

Wilson, M., and Daly, M. (1992b) Who kills whom in spouse killings? On the exceptional sex ratio of spousal homicides in the United States. *Criminology*, 30: 189–215.

Wilson, M. and Daly, M. (1997) Life expectancy, economic equality, homicide, and reproductive timing in Chicago neighbourhoods. *British Medical Journal*, 314: 271–1274.

Wilson, M., Daly, M. and Weghorst, S.J. (1980) Household composition and the risk of child abuse and neglect. *Journal of Biosocial Science*, 12: 333–340.

Winterhalder, B. and Smith, E. (2000) Analyzing adaptive strategies: human behavioral ecology at twenty-five. *Evolutionary Anthropology*, 7: 51–72.

Wolfgang, M.E. (1958) *Patterns in Criminal Homicide*. Philadelphia, PA: University of Philadelphia Press.

Wolpoff, M.H. (1999) *Palaeoanthropology* (2nd edn). Boston, MA: McGraw Hill.

Wood, B. and Hill, K. (2000) A test of the 'showing–off' hypothesis with Ache hunters. *Current Anthropology*, 41: 124–125.

Wood, B.A. (1992) Evolution of *australopithecines*. In Jones, S., Martin, R. and Pilbeam, D. (eds) *The Cambridge Encyclopedia of Human Evolution*. Cambridge: Cambridge University Press. pp. 231–240.

Wood, B.A. and Brooks, A. (1999) We are what we ate. *Nature*, 15: 219–220.

Woods, R. (1995) *The Population History in Britain in the Nineteenth Century*. Cambridge: Cambridge University Press.

Woodside, D.B. and Kennedy, S.H. (1995) Gender differences in eating disorders. In Seeman, M.V. (ed.) *Gender and Psychopathology*. Washington, DC: American Psychiatric Press. pp. 253–268.

Wynne-Edwards, V.C. (1962) *Animal Dispersion in Relation to Social Behaviour*. London: Oliver and Boyd.

Yerkes, R.M. (1911) Instinct. *Psychological Bulletin*, 8: 395–402.

Zahavi, A. and Zahavi, A. (1997) *The Handicap Principle: A Missing Piece of Darwin's Puzzle*. Oxford: Oxford University Press.

Zipes J. (2006) *Why Fairy Tales Stick: The Evolution and Relevance of a Genre*. London: Routledge.

Zvoch, K. (1999) Family type and investment in education: a comparison of genetic and stepparent families. *Evolution and Human Behavior*, 20: 453–464.

INDEX

Note: Page references for figures are in **bold**